REVEI

MW01534763

TIMELINE

DECODED

Messiah's apocalyptic vision is a war manual that uses symbols and layers to hide the fulfillment.

Blessed is he that readeth, and they that hear the words of this prophecy, and keep those things which are written therein: for the time is at hand.
Revelation 1:3

The enemy has tried to hide the fulfillment of Revelation as it validates the authority of Scripture and the deity of Messiah. Our adversary has worked hard to mislead the end-times saints, but the Spirit is moving to reveal the truth and to expose the deceptions of the enemy.

When I learned about the amazing fulfillment of the prophecies in Revelation, it gave me tangible evidence of my faith and I became that much more in awe of Messiah who foretold the apocalyptic vision in the first century. I long for Messiah's return, but until then I will fight the good fight for His kingdom. All glory goes to our Heavenly Father, our beloved Messiah and the Spirit of Truth who guides us.

David Nikao Wilcoxson

Unless otherwise indicated, Scripture quotations are taken from the King James Bible Version. Unless otherwise noted, all dates are AD. Verses are from the book of Revelation, unless otherwise noted.

TABLE OF CONTENTS

The Pope Takes Power Over The Roman Beast

The Fall Of The Eastern Roman Empire

The Revival Of The True Faith

FOREWORD

The great theologians of the 16ᵗʰ-19ᵗʰ centuries taught the same core concepts that I give in this book. It's only during the last century that the enemy's false explanations have become accepted by the saints.

In this book, I often cite Henry Grattan Guinness, who wrote *The Approaching End Of The Age* (1881), *Romanism And The Reformation* (1887), *Light For the Last Days* (1888), *Key To The Apocalypse* (1899), and *History Unveils Prophecy* (1906). He is one of my heroes of the faith as he helped me see the truth about the glorious fulfillment of Messiah's apocalyptic vision. He wrote books to counter the futuristic prophecy fulfillment explanations which were starting to take hold among the saints.

In *The Approaching End Of The Age,* **Guinness says,** *And the views thus thoughtlessly imparted, and thoughtlessly received, are yet firmly held; for mental habits are strong. That which we have always heard and supposed to be true, that which most people appear to hold as true, assumes the authority of ascertained truth in the mind, and the moment it is attacked, prejudice rises in arms to defend it.*

Guinness would be appalled at how effective the enemy has been since his day. I stand on his shoulders to bring his words back to life for the end-times saints to read. When you read his comments, you'll see why.

I cite E.B. Elliot, who wrote *Horae Apocalypticae* (1844), which means 'Hours With The Apocalypse,' the most elaborate work ever produced on Revelation. 10,000 invaluable references buttress its 2,500 pages.

I reference Roman Empire authority Edward Gibbon, who wrote the epic six-volume *The History Of The Decline And Fall Of The Roman Empire* (1776). He was not a believer, but he was used to document what took place in the Roman Empire, which amazingly aligns with what took place from the first seal through the sixth trumpet.

Here's a list of Bible commentaries that were written by esteemed theologians. Their extensive writings give profound insight into the fulfillment of prophecy. They expounded on Scriptural truth to prove the historical fulfillment of prophecy, without the enemy's deceptions clouding their minds. They don't all agree on every prophecy, but they have the same historical narrative.

Adam Clarke Commentary
Adam Clarke (1760-1832) was a British Methodist theologian and Biblical scholar. He is chiefly remembered for writing a commentary on the Bible, which took him forty years to complete and was a primary theological resource for two centuries—consisting of six volumes of nearly 1,000 pages each. It was considered the most comprehensive commentary on the Bible ever prepared by one man.

Albert Barnes Notes on the Whole Bible

Albert Barnes (1798-1870), an American theologian, graduated from Hamilton College, Clinton, NY, and Princeton Theological Seminary. Of the well-known *Notes on the Whole Bible*, it is said that more than a million volumes had been issued by 1870.

The Geneva Study Bible

The margin notes are authored by John Calvin, John Knox, Miles Coverdale, and other Reformation leaders. Owing to the commentary and the translation's superior quality, the Geneva Bible became the most widely read and influential English Bible of the 16th and 17th centuries.

Jamieson-Fausset-Brown Commentary

This one-volume commentary was prepared by Robert Jamieson, A. R. Fausset, and David Brown and published in 1871.

John Gill's Exposition of the Whole Bible

John Gill (1697-1771) was an English Baptist pastor for fifty-one years and a biblical scholar. His *Exposition of the New Testament* is in three volumes, and his *Exposition of the Old Testament* is in six volumes.

Joseph Benson's Commentary on Revelation

Joseph Benson (1749-1821) was one of the most eminent early Methodist ministers in England. John Wesley appointed him a classical master at Kingswood School. He devoted himself closely to philosophy and theology, studying constantly and zealously.

Matthew Poole's English Annotations on the Holy Bible

Matthew Poole (1624 - 1679) was an English nonconformist theologian. His *English Annotations on the Holy Bible*, a work completed by several of his nonconformist brethren, was published in two volumes.

The People's New Testament by Barton Johnson

B.W. Johnson wrote this work for the novice student to help them understand every verse. He also wrote *Vision Of The Ages – Lectures On The Apocalypse* in 1881.

The Pulpit Commentary

Written in the nineteenth century, it consists of 23 volumes with 22,000 pages and 95,000 entries. The *Pulpit Commentary* drew from over one-hundred authors over a thirty-year year span to assemble this conservative and trustworthy homiletical commentary set.

These theologians taught a very different explanation of the fulfillment of Revelation than what is given by pastors today. The enemy has created many prophecy fulfillment deceptions to fool the end-times saints and to hide the identity of the *antichrist beast* and the *false prophet*.

I provide explanations of the Revelation prophecies and then add commentaries from theologians, which give more information. Some of the explanations are redundant, but that's a good thing as it helps us comprehend the truth about the fulfillment.

When studying prophecy, these Hermeneutic principles need to be applied: 1) Scripture interprets Scripture. The Bible is its own dictionary. 2) Context interprets Scripture. The surrounding verses, chapter and book provide context to any Bible verse. 3) Intent interprets Scripture. Prophecy points to one historical fulfillment while it many have many applications. 4) The clear interprets the obscure. No verse should be interpreted to contradict the overall message of the prophecy.

You may think that you already know the fulfillment of the prophecies in Revelation, but my friend, the enemy has worked hard to deceive us. Please put aside any preconceived notions. I'm not asking you to be empty-minded, but I hope that you will be open-minded.

I pray that your goal is to seek the truth, not to defend a belief.
As your brother in Messiah, I'm lovingly admonishing you to read the whole explanation, compare it to Scripture, and pray about it. The saints who have gone before us taught the historical fulfillment explanations, but the enemy has pushed their witness aside to hide the truth. I pray for a great awakening in these end times, to bring their testimony back to life, to expose the deceptions of the enemy, and set the captives free!

INTRODUCTION

Messiah's apocalyptic vision is a war manual designed to conceal the message from those who shouldn't understand it. He uses symbols defined in the Old Testament to point to a literal fulfillment. If you haven't studied the whole Word, you're left to take the prophecies either symbolically or literally, which hides the explanation.

The apocalyptic vision has four chronological layers, all of which span from when it was written until Messiah returns. Like the four Gospels, none of them give the complete narrative, but you see the whole message when you overlay them on a timeline.

If you read Revelation literally, as one chronological narrative, then the sixth seal seems like it takes place in the end times because it declares that the *sun becomes black and the moon as blood*. Messiah uses symbolic language using the heavenly bodies to point to leaders being removed from power, so it's not pointing to the literal sun and moon.

Revelation prophecy fulfillment is fairly straight-forward. It's all of the deceptions of the enemy, which makes it hard to see the truth.

Messiah started His apocalyptic vision with these words.

> *The Revelation of Jesus Christ, which God gave unto him, to show unto his servants <u>things which must shortly come to pass</u>; and he sent and signified it by his angel unto his servant John. Who bare record of the word of God, and of the testimony of Jesus Christ, and of all things that he saw. Blessed is he that reads, and they that hear the words of this prophecy, and keep those things which are written therein: <u>for the time is at hand</u>.* Revelation 1:1-3

Messiah did not say that most of the prophecies in Revelation would be fulfilled in the end times. That is a deception from the enemy, who had hidden the historical fulfillment of most of Revelation because it authenticates Scripture's authority and the deity of Messiah.

I'm going to present a lot of evidence that will challenge you. But this isn't just my interpretation, for the saints who have gone before us understood a completely different narrative of how Revelation is fulfilled. It's only during the last century that the enemy's futuristic deceptions have gained a stronghold in Messiah's assembly of saints.

Put aside any preconceived notions and ask yourself what makes more sense to you? That none of the Revelation prophecies would be fulfilled for 1,900 years, and then all of them would occur during the final few years? Or, that the Revelation prophecies would be fulfilled during the time from when they were written until Messiah returns?

If the futuristic view of prophecy is true, then that means that our Messiah had nothing to say to His saints about the following events, which have occurred during the last 1,900 years.

Satan using the Roman Emperors to kill millions of believers in his attempt to wipe out Messiah's Ekklesia of saints.

The pagan Roman Empire's *decline* from civil wars, financial distress, famine, and pestilence.

Emperor Constantine and the Roman bishops creating a new pagan religion of Roman Christianity, Romanism, in the name of Jesus Christ, proclaiming that it's the *'one true church,'* when all the while, it has deceived billions of people with a false salvation message.

Army after army attacking the mighty Roman Empire to desolate it, causing its *fall* and the last Western Roman Emperor being removed from power in 476 AD.

The rise of the Popes to power over the fallen Roman Empire to became the leader of the church-state of the Roman beast kingdom.

The Popes making declarations and empowering Catholics to burn the Holy Scriptures and torture and kill tens of millions of saints during the Dark Ages and the Inquisition.

6

The Popes of Rome proclaiming to lead Messiah's church but saying blasphemous things, such as they are God, they are Jesus Christ in the flesh, they can forgive sins, they provide salvation, and that Mary is the intercessor to the Father.

The translation of the Scriptures into English, German, and other languages; after it had been hidden during the Dark Ages by the Papal Church, who only taught in Latin.

The printing press's timely advent, which caused Bibles, the *little book* of Revelation 10, to be printed en masse and spread worldwide.

Catholic monk Martin Luther being led to read the Scriptures to see that the Papal Church is a false church, a *harlot* church. He responded by posting his 95 Thesis, sparking the Protestant Reformation, causing millions of people to be redeemed for the kingdom and come out of the Roman Catholic Church and form the Protestant Churches.

The rise of the Jesuit Order, which the Pope empowered to counter the Reformation and bring the Protestants back under their power, through the tortures of the Inquisition.

The French Revolution and Napoleonic Wars, which killed many Catholics in countries that had previously persecuted the saints.

The time of *The Great Awakening*, when missionaries traveled around the world, spread the Good News, and Bible societies sent the Scriptures around the world.

The futuristic view tells you that Messiah had <u>nothing</u> to say to His saints who endured all of those things. Friend, I promise you that our Messiah described all of those things in the book of Revelation, not by name, but the events and the people groups were all described in clear detail, and you'll see that history proves the fulfillment.

This book is about the glory of Messiah, as it shows how He has faithfully worked through His set-apart saints. This book is a proof of His deity, as His prophecies have been fulfilled in exacting detail.

This book shows you that Messiah wrote to the saints who exist from the time that Revelation was written until He returns, to foretell the events they would face to know where they're at on the fulfillment timeline. Revelation gives the historical battle narrative between the Satan-empowered leaders of the Roman beast kingdom, fighting against Messiah and His saints. We're at war, and the saints win the battle when they teach Scriptural truth about the fulfillment of prophecy, to expose the enemy's deceptions, and set the captives free!

There's more at stake here than just understanding the fulfillment of Revelation. The three primary prophecies that prove Scripture's authority and Messiah's deity are the 70th Week of Daniel 9, Messiah's Olivet Discourse, and Messiah's apocalyptic vision. This is why Satan has worked hard to hide the truth.

In my previous books, I proved the fulfillment of the 70th week of Daniel 9, which is the only prophecy that foretold the exact time that Messiah would carry out His ministry and confirm the *everlasting covenant* with His blood as the Spotless Lamb for our sins. And I proved the fulfillment of the Olivet Discourse, which is about the Jewish nation's judgment, for delivering Messiah up to be killed.

Nobody wants to learn that they've been deceived, but wouldn't you rather learn about it now before Messiah returns? We don't want to be caught off guard by how the end-times play out and appear as foolish virgins who didn't have the oil of Scriptural truth in our lamps.

In Revelation 3:15-17, Messiah chastises the end-times saints, proclaiming that *they're lukewarm, wretched, miserable, naked, poor, and blind.* My mission is to give you *eyesalve* so that you may see and be an overcomer, to help win the victory for our Warrior Messiah.

All praise goes to our Heavenly Father and His *faithful witness*, the *first begotten of the dead*, the *prince of the kings of the earth*, the *Alpha and Omega*, the *beginning and the ending*, the *Lion of the tribe of Judah*, the *root and the offspring of David*, and the *bright and morning star.* HalleluYah!

ABOUT DAVID

I was blessed to grow up in a family of believers and the community of a Baptist Church. Then the verse-by-verse studies at Calvary Chapel churches blessed me, and I visited Israel with one of my Pastors.

I have not been to a seminary or a Bible school, which is a blessing because the enemy has infiltrated the teachings in those places. Pastors are taught false explanations of prophecy fulfillment, making it difficult for them to see the truth, as they assume that the teachers have proved it all out. I'm simply a servant of our Heavenly Father and Messiah, who has the Scriptures as my guide and the Spirit as my teacher.

For most of my life, I simply believed what my pastors had told me about the end times. What they taught lines up with what my John MacArthur Study Bible says, which corresponds with what I heard popular pastors like David Jeremiah and Chuck Swindoll teach, which is reinforced in movies and books like *Left Behind*.

Those Pastors went to seminary, so I thought that they must know the proper explanations. I had no reason to doubt them because they seem like sincere men who love the Heavenly Father and Messiah.

But about ten years ago, the Spirit moved in my life to show me the many deceptions which the enemy has created to mislead the end-times saints. Since then, I've committed my life to learn and teach the truth about prophecy, and I work full-time in this ministry. I believe that the Spirit of Truth shows us insights when we hunger for knowledge.

I've written two other Bible prophecy books, *The 70th Week Of Daniel 9 Decoded* and *The Olivet Discourse Decoded*. None of my books are about me. I'm simply sharing what I've been blessed to learn in my studies so that you can compare it to Scripture and discern it for yourself. All glory goes to our Heavenly Father, our blessed Messiah, and the Spirit of Truth.

My friend, I encourage you to be a Berean and search these things out. Don't take my word for it; don't seek to defend your beliefs, just seek the truth. Until the end-times saints understand the grand deceptions that have blinded her, she cannot fight to overcome the enemy in the power of the Word, and she is powerless to set the captives free.

My heart breaks for believers who've been deceived by the enemy, who don't know how the future will play out so that they're like the foolish virgins who are unprepared for Messiah's return. My tears are shed for Pastors who are unknowingly teaching false prophecy concepts that originated from the enemy, for they will be held accountable.

When you read explanations that identify individuals and people groups who fulfill prophecy in a negative way, it can come across as cold, and some say that it's hate. So I want you to know that I declare these truths out of a heart of love for people. I want everyone, Jews, Muslims, Catholics, Protestants, etc., to see the truth about Messiah's declarations so that they come out of their Babylonian captivity. I desire all to have a covenant relationship with the Father through the Son.

I pray that our Heavenly Father causes a great revival, during which the enemy's prophecy fulfillment deceptions are exposed and many millions of captives are set free. I hope that my work brings honor to my father and mother, who blessed me so much by teaching me about our Heavenly Father and beloved Messiah. I pray that this book helps you be an *overcomer* who shares the truth of prophecy fulfillment, to conquer the enemy and get the victory for the kingdom! This book isn't about me; it's about seeing the glory of Messiah, the Lion of the tribe of Judah!

> *Worthy is the Lamb that was slain to receive power, and riches, and wisdom, and strength, and honor, and glory, and blessing. And every creature which is in heaven, and on the earth, and under the earth, and such as are in the sea, and all that are in them, heard I saying, Blessing, and honor, and glory, and power, be unto him that sitteth upon the throne, and unto the Lamb for ever and ever. Revelation 5:12-13*

DISCLAIMER

I've gathered a lot of information over the years from reading the great theologians' Bible study notes and books. If I've used some text from a source without giving credit, please accept my sincere apology.

I use the King James Bible version as it's based on a firm foundation of manuscripts, and it's a good word-for-word translation. Study tools like the Strong's Hebrew and Greek Dictionary are based on it, as are the commentaries of the great theologians of the 17th-20th centuries.

Instead of using the generic title of '*God*,' I use the name '*Yah*' which is based on the Tetragrammaton, the combination of four Hebrew letters, *yud-hey-vav-hey* (יהוה) that form the ancient Hebrew name of the Heavenly Father. Some use the Hebrew rendering of our Heavenly Father's name as *Yahuah*. Others use the Aramaic rendering of our Heavenly Father's name as *Yahweh*. HalleluYah means *Praise Yah!*

Could I be wrong about some of my explanations? Of course, but I'm confident that if you read the whole book, you'll see the truth about the fulfillment of Revelation so that you are not deceived.

I use these abbreviations to not fill the book up with the full titles and to reinforce them in your mind as you recall them.

RCC	=	The Roman Catholic Church
SOJ	=	The Society of Jesus, the Jesuit leaders in Rome
ACBP	=	The Antichrist Beast Pope, the White Pope
JSG	=	The Jesuit Superior General, the Black Pope
FPJSG	=	The False Prophet Jesuit Superior General

All verses are from Revelation unless otherwise noted. I apologize in advance for any mistakes, as I truly dislike seeing errors in books. I did not correct spelling or grammar errors in the quotes or commentaries. Thankfully, our gracious Heavenly Father and Messiah use flawed people when we're willing to step outside of our comfort zone.

CHAPTER 1 - THE BEASTS OF DANIEL

The proof that the beast kingdoms described in Daniel 2 and 7 are the same is evident. The number is the same, four in each. The starting point is the same, for each was given while Babylon was the ruling power. The order is the same, for the kingdoms in the first vision are successive. There is the same graduation, for the noblest metal (gold) and the noblest animal (lion) take the lead in each series.

Only five supreme and ruling kingdoms are announced by name in the Scriptures, from the time of Daniel to the close of the sacred canon. The first four kingdoms are established and ruled by men, the fifth by Messiah. The first four are smitten and broken in pieces; the last one, Messiah's kingdom, endures forever. HalleluYah!

The Babylonian beast kingdom was in power from 612-539 BC.

Babylon was used to destroy the temple and city of Jerusalem and take the House of Judah captive for seventy years because of their abominations of worshiping false gods. The book of Daniel was written while they were in Babylon. During this time, King Nebuchadnezzar had a dream, which Daniel interpreted for him.

> *This image's head was of fine gold, its chest and arms of silver, its belly and thighs of bronze, its legs of iron, its feet partly of iron and partly of clay.*
> Daniel 2:32-33

Daniel states that the first kingdom is Babylon.

> *Thou, O king, art a king of kings: for the God of heaven hath given thee a kingdom, power, and strength, and glory. And wheresoever the children of men dwell, the beasts of the field and the fowls of the heaven hath he given into thine hand, and hath made thee ruler over them all. <u>Thou art this head of gold</u>.* Daniel 2:37-38

Daniel 7:3 says: *And four great beasts came up from the sea, diverse one from another.*

Daniel 7:17 says: *These great beasts, which are four, are four kings, which shall arise out of the earth.*

This tells us that a *'beast'* in prophecy is a great kingdom, which is the same message of Daniel 2, about four pagan kingdoms.

Daniel 7:4 says, *The first was like a lion, and had eagle's wings: I beheld till the wings thereof were plucked, and it was lifted up from the earth, and made stand upon the feet as a man, and a man's heart was given to it.*

The kingdom of Babylon was strong, courageous, and fierce as a *lion.* A lion's image is found at the Ishtar Gate along the processional way into the city of Babylon. It was constructed around 575 BC by King Nebuchadnezzar II. Babylon had *eagle's wings* as it swiftly conquered several kingdoms, adding them to its empire, which brought their monarchy to a prodigious height in a short time.

Its wings, which once lifted it above other nations, were *plucked off* by the Medo-Persians, who stopped their conquests. The once-fierce beast lost its strength and became more mild and tractable. Their lion-like courage was reduced to being faint and cowardly like other men.

Jeremiah describes the Babylonian kingdom as a lion:

The lion is come up from his thicket, and the destroyer of the Gentiles is on his way; he is gone forth from his place to make thy land desolate; and thy cities shall be laid waste, without an inhabitant. Jeremiah 4:7

The king of Babylon hath heard the report of them, and his hands waxed feeble: anguish took hold of him, and pangs as of a woman in travail. Behold, he shall come up like a lion from the swelling of Jordan unto the habitation of the strong: but I will make them suddenly run away from her: and who is a chosen man, that I may appoint over her? for who is like me? and who will appoint me the time? and who is that shepherd that will stand before me? Jeremiah 50:43-44

13

Daniel 5 told the Babylonian king that his kingdom was at an end and would be given to the Medes and Persians. In the vision of the handwriting on the wall, Daniel told the Babylonian king.

This is the interpretation of the thing; God hath numbered thy kingdom, and finished it. Thou art weighed in the balances, and art found wanting. Thy kingdom is divided, and given to the Medes and Persians. Daniel 5:26-28

In that night was Belshazzar the king of the Chaldeans slain. And Darius the Median took the kingdom, being about threescore and two years old. Daniel 5:30-31

In those verses, we see the transition from the Babylonian beast kingdom to the Medo-Persian kingdom.

The Medo-Persian beast kingdom was in power from 539-331 B.C.

Daniel told Nebuchadnezzar that after the kingdom of Babylon would come a lesser kingdom.

Daniel 2:39 says, *And after thee shall arise another kingdom inferior to thee, and another third kingdom of brass, which shall bear rule over all the earth.*

Daniel 7:5 says, *And behold another beast, a second, like to a bear, and it raised up itself on one side, and it had three ribs in the mouth of it between the teeth of it: and they said thus unto it, Arise, devour much flesh.*

Silver is a lesser metal than gold, and the bear is less ferocious than a lion. The *chest of silver* in Daniel 2 and the *bear* of Daniel 7 point to the Medes and Persians, who were fierce, ravenous people. They destroyed many countries, and their hunger could not be satisfied.

The Medes first arose (*raised on one side*) and sent to Cyrus the Persian to assist him against Babylon. Babylon, Lydia, and Egypt were oppressed by the Medes and Persians, as the '*three ribs*' were ground in the mouth of a bear. Like a bear, their army was massive, up to 1.5 million people, and they overwhelmed the enemy with their size.

Daniel 6:1 spoke of the Medo-Persian leader, *It pleased Darius to set over the kingdom an hundred and twenty princes, which should be over the whole kingdom.*

Daniel was thrown into the lion's den because of the *law of the Medes and Persians.*

Daniel 6 ends with *Daniel prospered in the reign of Darius and in the reign of Cyrus, the Persian.*

Daniel 8:3 describes the Medo-Persian Empire, where the Persian portion was more substantial (*higher horn*).

Then I lifted up mine eyes, and saw, and, behold, there stood before the river a ram which had two horns: and the two horns were high; but one was higher than the other, and the higher came up last.

Daniel 9:1-2 points to Darius of the Medes.

In the first year of Darius the son of Ahasuerus, of the seed of the Medes, which was made king over the realm of the Chaldeans; In the first year of his reign I Daniel understood by books the number of the years, whereof the word of the LORD came to Jeremiah the prophet, that he would accomplish seventy years in the desolations of Jerusalem.

Daniel stayed in Babylon even after the Jews were released from captivity by Cyrus, the Persian king.

In the third year of Cyrus king of Persia a thing was revealed unto Daniel, whose name was called Belteshazzar; and the thing was true, but the time appointed was long: and he understood the thing, and had understanding of the vision. Daniel 10:1

Isaiah 44:28 foretold the role of Cyrus,

That said of Cyrus, He is my shepherd, and shall perform all my pleasure: even saying to Jerusalem, Thou shall be built; and to the temple, Thy foundation shall be laid.

History confirms that Persia's leaders set the Jews free from captivity and empowered them to rebuild Jerusalem and the temple. The book of Ezra focuses on the temple rebuilding, while the book of Nehemiah talks about the reconstruction of the walls of Jerusalem.

> *Now in the first year of Cyrus king of Persia, that the word of the LORD by the mouth of Jeremiah might be fulfilled, the LORD stirred up the spirit of Cyrus king of Persia, that he made a proclamation throughout all his kingdom, and put it also in writing, saying, Thus says Cyrus king of Persia, The Lord God of heaven hath given me all the kingdoms of the earth; and he hath charged me to build him an house at Jerusalem, which is in Judah.* Ezra 1:1-2

> *And the elders of the Jews built, and they prospered through the prophesying of Haggai the prophet and Zechariah the son of Iddo. And they built, and finished it, according to the commandment of the God of Israel, and according to the commandment of Cyrus, and Darius, and Artaxerxes king of Persia.* Ezra 6:14

The book of Haggai begins by noting that they are under King Darius of Persia, *in the second year of King Darius.*

> *In the second year of Darius the king, in the sixth month, in the first day of the month, came the word of the LORD by Haggai the prophet unto Zerubbabel the son of Shealtiel, governor of Judah, and to Joshua the son of Josedech, the high priest.*

The book of Zechariah also begins by noting that they are under King Darius of Persia in King Darius's second year.

> *In the eighth month, in the second year of Darius, came the word of the LORD unto Zechariah, the son of Berechiah, the son of Iddo the prophet.*

Daniel 11:1-2 points to the overthrow of Persia by the Greeks.

> *Also I in the first year of Darius the Mede, even I, stood to confirm and to strengthen him. And now will I show thee the truth. Behold, there shall stand up yet three kings in Persia; and the fourth shall be far richer than*

they all: and by his strength, through his riches, he shall stir up all against the realm of Grecia.

Daniel, and the other prophets, spoke about the Medo-Persian Empire and then the transition to the Grecian Empire.

The Grecian beast kingdom was in power from 331-168 BC.

Daniel told Nebuchadnezzar that a third kingdom shall arise, that is represented by *brass*, which is inferior to silver and gold.

And after thee shall arise another kingdom inferior to thee, and another third kingdom of brass, which shall bear rule over all the earth. Daniel 2:39

The *brass waist* represents the kingdom of Greece, as Alexander the Great defeated the kingdom of Medo-Persia.

Daniel 7:6 says, *After this I beheld, and lo another, like a leopard, which had upon the back of it four wings of a fowl; the beast had also four heads; and dominion was given to it.*

Alexander the Great and his Grecian army gained control over the known world of his day in only ten years, by the time he was 32. His army was small compared to those they faced, making them agile like a *'leopard.'* Their weapons and strategies made them very effective.

Daniel 8:5 points to Alexander the Great as the *'notable horn.'*

And as I was considering, behold, an he goat came from the west on the face of the whole earth, and touched not the ground: and the goat had a notable horn between his eyes.

Daniel 8:6 points to Alexander the Great overthrowing the Persian Empire.

And he came to the ram that had two horns, which I had seen standing before the river, and ran unto him in the fury of his power.

Daniel 8:8 points to Alexander the Great subduing the world and then dying at a young age.

Therefore the he goat waxed very great: and when he was strong, the great horn was broken; and for it came up four notable ones toward the four winds of heaven.

Alexander died in his 30's with no surviving heirs, so his kingdom was divided. The *'four wings'* represent Alexander's four chief captains (Cassander, Lysimachus, Seleucus, and Ptolemy) who helped him conquer and then became heads of the empire after his death.

Daniel 8 gives the vision of Medo-Persia being destroyed and succeeded by the kingdom of Greece.

The ram which thou saw having two horns are the kings of Media and Persia. And the rough goat is the king of Grecia: and the great horn that is between his eyes is the first king. Daniel 8:20-21

The *little horn* of Daniel 8:9 is Antiochus Epiphanes, who arose out of the Seleucidae of Syria. He was called a *little horn* because he was much less of a leader than Alexander the Great.

And out of one of them came forth a little horn, which waxed exceeding great, toward the south, and toward the east, and toward the pleasant land.

Daniel 10 speaks of the change of power from Persia to Greece.

Then said he, knowest thou wherefore I come unto thee? and now will I return to fight with the prince of Persia: and when I am gone forth, lo, the prince of Grecia shall come. Daniel 10:20

Daniel 11 gives the continuous historical narrative of Medo-Persia, Greece and Antiochus Epiphanes, and then Rome. Alexander the Great, the Mighty King, rose and ruled with great dominion.

The Seleucid Empire was a Hellenistic state ruled by the Seleucid dynasty founded by Seleucus I Nicator following the division of the empire. The Seleucids (kings of Syria, *"the north"*) and the Ptolemies (kings of Egypt, *"the south"*) had incessant wars.

Daniel 11:21 points to Antiochus Epiphanes.

And in his estate shall stand up a vile person, to whom they shall not give the honor of the kingdom: but he shall come in peaceably, and obtain the kingdom by flatteries.

The Jewish Maccabean Revolt lasted from 167 to 160 BC, between a Judean rebel group known as the Maccabees and the Seleucid Empire. The Maccabean uprisings delivered the Jews in the reign of Antiochus, and faithfully served their people as rulers and priests for 130 years.

The Grecian Empire ended with the overthrow and subduing of Greece and Carthage in the decisive *Battle of Pydna* against King Perseus.

This entirely broke the power of the ancient kingdom of Macedon, with the final demise coming some years later.

The Roman beast kingdom rose in 168 BC and is still in power.

Iron is a base metal, compared to gold, silver, and bronze, but it is very strong.

His legs of iron, his feet part of iron and part of clay. Daniel 2:33

The two legs represent the iron kingdom of Rome, which split into the Western Roman Empire and the Eastern Roman Empire.

And the fourth kingdom shall be strong as iron: forasmuch as iron breaks in pieces and subdues all things: and as iron that breaks all these, shall it break in pieces and bruise. Daniel 2:40

The iron Roman Empire conquered the many nations around it with ruthless barbarity and efficiency.

Daniel 7 expands on the description of the fourth beast kingdom

After this I saw in the night visions, and behold, a fourth beast, dreadful and terrible, exceedingly strong. It had huge iron teeth; it was devouring, breaking in pieces, and trampling the residue with its feet. It was different from all the beasts that were before it, and it had ten horns. Daniel 7:7

In the fourth kingdom of both Daniel 2 and Daniel 7, we see the *iron,* which represents its *strength.* The *iron teeth* point back to the *iron legs* of the Roman Empire of Daniel 2. We see that it's *breaking* other kingdoms, confirming that both Daniel 2 and 7 are pointing to the same kingdom.

The Roman Empire was diverse from the other beast kingdoms in power and greatness, the extent of dominion, and duration. There was no one beast in nature to which it could be compared; it had all the ill properties of the other beasts, for craft, cruelty oppression, and tyranny; and therefore John describes this same beast as being like a *leopard,* having the feet of a *bear* and the mouth of a *lion.*

Though Daniel 11:20 seems to point to the Grecian Empire raising taxes, it is interesting that we see in Luke 2:1-3 that Roman Caesar Augustus was also a raiser of taxes.

> *And it came to pass in those days, that there went out a decree from Caesar Augustus, that all the world should be taxed. (And this taxing was first made when Cyrenius was governor of Syria.) And all went to be taxed, every one into his own city.*

The book of Revelation is about the fourth kingdom, the legs of *iron* in Daniel 2, the *dreadful* beast of Daniel 7 whose teeth were made of *iron,* the Roman Empire, which split into two parts, the Western and Eastern Divisions. It trampled everything in its path. It was in power during Messiah's ministry and when John wrote Revelation.

Daniel 12 describes the *Jewish people's desolation* at the Romans' hands during the Jewish-Roman War of 66-70 AD, prophesied in Daniel 9 and Messiah's Olivet Discourse. The *abomination of desolation* that Messiah warned about was fulfilled in 66 AD, when the first division of the Roman army surrounded Jerusalem (Luke 21:20-21), built ramps up the walls, and was ready to take it captive. Then they left for no apparent reason, other than the hand of Yah. The saints saw the *sign,* and they took the opportunity to flee Judea to the mountains of Pella for safety. The Jews were encouraged, and they stayed in Jerusalem.

Then three divisions of the Roman army surrounded Jerusalem and camped out, which led to hundreds of thousands of Jews dying from famine, pestilence, infighting, suicide, evisceration, and crucifixion.

One thousand two hundred ninety days after the *abomination of desolation* appeared, the Roman army *flooded* the city and killed hundreds of thousands of Jews by the sword. The siege lasted for forty-five days when it ended abruptly after the last stronghold of Jews surrendered. That fulfilled the 1,335 days of Daniel 12. I cover this in detail in my **The Olivet Discourse Decoded** book.

The book of Revelation is about the fourth beast kingdom of Rome, which stays in power until Messiah returns to destroy it. The *little horn* of Daniel 7 is fulfilled by the Popes, once again proving that the four kingdoms in Daniel 2 and 7 are only about four beast kingdoms, the last of which is Rome.

John picks up the story of the Roman beast kingdom and describes three different phases in Revelation 12-13.

In *Key To The Apocalypse*, Henry Grattan Guinness says,
The four great empires of prophecy plainly agree with the four great empires of history. Their number is the same, their order is the same; they have the same commencing-point and the same course, character, and termination. The first kingdom of Ptolemy and Daniel is the Babylonian, the second the Medo-Persian, the third the Grecian, the fourth the Roman.

Daniel doubly represents these four empires by four distinct metallic parts of a single image, by four successive Wild Beasts. The fourth kingdom of Daniel reappears three times in the Apocalypse of John, while the fifth kingdom of Daniel, the eternal kingdom of the God of heaven, is the terminal kingdom of the Apocalypse.

The kingdom of the Mountain in Daniel 2, represented as the kingdom of the Son of Man and of the saints in Daniel 7, is identical with the kingdom of Christ and the saints in Revelation 20-22.

Further, the three great visions of the fourth empire in the Apocalypse represent successive stages in its history. The first of these represents the Roman Empire under the regnancy of its crowned Heads; the second under the regnancy of its crowned Horns; the third as carrying the Harlot Babylon, whom it subsequently casts off and destroys.

Sir Isaac Newton said, *The Apocalypse of John is written in the same style and language with the prophecies of Daniel, and hath the same relation to them which they have to one another so that all of them together make but one complete prophecy.* (1)

In *The Seventh Vial* **(1848), James Aitken Wylie says,** *There is a close resemblance, as anyone may see who compares the two descriptions, between the fourth beast of Daniel and the beast of the sea seen by John. The description given by Daniel is such as to lead us to conclude that the fourth beast was a compound of the preceding three. It had the teeth of the Babylonian lion, the claws of the Persian bear, and the spotted skin of the Macedonian leopard; that is, it possessed all the propensities of its predecessors, in addition to its own characteristic qualities. Now, such is precisely the appearance of the beast of the sea, verse 2: "And the beast which I saw was like until a leopard, and his feet were as the feet of a bear, and his mouth as the mouth of a lion."*

The summary is that Daniel only describes four beast kingdoms and that John picks up the narrative of the fourth, the Roman beast kingdom, in the apocalyptic vision. This becomes important when we discuss the *sea beast* and the *earth beast* of Revelation 13 and the *harlot* church of Revelation 17.

The countries of Israel and the United States of America are referred to in Revelation, but not as the controlling beast kingdom. You'll see that Revelation is predominantly pointing to the Roman beast kingdom, as Satan empowers its leaders to make war with Messiah and His saints. The saying *'All roads lead to Rome'* will take on new meaning as you read the explanation of the prophecies in Messiah's apocalyptic vision.

CHAPTER 2 - HISTORICISM VS. FUTURISM

The enemy has caused people to believe that the 70th week of Daniel 9, 2 Thessalonians 2 and most of Revelation are yet to be fulfilled. Here's the basic false narrative that we have been led to believe.

A one-man antichrist will make a seven-year Israeli peace agreement, which marks the start of a futuristic 7-year tribulation period.

Some believe that they will be raptured out at this point.

There will be 3 ½ years of relative peace, in which time the temple will be rebuilt in Jerusalem.

Then at the midpoint, the antichrist will enter the temple, desolate it and proclaim to be God.

Then there will be 3 ½ years of *great tribulation*, in which most of Revelation will be fulfilled.

That false narrative is based on the concept of a futuristic 70th week of Daniel 9. Friend, there will be no future 7-year tribulation period! The 70th week of Daniel 9 was fulfilled on time, from 27-34 AD, when Messiah *confirmed* the *everlasting covenant* in the midst of the seven years of the 70th week, with His blood as the Spotless Lamb. I prove it out in my *The 70th Week Of Daniel 9 Decoded* book, which you can get @ **www.70thweekofdaniel.com**

This is one of Satan's grandest deceptions, for he has taken a passage that points to the promised Messiah and has assigned it to an end-times antichrist making an Israel peace agreement. We are not waiting on a futuristic one-man antichrist to make an Israel peace agreement because the *covenant* of Daniel 9:27 was the *everlasting covenant* that Daniel pleaded with our Heavenly Father to remember in Daniel 9:4.

The *antichrist beast* of Revelation is not just one man; it's an office, like the President of the USA or the King of England. Since 900 AD, when the Popes were rising to great power, the saints have proclaimed that the Popes fulfill Bible prophecy as the *little horn* of Daniel 7, the *son of perdition* of 2 Thessalonians 2, and the *antichrist beast* of Revelation, who leads the *harlot* church of Rome.

The Protestant Reformers all proclaimed the same thing, which caused millions of Catholics to be saved by faith in Messiah and come out of Rome's *harlot* church. The Popes responded by empowering the SOJ to counter the Reformation, part of which was to write futuristic explanations of a one-man antichrist in a futuristic 70th week of Daniel; to deflect blame away from the Popes.

The great theologians of the 16th-19th centuries all proclaimed the historical fulfillment of the 70th week of Daniel. With one accord, they all proclaimed that Revelation has been in the process of being fulfilled since it was written.

In the late 16th century, SOJ priest Francisco Ribera, a brilliant man with a doctorate in theology, wrote a 500-page commentary with an opposing view, where he manipulated the 70th week of Daniel 9 prophecy to create an end-time 7-year tribulation that features a one-man antichrist, and most of Revelation fulfilled in the last few years.

Following close behind was another brilliant SOJ scholar, Cardinal Robert Bellarmine of Rome. He promoted Ribera's concepts in his work *"Polemic Lectures Concerning the Disputed points of the Christian Belief Against the Heretics of this Time."*

In 1812, a Roman SOJ priest named Manuel de Lacunza published the work *'The Coming of Messiah in Glory and Majesty.'* Knowing that Protestants would not embrace a Jesuit's teachings, Lacunza wrote the book under the pen name of *'Juan Josafat Ben-Ezra,'* a supposed converted Jew, to get Protestants to read it.

In the 19th century, Dr. Samuel Roffey Maitland advanced the SOJ teachings. James H. Todd published pamphlets and books supporting their teachings.

John Henry Newman promoted their explanations in England. Minister Edward Irving created the concept of the *'secret rapture.'* John Nelson Darby created the concept of *dispensationalism*.

The *Scofield Reference Bible* established the deception in America. It was received by Congregationalists, Baptists, and some Presbyterian denominations. Lewis Sperry Chafer, an American theologian, became associated with Scofield's ministry, who became his mentor. When Scofield died in 1921, Chafer moved to Dallas, Texas, to pastor the *First Congregational Church of Dallas*, where Scofield had ministered. Chafer went on to found *Dallas Theological Seminary*, taking with him the false, futuristic explanations.

DTS is the key place where the SOJ concepts are taught to thousands of Pastors, including today's top TV and radio personalities. Graduates of DTS include the following people. Author John F. Walvoord. Charles Caldwell Ryrie promoted futurism in his *Ryrie Study Bible*. Hal Lindsey brought their deceptions to the mainstream. Chuck Swindoll and *Insight For Living*. David Jeremiah and *Turning Point Broadcast Ministries*. J. Vernon McGee and *Thru the Bible Radio Network* program. Ron Rhodes and *Reasoning from the Scriptures Ministries*. Dr. Thomas Ice of the *Left Behind* series of books and movies.

DTS graduates go to work for Christian denominations, seminaries, Bible colleges, and publishing companies. They become pastors throughout the world. And that's how the leaven of the SOJ's deceptions have spread around the world during the last century.

So when you look around and see the majority of people believe in the futuristic explanations of prophecy fulfillment, now you understand how the enemy has worked to push the false explanations, to hide the truth of the fulfillment of Revelation, which authenticates Scripture and the deity of Messiah. The enemy programs people's minds through repetition. *If you tell a lie big enough and keep repeating it, people will eventually come to believe it.*

So are these Pastors misled? Are they ignorant? Are they wolves in sheep's clothing? The prophecy fulfillment explanations in this book prove that the majority of today's pastors are teaching end-time prophecy concepts that are false, which makes them false prophecy teachers. They may be sincere Christians, but they teach false doctrine, and they will be held accountable! Most of them have been deceived at seminaries and Bible schools, where the SOJ infiltrated the ranks to deceive them. Others are wolves in sheep's clothing, who have sold out to the riches of Rome.

There are definite strongholds in Pastors' lives that aren't allowing them to see the truth, so they desperately need our prayers. The witness of history proves that most of Revelation has already been fulfilled during the last 1,900 years, which validates the historical view of prophecy.

We will all stand before our Righteous Judge, saying that your pastor taught you these concepts would not be an acceptable excuse, for we are all called to compare what men teach with Scripture. That applies to this book. Please don't blindly trust what I say. Pray about it and compare it to Scripture.

Timothy foretold what would take place in the end times.

> *For the time will come when they will not endure sound doctrine; but after their own lusts shall they heap to themselves teachers, having itching ears.* 2 Timothy 4:3

We're in one of the most important eras in the history of the world. If your pastor is just teaching you how to live a better life and they're not giving you the proper explanations of the fulfillment of prophecy, to let you know how the end times are going to play out and to give you the context of Messiah's return, then that's problematic.

When you read the explanations in this book and see how the prophecies in Messiah's apocalyptic vision are fulfilled, you will understand why I emphasize the importance of Pastors teaching primarily about prophecy fulfillment.

CHAPTER 3 - THE EARLY SAINTS PERSPECTIVE

Some people cite the early church fathers' perspective of Revelation prophecy fulfillment, proclaiming that they must know the true fulfillment because they lived close to the disciples' time. But the early church saints' perspective during the first few centuries has to be seen in its proper context.

For example, early church fathers thought that the length of the *antichrist beast's* reign of power and the time of *great tribulation* foretold in Revelation 13 would be 3 ½ years long. They expected an individual antichrist who would rise to power out of the fallen Rome Empire, rule for 1,260 days, and then Messiah would return. They had no concept that the *antichrist beast* would reign for 1,260 years, as they weren't in the frame of mind to see that one day was pointing to one year.

So we have to keep that in mind when people cite the beliefs of early church fathers of the first few centuries; because some people proclaim that their views are as authoritative as Scripture.

In *History Unveiling Prophecy*, Henry Grattan Guinness says,
To have interpreted the 1,260 days as symbolically representing 1,260 years of suffering and subjected condition of witnesses to gospel truth, was of course impossible at that early period of the church's history. The latter view only dawned upon the minds of Apocalyptic interpreters during the actual fulfillment of the prophecy of the middle ages.

It was universally believed that after the Roman Empire split and the Antichrist appeared, it was the end of the world and the kingdom of heaven was at hand. They no doubt believe in 3 1/2 years of tribulation based on the 42 months prophecy, but it was unimaginable to think it would last 1,260 years.

27

CHAPTER 4 – THE DOCTRINE OF PRETERISM

Before we get to the fulfillment of Revelation, let me address an association that some people make when you explain Revelation's historical fulfillment. Because it's contrary to the futuristic explanations that they've been taught, they put you in a box and call you a *'Preterist.'*

So what is Preterism? It's another false prophecy fulfillment perspective created by the SOJ to deflect blame away from the ACBP.

In the 16th century, Spanish Jesuit Luis De Alcazar wrote a 900-page commentary called *Investigation of the Hidden Sense of the Apocalypse.* He proposed that all of Revelation applied to the era of pagan Rome.

Most Preterists believe that Revelation is symbolic and that all or most of it was fulfilled in the first century or the first few centuries, and Roman Emperor Nero was the *antichrist beast.*

That is not what I teach, so I am not a Preterist. I'm a Historicist who proves in this book that most of the prophecies in Revelation have been fulfilled during the last 1,900 years, and there's not much left to be fulfilled before Messiah returns.

Don't let people put you in a box when you try to help them see the historical fulfillment of prophecy. The exacting historical fulfillment of the prophecies in Revelation proves Futurism and Preterism wrong.

Keep in mind Paul's admonition in 1 Corinthians 8:2.

And if any man think that he knows any thing, he knows nothing yet as he ought to know.

REVELATION BASICS
CHAPTER 5 - HISTORY UNVEILS PROPHECY

People try to figure out Revelation based on what's going on in the world today, but to their detriment, they ignore what has happened to the saints during the last 1,900 years. History unveils prophecy. Unless you understand the history of the persecution of the saints, the Roman Empire, the Roman Popes, the Dark Ages, the Inquisition, and the Protestant Reformation, you can't understand Messiah's Revelation because He was foretelling the narrative of those things.

In its simplest form, the apocalyptic vision is the narrative of the historical battle between the Satan-empowered leader of the Roman beast kingdom fighting against Messiah and His saints. We can look back and see how most of it has been fulfilled in exacting detail. Based on that, we can see where we are on the fulfillment timeline and what will happen next as we await Messiah's glorious return.

In the 18th century, Edward Gibbon wrote the epic 6-volume *The History of the Decline and Fall of the Roman Empire.* Gibbon had no belief in the divine origin of the true faith. We can use it as an impartial and fair witness, for he didn't write it to refute or vindicate the prophecies in the Bible. Amazingly, it documents the time from the first seal until the sixth trumpet, from its height of power to its fall.

In *Vision Of The Ages* (1881), Barton Johnson says, *The Greek word for Revelation is transferred into the English by the word Apocalypse. This means 'uncovering.' In the fourth verse of the opening chapter a blessing is pronounced upon those who 'read, hear, and keep' the words of this prophecy. No more emphatic blessing is pronounced upon the study of any part of the word of the Lord. The reader will turn to the fifth chapter he will find that a sealed book, the book of the unknown future, sealed from mortal eyes, was in the hands of Him who sat on the throne and that the Lion of the tribe of Judah prevailed to open the book.*

One after another, in succession, the seals are loosed, and the map of the future, especially the history of the Church and its enemies, is unrolled until its final triumph. Not only are the seals opened and the future disclosed, but the predictions have been in a great part fulfilled and can be read upon the pages of history.

Too many have failed to study it in the light of history. John says that the things referred to were "shortly to come to pass." They were future when he wrote, prophecy then; they are nearly all in the past, history now. The book of prophecy must be held in one hand and the book of history in the other. Too many would-be interpreters have been shamefully ignorant of the history of the Church, and of the perils of the Church from its political or spiritual foes. A familiarity with the great work of the infidel Gibbon, The History of the Decline and Fall of the Roman Empire, a history of mankind for over 1300 years, will flood the meaning of Revelation with light. The infidel historian has unwittingly fortified the word of God.

The Spirit used Jewish-Roman historian Josephus to document the events of the first century, which led to the Jewish-Roman War of 66-70 AD, and the desolation of Jerusalem, the temple, and the Jewish nation.

And the Spirit used Roman historian Edward Gibbon to help us see the fulfillment of Revelation's seals and trumpets. How amazing is our Heavenly Father, who uses men to accomplish His purposes for His saints? HalleluYah!

Today, we have an even greater viewpoint than the Protestant Reformers and the theologians of the 16th-19th centuries. Because we have so much evidence before us, we are more accountable. I disliked history class in school, but now that I've learned the truth about prophecy fulfillment, I love learning history because it tangibly proves the authority of Scripture and edifies my faith.

CHAPTER 6 - REVELATION IS A LAYERED WAR MANUAL

Messiah's apocalyptic vision is a war manual, which is layered and coded with symbols to hide the message from those who should not understand it. That includes people who don't study the whole Word, who don't hunger and pray for the truth about prophecy fulfillment.

If you've tried to make sense of it as one chronological narrative, the narrative seems disjointed. That's because it has four chronological layers whose fulfillment spans from when it was written until Messiah returns. When the four layers are all overlapped onto a timeline, they all fit together and reveal the apocalyptic vision.

I made this Revelation Fulfillment Chart to help you see how the four chronological layers interact. To print out a high-quality image of it, go to the **www.RevelationTimelineDecoded.com** website. On the home page you can save the **Revelation Timeline Decoded summary image**. Print it out in landscape mode, in color if possible.

4th Layer - The *antichrist beast* Popes rose to power out of the fallen Roman Empire, leads *harlot* church - Revelation 17-19

Five forms of Roman government (heads) had passed. The 6th, the Emperors ruled in John's time. Last Western Emperor was removed in 476. The 7th ruled for a short space from 476-538.	The 8th head is the *antichrist beast* Popes who rose to power out the Roman Empire. His *harlot* church priests dress in scarlet and purple, and have the golden Eucharist cup. False religion came from Babylon, the beast who was, who was not in John's day, *but is* alive again in the Roman Catholic Church. She is called 'Mystery, Babylon the Great.'	The Jesuits empower and enrich the kings of the earth. They were used to carry out the bowl judgments, and their New World Order, they will cause the judgment of the *harlot* church.

3rd Layer - Seal, Trumpet and Bowl Judgments against the Roman beast - Revelation 4-11, 14-16

Seal 1 - Mighty Roman Empire conquering (white). Messiah setup kingdom, Gospel spread quickly. Seal 2 - Bloody civil wars. Emperors killed (red). Seal 3 - Economic dispair from high taxes (black). Seal 4 - Famine. 1/4th of Romans died (pale). Seal 5 - Smyra Church era martyrs. Their blood cried out for vengeance, which came shortly. Seal 6 - Constantine ended the persecutions. *Earthquake* = political upheaval. Darkened sun, moon, stars = Rome divided, leaders cast down. Seal 7 - Sealing of saints before Rome attacks. Trumpet 1 - Goths led by Alaric 400-410 Trumpet 2 - Vandals led by Genseric 425-470 Trumpet 3 - Huns led by Attila, *the scourge of God.* Trumpet 4 - Heruli led by Odoacer, removed the last Western Roman Emperor from power in 476.	Trumpet 5 represents the rise of Mohammed / Islam, who were used to attack the Western Roman Empire for 5 months (150 days = 150 years), from 612-762. They had gold turbans (*crowns of gold*), beards (*faces of men*), long hair (*like women*), they wore chain-mail (*breastplates of iron*) and were fierce (*teeth of lions*). Trumpet 6 - the Turks crossed the Euphrates River to attack the Eastern Roman Empire, for 391 years, from 1062-1453; ending in them conquering Constantinople with large cannons (*fire, smoke and brimstone*). Priests escaped Constantinople and took the Holy Scriptures to Europe, to be translated into English. The *iron/clay feet* of Daniel 2 represents the Roman Church (iron) helping write the Qur'an and prop up Mohammed as the prophet. They did this to prevent Arabs (clay) from being saved, to use them to kill Jews and the saints, and to conquer territory. They don't mix well with Christians, to take over countries, and to attack Israel in WW III, which will push the world into their New World Order.	The Little Book of Revelation 10 is the printed Bible. With the advent of the printing press, this Witness came back to life and was spread around the world. Martin Luther measured the temple and found that the Papal Church is an apostate *harlot* church. Revelation 14 points to the harvest, as millions came out of the *harlot* church; and to coming bowl judgments.	Bowl 1 - Sore of athiesm poured on France Bowl 2 - Bloody French Revolution 1793 Bowl 3 - Killing Catholics spread to rural France Bowl 4 - Bloody Napoleonic wars killed Catholics Bowl 5 - Pope captured in 1798, lost power Bowl 6 - Ottoman Empire *dried up* by 1922. *Kings of the east* = fake Khazar Jews in Israel. Gog = Lord Rothschild, Magog = Khazar Jews 3 spirits = 3 World Wars. **We're here**, waiting on WW III, and a worldwide economic collapse. Bowl 7 - NWO controlled by the 3 city-states of Vatican City, London and Washington D.C.

2nd Layer - The seven Church eras which have battled against the different phases of the Roman beast - Revelation 2-3

Ephesus	Smyrna	Pergamos	Thyatira	Sardis	Philadelphia	Laodicea
Ephesus spread the Gospel in Roman Empire. Their love grew cold when Messiah didn't return soon.	Smyrna saints were persecuted by the pagan Emperors, especially from 303-312, the 10 days of 5th Seal.	Pergamos Many saints fell away from the Scriptural faith, when they compromised with Rome.	Thyatira means 'ruled by a woman,' the *harlot* Roman Church. The *antichrist beast* Popes sought to eliminate the Two Witnesses against them. They killed the Saints and burned the Scriptures so relentlessly that in May 1514, they proclaimed that the Two Witnesses were dead, silenced, and that all of Christendom was under their authority. And they held great feasts to celebrate.	Sardis means 'escaping one.' Messiah called them 'dead.' Exactly 3.5 years after the Pope said they were *dead*, Luther posted his 95 Thesis, sparking the Protestant Reformation, and the Witnesses came back to life.	The Philadelphia saints led many worldwide missions. Bible Societies spread Word / Gospel. Millions saved.	The end-times saints of this era think that they're rich in truth; but they've been blinded by the enemy; as the Jesuits have deceived them with false, futuristic prophecy explanations.

The Roman Emperor (the *restrainer of 2 Thes 2*) was removed from power in 476, which was the *deadly head wound* (Rev 13). This allowed the Son of Perdition Popes to take the Emperors place as Pontifex Maximus, healing the *head wound.*	This 1,260 year period from 538-1798 fulfilled the prophecies about 'time, and times and half a time', '1,260 days', and 'forty two months' as one day pointed to one year. During this time of great tribulation, the Two Witnesses, the Saints and the Scriptures, were almost wiped out by the *antichrist beast* Popes. The saints were tortured with brutal devices and over 50 million saints were killed, many were burned at the stake.	We're called to protest against the *antichrist beast* Popes & false prophet Superior Generals; to expose their prophecy deceptions, to preach the Gospel and help people come out of Babylon. www.RevelationTimelineDecoded.com

1st Layer - The three phases of the Satan-empowered Roman Beast - Revelation 12-13

Revelation 12 describes the pagan Roman Empire, which Satan used to try to wipe out the early Church (woman), killing millions of saints. Judgement came, the seal judgments caused its decline, and the trumpet judgments caused its fall. The Empire split into ten kingdoms, the ten horns. Satan countered by creating a false, *harlot* Roman church to be led by the *antichrist beast* Popes. The Popes are the *little horn of Daniel 7* that plucked out three leaders who didn't bow down to the Pope's authority.	The Revelation 13 *sea beast* was the next phase of the Roman beast, as the Popes rose to power out of a sea of people, out of the 10 civil kingdoms of the fallen Roman Empire. The *antichrist beast* Popes were given power and authority for 1,260 years, from 538-1798. They took the title Pontifex Maximus, the head of church and state, healing the *deadly head wound.* The Popes of Rome are the Son of Perdition, as they pretend to be the leader of Messiah's Church, thus they sit in the *temple of God.* They proclaimed to be God, forgive sins, and provide salvation, which is blasphemy. They persecuted the saints, so they're *anti-Christ.* Their teachings are contrary to Christ, saying that Mary is the Intercessor, and is *anti-Christ.* And they have the title of the 'Vicar of Christ,' taking the place of Christ. Pope removed from power in 1798, ending their 1,260 year reign of power. The *mark of the beast* = revering and obeying the Pope.	The Revelation 13 *earth beast* is the last phase of the Roman beast, which is led by the *false prophet* Superior General and *antichrist beast* Pope; the *two horns* (leaders) who pretend to be Christ-like (*like a lamb*), but really serve Satan. The Superior General (Black Pope) controls the Vatican and is using it to gather the world under their power. He controls the U.S. to use as his war machine, to overthrow leaders who don't bow down to his authority, setup Rothschild central bank. 666 = crucifix, Lateinos = Pope

| 313 | 476 | 538 | 1514 | 1798 | All dates are A.D. |

The first layer describes three phases of the Roman beast kingdom.

Daniel pointed to Rome in describing the fourth beast kingdom, which stays in power until Messiah returns to destroy it. The first layer is given in Revelation 12-13, where John describes the three phases of the Roman beast kingdom and the Satan-empowered leaders (the pagan Emperors > the ACBP > the FPJSG) that His followers battle against.

The second layer describes the seven church eras of Revelation 2-3.

In Revelation 2-3, John describes seven church eras which have spanned from when John wrote the vision until Messiah returns. The saints of Messiah in these church eras have had to battle against the different phases of the Roman beast kingdom.

The third layer describes the seal, trumpet, and bowl judgments.

On the Revelation Fulfillment Chart, you can see how the seal, trumpet, and bowl judgments occur during the different Roman beast kingdom phases and the different church eras.

The fourth layer describes how the Pope's *harlot* church came to be.

Revelation 17-18 describes the *harlot* church of Rome, which is led by the ACBP. It gives many details about the apostate church so that she is unmistakable. And it describes the judgment of the *harlot* church.

Revelation 19 describes the bride of Messiah being made ready, the capture of the ACBP and FPJSG, the desolation of the armies with them, Satan being bound, and the saints reigning in power. HalleluYah!

I think that it's very interesting that Messiah proclaims that He's the *'Alpha and Omega'* four times in Revelation. Is He pointing to the four chronological layers which span from the first century until His return?

This book explains the prophecies as they're fulfilled on the timeline so that you see how the four chronological layers interact to comprehend the whole vision.

CHAPTER 7 - THE SEVEN CHURCH ERAS

Messiah's message to the seven churches of Revelation 2-3 has a general application to the saints of the 1st century, and His admonition and encouragement apply to saints in every generation. But suppose Messiah's message was only to the saints when Revelation was written. In that case, it makes no sense that each of the churches would face dramatically different situations since they are in such close proximity.

There were much bigger churches in Corinth, Philippi, Colossae, Thessalonica, etc. Why did Messiah speak only to these churches?

Revelation 1:20 sets up the narrative of the seven church eras and provides some definitions that we will see applied in the prophecies.

The mystery of the seven stars which thou saw in my right hand, and the seven golden candlesticks. The seven stars are the angels of the seven churches: and the seven candlesticks which thou saw are the seven churches.

Messiah is telling us that there's a *'mystery'* to be solved to unlock the apocalyptic vision.

The *secret* is that Messiah is pointing to seven church eras, which span from when Revelation was written until He returns. He chose these seven assemblies because their names and culture provide symbolism that points to what the saints' face during the seven church eras. Interestingly, these seven assemblies were founded by the Apostle John, to whom Messiah gave the vision.

A *'star'* in prophecy can point to a *'leader.'* The word *angel* is Greek Strong's 32 *aggelos*, which means: *a messenger; especially an "angel"; by implication, a pastor:—angel, messenger.* The seven stars are pointing to the leaders of the seven church eras.

John is told to write to these *angels*, and certainly, the letters were not sent to the angels of heaven. Therefore, it becomes evident that the *angels* are the *'star'* of the church, the leader. Messiah then defines that the *seven golden candlesticks* represent the *seven church eras*.

The Strong's Greek word for *'church'* is 1577 *ekklesia* from a compound of 1537 *ek* and a derivative of 2564 *kaleo*; which means: *a calling out, i.e. (concretely) a popular meeting, especially a religious congregation (Jewish synagogue, or Christian community of members on earth or saints in heaven or both):—assembly, church.*

Most Pastors teach that Messiah's letters to the seven churches only apply to the current state of those assemblies, but you will see a different picture: Messiah walking amid the *seven candlesticks* reveals His intimate involvement, interest, and loving care for His saints during the seven church eras, which span until He returns.

Regarding the church era of Ephesus, the saints spread the Gospel in many countries and planted new churches, which required a lot of patience. They were burdened by opposition, and many were persecuted and killed. All of the Apostles except John were killed by a violent death, which no doubt was disheartening to the saints. When Messiah didn't return after Jerusalem's destruction, they may have relaxed their efforts and lost their love and zeal for good works.

CHAPTER 8 - REVELATION IS SYMBOLIC AND LITERAL

One way to hide the message from those who shouldn't understand it is to use symbols that are defined in the Old Testament. It's like a Scriptural final exam, which tests to see who studies the whole Word. People tend to take Revelation literally and try to apply it to current events, which results in bizarre, out of context explanations.

In *Vision Of The Ages* (1881), Barton Johnson says, *We are to remember that it is a picture of some event or events of future history. We are to remember that it is symbolical and that, instead of looking for a literal fulfillment, we are to ask the meaning of the symbols.*

In *The Seventh Vial* (1848), James Aitken Wylie says, *The Apocalypse is, in brief, a history of the Church, written in grand symbolical characters, from the ascension of Christ to his second and glorious coming. The key of the Apocalypse is to be sought on the Old Testament Scriptures. This is the briefest, and perhaps the best, rule that can be laid down for the interpretation of this book. In the prophets, the heavenly bodies uniformly symbolize the rulers of kingdoms. We find this symbol employed, particularly in the denunciations against Egypt and Babylon. Of Egypt, Ezekiel says, "I will cover the sun with a cloud, and the moon shall not give her light. All the bright lights of heaven will I make dark over thee."*

In Ezekiel and other books of Scripture, we find the false church exhibited under the symbol of a harlot. Rivers point to nations. Mountains and islands point to great and small kingdoms. Air points to the political atmosphere. Heaven, to the civil or ecclesiastical firmament; the sun, the monarch; the Stars, inferior rulers. Hail and thunder point to wars. Earthquakes point to revolution. A head points to a form of government. A horn to a leader. An altar, to martyrdom. Coals, to severe judgment. A vine, to a church. An angel, to a minister of God's purposes.

Thus, when we are shown in the Apocalyptic drama, coals of fire taken from the altar and cast upon the earth, we understand that the action indicated is the infliction of terrible judgments, on account of the martyrdom of the saints, on the inhabitants of the Roman world.

In *Horae Apocalypticae*, **Edward Bishop Elliott says,** *Allusions shared between John and his audience ensured each word meant much more than its dictionary definition. In particular, John's audience was attuned to images and emblems in a way modern interpreters find hard to grasp. For example, when John said of the locusts of the fifth trumpet, "and they had hair as the hair of women, and their teeth were as the teeth of lions. And they had breastplates, as it were breastplates of iron," clear and defined metaphors were being used which the audience could pick up upon; there was no fanciful or poetic superfluity to the words chosen.*

In *Romanism And The Reformation*, **Henry Grattan Guinness says,** *The prophecies of Daniel and the Apocalypse being symbolic in their language are not to be interpreted literally. In these books, the sun, moon, stars, earth, fire, meteors, winds, storms, lightning, hail, rain, waters, sea, rivers, floods, dry land, overflowing of waters, drying up of waters, fountains, islands, trees, mountains, wilderness, beasts, as the lion, bear, leopard, goat, with their horns, heads, feet, wings, teeth, etc., are all symbolic; they are symbols of things of a different nature, though things analogous to these, or in some sense resembling them.*

Keep in mind that John is conveying visions about prophecies that are fulfilled during a span of 2,000 years, from when they were written down until Messiah returns. So a picture is worth a thousand words. He's using the symbolism of hieroglyphs to point to a literal fulfillment.

I'll explain the symbolism of the prophecies as they come up on the timeline.

CHAPTER 9 - REVELATION IS FROM JOHN'S PERSPECTIVE

The narrative of Revelation can seem confusing when we try to apply it to what's going on in the world today. This is why Messiah gave the narrative from John's perspective in the first century so that we have a solid frame of reference for what the terms meant in John's day. Messiah declared this perspective in Revelation 1:19.

> *Write the things which thou hast seen, and the things which are, and the things which shall be hereafter.*

'*Things that thou has seen*' points to what John saw in the past. '*Things which are*' points to the current circumstances when Revelation was written. And then *the things which shall be hereafter* are future from John's perspective. Messiah did this because it gives us a precise timestamp to be able to understand the prophecies.

So when we go through the explanations of the prophecies, just keep in mind that it's from John's perspective; and we have to reference that historical view to unlock the truth. In the first three verses of Revelation, Messiah said that the things He describes in His apocalyptic vision must start shortly.

> *The Revelation of Jesus Christ, which God gave unto him, to show unto his servants <u>things which must shortly come to pass</u>; and he sent and signified it by his angel unto his servant John: Who bare record of the word of God, and of the testimony of Jesus Christ, and of all things that he saw. Blessed is he that reads, and they that hear the words of this prophecy, and keep those things which are written therein: <u>for the time is at hand</u>.*

With that in mind, let's start looking at how the prophecies in Revelation are fulfilled chronologically, as we see the historical narrative of the Satan-empowered leaders of the Roman beast kingdom fighting against Messiah's saints.

CHAPTER 10 - REVELATION 12 - THE ROMAN EMPERORS

Look at the Revelation Fulfillment Chart. On the bottom, you see the three phases of the Roman beast kingdom. Read through the 1st layer summary of the Revelation 12 Roman Empire phase. Above it, you see that the Western Roman Emperor is the *'restrainer'* of 2 Thessalonians 2, who prevents the *'son of perdition'* from taking power.

On the 2nd Layer, we see the narrative of the three church eras which existed during this phase of the Roman beast kingdom (Ephesus > Smyrna > Pergamos). On the 3rd Layer, we see a summary of the seal and trumpet judgments that caused the decline and fall of the Roman Empire. I'll explain all of this in the upcoming chapters.

Revelation 12 describes the mighty Roman Empire, which Messiah described as a *great, fiery red dragon*. The *woman* is Messiah's assembly of saints. We know this because Revelation 12:17 points to the actions of the woman, who have the testimony of Messiah.

Revelation 12:3 describes the pagan Roman Empire.

And another sign appeared in heaven: behold, a great, fiery red dragon having seven heads and <u>ten horns</u>, and seven diadems on his heads.

Messiah is pointing to the fourth beast that Daniel foretold:

After this I saw in the night visions, and behold, a fourth beast, dreadful and terrible, exceedingly strong. It had huge iron teeth; it was devouring, breaking in pieces, and trampling the residue with its feet. It was different from all the beasts that were before it, and it had <u>ten horns</u>. Daniel 7:7

The dragon figure represents the Satan-empowered pagan Roman Empire, whose armies used the symbol of the *dragon* on their ensigns. As Daniel foretold, the Roman Empire was *great and dreadful*, much like a dragon, as they conquered and crushed the nations. The *'red'* represents the bloodshed of war and persecution.

The *'ten horns'* represent the ten civil kingdoms that were formed after the Roman Empire collapsed. This matches the description of the Roman beast in Daniel 7. The *seven crowns* match up with the description of the *seven kings* in Revelation 17:10, which represent the seven different forms of the Roman government.

Notice that the *diadems* are on the *seven heads*. John is telling us that the Roman Empire, which had *seven* forms of government, is in power. When it falls, and the Western Roman Emperor is removed from power, the Popes seize control, and the diadems will move to the *ten horns*.

Satan failed in his attempt to stop the promised Messiah, so he turned his wrath on His saints to try to wipe them out. The early assembly of saints was *birthed* out of much pain, as all of the disciples but John died from a violent death. Millions of saints were killed by the pagan Roman Empire. They cried in pain as they were tortured and killed. And they also had to expose the false teachings that arose.

Revelation 12:4-6 is pointing to Satan using the mighty Roman Empire to persecute the Messiah's early assembly of saints and destroy their Scriptures, the *rod of iron*. Her child, the early assembly of saints, was persecuted for their faith, and these martyrs were the first fruits of the Kingdom, who were symbolically *caught up* to Yah.

The martyrs who were killed by the Emperors did not deny their Messiah to preserve their lives; rather, they honored Him with the words of their testimony before the persecuting Romans, who must have marveled at their faith. The victory of the saints caused rejoicing in heaven, but it enraged Satan. The Roman Empire was *declining*, and he only had a *short time* to use the Emperors to try to wipe out the saints.

The Spirit caused a people group called the Vaudois to take the Scriptures to the Piedmont Valley of the Alps, away from the Satan-empowered Roman Empire's influence. They were *the Church in the wilderness*, by which the spirit of Scriptural doctrine was kept alive during the epoch of the Roman Empire persecutions.

CHAPTER 11 - THE CONQUERORS OF THE FIRST SEAL

And I saw when the Lamb opened one of the seals, and I heard, as it were the noise of thunder, one of the four beasts saying, come and see. And I saw, and behold a white horse: and he that sat on him had a bow; and a crown was given unto him: and he went forth conquering, and to conquer. **Revelation 6:1-2**

In Revelation 1:1, Messiah began to *show unto his servants things which must shortly come to pass.* In Revelation 1:3, Messiah proclaimed that *the time is at hand.* Both of those statements tell us that the prophecies began to be fulfilled shortly after they were written.

John uses symbols that the saints knew because the Roman Empire was conquering much of the territories of the three preceding empires of Babylon, Medo-Persia, and Greece. Their military conquests were celebrated by riding *white horses* in their victory parades.

At the death of Emperor Domitian, the Roman Senate appointed an elder statesman named *Nerva* in his place, a descendent from the Island of Crete. He was the first to occupy the throne of Augustus, who was not of Roman descent. He was selected on the merit of his ability.

The *bow* relates to the Cretan Dynasty of Nerva, as their warriors were known as the most famous race of *bowmen* in the ancient world. Alexander the Great used large companies of Cretan archers, and Roman armies used them during Julius Caesar's time.

Emperor Nerva reigned from 96-98, shortly after Revelation was give to John. Emperor Trajan reigned from 98-117 and he sought to extend the boundaries of the Empire to the east. They had victory parades, rode white horses and wore laurel wreath crowns. Trajan proved his greatness among scholars as perhaps second only to Augustus.

Marcus Aurelius, and the sometimes forgotten Lucius Verus, continued that pattern while re-establishing military superiority among the bordering Germanic tribes. Cretan Roman Emperor Hadrian had a coin struck that has him wearing his laurel *crown* on the front, and on the back, he is riding on a *horse* to celebrate their military victory.

This was a time of the Roman Empire's greatest expansion and their military conquests. *White* is the color of prosperity, happiness, and triumph. This *crown* is not *the diadem* that Messiah is wearing in Revelation 19:12, but the *garland crown* (*stephanos*), which is given as a reward for victory in battle and games and great achievements.

The period would come to an end amidst plague and the weariness of war with the death of Aurelius in 180. As his son Commodus ascended the throne as sole emperor, thus ending the period of 'adoptive' authority, the Empire's stability began to unravel.

Edward Gibbon documented, *In the second century of the Christian Era, the empire of Rome comprehended the fairest part of the earth, and the most civilized portion of mankind. If a man were called to fix the period in the history of the world, during which the condition of the human race was most happy and prosperous, he would, without hesitation, name that which elapsed from the death of Domitian to the accession of Commodus.*

In *Vision Of The Ages* (1881), Barton Johnson says, *John was an exile on Patmos in the last year of the reign of Domitian, A. D. 96. In that year the tyrant was slain. The humane Nerva succeeded him upon the Roman throne. With his reign begins a new epoch, it once the most brilliant and the most prosperous in Roman history. He was the founder of a new family of Caesars. He adopted, as his son and successor, the warlike Trajan, and four years later, that distinguished warrior and conqueror received the crown. His reign, beginning some four or five years after John wrote, constitutes one of the most remarkable eras in Roman history.*

The mighty kingdom of Parthia, in the heart of Central Asia, which had before successfully hurled back the Roman armies, was laid prostrate at his feet, and his victorious legions then turned southward, until they stood upon the shores of the southern seas. The terror of the Roman name was carried into kingdoms that had never before seen the face of a Roman soldier. While his greatest conquests were in Asia, in Europe, also, he ruled a vaster empire than any Roman, either before or after him. The fierce nations in the dark forests of the vast regions north of the Danube and east of the Rhine had, until his time, successfully resisted the progress of the Roman arms; but his legions forced the passage of the Danube, and, after five years conflicts, conquered the kingdom of Dacia, occupying the regions now marked upon the maps as Hungary and Romania.

Trajan was a distinguished general when John wrote. Before John had passed from earth, Trajan had received the diadem, and before a generation had passed, he stood, the mightiest conqueror of the Roman name, save Julius Caesar, upon the shores of the Southern Ocean. His age was not only an age of conquest and triumph, fitly symbolized by the white horse and his rider but an age of internal peace and prosperity. Of this happy period, Trajan, who ascended the throne four years after the death of Domitian, is the chief figure.

In all Grecian history, the bowmen of their armies are Cretans. The Rhodian slingers, the Thessalian horsemen, the Spartan spearmen, and the Cretan bowmen are constant features of Grecian history. The bow, the national weapon, might signify someone connected with Crete.

A remarkable historical fact is illustrated by the bow. Beginning with Julius, the "Twelve Caesars" who ruled the empire in succession were all of pure Roman blood. Domitian, the last of the "Twelve Caesars," the persecutor of John, was of the Roman stock, but he was the last emperor of an old Roman family that ruled for ages. He was succeeded by Nerva, the founder of a family that furnished five Caesars in succession, Trajan being the adopted son and successor of Nerva, as was Adrian, of Trajan, Antoninus, of Adrian, and Aurelius, of Antoninus. Nerva, the first emperor of this new family, the inaugurator of this epoch of Roman history, was not of the Roman blood. Dion Cassius, a historian of that age, states that he was of Greek descent, and another Roman historian, Aurelius Victor, says that his family came from the Greek island of Crete; or, in other words, he was a Cretan. We have already found that the national weapon of the Cretans was the bow and that they were famous as bowmen in all the ancient armies.

The Roman beast kingdom conquered nations thanks in part to its use of *iron weapons,* which made it very effective at destroying the enemy. The mighty Roman Empire was conquering nations, fulfilling its role as the fourth beast kingdom of Daniel 2.

> *And the fourth kingdom shall be strong as iron: forasmuch as <u>iron breaketh in pieces and subdues all things</u>: and as iron that breaketh all these, shall it break in pieces and bruise.* Daniel 2:40

The Roman Empire fulfills the fourth kingdom of Daniel 7:7

> *After this I saw in the night visions, and behold a fourth beast, dreadful and terrible, and strong exceedingly; and it had <u>great iron teeth</u>: it devoured and brake in pieces, and stamped the residue with the feet of it: and it was diverse from all the beasts that were before it; and it had ten horns.*

The first seal points to a time of temporary prosperity of the Roman Empire immediately after John wrote down the apocalyptic vision. But the first seal has another association.

CHAPTER 12 - MESSIAH SET UP HIS FATHER'S KINGDOM

In *History Unveiling Prophecy,* **Henry Grattan Guinness says,** *The early Church interpreted the first vision, that of the crowned rider seated upon a white horse, armed with a bow, going forth "conquering and to conquer," as a representation of Christ going forth on His victorious mission. The words of Origen in his answer to Celsus strikingly exhibit the conviction of the primitive Church, that its marvelous progress could only be explained by attributing it to the action of supernatural power.*

And in the vision thus interpreted is found a key to the entire prophecy; for this is the starting point of the whole. Seals, trumpets, and vials set forth a continuous course of history stretching to the consummation, having as its commencement the going forth of the Gospel of Christ to accomplish its world-subduing work. The inference is unavoidable that the Apocalypse presents a prophetic foreview of the entire course of Christian history, from the foundation of the Church to the end of the world. Nor was any other interpretation ever known in the Christian world till the rise of modern futurism.

Daniel foretold that Messiah would set up His kingdom *in the days of* the four beast kingdoms, not *after* them.

> *And in the days of these kings the God of heaven will set up a kingdom which shall never be destroyed; and the kingdom shall not be left to other people; it shall break in pieces and consume all these kingdoms, and it shall stand forever.* Daniel 2:44

> *I saw in the night visions, and, behold, one like the Son of man came with the clouds of heaven, and came to the Ancient of days, and they brought him near before him. And there was given him dominion, and glory, and a kingdom, that all people, nations, and languages, should serve him: his dominion is an everlasting dominion, which shall not pass away, and his kingdom that which shall not be destroyed.* Daniel 7:13-14

It took place in the first century when the fourth beast kingdom of Rome was in power. When you read the Gospels, you see Messiah continually saying that *'the kingdom is at hand.'* He isn't pointing to when He returns; He's proclaiming that it was set up at that time. He declared that the kingdom of Yah was setup while some of His disciples were still alive.

> *And he said unto them, Verily I say unto you, That there be some of them that stand here, which shall not taste of death, till they have seen the kingdom of God come with power. Mark 9:1*

The *desolation* of Jerusalem, the temple, the Jewish leadership system, and the unbelieving Jewish nation in 70 AD, led to the Messiah's kingdom being set up with the believing Jews and Gentiles.

In Revelation, the bride of Messiah is called *New Jerusalem.* With physical Jerusalem destroyed, Jew and Gentile believers, the *Ekklesia*, the *called-out ones* are the citizens of *Holy Jerusalem*.

Messiah and the saints form the temple, in which Yah dwells. With the physical temple in Jerusalem destroyed, the true temple was set up, for the Father does not dwell in a temple made with hands. Messiah is the cornerstone, the disciples the foundation, and the saints are the stones that make up the temple walls.

Messiah became the High Priest of His temple. With the physical type of the Jewish High Priest removed from power, Messiah took His rightful place as our High Priest who intercedes for us.

The saints are the priests of Messiah's kingdom. With the Jewish priest system removed, Messiah's saints are His priests. I cover this in detail in my ***The Olivet Discourse Decoded*** book, but the bottom line is that Daniel 7:13-14 foretold that the Son of Man would set up the Father's kingdom during the reign of the four beast kingdoms. Messiah's kingdom expanded rapidly by supernatural power during the first few centuries. Messiah has empowered His saints with the Word, the *rod of iron*, the Scriptures to take control of the nations.

The early church interpreted the first seal with Messiah going forth on His mission to conquer the enemy, Satan, and his Roman beast kingdom; by preaching the Gospel through His army of saints. Messiah's *Ekklesia* is the set-apart ones who advance Yah's kingdom.

> Daniel 2:34-35 says that *a stone was cut out without hands, became a great mountain (nation) which filled the whole earth, and it was cast at the iron-clay feet of the statue.*

Since then, Messiah's Kingdom has become a large *mountain*, a great nation. And someday, He will return for His kingdom saints. The battle between good and evil, Messiah vs. Satan, the saints of Holy Jerusalem vs. the leaders of the *great city* of Rome, begins in the first seal. Two kingdoms are going forth and conquering at this time: the mighty Roman beast kingdom and Messiah's Spirit-filled assembly of saints.

Interestingly, in Roman mythology, Cupid is the son of Venus, the goddess of love and beauty. And he is known as the god of affection. Legend has it that Cupid shoots magical gold-tipped arrows at gods and humans alike. By piercing their heart with an arrow, he causes individuals to fall deeply in love. The Roman beast kingdom conquers by force using the strength of iron. Amazingly, Messiah's kingdom conquers with a bow, shooting arrows of the Gospel of love, to cause people to fall in love with the Heavenly Father and His beloved Son.

In *Key To The Apocalypse*, Henry Grattan Guinness says, *It pleased God to order it in His providence," says Jonathan Edwards, "that earthly power and dominion should be raised to its greatest height, and appear in its utmost glory, in those four great monarchies that succeeded one another, and that everyone should be greater and more glorious than the preceding before He set up the Kingdom of His Son. By this, it appeared how much more glorious His spiritual Kingdom was than the most glorious temporal kingdom. The strength and glory of Satan's kingdom in those four mighty monarchies appeared in its greatest height; for, being the monarchies of the heathen world, the strength of them was the strength of Satan's kingdom."*

The 16ᵗʰ century Geneva Bible says, *The white horse signifies innocence, victory, and felicity – which should come by the preaching of the Gospel.*

Adam Clarke's Commentary on the Bible (1832) says, *A white horse – Supposed to represent the Gospel system and pointing out its excellence, swiftness, and purity. He that sat on him – Jesus Christ. A bow - The preaching of the Gospel, darting conviction into the hearts of sinners. A crown - The emblem of the kingdom which Christ is to establish on earth.*

Matthew Poole's Commentary on the Holy Bible (1684) says, *Some, by this white horse, understand the gospel; others, the Roman empire. And by him that sat thereon with a bow, some understand Christ going forth with power to convert the nations; others (and in my opinion more probably) the Roman emperors, armed with power, and having the imperial crown, carrying all before them. So as that which God intended by this to reveal to St. John, was that the Roman emperors should yet continue and use their power against his church.*

John Gill's Exposition of the Entire Bible (1748) says, *And I saw, and behold a white horse, represents the ministration of the Gospel in the times of the apostles, which were just now finishing, John being the last of them, who saw this vision. Its "white" color may denote the purity of Gospel truths, the peace it proclaims, the joy brings, and the triumph that attends it, on account of victories obtained by it, and which is afterward suggested. The bow is the word of the Gospel, and the arrows the doctrines of it. And a crown was given unto him; by God the Father; expressive of Christ's regal power and authority, of his honor and dignity, and of his victories and conquests.*

The People's New Testament by Barton Johnson (1891) says, *And in the vision thus interpreted is found a key to the entire prophecy; for this is the starting point of the whole. Seals, trumpets, and vials set forth a continuous course of history stretching to the consummation, having as its commencement the going forth of the Gospel of Christ to accomplish its world-subduing work.*

Like a grain of mustard-seed, the kingdom of Messiah grew up and became greater than the mighty Roman Empire.

CHAPTER 13 - THE MYSTERY OF INIQUITY

In 2 Thessalonians 2:7, the Apostle Paul proclaimed that the *mystery of iniquity* was already at work in the first century.

> For the mystery of iniquity doth already work: only he who now letteth will let, until he be taken out of the way.

He's saying that the false beliefs that would cause some to *fall away* and lead to the false religion of the *son of perdition* had already permeated the early assembly of saints. To counter Messiah's kingdom assembly of saints, Satan laid the foundation for his own *'Christian'* church. We see the fulfillment of that in Acts 8:20-23 when Luke tells us about Simon Magus, whom the Samarians deemed was a *'great power of God.'*

He tried to buy the power of the Holy Spirit and was rebuked by Peter. Magus's name means *Zoroaster*, a *practitioner*, a *priest*, of astrology and magic, a *sorcerer*. Deuteronomy 29:16-18 points to the iniquity of *idol worship* being *gall and wormwood* (bitterness). Peter was proclaiming that Simon the Sorcerer was a cause of *'bitterness and corruption'* to others.

Peter was making a prophetic statement, foretelling Simon's sinful role and how his teachings would mislead people. The *Babylonian Mystery Religion* influenced those in *Samaria*, which is where Simon Magus originated. He used magic to deceive people, which gained him fame. *Magus* is the Chaldean word for *priest*, making Simon a *false priest*.

> Messiah warned, *Beware of false prophets, which come to you in sheep's clothing, but inwardly they are ravening wolves.* Matthew 7:15

Simon the Sorcerer appears to be the forerunner of the ACBP, who pretend to be priests of Messiah, but really serve Satan's agenda. After Peter admonished Simon, it appears that the sorcerer went to Rome to proclaim to be an apostle of Messiah, deceive people and draw them under his authority. I'll include links to in-depth studies about the role of Simon Magus on the book resource page.

It appears that he formed his own church in the name of Jesus (Iesous), in which he was the Bishop, the leader of a church designed by Satan to seek to overthrow the true Assembly of Messiah. He blended the *Babylonian Mystery Religion* with Messiah's teachings to create a universal church that would attract all of Rome.

Does that sound familiar? Is that not what the RCC is, a false church led by a Roman Bishop, filled with idols, which teaches a false Messiah and a false Gospel; to deceive people?

From Simon's Gnostic teachings, a sect of Simonians flourished, preached a false messiah and false gospel; and even taught that Simon was the *'Holy Father'* in human form to bring salvation to them. We can see a direct connection with the sect of Simonians, who revered Simon as the sun god, and Helen as the moon goddess; to what became the RCC, where the Pope is revered as the sun god, and Mary is the moon goddess, the *Queen of Heaven*.

In 152, in the *First Apology of Justin Martyr*, Justin noted that the sect of the Simonians appears to have been formidable, as he spoke of the founder, Simon, four times. He describes him as a formidable magician who came to Rome in the days of Claudius Caesar. He was honored as a god, with a statue erected on the Tiber, between the two bridges, bearing the inscription *'Simoni deo Sancto'* (the holy god Simon).

The word *pater* means *father*, as we find in the word *paternal*. We find this *other Peter* calling himself *Simon the Father*. Bishops of Rome pre-empted the old Mithraic high priest's ancient title of *Pater Patrum*, which became *Papa*, or *Pope*, meaning *Father*. The Popes of Rome call themselves by the *Holy Father*, the *Holy Peter*.

The RCC proclaims that Peter spent twenty-five years in Rome as the first Bishop (Pope) until he was martyred by being crucified upside-down in the last year of Nero's reign. But the narrative of Peter being in Rome that long is easily proven to be false.

We can see that it was not the Apostle Peter, who was the first Pope, but instead, it was Simon the Sorcerer. He set up the Babylonian priesthood of what became the RCC. The *mystery of iniquity*, which was started in the 1st century, became the false religion of Romanism. Pagan sun gods are symbolized by a pole or upright stake, which are phallic symbols, *sacred Peters*. An Egyptian obelisk was erected in St. *Peter's* Square at the Vatican, in the middle of a sun wheel. It sits in front of St. *Peter's* Basilica, the temple of their chief god; Simon Magus, the *Holy Peter*, and his successors; the Popes of Rome.

Simon Magus sought to prove His power and perhaps parody when Satan tempted Messiah to throw Himself off the temple's pinnacle. In the *St. Pietro Basilica* in Vatican City, stucco bas-relief panels in the portico present the events in the life of St Peter, including *The Fall of Simon Magus*. Google images of *'the fall of Simon Magus.'*

A mosaic of *The Death of Simon Magus* was made in the 12th century at the *Mosaic Palatine Chapel* in Palermo, Sicily. It shows the Apostle Paul knelt while Peter commanded the demons to let Simon fall. Magus reportedly broke his leg and was severely hurt, and died a few days later. Losing Simon Magus, his top magician, no doubt enraged Nero against Peter and Paul. And, interestingly, Nero killed both of them.

We can see that the *'mystery of iniquity'* pointed to Simon Magus, the founder of what became the RCC of the ACBP. Satan's use of Simon the Sorcerer, who pretended to be an apostle of Messiah, set up the *wheat and tares* narrative.

> *But while men slept, his enemy came and sowed tares among the wheat and went his way.* Matthew 13:25

> *Let both grow together until the harvest: and in the time of harvest, I will say to the reapers, Gather ye together first the tares, and bind them in bundles to burn them: but gather the wheat into my barn.* Matthew 13:30

Interestingly, in pointing to the desolation of Rome's *harlot* church, Revelation 18:23 declares *for by thy sorceries were all nations deceived.*

The Decline Of The Pagan Roman Empire

CHAPTER 14 - THE SECOND SEAL JUDGMENT
193-284 AD

And when he had opened the second seal, I heard the second beast say, Come and see. And there went out another horse that was red: and power was given to him that sat thereon to take peace from the earth, and that they should kill one another: and there was given unto him a great sword. **Revelation 6:3-4**

This represents a bloody time in the Roman Empire, as judgment was poured out on them for killing millions of saints. The color changing from *white* to *red* indicates the shift from *peace* to *bloodshed*. When the Cretan Dynasty came to an end, this led to Rome's downfall. The *'earth'* (Greek *ghay, a region, land*) envisioned by John was the Roman territories of Europe and the Mediterranean, not the whole world.

An attempt was made to kill Commodus. To try to protect himself, he exalted his captain of the Praetorian Guards to high authority. The Roman Empire went into a phase of revolution and civil war, during which there were thirty-four emperors and many contenders for the throne. All but two of them were poisoned or killed by the *sword*. The Romans blamed the saints for their cursed situation.

In *History of the Fall of the Roman Empire* **(1834), Jean Charles Léonard de Sismondi says,** *With Commodus' death commenced a most calamitous period. It lasted ninety-two years, from 193 to 284. During that time, 32 emperors, and 27 pretenders to the empire, alternately hurled each other from the throne by incessant civil warfare. Ninety-two years of almost incessant civil warfare taught the world on what a frail foundation the virtue of the Antonines had reared the felicity of the empire.*

The second seal's *red horse* points to the rule of military despotism, which incited a time of *bloody* civil war in the Roman Empire.

Edward Gibbon said _The power of the sword had begun its reign,_ and military rule was supreme. _The tyranny of Commodus, the civil wars occasioned by his death, and the new policy introduced by Severus, had all contributed to increase the dangerous power of the army, and to obliterate the faint image of laws and liberty that was still impressed upon the minds of the Romans. This internal change undermined the foundations of the Empire. The "giving of the sword" was fulfilled when Commodus exalted Perennis (who aspired to the Empire) to practically despotic authority as Captain of the Praetorian Guards (ch.4, Gibbon). In theory, the Praetorian commander represented the Emperor; the action of Commodus transferred in practice supremacy to the army ("a great sword"), which it wasn't slow to use. Then Septimus Severus (193-211) increased their number to 50,000 and doubled their pay, making the Praetorian Guard a very "great sword," thereby leading to further revolutions and bloodshed._

Commodus rapidly degenerated in character after an attempt was made upon his life in 183. He assassinated any people of distinction without pity. In 193, he was strangled to death and was succeeded by the virtuous Pertinax, who endeavored to repair the damage caused by his predecessor and to restore peace. But he was prevented by the Praetorian Guard ("great sword"), who, fearing the suppression of their privileges, power, and vices, assassinated him. Then they put the Empire up for auction to the highest bidder, and Didius Julianus, a vain old senator, gained it by paying £200 to each of the Guards. This aroused the anger of three generals commanding various divisions of the Roman Legions: Clodious Albinus, Pescennius Niger, and Septimus Severus.

Each marched on Rome to defend its honor. The first to reach the capital was Severus, and with his legions, trained in war, he prepared to attack the Praetorian Guard, who were soldiers in name only and were not prepared to contest the issue, nor defend Julianus in the face of the skilled, determined warriors of Severus. To appease Severus and his warriors, they beheaded Julianus and pronounced Severus Emperor. Severus subsequently disbanded the Praetorian Guard, replacing it with his legions. Meanwhile, the two other generals converged on Rome from different directions. Severus met them each in battle and successfully defeated both. (2)

CHAPTER 15 - THE THIRD SEAL JUDGMENT
212-235 AD

And when he had opened the third seal, I heard the third beast say, Come and see. And I beheld, and lo a black horse; and he that sat on him had a pair of balances in his hand. And I heard a voice in the midst of the four beasts say, a measure of wheat for a penny, and three measures of barley for a penny; and see thou hurt not the oil and the wine. **Revelation 6:5-6**

The *black horse* represents the despair and gloom of the Roman people, as they were taxed excessively to pay for all of the wars, which caused a major economic depression.

As you can see on this coin, the pair of scales represents the Roman Empire's justice and commerce. As the taxes increased, the burden got heavier on the people, and they were ground down, and they suffered as the economy declined. The denarius of Emperor Tiberius was referred to as the *Tribute Penny*, which represented a laborers' daily wages.

A shortage of coins may have led to the government receiving tax payments with food products. If citizens couldn't pay their taxes in coinage, they were allowed to pay with the equivalent value of *wheat, barley, wine, and oil.*

To '*hurt not the oil and the wine*' means to be not unjust to them. In other words, let the taxation be fair as compared to the prices of wheat and barley, instead of raising the prices of oil and wine even more. Emperor Caracalla gave non-citizens in the Roman Empire the name and privilege of being a '*Roman citizen.*' This was not out of generosity but greed for wealth so that he could tax them more.

Fines and confiscations ruined wealthy families. Taxes on farming land were levied, the flocks and herds of ranchers were numbered and taxed, and the agricultural industry was ruined under this heavy taxation. Farmers stopped growing food because of the taxes, and also barbarians were starting to invade territories of the Roman Empire. Farmers moved into the cities to get jobs and to have protection.

The industry of the people in the Roman Empire waned, as there was no incentive to produce goods and food, which were going to be taxed so heavily. Interestingly, before his death from an illness, Emperor Caracalla told his two boys, *"Be good to each other, enrich the army."*

Edward Gibbon documented, *The most important edict Emperor Antoninus Caracalla (in 212) communicated to all the free inhabitants of the empire the name and privileges of Roman citizens. His unbounded liberality flowed not, however, from the sentiments of a generous mind; it was the sordid result of avarice (extreme greed for wealth or material gain). The most wealthy families were ruined by partial fines and confiscations, and the great body of his subjects oppressed by ingenious and aggravated taxes.*

The land tax, the capitation, and the heavy contributions of corn, wine, oil, and wheat, exacted from the provinces for the use of the court, the army and the Capital. The great body of Caracella's subjects were oppressed by the aggravated taxes, and every part of the Empire crushed under the weight of his iron scepter.

The animating health and vigor (of the Roman state) was fled; the industry of the people was discouraged by a long series of oppressions, and the financial oppression was a noxious weed of luxurious growth, darkening the Roman world with its deadly shade. And the general famine, which (soon after Philip's death) befell the empire, was the inevitable consequence of the rapine and oppression, which extirpated the produce (wheat and barley) of the present, and the hope of future harvests.

Swarms of exactors sent into the provinces filled them with agitation and terror, as though a conquering enemy were leading them into captivity. The fields were separately measured, the trees and vines, the flocks and herds were numbered, and an examination made of the men. A reckoning was made of the age of each, years were added to the young and subtracted from the old in order to subject them to the higher taxation the law imposed. The whole scene was filled with wailing and sadness.

In *Horae Apocalypticae,* **Edward Bishop Elliott says,** *The third black horse and rider with a balance scale represented a time of unjust taxation whereby the producing provinces of the empire were robbed to satisfy the legions and to provide handouts for the populace of Rome. Economic depression resulted, but no famine. The words used in Revelation are a mocking reference to the sort of laws that were supposed to guarantee fair dealing but were, in reality, merely "records of the crime." The proclamation by Severus, "A modius of wheat for a denarius," proves to have given the literally true expression of its average price for that particular area.*

In *Vision Of The Ages* **(1881), Barton Johnson says,** *In the course of this history, we shall be too often summoned to explain the land tax, the capitation, and the heavy contributions of corn (wheat), wine, oil, and meat, which were exacted of the provinces for the use of the army, the court, the capital. Swarms of exactors sent into the provinces filled them with agitation and terror, as though a conquering enemy were leading them into captivity. The fields were separately measured, the trees and vines, the flocks and herds were numbered, and an examination made of the men. The sick and weak were borne to the place of inscription, a reckoning was made of the age of each, years were added to the young and subtracted from the old, in order to subject them to the higher taxation the law imposed. The whole scene was filled with wailing and sadness.*

The *black horse* of the third seal points to oppressive taxation, which caused farmers to stop producing and pushed the Roman Empire into a time of famine and pestilence.

CHAPTER 16 - THE FOURTH SEAL JUDGMENT
250-300 AD

And when he had opened the fourth seal, I heard the voice of the fourth beast say, Come and see. And I looked, and behold a pale horse: and his name that sat on him was Death, and Hell followed with him. And power was given unto them over the fourth part of the earth, to kill with sword, and with hunger, and with death, and with the beasts of the earth. **Revelation 6:7-8**

The *pale horse* represents an era of death in the Roman Empire, from 250-300. The Roman Empire is the *land/earth* of the apocalyptic vision. The pale horseman rode force, and the Roman Empire crumbled into the most dreadful state of disorder and chaos, where their society had almost completely broken down.

'Hell' or 'Hades' is better translated as the *grave*, as many people died. Acts 2:27 says, *For You will not leave my soul in Hades, Nor will You allow Your Holy One to see corruption,* meaning Messiah was in the grave. *'Helling your potatoes'* means a farmer digs a hole and buries them.

Edward Gibbon documented, *But a long and general famine was a calamity of a more serious kind. It was the inevitable consequence of rapine and oppression, which extirpated the produce of the present, and the hope of future harvests. Famine is almost always followed by epidemical diseases, the effect of scanty and unwholesome food. Other causes must however have contributed to the furious plague, which, from the year two hundred and fifty to the year two hundred and sixty-five, raged without interruption in every province, every city, and almost every family, of the Roman empire. During some time, five thousand persons died daily in Rome, and many towns, that had escaped the hands of the barbarians, were entirely depopulated.* (1)

An exact register was kept at Alexandria of all the citizens entitled to receive the distribution of corn. It evidently proves that above half the people of Alexandria had perished; and could we venture to extend the analogy to the other provinces, we might suspect, that war, pestilence, and famine, had consumed, in a few years, the moiety of the human species

In *The Last Prophecy*, Edward Bishop Elliott says, *About fourteen years after the death of Alexander Severus, beginning with the reign of Philip, about 248 AD, Gibbons speaks of the twenty years of "shame and misfortune, of confusion and calamity," that then ensued. And, all unconsciously speaking of the voice of Scripture, he says that at that time, "The ruined empire seemed to approach the last and fatal moment of its dissolution." We have it on record that at an epoch twenty or thirty years after the death of Gallienus, the multiplication of wild beasts of prey had arisen to such an extent in parts of the empire as to become a crying evil: Arnobius, the Roman writer, alludes to wild beasts as one of the plagues with which the land was then afflicted, about 296 AD, near thirty years after the death of Gallienus.*

In *Vision Of The Ages* (1881), Barton Johnson says, *Let all notice the correspondence. The prophet asserts that one-fourth of mankind would be destroyed, but the infidel historian goes beyond the prophet and doubtless exceeds the facts when he makes the mortality twice as great. The prophet names the sword, famine, pestilence, and beasts of the field as instruments of destruction. The historian affirms that half the human race were destroyed by the first three of these agencies but fails to mention the fourth. We might, without historical proof, dare to assert that on the terrible depopulation of large districts, the beasts of prey, wolves, hyenas, and lions, would so multiply as to become objects of terror, but we are not left to this necessity.*

The *pale horse* of the fourth seal points to a time when the Roman Empire suffered from famine, pestilence, and wild beast attacks. Messiah is talking about one-fourth of the Roman Empire's population dying. The Roman Empire's calamity was blamed on Messiah's followers, as they did not bow down to the Roman pagan gods. This served to increase the persecution of Messiah's saints by the Roman Emperors.

CHAPTER 17 - THE FIFTH SEAL MARTYRS

And when he had opened the fifth seal, I saw under the altar the souls of them that were slain for the word of God, and for the testimony which they held: And they cried with a loud voice, saying, How long, O Lord, holy and true, dost thou not judge and avenge our blood on them that dwell on the earth? And white robes were given unto every one of them; and it was said unto them, that they should rest yet for a little season, until their fellow servants also and their brethren, that should be killed as they were, should be fulfilled. **Revelation 6:9-11**

The Roman Empire was in decline, and they blamed the saints of Messiah for their refusal to worship the Roman gods.

Edward Gibbon noted, *If the empire had been afflicted by any recent calamity, by a plague, a famine, or an unsuccessful war; if the Tiber had, or if the Nile had not, risen beyond its banks; if the earth had shaken, or if the temperate order of the seasons had been interrupted, the superstitious Pagans were convinced that the crimes and the impiety of the Christians, who were spared by the excessive lenity of the government, had at length provoked the divine justice.* (1)

The fifth seal judgment represents the millions of martyrs killed by the Roman Empire, as Satan used the Emperors to try to wipe out Messiah's assembly of saints. They endured ten persecution periods, starting with Emperor Nero, who blamed them for the fire in Rome to justify killing them. Emperors Maximinus and Gallienus were both great butchers, both to their own subjects that were heathens and to the saints. Gallienus is said to have killed three or four thousand every day.

The most terrible, most prolonged persecution in the history of the early assembly of saints occurred during the Tenth Persecution, as Diocletian and Maxentius sought to root out Messiah's Ekklesia from the very face of the earth, from 303-313.

When facing a critical battle, Emperor Maximin made a vow to the god of Jupiter (which symbolizes Satan) that if victory were given to him, then the Roman Emperor would seek to abolish Messiah's saints. We see the pagan god Jupiter on the coin of Emperor Diocletian.

The martyrs' blood is symbolically *crying out for vengeance*. There are two groups of martyrs spoken of in Revelation. The first was killed by the pagan Roman Empire. The second group is killed during the Dark Ages and the Inquisition when tens of millions of martyrs were slain by Papal Rome and the countries they controlled.

Edward Gibbon documented, *Perhaps it was represented to Diocletian that the glorious work of the deliverance of the Empire was left imperfect so long as an independent people (Messiah's saints) were permitted to subsist and multiply in it. The resentment or the fears of Diocletian at length transported him beyond the bounds of moderation, which he had hitherto preserved, and he declared, in a series of edicts, his intention of abolishing the Christian name.*

Now let's relate this to Revelation 12, which is about Satan using the pagan Roman Empire to try to wipe out Messiah's saints.

Look at the Revelation Fulfillment Chart, and you see that the fifth seal took place when the Roman Emperors were in power. The victors are declared to have overcome not by sword and spear, as in a carnal conflict, but by spiritual weapons. They put on the armor of Yah described in Ephesians 6:11-18. The martyrs who were killed by the Roman Empire did not deny their Messiah to preserve their lives; rather, they honored Him with the words of their testimony before the persecuting Romans.

Now let's connect the fifth seal with the Smyrna church era.

Smyrna's name comes from the word *'myrrh,'* a tree resin with a bitter taste that was crushed and used in perfume, incense, and as a preservative in burial. It's a symbol of death, which is appropriate for this church era. Messiah pointed to *ten days*, ten prophetic years.

> *Fear none of those things which thou shall suffer: behold, the devil shall cast some of you into prison, that ye may be tried; and ye shall have tribulation ten days: be thou faithful unto death, and I will give thee a crown of life.* Revelation 2:10

Messiah had only words of encouragement and comfort in her sufferings at the hands of her persecutors. *Their blood was crying out* for Him to avenge their deaths. And *vengeance* came soon, as the trumpet judgments were poured out on the pagan Roman Empire. Look at the Revelation Fulfillment Chart. The Smyrna church era faces harsh persecution for ten years, from 303-312. And the fifth seal is describing the martyrs crying out for vengeance. The perfect synchronicity of the four chronological layers of Messiah's apocalyptic vision is amazing! HalleluYah!

Interestingly, there's a connection to the normal gestation period for a human, 280 days. If we count from the Holy Feast Day of Pentecost, when the Ruach (Spirit) was poured out on the saints in 31 AD, we see that 280 years (one day = one year) later is 311. The most painful part happened in the last part of those 280 years when the saints *travailed* and were *pained* the most from 303-312. Indeed, Messiah's kingdom of saints was *birthed* with much pain, fulfilling Revelation 12:2. *And she being with child cried, travailing in birth, and pained to be delivered.*

The *white horse* of the first seal points both to the conquering Roman Empire and Messiah gaining victory over the Satan-empowered Roman beast kingdom through the witness of the saints of His kingdom. The story of George of Lydda gives us a perfect example of victory over Satan. His father served in the Roman army, and George also served as a Roman soldier and became a Praetorian Guard for Roman Emperor Diocletian. George was a follower of Messiah, and when Diocletian found out about his faith, he was sentenced to torture and death for refusing to recant his faith.

Diocletian's wife, Empress Alexandra of Rome, witnessed George's torture, and she bowed before him and professed her faith in Messiah openly. When she questioned whether she was worthy of paradise and martyrdom without being baptized, George told her, *"Do not fear, for your blood will baptize you."* Diocletian was outraged by her conversion and is said to have uttered, *"What! Even thou hast fallen under their spell!"* She was denounced by Diocletian and sentenced to death.

George of Lydda was tortured for an extended period, as Diocletian was taking out his anger about Alexandra's faith profession. He was executed by decapitation before Nicomedia's city wall on April 23, 303.

When you read about how Diocletian vowed to wipe out Messiah's Ekklesia, and he persecuted them from 303-312, now you understand why he was so emotionally charged with carrying out this mandate. Recall how Messiah's saints gained the victory during the persecutions.

> *And they overcame him by the blood of the Lamb, and by the word of their testimony; and they loved not their lives unto the death.* Revelation 12:11

Revelation 12:9 points to Satan losing power in the heavenly realm because of the witness of the saints.

> *And the great dragon was cast out, that old serpent, called the Devil, and Satan, which deceiveth the whole world: he was cast out into the earth, and his angels were cast out with him.*

George of Lydda is called Saint George for his heroic stance against the pagan Roman Emperor and defense of his faith. Paintings have him on a white horse, representing his victory, and he's piercing a dragon. His martyrdom for the faith, along with the other Smyrna martyrs, cast Satan down from power. This is how we win the battle over the enemy.

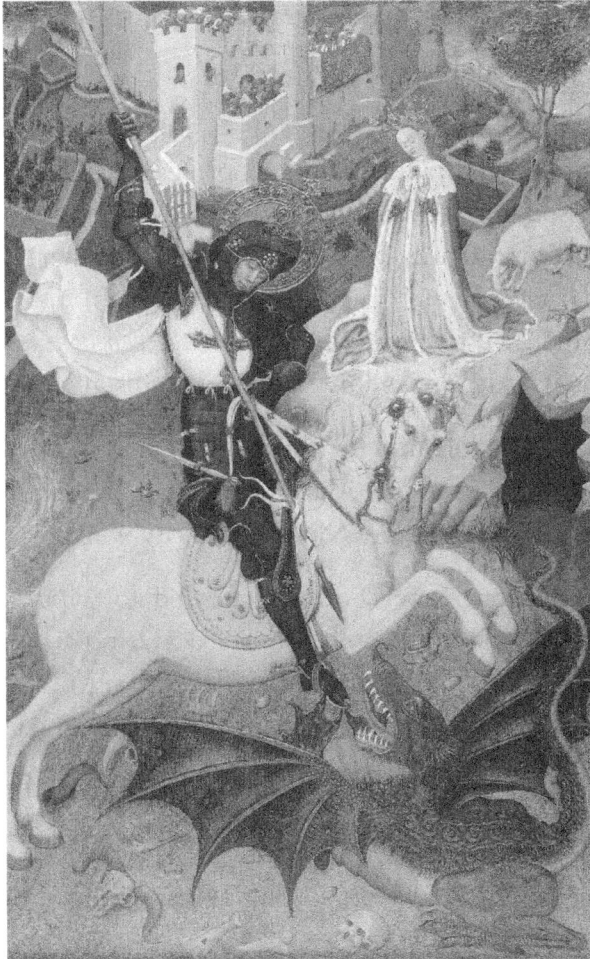

The fifth seal points to the church era of Smyrna martyrs who were killed during the persecutions of the Roman Emperors, whose blood is symbolically *crying* out for vengeance.

CHAPTER 18 - THE SIXTH SEAL JUDGMENT
312-324 AD

And I beheld when he had opened the sixth seal, and, lo, there was a great earthquake; and the sun became black as sackcloth of hair, and the moon became as blood; And the stars of heaven fell unto the earth, even as a fig tree casts her untimely figs, when she is shaken of a mighty wind. And the heaven departed as a scroll when it is rolled together; and every mountain and island were moved out of their places.
Revelation 6:12-14

Many people teach that it's pointing to a literal *earthquake* and the darkening of the literal *sun*, *moon*, and *stars*. This causes them to mistakenly assign this prophecy to the end times. But the context of the seal judgments is the decline of the pagan Roman Empire, from bloody civil wars, economic strife, and severe famine and pestilence.

It's not pointing to a literal *earthquake*, the literal *sun becoming black*, the literal *moon as blood*, or the literal *stars falling onto the earth*.

Though I've not found a precedent in Scripture for an *earthquake* symbolizing a *great social upheaval*, history unveils prophecy. We can see that is what is taking place in the pagan Roman Empire. And in the seventh bowl, we'll see that the *greatest earthquake ever* will occur when all nations lose power from a worldwide economic collapse and become subservient to the One World Government.

One of the most misunderstood uses of symbolism in Revelation is regarding heavenly bodies and events.

If you don't understand the symbolism that is used by Messiah to point to a literal fulfillment, then you're left to the literal interpretation and conclude that the sixth seal is about the end times, as the sun is blackened and the moon becomes as blood; and the meaning of Revelation is hidden from you.

Joseph's dream in Genesis 37:8-10 gives a perfect example of the *sun, moon, and stars*, symbolizing *leadership structure*. He's pointing to his dad (*sun*), mom (*moon*), and eleven stars (*brothers*).

Isaiah 13:10 points to Yah's judgment against Babylon's leadership when He sent the Medo-Persian Empire to remove them from power.

> *For the stars of heaven and the constellations thereof shall not give their light: the sun shall be darkened in his going forth, and the moon shall not cause her light to shine.*

Isaiah 34:4-5 points to judgment against Edom, describing its downfall with the symbolism of the *stars* (leaders) being dissolved.

> *And all the host of heaven shall be dissolved, and the heavens shall be rolled together as a scroll: and all their host shall fall down, as the leaf falleth off from the vine, and as a falling fig from the fig tree. For my sword shall be bathed in heaven: behold, it shall come down upon Idumea, and upon the people of my curse, to judgment.*

Daniel 8:10 points to Antiochus Epiphanes killing some Jewish priests.

> *And it waxed great, even to the host of heaven; and it cast down some of the host and of the stars to the ground, and stamped upon them.*

In Matthew 24:29, Messiah is pointing to the Jewish leadership system of the High Priest (*sun)*, the Sanhedrin (*moon)*, the many priests (*stars)*, *being* removed from power, as their punishment for rejecting Him and delivering Him up to be killed.

> *Immediately after the tribulation of those days shall the sun be darkened, and the moon shall not give her light, and the stars shall fall from heaven, and the powers of the heavens shall be shaken.*

This was fulfilled in 70 AD when the Roman army desolated Jerusalem, the temple, and the Jewish nation. My **Olivet Discourse Decoded** book proves out the fulfillment.

64

Revelation's sixth seal points to great political upheaval (*earthquake*) and the *darkening* of the Roman Empire as it was declining. The leadership structure Emperor (*sun*), Senate (*moon*), and leaders (*stars*) were losing power due to the previous seal judgments. The Roman Empire was vast, with many leaders overseeing provinces, so the *sky receding as a scroll* represents the Roman Empire losing its power over the nations.

Now let's look at the events of the Roman Empire's great political upheaval during the sixth seal judgment. Recall that just two centuries prior, the Roman Empire was at its height of power. And now it's falling apart.

In 285, Emperor Diocletian decided that the Roman Empire was too big to manage. He divided the Empire into two parts, the Eastern Roman Empire and the Western Roman Empire. And now, the Emperors of the Roman Empire are warring against each other.

Before *The Battle of the Milvian Bridge*, Eastern Emperor Constantine was given a vision of a cross in the sky, and told *'In this sign, conquer.'* Pastors proclaim that Yah gave him the sign as he supposedly went on to become a Christian, but it's quite the opposite. No doubt it was Satan who gave Constantine the sign because he was used to create the false religion of Romanism, which is based on pagan god worship.

Constantine's victory at the *Milvain Bridge* counts among the most decisive moments in world history. Constantine defeated Eastern Emperor Diocletian's army. Diocletian died an insane man, as he refused to eat or sleep, and he wandered the halls of his palace wracked with grief and regrets until he died.

This was an inauspicious end to the life of one of the most innovative men to rule the Roman Empire. Did he have regret about having his wife executed for becoming a believer?

The book *Paraphrase of the Revelation of Saint John According To E.B. Elliott* (1862) says, *On April 30, 313, Maximian was defeated by Licinius, and died, like Galerius, in agonies, confessing himself vanquished. "His death," says Gibbon, "delivered the Church from the last and most implacable of her enemies."*

Constantine defeated Western Emperor Maxentius (the *sun*) to become sole ruler of both west and east by 324. Maxentius drowned in the Tiber during the battle; his body was later taken from the river and decapitated, and his head was paraded through the streets of Rome.

The Romans had been the *kings of the earth* for many years. They had gathered the riches of the world as they conquered. Their military had no equal. The leaders were spoiled by their conquests, as nobody was able to oppose them.

As the Empire collapsed around them, the kings and mighty men would remember all the saints' warnings of Yah's coming wrath and also remember their courage to die for their faith.

In *Horae Apocalypticae*, Edward Bishop Elliott says, *In the sixth unsealing, a complete breakdown of the natural world occurred from which rich and poor flee in terror. No earthly foe caused their panic. Constantius, father of Constantine, appointed "Constantine the Great" as his successor. This prince was already known to favor Christians, while yet Maxentius was in possession of Rome – the son of the persecuting emperor, Maximian.*

Constantine (306 AD) bored down against Maxentius, he avowed his belief in and his adherence to Christianity. We are told (and before his death, he asserted it) that on his march toward Rome, as the sun was declining, there appeared suddenly in the heavens a pillar of flight in the form of a cross, with this inscription, "In this overcome."

Constantine immediately adopted the cross as his ensign; that object of hatred to the Pagans was seen "glittering on the helmets, engraved on the shields, and interwoven into the banners of his soldiers." The emperor's own person was adorned with it. Moreover, there was displayed on his principal banner this once accursed emblem, above which was set a crown of gold and gems, and the initials of Him who suffered on the one and now wears the other were inscribed upon it. "By this ensign thou shalt conquer."

Well was the promise fulfilled to Constantine. Army after army, emperor after emperor, were routed and fled or perished before the warriors of the cross. The terror of Maxentius and that of his army, in their flight over the Milvian bridge across the Tiber, is portrayed in sculpture, which may be seen at Rome on the arch of Constantine. Similar was the terror of the other two commanders, Maximin and Licinius.

As memorials of the persecution just before, the two joint emperors, Diocletian and Maximian, had medals struck of themselves, in the characters of Jove and Hercules, destroying the hydra-headed serpent monster, Christianity! Their successors had adopted these titles. When Maxentius went forth to battle, he went fortified by heathen oracles, and in the character of "the champion of heathenism" against "the champion of the cross."

Licinius again, haranguing his soldiers, ridiculed the cross, and staked the falsehood of Christianity on its success. In the hour of danger and death, however, his boldness forsook him. "Licinius," says Gibbon, "dreaded the power of the consecrated banner, the sight of which animated the soldiers of Constantine with invincible enthusiasm, and scattered terror and dismay through the adverse legions.

The dying terrors of these persecutors have been recorded. A dark cloud brooded over the death beds of Maximian and Diocletian; the former of whom, oppressed by remorse, is said to have strangled himself, and the latter to have died raving mad. Galerius, from an agonizing death bed illness, sent to entreat the Christians to pray for him; and Maximin confessed his guilt in his last moments and called on Christ to compassionate his misery.

Revelation 12:9 points to Satan losing spiritual authority over the pagan Roman Empire, in which he was exalted in their worship of false gods.

And the great dragon was cast out, that old serpent, called the Devil, and Satan, which deceiveth the whole world: he was cast out into the earth, and his angels were cast out with him.

Satan is *the prince of the power of the air*, who is using the Roman beast kingdom to fight against Yah, His Son, and His set-apart people. It's not pointing to him being kicked out of heaven, but to him losing power in the heavenly realm over the pagan Roman Empire. Satan was in his glory in the powerful Roman Empire, as they worshiped many pagan gods, which ultimately honored him; so he was exalted in the spiritual heavens. But now he is being cast down, as the Roman Empire was collapsing from the seal judgments.

Recall that when the disciples cast out demons, Messiah proclaimed that He *'beheld Satan fall as lighting from heaven.'* Satan is cast down from power when his deceptions are exposed, and people are saved. That's how we win the war!

We expose the enemy's deceptions, to cast down Satan's power over people, to set the captives free. I repeat this point many times in this book because I want you to know how we overcome the enemy.

Ye are of God, little children, and have overcome them: because greater is he that is in you, than he that is in the world. 1 John 4:4

CHAPTER 19 - THE FALLING AWAY OF 2 THESSALONIANS
FOURTH CENTURY

The Roman Empire declined dramatically from bloody civil wars, economic strife from paying for the vast military, excessive taxation, famine, and pestilence. Satan's time was running short to use the mighty Roman Empire to fight against Messiah's kingdom saints.

Satan found out that the more he caused the Emperors to persecute the saints, the faster Messiah's kingdom grew. So he changed strategies and used Emperor Constantine and the Roman bishops to create a false version of the Scriptural faith, called *Romanism*.

A fresco by Raffaello in the Vatican depicts Emperor Constantine being given the *sign of the cross*, and it shows a *dragon* (Satan) on the banner (standard) of the pagan Roman Empire. It's fitting that the Romans used the dragon to represent them, as Revelation 12 points to a *great red dragon*, in describing the pagan Roman Empire.

Ever since Constantine was given the vision, the cross was put on the military banners. This symbolizes the change from Satan (the *dragon*) using the Romans to try to conquer the saints by force to Satan using a false Christian religion to conquer the saints.

There is a *falling away* from the truth during these end times. Still, the *'falling away'* that the Apostle Paul refers to in 2 Thessalonians 2 occurred before the *son of perdition* took power in the sixth century. Satan used Emperor Constantine and the Roman Bishops to expand on Simon the Sorcerer's false Christian teachings.

Like Simon, Constantine used the *Babylonian Mystery Religion* symbols and masked them with a veneer of the Scriptural faith, as he sought to draw all people under his authority. Constantine became the sole Emperor of Rome in 312; he took the title *Summus Pontifex Maximus*, which means *'The Supreme and Ultimate Bridge.'* This title implies that they're *the mediator* between the Creator and mankind!

Before Emperor Constantine, Messiah's saints stayed pure, and the saints were willing to die for the faith. But everything changed when Constantine ended the persecutions, as he offered positions of power and prestige to people who joined with him, which caused many saints to compromise their faith.

Satan couldn't destroy Messiah's church through persecution, so he changed his strategy to destroy it from within. He caused Constantine to unite the Scriptural faith with pagan idol worship and feasts to create Romanism, the false gospel of the RCC.

Pagan Rome had many gods and idols, which they weren't going to give up. To make Satan's Roman church more acceptable to them, they gave the idols new names, to give them a veneer of the Scriptural faith. The statue of St. Peter was the god Jupiter. Mary represents the Babylonian Goddess Semiramis. Her son, Tammuz, represents Messiah.

Pastors today teach that Constantine became a follower of Messiah, and they champion that he made it the official religion of the Roman Empire.

70

But that is far off the mark, as the very opposite took place. The Roman beast didn't die; it simply changed its appearance and its approach, as Satan empowered the RCC to try to destroy Messiah's kingdom from within. He caused the Bishops and Emperor Constantine to create the cult of Roman Christianity.

Romanism is based on the worship of pagan gods, primarily the sun god, which is why Sunday became the first day of the week, and why the RCC has so many sun symbols, such as an Egyptian obelisk in the middle of a sun wheel in St. Peter's Square.

In Constantine's Christian Creed, he banned observing Yah's Holy Feast days. It reads: *I renounce all customs, rites, legalisms, unleavened breads and sacrifices of lambs of the Hebrews, and all the other feasts of the Hebrews, sacrifices, prayers, aspirations, purifications, sanctifications, and propitiations, and fasts and new moons, and Sabbaths, and superstitions, and hymns and chants, and observances and synagogues; absolutely everything Jewish, every Law, rite, and custom.*

At the *First Council of Nicaea* in 325, they changed the calendar to be based on the Sun, which is contrary to the ordained Scriptural calendar. Constantine outlawed the Sabbath and made it punishable by death for any follower of Messiah who was caught keeping the Sabbath Day, Passover, or any of the Scriptural feasts found in Leviticus 23. What the Popes of Rome declared as '*Jewish*' was, in fact, Yah's commandments, which all of His followers are to observe. Satan was creating a new Christian sect, the RCC, which perverts the commands of Yah.

In place of Yah's Holy Feast days, they created holidays that were based on pagan Roman dates. In 325, at the *First Council of Nicaea*, they established the date of Easter as the first Sunday after the full moon following the March equinox. Before this, the Romans worshiped Cybele and her lover/son Attis on this day. Supposedly born of a virgin, Attis died and was reborn annually. The festival began as a day of blood on Black Friday and culminated after three days in a day of rejoicing over the resurrection.

Do you see the parallels between Good Friday and Resurrection Sunday? This appeased the pagan Romans, as they still had their holiday. And it drew in the followers of Messiah to celebrate the death and resurrection on these pagan days.

Here's a fresco that resides at the Vatican depicting the *Council of Nicaea*. Notice all of the mitres on their heads, indicating that they are all Roman bishops who defined the laws of Romanism. Pastors today proclaim that it was a *Christian* council, but it was Roman Christianity. And their false doctrines are still a part of Protestant churches today.

In 350, Pope Julius I declared December 25 as the official date of Christmass. Before this, December 25th had been the Roman feast of *Sol Invictus* (the *Unconquered Sun*), where they celebrated sun-god worship. They believe that the sun god dies on 12/21, the winter solstice when the sun is furthest away and daylight is shortest. Then after three days of being dead, they celebrate its rebirth on 12/25.

This strategy of creating the false religion of Romanism has done more harm than the Roman Emperors' persecutions!

In the fourth century, the veneration (worship) of angels and dead saints and the institution of the sacrament of the Mass was instituted. In the fifth century, the Roman bishops were misleading people into worshipping Mary, the Queen of Heaven, the ever-virgin, the Mediatrix.

Most end times saints know nothing of the *falling away* from the faith in the 4th century, which causes believers to follow some of the Babylonian harlot church's teachings.

Believers have been misled to follow the pagan teachings of Rome, which were set up during the time of the *falling away*. They follow the Roman holidays of Easter, which is based on the fertility goddess, thus the symbolism of the rabbits and the eggs. They celebrate Christ-mass, which is based on the pagan sun god being re-born on 12/25.

People proclaim that observing Yah's Holy Feast Days is no longer required, but that's not valid as they're divine appointments which Messiah is still in the process of fulfilling to redeem His set-apart saints.

The spring feasts pointed to Messiah's fulfillment of them as the *Passover* Lamb, as the sinless Savior who was in the grave on the *Feast of Unleavened Bread*, and as the victorious King who rose again on the *Feast of First Fruits*. Then in summer, as Messiah promised, the Comforter, the Ruach Spirit, was sent to infill the set-apart saints on the Feast of *Pentecost*. But the fall three Feast Days have not been fulfilled yet. The fall *Feast of Trumpets* represents Messiah's return, the *Day of Atonement* to His judgment, and the *Feast of Tabernacles* points to the wedding to His bride.

So let me ask you: should we not celebrate these Holy Feast Days, which our Heavenly Father ordained for His Son to fulfill, to redeem His set-apart saints? And should we not set ourselves apart by not participating in the Roman holidays, which are based on pagan gods?

Don't let the Pharisaical attitudes of some Hebrew Roots Movement people cause you to throw the baby out with the bathwater.

Seek Scriptural truth to make sure that you're not following any teachings of Babylon/Rome. You can read more about the fulfillment of the *falling away* of 2 Thessalonians 2 and how to return to the ancient path of the true Scriptural faith on this website: www.ComeOutOfHer.org

This *falling away* lines up with the church era of Pergamos.

Read Revelation 2:12-17. The name *Pergamos* is based on two Greek words, *'pergos'* and *'gamos,'* which can have two meanings. It can mean *'city'* or *'high tower;'* and *'married,'* or *'united by marriage.'* Therefore, the literal translation of Pergamos is *'married to the high tower,'* which symbolizes what happened during this church age as saints *fell away* from the Scriptural faith and joined with what became the *harlot* RCC.

Messiah selected the church of Pergamos for another reason, because of the city's history. Pagan god worship originated in Babylon, where the tower represented their ambition to become gods. When the Medo-Persians conquered Babylon, the Babylonian priests moved to Pergamos and established satanic cultic idolatry of pagan god worship, where the worship of Aesculapius the serpent child of the *'incarnate sun'* continued. The title of *Pontifex Maximus* (*Supreme Pontiff*) was then transferred to the Roman Emperors and then to the Popes. Pergamos is a perfect name for this church age, as *'Mystery, Babylon the Great,'* the RCC, was formed during this church era.

When Messiah spoke to the first church era of Ephesus, He pointed to the *"deeds of the Nicolaitans,"* but now to the third church era of Pergamos, He's pointing to the *"doctrine of the Nicolaitans."* During this church era, Emperor Constantine and others held councils, like the *Council of Nicaea*, in which they defined the *'doctrine'* of the false religion of Romanism. Protestant Churches still proclaim doctrine based on the *Council of Nicaea*; thus, they follow Rome's doctrine of the Nicolaitans. The name Nicolaitans may be pointing to them being *'lay conquerors'* or *'conquerors of the laypeople,'* which the Roman church has done, as they set up a false priest system to rule over the laypeople.

In *Romanism And The Reformation*, Henry Grattan Guinness says,
In the fourth century, with the fall of paganism, began a worldly, imperial Christianity, wholly unlike primitive apostolic Christianity, a sort of Christianized heathenism; and in the fifth and sixth centuries sprang up the Papacy, in whose career the apostasy culminated later on.

As our alone Mediator, High-Priest, and Intercessor at the right hand of Yah, the glory of Messiah was becoming obscured. The invocation of saints and martyrs was coming in, new means of propitiation were now invented, the worship of relics and images, and fictitious miracles followed; first, departed-saints, and then the priests of the temples dedicated to their memory, were sought after as the mediators and intercessors of the people.

The judgment of the *harlot* RCC is coming.

And after these things I heard a great voice of much people in heaven, saying, Alleluia; Salvation, and glory, and honor, and power, unto the Lord our God: For true and righteous are his judgments: for he hath judged the great whore, which did corrupt the earth with her fornication, and hath avenged the blood of his servants at her hand. And again they said, Alleluia. And her smoke rose up for ever and ever. And the four and twenty elders and the four beasts fell down and worshipped God that sat on the throne, saying, Amen; Alleluia. And a voice came out of the throne, saying, Praise our God, all ye his servants, and ye that fear him, both small and great. And I heard as it were the voice of a great multitude, and as the voice of many waters, and as the voice of mighty thunderings, saying, Alleluia: for the Lord God omnipotent reigneth. Revelation 19:1-6

CHAPTER 20 - SEALING OF THE 144,000

People today like to think that they're part of the 144,000, but this takes place before the trumpet judgments to protect them from the barbarian armies which were ready to attack the Roman Empire.

It points to people being sealed from the twelve tribes, and there's no reason to believe that didn't happen, as they had spread through the Roman Empire and needed to be protected. The *earth*, *sea*, and *trees* would be impacted by the trumpet judgments.

The takeaway is that they were marked before the trumpet judgments began, and the reference is not to the end-times.

John saw a vision of the millions of saints who had been killed during the pagan Roman Emperors during the ten persecution periods.

> *After this I beheld, and, lo, a great multitude, which no man could number, of all nations, and kindred, and people, and tongues, stood before the throne, and before the Lamb, clothed with white robes, and palms in their hands. And one of the elders answered, saying unto me, What are these which are arrayed in white robes? And whence came they? And I said unto him, Sir, thou knows. And he said to me, These are they which came out of great tribulation, and have washed their robes, and made them white in the blood of the Lamb.* Revelation 7:9, 13-14

They are the fifth seal martyrs, who lived during the Smyrna church age, who were killed by the pagan Roman Emperors.

> *And they overcame him by the blood of the Lamb, and by the word of their testimony; and they loved not their lives unto the death.* Revelation 12:11

This is something that we need to keep in mind in the end times. Being martyred is not defeat; it's a victory for the kingdom! Messiah died the most painful death, which declared His great love for us. HalleluYah!

CHAPTER 21- THE SEVENTH SEAL SILENCE

When He opened the seventh seal, there was silence in heaven for about half an hour. **Revelation 8:1**

This is a retrospective chapter inserted between the historical series of the seal judgments and the pending trumpet judgments.

In the context of the historical fulfillment of the seals of Revelation, when Constantine gave the *Edict of Milan* in 313, it gave liberty to the saints, and there was *peace* for a little while. Amazingly, a Roman coin was minted in 322 that had Constantine on the front and '*Beata Tranquillitas*' on the back, which means '*Blessed Tranquility.*'

There was relative peace for the saints in the Roman Empire from the time Constantine took control until after Emperor Theodosius I, who ruled from 378-395. While the Romans enjoyed a time of peace, the savage nations were amassing on the borders, awaiting their time to attack the mighty Empire. The Goths revered Emperor Theodosius, so while he was alive, they didn't attack. When he died in January 395, the Empire was left to his weaker sons, Arcadius and Honorius, and the time of peace ended.

'*Trumpets*' are used to signify *war*, and the seven trumpet judgments represent Yah pouring out His wrath on the Roman Empire via attacks from people groups. The seven trumpets describe Yah's judgment against the Middle and Eastern Roman Empire, with the first trumpet symbolized by a *hail storm*.

The seventh seal is divided into seven trumpet judgments, as the armies of the Goths, Vandals, Huns, Heruli, Saracens, and Turks were sent to invade and scourge the Roman territory.

The prayers of the saints who suffered persecution at the Romans' hands were collected and offered up to Yah. The pagan Roman Empire had supposedly converted to Christianity and made it the official state religion, so why was judgment still coming against it? Because Romanism is a perversion of the true Scriptural faith, as it's based on the worship of pagan gods and a false Gospel.

The truth about what they're worshiping is revealed by their rituals, symbols, and proclamations. It has the veneer of the true faith, using the names of Scripture, but it's the *Babylonian Mystery Religion* in disguise. During the councils of *Nicaea* and *Constantine*, the true faith was adulterated and corrupted.

While the Roman Empire enjoyed a time of tranquility, Edward Gibbon documented that the barbarian armies gathered like a hail storm, waiting to attack the Empire. *The correspondence of nations was so imperfect and precarious that the revolutions of the North might escape the knowledge of the court of Ravenna; till the dark cloud which was collected along the coast of the Baltic, burst in thunder upon the banks of the Upper Danube.* (1)

In 364, Ammianus Marcellinus, a Roman soldier, and historian, wrote this prophetic statement, which points to the pending trumpet war judgments. *At this time, it was as if the trumpets were sounding the signal for the battle throughout the entire Roman world. The most savage nations rose and poured across the nearest frontiers.* (2)

In *Early European History* **(1917), Hutton Webster noted,** *Until his death, the Goths remained quiet – but it was only the lull before the <u>storm</u>. Theodosius, "the friend of the Goths," died in 395 A.D., leaving the defense of the Roman world to his weakling sons, Arcadius and Honorius. In the same year, the Visigoths raised one of their young nobles, named Alaric, upon a shield and with joyful shouts, acclaimed him as their king. The Visigoth leader despised the service of Rome. His people, he thought should be masters, not servants. Alaric determined to lead them into the very heart of the empire, where they might find fertile lands and settle once for all.*

In *Philosophy of History* **(1820), Karl Wilhelm Friedrich Schlegel pointed to this time of relative peace.** *The Goths, moved by the representations of their prince, declared to Theodosius that as long as he lived, they wished to have no other king but himself. But the case was altered under the sons of Theodosius; and, to defend themselves from this people, these princes knew no other expedient than to let loose on Italy these barbarians, and to divert and point <u>the storm of invasion</u> towards that quarter.*

The book *Paraphrase of the Revelation of Saint John According To E.B. Elliott* **(1862) says,** *The <u>threatening tempest of barbarians</u>, destined soon to obliterate all remaining traces of Roman greatness, was still repelled or suspended on the frontiers" of the empire and was only kept for a season from bursting upon it with destructive violence by the overruling hand of Divine Providence.*

The saints were sealed to protect them, and the pagan Roman Empire enjoyed a slight reprieve before the barbarian armies were sent to attack it, which led to the fall of the once-mighty Empire.

The Fall Of The Western Roman Empire

CHAPTER 22 - THE FIRST TRUMPET JUDGMENT
395-410 AD

The first angel sounded, and there followed hail and fire mingled with blood, and they were cast upon the earth: and the third part of trees was burnt up, and all green grass was burnt up. **Revelation 8:7**

The first trumpet represents the Goths' invasion, from 395-410, led by Alaric. The Bible defines *'hail'* as symbolic of *war*.

> *Have you entered the treasury of snow, Or have you seen the treasury of hail, Which I have reserved for the time of trouble, For the day of battle and war?* Job 38:22-23

This symbolism is used of the King of Assyria and his army, who were sent against the House of Israel.

> *Behold, the Lord has a mighty and strong one, like a tempest of hail and a destroying storm, Like a flood of mighty waters overflowing, Who will bring them down to the earth with His hand.* Isaiah 28:2

Fierce Gothic tribes had been at war with the Romans along the Northern frontier for many years, but they were restrained by Roman military leader Theodosius. But when he died in 395, the northern cloud of warriors, who had so long been gathering, discharged itself with fury upon the Roman Empire.

The barriers of the Danube were thrown open, as the uncommon severity of the winter allowed them to roll their large wagons over the broad and icy back of the river. The Goths moved south in the direction in which literal hail came and attacked the Roman Empire in Greece, Gaul, Spain, and then 300,000 Goths invaded Italy.

The *'fire'* represents their *scorched earth* policy in their invasions of enemy territory, as they burned everything in their path, and there was much *blood* being poured out. Thus did the first great storm of *hail* lay waste the Roman Empire.

Alaric confirmed that Yah sent him to attack the Romans when he said, *It is not of my own will that I do this; there is One who forces me on and will not let me rest, bidding me spoil Rome.*

Edward Gibbon documented, *The frontiers of Gaul had enjoyed for many years <u>a state of quiet and prosperity</u>; but <u>the consuming flames of war</u> spread from the banks of the Rhine over the greatest part of the seventeen provinces of Gaul. The scene of peace and plenty was suddenly changed into a desert; and the prospect of the smoking ruins could alone distinguish the solitude of nature from the desolation of man. At the hour of midnight the Salarian gate was silently opened, and the inhabitants were awakened by the tremendous sounds of the <u>Gothic trumpets</u>.*

They fired the adjacent houses to guide their march and to distract the attention of the citizens; <u>the flames</u>, which encountered no obstacle in the disorder of the night, consumed many private and public buildings. This awful catastrophe of Rome filled the astonished empire with grief and terror. Eleven hundred and sixty-three years after the foundation of Rome, the imperial city, which had subdued and civilized so considerable a part of mankind, was delivered to the licentious fury of the tribes of Germany and Scythia

The Roman Empire killed the saints for their witness. They were burned at the stake, fed to lions, and their blood was shed. Now the barbarians were sent against the Romans, spilling their blood and burning everything in their path.

In *Ecclesiastical History* (425), Philostorgius documented, *The sword of the barbarians carried off large multitudes, and pestilence and famine pressed upon them at the same time together with large herds of wild beast. Hail, too, fell in many places, bigger than a stone which would fill the hand. It was found in some parts of such size that it weighed no less than eight pounds, most clearly revealing the anger of God.*

In *The Fall of Rome*, **Mike Duncan uses weather terms to describe Alaric and his army.** *Far into the dark frontier, an unrepairable <u>rain of destruction</u> was about to befall the Roman world. The Visigoths were temporarily pacified by Emperor Theodosius, who granted them more land in northern Greece. After the death of Theodosius, <u>the Visigoths were on the move like a thunderstorm</u>. Led by Alaric, the Visigoths reached the imperial city uncontested in 410. For the first time in over a millennium, barbarian hordes stormed into the eternal city.* (4)

In *The Last Prophecy*, **Edward Bishop Elliott says,** *And then the first trumpet sounds. Alaric's course was to Italy. As he said himself, "He felt a secret impulse that impelled him to the gates of Rome." Thrice did he descend from the Alps, marking each step of his course with conflagration and blood, till the city was opened to the conqueror, and the <u>Gothic fires blazed around the Capital</u>. Meanwhile, Radagaisus, with 300,000 Vandals from the Baltic, broke <u>"like a dark thunder cloud,"</u> as Gibbon writes it, on the Italian valleys. "Over the greatest part of the seventeen provinces of Gaul, the scene of peace and plenty was suddenly changed into a desert, and the prospect of the smoking ruins could alone distinguish the solitude of nature from the desolation of man. <u>The consuming flames of war</u> spread from the banks of the Rhine over the greatest part of the seventeen provinces of Gaul; the scene of plenty was suddenly changed into a desert.*

How amazing is the exact fulfillment of our Messiah's prophecy! He heard the saint's cries and prayers and carried out vengeance against the enemies of His saints!

In *Vision Of The Ages* (1881), **Barton Johnson says,** *There is one expression that I have not yet noticed, which occurs several times in the book of Revelation, and about which there has been considerable discussion. Under the first of the trumpet angels, "one-third part of the trees was burned up, and all green grass." As we have already found that the "earth" meant by John is the Roman Empire, this would imply that one-third of that empire was particularly scourged. When the second angel sounds (verses 8 and 9), the third part of the sea became blood, a third part of the creatures in the sea died, and a third part of* the ships were destroyed. When the third angel (verses 10 and 11) sounded, a burning star fell upon a third part of the rivers, and a third part of the waters became wormwood.

When the fourth angel sounded (verse 12), a third part of the sun and or the moon and stars was smitten. If the reader will observe the reading closely, he will see that these four "third parts" described may all refer to the same third of the Roman world. The first third refers to the scourging of one-third of the land; the second, to one-third of the sea; the third, to one-third of the rivers; and the fourth, to one-third of the heavens above. All combined, land, sea, rivers, and sky, would imply the scourging of one-third part of the world. Let it be noted particularly that these need not be in different quarters of the earth, but all together, and that the first four of the trumpet angels may unitedly scourge the land, sea, rivers, and heavens of one-third of the earth which was present to the mind of the prophet or one-third of the Roman Empire.

The first four angels desolate Western Europe, the Latin portion of the earth, and the Mediterranean sea, and together put an end to the western Roman Empire. The fifth angel lets loose the Saracen invasion, which scourges and conquers the Saracen third of the world. With the blast of the sixth angel, the Euphratean horsemen are loosed to pour their myriads on the Greek third of the world, to overthrow it, and to establish the Turkish Empire upon its ruins.

The book *Paraphrase of the Revelation of Saint John According To E.B. Elliott* **(1862) says,** *The first four were to reveal under successive emblems the fearful desolations which God would bring by the Goths and those who followed them, upon a "third part" of the "land" and the "sea" and the "rivers;" that is, upon the land and the sea and the rivers of the Western Empire, which was one of the three parts into which the empire at large was divided in the days of Constantine; the Eastern Empire and the Illyrian or central of the three divisions being as yet spared from the desolating judgments which were to visit the West.*

The Western Roman Empire is the area of the first four trumpet judgments. Alaric and the Goths devastated the land with their *scorched-earth* policy. Next, come attacks on its coastlines.

CHAPTER 23 - THE SECOND TRUMPET JUDGMENT
425-470 AD

And the second angel sounded, and as it were a great mountain burning with fire was cast into the sea: and the third part of the sea became blood And the third part of the creatures which were in the sea, and had life, died; and the third part of the ships destroyed. **Revelation 8:8-9**

A *'mountain'* can symbolize a great nation. In speaking of Babylon, Yah used this terminology.

> *Behold, I am against thee, O destroying mountain, says the LORD, which destroys all the earth: and I will stretch out mine hand upon thee, and roll thee down from the rocks, and will make thee a burnt mountain.* Jeremiah 51:25

The *'sea'* in Scripture can symbolize large centers of people — nations, such as when the great army of Medo-Persia came against Babylon.

> *The sea is come up upon Babylon: she is covered with the multitude of the waves thereof.* Jeremiah 51:42

A *great mountain* (kingdom) *being cast into the sea* points to maritime warfare against the Roman Empire. The second trumpet represents the Vandals, a branch of the Goths, attacking Rome. They fought naval battles in the Mediterranean Sea between 425-470 and destroyed many Roman ships by pirating the seas.

The Vandals were led by Genseric, who is known as the *'tyrant of the seas.'* They were like a *great burning mountain* that attacked the coast-lands on the Mediterranean and all the islands, leaving bloodshed and confusion in their wake. Many portions of the sea were turned to blood, as ships were captured and many sailors were killed. The word *vandalism* comes from this time, as they plundered the Empire and stripped it of gold and silver, and ornaments and trophies. By former ravages, Rome's power had been greatly weakened, but Genseric utterly broke it.

The *third part* points to the Western part of the Roman Empire being attacked, which was a third part of the kingdom. During the fourth century, the Roman Empire was divided into three parts: The Western Roman Empire, the Eastern part of Constantinople (Greek), and the middle *Illyrian Prefecture*.

Genseric, like Alaric the Visigoth, believed himself to be an agent of divine wrath. At length, the work (of ravaging the coast) became almost monotonous and the choice of a victim hard. Once, when the fleet had weighed anchor and was sailing forth from Carthage's broad harbor, the helmsman turned to the king and asked for what part he should steer. Genseric replied, *"For the men with whom God is angry,"* answered the Vandal king and left the winds and the waters to settle the question who were the proper objects of the wrath of heaven. Leave the determination to the winds; they will transport us to the guilty coast, whose inhabitants have provoked the divine justice.

The Western Emperor's naval resources were exhausted, so he appealed to the Eastern Roman Empire for aid against the Vandals. A great fleet was gathered, and the Eastern Empire's powers were strenuously exerted to deliver Italy and the Mediterranean from the Vandals.

Edward Gibbon documented, *Genseric again became the tyrant of the sea; the coasts of Italy, Greece, and Asia were again exposed to his revenge and avarice. Tripoli and Sardinia returned to his obedience; he added Sicily to the number of his provinces, and before he died, in the fullness of years and of glory, he beheld the final extinction of the empire of the west. The terrible Genseric, a name which, in the Vandals destruction of the Roman Empire, has deserved equal rank with the names of Alaric and Attila. Genseric cast his eyes towards the sea; he resolved to create a naval power to embrace a mode of warfare which would render every maritime country accessible to their arms. The Vandals repeatedly visited the coasts of Spain, Liguria, Bruttium, Apulia, Calabria, Venetia, Dalmatia, Epirus, Greece, and Sicily.*

Emperor Majorian was determined to break Genseric's power, and three years were spent building a fleet. The woods of the Apennines were felled; the arsenals and manufactures of Ravenna and Misenum were restored; Italy and Gaul vied with each other in liberal contributions to the public service; and the Imperial navy of three hundred galleys, with an adequate proportion of transports and smaller vessels, was collected in the secure and capacious harbor of Carthagena in Spain. But Genseric surprised the unguarded fleet in the Bay of Carthagena: many of the ships were sunk, or taken, or burnt; and the preparations of three years were destroyed in a single day.

The [Roman] fleet that sailed from Constantinople to Carthage consisted of eleven hundred and thirteen ships, and the number of soldiers and mariners exceeded one hundred thousand men. Genseric, who had so long oppressed both the land and sea, was threatened from every side with a formidable invasion. He beheld the danger and developed a plan. He positioned that he was ready to yield to the Emperor, but he requested a five-day truce to arrange the terms; and it was granted. Guided by their secret intelligence, Genseric surprised the unguarded fleet in the bay of Carthagena; many of the ships were sunk, or taken, or burnt; and the preparations of three years were destroyed in a single day. (2)

The wind became favorable to the designs of Genseric. He manned his largest ships of war with the bravest of the Moors and vandals; and they towed after them many large barges, filled with combustible materials. In the obscurity of the night, these destructive vessels were impelled against the unguarded and unsuspecting fleet of Romans, who were awakened by the sense of their instant danger. Their close and crowded order assisted the progress of the fire, which was communicated with rapid and irresistible violence; and the noise of the wind, the crackling of the flames, the dissonant cries of the soldiers and mariners, who could neither command nor obey, increased the horror of the nocturnal tumult. Whilst they labored to extricate themselves from the fire-ships and to save at least a part of the navy, the galleys of Genseric assaulted them with temperate and disciplined valor; and many of the Romans who escaped the fury of the flames, were destroyed or taken by the victorious Vandals. (3)

86

As you read the following two quotes from historians, keep in mind that Messiah describes the Vandals as a *'great burning mountain.'*

In *An History of Marine Architecture* **(1810), John Charnock is not documenting Revelation's fulfillment but describing the naval battle against the Roman Empire.** *The <u>irruption of the Vandals</u>, the successors to the Goths, and equal claimants with them as to the extent of the share they separately held in the destruction of the Roman Empire, <u>forced its way like a slow but terrific eruption of a volcano</u> and passed from the Elbe, the crater whence it last issued, even to the Pillars of Hercules, now more commonly known as the Straights of Gibraltar*

In the book *Rome's Enemies: The Desert Frontier* **(2005), David Nicolle says,** *Increasing resistance by the Berbers had greatly weakened Rome's hold by the time the <u>Germanic Vandals erupted</u> on the scene in the 5th century.*

In *Italy and Her Invaders* **(1880), Thomas Hodgkin says,** *The Vandals leader, Genseric, put all his energies to shipbuilding; and soon possessed incomparably the most formidable naval power in the Mediterranean. From Carthage's port, he repeatedly made piratical sallies, preyed on Roman commerce, and waged war with the empire.*

John Wesley's Notes on the Bible (1765) says, *By the sea, particularly as it is here opposed to the earth, we may understand the west of Europe; and chiefly the middle parts of it, the vast Roman Empire. A mountain here seems to signify a great force and multitude of people. Jeremiah 51:25; so this may point at the irruption of the barbarous nations into the Roman Empire. The warlike Goths broke in upon it, and from that time, the irruption of one nation after another never ceased till the very form of the Roman Empire, and all but the name, was lost. The fire may mean the fire of war and the rage of those savage nations. And the third part of the sea became blood - This need not imply that just a third part of the Roman was slain, but it is certain an inconceivable deal of blood was shed in all these invasions.*

CHAPTER 24 - THE THIRD TRUMPET JUDGMENT
451 AD

And the third angel sounded, and there fell a great star from heaven, burning as it were a lamp, and it fell upon the third part of the rivers, and upon the fountains of waters; And the name of the star is called Wormwood: and the third part of the waters became wormwood; and many men died of the waters, because they were made bitter.
Revelation 8:9-11

The third trumpet represents the invasion of Attila the Hun, who came on the scene in 451. A *'star'* can symbolize a leader; in this case, the *great burning (destroying) star* was the king of the Huns, Attila, who was called *'the scourge of God.'*

Attila and his 800,000 man army rose quickly and flashed across the land, and desolated the Italian Alps, which is the source of the Danube, Rhine, and Po rivers. This is an area with over forty rivers that covered one-third of the Roman Empire.

The *Bitter Absinthe* plant, called *Wormwood*, grows freely in the Alps. Therefore the same name gives us both the location of the *'great star'* and his war's effect. Attila burnt cities, massacred and enslaved inhabitants, and generally caused despair, famine, and bitterness.

His strategy was to lure Roman armies into crossing rivers after he had feigned a retreat. While the armies were crossing the rivers, he ordered his troops to attack. Historians estimate that 300,000 men lay slaughtered in the rivers, making the water contaminated (*bitter*), causing thousands of people to die downstream from disease.

Attila and his vast army attacked the areas of the great rivers and then moved out to the Alps, the springs' sources; fulfilling the description, he *'fell upon rivers and springs of water.'* Attila's attack only stopped when he died on his wedding night, after he got drunk, suffered a severe nosebleed, and choked to death on his blood. Thus his attack on the West was like the passing of a transitory meteor, a *falling star*, who shined brightly, illuminated the sky, and then disappeared.

Edward Gibbon documented, *The western world was oppressed by the Goths and Vandals, who fled before the Huns; but the achievements of the Huns themselves were not adequate to their power and prosperity. In the reign of Attila, the Huns again became the terror of the world; and I shall now describe the character and actions of that formidable barbarian who alternately invaded and insulted the East and the West, and urged the rapid downfall of the Roman Empire. Attila spread his ravages over the rich plains of modern Lombardy, which are divided by the Po, and bounded by the Alps and the Apennines*

In *Attila the Hun: The Scourge of God - Demonic Savage or Inspired Leader?* (2007), Alexander Knights says, *Attila's barbaric savagery is exemplified through his self-dubbing title "The Scourge of God." The "Scourge" was an ancient Roman type of whip, designed to inflict the most damage and pain possible on the victim. Attila believed himself to be God's whip to inflict as much pain and damage to the Roman Empire as possible. Attila the Hun, in his decade of military ventures, managed to contribute more to the fall of the Western Roman Empire than any other figure*

In *Revelations from Revelation*, Patrick M. Jones says, *As Attila approached Rome, the people were desperate, knowing that they had no power to resist such an army as accompanied Attila. It was then that Leo, the Bishop of Rome, volunteered his services and went out to meet the coming army. He appealed that the city be spared. The barbarian monarch listened with favorable and even respectful attention, and the deliverance of Italy was purchased by the immense ransom, or dowry, of the princess Honoria. Attila added a beautiful maid, whose name was Ildico, to the list of his numerous wives. Their marriage was celebrated with barbaric pomp and festivity at the wooden palace beyond the Danube: and the monarch, oppressed with wine and sleep, retired at a late hour from the banquet to the nuptial bed. Then an artery suddenly burst, and as Attila lay in supine posture, he was suffocated by a torrent of blood.*

In *Italy and Her Invaders* (1880), **Thomas Hodgkin says,** *With dramatic suddenness, the stage after the death of Attila is cleared of all the chief actors. The death of Attila was followed by a dissolution of his empire, as complete and more ruinous than that which befell the Macedonian monarchy on the death of Alexander.* (4)

Keep in mind that Messiah described him as a *'great burning star.'*

The 1910 New Zealand *Hawera and Normanby Star* newspaper article called 'When Comets Do Appear' says, *The comet brought tragedy and devastation in its train, as it followed the fortunes of the "Scourge of God" – the great Hun leaders, Attila. Conquerer of the world, the warrior hastened in triumph to the bridal feast… and there fell lifeless, mysteriously stricken, under canopy of a sky where <u>blazed the wonder-star.</u>* (5)

In *History of the Later Roman Empire* (1923), **J.B. Bury says,** *The rise of the great Hunnic power which threatened European civilization in the fifth century was as sudden and rapid as its fall.* (6)

In *The Cambridge Medieval History* (1911), **J.B. Bury says,** *The empire of Attila was of too ephemeral a nature to be crucially dangerous, and <u>his attack on the West was like the passing of a transitory meteor</u>, which affected its destinies far less than the steady and deliberate menace of the policy of Gaiseric. But the <u>meteor</u> was not yet exhausted, and Italy had to feel in 452 what Gaul had experiences in 451.* (7)

In *A View of Ancient Geography and Ancient History* (1813), **Robert Mayo says,** *Attila again comes upon Italy but spares Rome. And dies the next year. His vast empire, being now divided among his discordant sons, <u>falls at once like a meteor that passes over one half the globe and then in an instant vanishes forever.</u>* (8)

We see the historical evidence of Attila the Hun fulfilling the third trumpet judgment, but there's more to the story. In the perfect timing of Yah, He caused this sign in the heavens. In 451 AD, a comet (Halley's Comet) blazed overhead as Attila the Hun overran Gaul on a march that culminated in the invasion of Italy. (9)

CHAPTER 25 - THE FOURTH TRUMPET JUDGMENT
476 AD

And the fourth angel sounded, and the third part of the sun was smitten, and the third part of the moon, and the third part of the stars; so as the third part of them was darkened, and the day shone not for a third part of it, and the night likewise. And I beheld, and heard an angel flying through the midst of heaven, saying with a loud voice, Woe, woe, woe, to the inhabiters of the earth by reason of the other voices of the trumpet of the three angels, which are yet to sound! **Revelation 8:12-13**

The war trumpets were sounding, and the first three trumpet judgments had brought the Western Roman Empire to the brink of annihilation. The fourth trumpet judgment represents the final overthrow of Rome by Odoacer and the Heruli in 476. The *'sun, moon, and stars'* can symbolize leadership structure. Here it represents Yah using Odoacer and the Heruli, a branch of the Goths, to cause the downfall of Roman leadership when Romulus Augustus, the last Western Roman Emperor (the *sun*) of the West, was captured in 476. The Senate (the *moon*) and the Roman government's entire framework (the *stars*) were diminished and later faded out completely.

The deposition of Romulus Augustus by Odoacer traditionally marks the end of the Western Roman Empire, the fall of ancient Rome, and the beginning of the Middle Ages in Western Europe.

Edward Gibbon documented, *I have now accomplished the laborious narrative of the decline and fall of the Roman Empire, from the fortunate age of Trajan and the Antonines to its total extinction in the West, about five centuries after the Christian era.* *The splendid days of Augustus and Trajan were eclipsed by a cloud of ignorance, and the barbarians subverted the laws and palaces of Rome.*

In *Horae Apocalypticae*, **Edward Bishop Elliott says,** *Odoacer, chief of the Heruli, a barbarian host left by Attila on the frontiers of Italy gave command that the name and office of Roman Emperor of the West should be abolished.* (3)

The 2000 Encyclopedia Britannica says, *In 476, the Germanic soldiery proclaimed Odoacer, a barbarian general, as king of Italy, and, when Odoacer deposed the Emperor Romulus Augustulus at Ravenna, the empire in the West was at an end.* (4)

In *Outlines of History* **(1864), Marcius Willson says,** *Under their leadership Odoacer, a chief of the barbarian tribe of the Heruli, they overcame the little resistance that was offered them; and the conqueror, abolishing the imperial titles of Caesar and Augustus, proclaimed himself king of Italy. The Western empire of the Romans was subverted: Roman glory passed away.* (5)

In *The Rise of Dennis Hathnuaght* **(1915), James Philip MacCarthy says,** *The world's midnight began in 476 AD when the triumph of Odoacer in Italy put an end to the Roman Empire. The Dark Ages, when intellect was in <u>eclipse</u>, are usually held to include the period from the time of Odoacer until the thirteenth century.* (6)

In *A History of the Later Roman Empire* **(2007), Stephen Mitchell says,** *The destinies of the eastern and western provinces of the empire parted ways during the fifth century. During this period, the supremacy of the western emperors was challenged and eventually superseded by the Germanic kingdoms, which led to their <u>eclipse</u> in 476. However, the eastern rulers remained closely involved in the immensely complicated political events which encompassed the <u>eclipse</u> of the western emperors in 476.* (7)

Interestingly, the last Western Roman Emperor's name was Romulus Augustus, as *Romulus* was the founder of Rome, and *Augustus* was the first Emperor of the Roman Empire.

It's amazing to see how Messiah's apocalyptic vision is pointing to the fall of the Western Roman Empire, which was a momentous event.

Pope Takes Power Over The Roman Beast
CHAPTER 26 - TRANSITION FROM EMPERORS TO POPES

This transition was foretold by Daniel, Paul, and John, yet most of today's Pastors don't teach about it. I'll give you the big picture here and then expand on the fulfillment in the next few chapters.

Daniel described the fourth beast kingdom of Rome in *civil* terms. The beast has *ten horns*, which pointed to the ten leaders of the ten civil kingdoms of the fallen Roman Empire. Daniel 7 describes a *little horn*, a small leader, the Pope of Rome, rising to power among them. The Pope demanded that the ten kings submit to his authority. Three kings said no, so the Pope caused their kingdoms to be *'plucked out,'* ended.

Paul described the Roman beast kingdom in *ecclesiastic* terms. The Popes and Bishops of Rome gained ecclesiastic power and followers after Constantine created Romanism, but the prophecy dictates that they couldn't take full power until the Roman Empire falls, as the Western Roman Emperor *restrained* the Popes from taking power.

The *man of sin*, the *son of perdition*, the Popes of Rome, rose to power after Romulus Augustus was removed from his office in 476, as part of the fourth trumpet judgment. This is referred to as the *'deadly head wound,'* as the office of the Western Roman Emperor ceased to exist.

In both ecclesiastic and civil terms, John described the Popes as the *'beast,'* the church and state leader. Revelation 13 describes the Popes rising to power out of a *sea* of people, out of the ten kingdoms of the fallen Roman Empire. In 538, they were given civil and ecclesiastic authority, and they took the Western Emperor's place and his title of *Pontifex Maximus*, *'healing the deadly head wound.'*

In Revelation 17, John describes the *harlot* church of the ACBP. They are the *'eighth king,'* who rose to power after seven previous forms of government of the Roman Empire.

When John wrote Revelation, *five* forms of government had passed; the *sixth* was the Emperors who were in power until 476; the *seventh* lasted a short time until 538 when the *eighth king*, the Popes, took power.

In *The Seventh Vial* (1848), James Aitken Wylie says, *Another chance, so to speak, was to be given to Satan. All his attempts hitherto had been abortive. He had seen the labors of long ages swept away by the seals and the trumpets: another cycle of centuries was to be given him, that he might do his very utmost to render frustrate the grand design of Christ's mediation.*

Accordingly, putting his ingenuity and malignity to the stretch, he now brings forth his masterpiece, even Popery, the most finished system of imposture, the most complete embodiment of Satanic malice and cunning, and the most skillfully organized plan of opposition to the cause of God, which the world ever saw. This is the grand subject which is not introduced on the Apocalyptic scene. It was necessary that the throne of the Emperor should be abolished, in order that the chair of the Bishop might be erected in its room. (1)

In *Romanism And The Reformation*, Henry Grattan Guinness says, *The casting down of the dragon in Revelation 12, and his restoration in a new form under the beast of Revelation 13, Brightman's "Commentary on the Apocalypse" applies to the casting down of the rule of heathen Rome under Constantine, and the subsequent revival of Roman rule under the Popes.*

Historian Frank Frost Abbot (1860-1924) wrote, *The transfer of the emperor's residence to Constantinople was a sad blow to the prestige of (Imperial) Rome, and at the time one might have predicted her speedy decline. But the development of the Church, and the growing authority of the Bishop of Rome, or the pope, gave her a new lease of life and made her again the capital – this time the religious capital – of the civilized world.* (2)

Knowing that he had no genuine claim to the Roman Caesars' empire, the Bishop of Rome created a fiction called the *Donation of Constantine*, which was legislated into canon law. This was a massive forgery commissioned by the Pope himself to justify his authority over the Roman Empire.

94

In *Vision Of The Ages* (1881), **Barton Johnson says,** *The fall of Rome introduced the period when, intellectually and spiritually, the day and night were darkened; when the minds of men were blinded, and when the Church, falling gradually into apostasy, gave forth for ages only a feeble light to human souls. In the period that follows, the barbarians who had ruined Rome fell gradually under the sway of an artful priesthood, the Bible was wrested from the hands of the people, and buried in the recesses of monasteries, superstition usurped the place of religion, and the gloom of the "Dark Ages" diffused itself over the Latin third part of the world.*

Thus, in the overthrow of the Western Roman Empire ends the work of the four hurtful angels, who were held back, for a season, from destruction. There remain three angels, the woe angels, who are grouped together by the angel that flits across the heavens and who foreshadows the terrible calamities that shall fall upon the earth when they blow their trumpets.

The bulk of the narrative of Revelation is about the ACBPs, yet today's Pastors can't see him because the antichrist is *hidden in plain sight*. Daniel, Paul, and John all described the office of the papacy and their *harlot* church, yet people are still trying to figure out who is the *antichrist* and *Mystery Babylon.*

The great theologians of the 16-20th centuries have proclaimed the same basic narrative about the historical fulfillment of Revelation's prophecies, yet today's pastors ignore their insight.

I pray that the upcoming chapters will leave no doubt in your mind about who is the *son of perdition* and the *antichrist*, and who is *Babylon the Great*. The world is getting crazy as the *antichrist* and *false prophet* work hard to push countries into their One World Government.

The world needs the saints to shine the *light* of Scriptural truth and expose the enemy's *dark works* so that they understand where to find hope and love in the arms of the Heavenly Father and Messiah of the Holy Scriptures.

CHAPTER 27 - 538 AD TIMELINE ANALYSIS

Looking at the Revelation Fulfillment Chart, on the 1st Layer, we see the transition from the pagan Emperors to the ACBP's controlling the Roman beast kingdom.

On the 2nd Layer, we see that the church eras of Ephesus, Smyrna, and Pergamos, are past. We see how the *'falling away'* of 2 Thessalonians 2 took place during the Pergamos church era, when the false religion of Romanism, which became the RCC, was created by Emperor Constantine and the Roman bishops. After centuries of persecution, many saints *apostatized* away from the Scriptural faith to take positions of power in Rome.

On the 3rd Layer, we see that the six seal judgments and the first four trumpet judgments caused the Roman Empire to decline and fall. The Western Roman Emperor had *'restrained'* the *'son of perdition,'* the Pope, from taking power, but when the last Western Emperor was removed in 476, as part of the fourth trumpet, the Pope was given power over the Roman beast kingdom. The office of the Western Roman Emperor ceased to exist, which was the *'deadly head wound.'*

On the 4th Layer, on the top left, we see that after seven forms of government of the pagan Roman Empire, *the eighth king* of Revelation 17, the ACBP, took power. At this point on the timeline, the pagan Roman Empire phase is past. The Popes have taken the Roman Emperors' place as *Pontifex Maximus*, as the leader of church and state, which marks *'the deadly head wound being healed.'*

Now we'll see how the Popes have fulfilled prophecy as the *little horn* of Daniel 7, the son *of perdition* and *man of sin* of 2 Thessalonians 2, the *antichrist beast* of Revelation, the leader of the *harlot* church of Rome, called *'Mystery, Babylon the Great,'* and the *eighth king* of Revelation 17.

CHAPTER 28 - REVELATION 13 - THE ROMAN POPES
538-1798 AD

In Revelation 13:1-10, Messiah describes a new phase of the Roman beast kingdom. It describes the Pope's reign over the Roman beast kingdom for 1,260 years (one day = one prophetic year) starting in 538, when Eastern Roman Emperor Justinian gave power to the Pope, and ending when the Pope was taken captive in 1798.

John doesn't use the word '*antichrist*' in the apocalyptic vision. Instead, he calls the main leader who opposes Messiah and His saints '*the beast.*' Recall that Simon Magus, a sorcerer, was effectively the first Roman Pope. Then Emperor Constantine and the Roman bishops codified the false religion of Romanism in their councils. And now the ACBP is being empowered by Satan

You will see that the Popes are the primary *antichrist* figure. Revelation's *antichrist beast* is not just one man, as so many people have been led to believe; it's the office of the papacy, the Popes of Rome.

And I stood upon the sand of the sea, and saw a beast rise up out of the sea, having seven heads and ten horns, and upon his horns ten crowns, and upon his heads the name of blasphemy. **Revelation 13:1**

Revelation 17:15 tells us that '*water*' points to *people*.

> *And he said unto me, the waters which thou saw, where the whore sitteth, are peoples, and multitudes, and nations, and tongues.*

The '*ten horns*' of the fourth beast in Daniel 7 point to the fallen Roman Empire splitting into ten civil kingdoms. The Popes of Rome rose to power over those ten civil kingdoms, which spoke different languages. The '*seven heads*' are pointing to the seven previous forms of government in the Roman Empire, which had passed. In Revelation 12, the *crowns* were on the *seven heads*, indicating that the pagan Roman Empire was in power.

In Revelation 13, the *crowns* are on the *ten horns*, telling us that power has transferred to those ten kingdoms. The *ten horns* point to the ten civil kingdoms' ten leaders, who submit their authority to the ACBP.

These have one mind, and shall give their power and strength unto the beast. Revelation 17:13

Here's a Vatican mural of Pope Leo X, showing his authority, which matches the narrative of Revelation 13:1 that the ACBP would rise out of a *sea* of people. The Popes openly declare their identity as the antichrist. They are hidden in plain sight!

And I stood upon the sand of the sea, and saw a beast rise up out of the sea.

In *The Last Prophecy*, Edward Bishop Elliott says, *A painting in the arc of the Florentines represents Pope Leo X with one foot on the land, the other on the sea, having a key in his right hand with which he opens heaven, and in the other another key (of hell, or perhaps of purgatory); with the legends beneath, "In thy hand I behold the empire of the earth, and sea, and heaven."*

Here's the painting that Elliott is describing. Look at how that declaration mimics these passages in Revelation 10, which shows the depth of the blasphemy of the ACBP.

And he set his right foot upon the sea, and his left foot on the earth. 10:2

And the angel which I saw stand upon the sea and upon the earth lifted up his hand to heaven. 10:5

Interestingly, the Popes refer to the Roman Catholic Church's central governing body, which rules over the different parts of the world, as the 'Holy See.' It is pointing to the people that they control. *The Holy See,* also called the *See of Rome,* is the jurisdiction of the Bishop of Rome, known as the Pope. It includes the apostolic Episcopal See of the Diocese of Rome with universal ecclesiastical jurisdiction of the worldwide Catholic Church, as well as a sovereign entity of international law governing the Vatican City. The *Holy See* fulfills Revelation 13:1 perfectly.

And the beast which I saw was like unto a leopard, and his feet were as the feet of a bear, and his mouth as the mouth of a lion: and the dragon gave him his power, and his seat, and great authority. **Revelation 13:2**

This confirms that it's the Roman beast kingdom. It describes the three previous kingdoms of Babylon, symbolized by a *lion*; Medo-Persia, symbolized by a *bear*; and Greece, symbolized by a *leopard*; the territories of which the Roman beast kingdom took control.

When a kingdom captures a territory, they tend to take on the characteristics of the people who live there. The Roman Empire had Greek characteristics, which put education and logic above revelation; Medo-Persian characteristics, which put the rule of law above mercy; and Babylonian characteristics, which was steeped in astrology, and the spirits of the occult. Just as the High Priest of Babylon carried out the *Babylonian Mystery Religion,* so do the Popes of Rome through their symbolism and reverence to Mary.

It's telling us that Satan, who had used the Roman Emperors to try to wipe out Messiah's saints and then caused Constantine and the Roman bishops to create Romanism to try to defeat Messiah and His saints by infiltrating His Ekklesia (his temple), is now empowering the ACBP to make war with the saints. The name 'Vatican' means 'divining serpent' in Latin (*Vatis=diviner* and *can=serpent*). Interestingly, there are several dragons/serpents in the crests of the Popes at the Vatican. Google images of '**Vatican dragons.**'

There's a dragon in Pope Gregory XIII's crest, and there is another one under his monument, which is fitting as he was an agent of Satan. Google images of '**Pope Gregory XIII Vatican monument**' and '**Pope Gregory XIII Vatican crest.**'

In European bestiaries and legends, a *basilisk*, from the Greek *basilískos*, which means a *'little king,'* is a legendary reptile reputed to be *king of serpents* and said to have the power to cause death with a single glance. Merriam Webster Dictionary defines *basilisk* as a legendary reptile with fatal breath and glance. So we can see that a basilica is a place of a *little king*, the abode of the *basilisk*, the *abode of the serpent*.

Here's a 1582 papal medal of Pope Gregory XIII, marking the Gregorian calendar reform year. On the reverse is a winged dragon, called an *Ouroboros*, a symbol of a serpent that grew so large that it surrounded the Earth and grasped its tail. It's a symbol of Satan.

And the great dragon was cast out, that old serpent, called the Devil, and Satan, which deceiveth the whole world. Revelation 12:9

The ram's head symbolizes *Baphomet*, Satan. It's telling you who the ACBP serves, who empowers him. It doesn't get any clearer than this!

Google images of '**Monument to Pope Gregory XIII**,' and you see a statue that designates him as Pont. Max., which is the title that the Roman Emperors used. You see kings kneeling, paying reverence to him, bowing to his authority. You see a priest holding a globe, representing the Pope's power over the world. And you see a dragon under his throne, symbolizing Satan, who gives the ACBP his powers.

And I saw one of his heads as it were wounded to death; and his deadly wound was healed: and all the world wondered after the beast. **Revelation 13:3**

The *sixth head* of Revelation 17:10 were the Caesars, the Emperors, who ruled in John's day. When the Western Roman Emperor was removed from power during the fourth trumpet judgment, the office ceased to exist, thus the term the *'deadly head wound.'*

The ACBP took power over the ten civil kingdoms of the fallen Roman Empire, and they took the title that the Emperors used, *Pontifex Maximus*; thus, the *'deadly head wound'* was healed. The leader of the Roman church and state was alive again in the Popes.

In *Daniel and the Revelation* (1898), **Joseph Tanner says,** *Pope Boniface III showed himself to the crowding pilgrims at the jubilee of 1300, seated on the throne of Constantine, arrayed with sword and crown and scepter, shouting aloud. "I am Caesar. I am Emperor!"* (2)

In *Horae Apocalypticae,* **Edward Bishop Elliott says,** *But in the pontificate, it (the Roman Empire) revived as with a second birth; its empire in magnitude not indeed equal to the old empire, but its form not very dissimilar: because all nations, from East and from West, venerate the pope, not otherwise than they before obeyed the Emperor.*

In *Historie de L'Eglise,* **Due de Broglie says,** *The Bishop of Rome mounted the throne whence the Emperors fell, and took, little by little, the position rendered vacant by the desertion of the successor of Augustus.* (3)

Said of Pope Pius IX, *'The captain who gloriously fills the place of the ancient Caesars.'*

Pope Pius IX said, *'The Caesar who now addresses you, and to whom alone are obedience and fidelity due.'*

In 607, the cruel Eastern Emperor Phocas conceded to Pope Boniface III the headship over all the Churches of Christendom. This *'wound'* was fully healed by Pepin and Charlemagne, who enthroned the Bishop of Rome in his full position when the ten kings, the ten civil kingdoms' leaders, submitted their power to him.

The structure of the RCC is based on the Roman Empire. The office of the papacy is based on Caesar. The Popes use the title of *Pontifex Maximus* just as the Emperor used this title, which means *'greatest bridge-builder'* in reference to building bridges in society that connects back to Rome. The Pope can be seen waving Caesar's salute today. The Vatican and Holy See use Latin for the official language and official documents, just as Latin was used in ancient Rome.

And they worshipped the dragon which gave power unto the beast: and they worshipped the beast, saying, Who is like unto the beast? Who is able to make war with him? Revelation 13:4

Satan, the god of this world, tempted Messiah to bow down and worship him, and said that he would give Messiah the kingdoms of the world. The ACBP of Rome took Satan up on his offer. Satan has given the office of the papacy, the Popes of Rome, his authority over the kingdoms of the world. And he uses them to steal worship away from the Heavenly Father.

Worshiping Satan doesn't imply *revering* him personally but *worshiping* idols, ultimately stealing worship from Yah and giving it to Satan. When the Virgin Mary, who is the Babylonian moon goddess Semiramis, is worshiped and prayed to by Catholics, Satan is exalted. When Catholics pray to dead saints and idols, worship is given to Satan and his demons that hide behind the idols.

It says that *'they worship the beast.'* It's referring to the kings and leaders of the European countries of the ten kingdoms of the Fallen Roman Empire, who have committed fornication with the Pope, who have become rich because of their allegiance to the Pope.

In *The Approaching End Of The Age*, **Henry Grattan Guinness says,** *In his full fame, and flushed with victory, the great Francis I of France, in his interview with Leo X at Bologna, just before the Reformation, "knelt three times in approaching him, and then kissed his feet." The Emperor Henry of Germany, driven to the most abject humiliation by the terror of a papal interdict, sought pardon, barefoot and clothed in sackcloth, and was kept waiting three wintry days and nights at the doors of the supreme Pontiff, ere he could secure an interview.*

The Strong's Greek Dictionary word for *'worshipped'* is 4352 *proskuneo*, which means: *to kiss, like a dog licking his master's hand; to fawn or crouch to, i.e. (literally or figuratively) prostrate oneself in homage (do reverence to, adore):—worship.*

Is that not what the Roman Cardinals and Bishops do as they fawn and crouch before the Pope, lying prostrate before him, kissing his hand and kissing his foot? Have we not seen the representatives of Christian denominations and people of other faiths bowing before the Pope and kissing his hand? This has been going on for many years.

Pope Pius XI said, *"To the hand of God, who guides the course of history, has set down the Chair of His Vicar on earth, in this city of Rome which, from being the capital of the wonderful Roman Empire, was made by Him the capital of the whole world, because He made it the seat of a sovereignty which, since it extends beyond the confines of nations and states, embraces within itself all the people of the whole world."* (6)

In 1439, Pope Eugene IV proclaimed, *"We define that the Holy Apostolic See and the Roman Pontiff hold the primacy over the whole world."* (7) At one time, it was even declared at the coronation of every Pontiff: *"Know thyself the Father of Kings and Princes, Ruler of the World."*

Let's see how the Pope-led *sea beast* of Revelation matches with the fourth beast of Daniel 7.

And four great beasts <u>came up from the sea</u>, diverse one from another. Daniel 7:3

> *And I stood upon the sand of the sea, and saw <u>a beast rise up out of the sea</u>, having seven heads and ten horns, and upon his horns ten crowns, and upon his heads the name of blasphemy.* Revelation 13:1

The first was like a <u>lion</u>, and had eagle's wings: I beheld till the wings thereof were plucked, and it was lifted up from the earth, and made stand upon the feet as a man, and a man's heart was given to it. And behold another beast, a second, like to a <u>bear</u>, and it raised up itself on one side, and it had three ribs in the mouth of it between the teeth of it: and they said thus unto it, Arise, devour much flesh. After this I beheld, and lo another, like a <u>leopard</u>, which had upon the back of it four wings of a fowl; the beast had also four heads; and dominion was given to it. After this I saw in the night visions, and behold a fourth beast, <u>dreadful and terrible</u>, and strong exceedingly; and it had great iron teeth: it devoured and brake in pieces, and stamped the residue with the feet of it: and it was diverse from all the beasts that were before it; and it had ten horns. Daniel 7:4-7

> *And the beast which I saw was like unto a <u>leopard</u>, and his feet were as the feet of a <u>bear</u>, and his mouth as the mouth of a <u>lion</u>: and the <u>dragon</u> gave him his power, and his seat, and great authority.* Revelation 13:2

I considered the horns, and, behold, there came up among them another little horn, before whom there were three of the first horns plucked up by the roots: and, behold, <u>in this horn were eyes like the eyes of man, and a mouth speaking great things</u>. Daniel 7:8

And of the ten horns that were in his head, and of the other which came up, and before whom three fell; even of that horn that had eyes, and <u>a mouth that spake very great things, whose look was more stout than his fellows</u>. Daniel 7:20

105

And there was given unto him a <u>mouth speaking great things and</u> <u>blasphemies</u>; and power was given unto him to continue forty and two months. <u>And he opened his mouth in blasphemy against God, to blaspheme</u> <u>his name</u>, and his tabernacle, and them that dwell in heaven. Revelation 13:5-6

I beheld, and the same horn <u>made war with the saints, and prevailed against</u> <u>them</u>. Daniel 7:21

And it was given unto him to <u>make war with the saints, and to overcome</u> <u>them</u>: and power was given him over all kindred, and tongues, and nations. Revelation 13:7

<u>And the ten horns out of this kingdom are ten kings that shall arise: and</u> <u>another shall rise after them</u>; *and he shall be diverse from the first, and he shall subdue three kings.* Daniel 7:24

And I stood upon the sand of the sea, and saw a beast rise up out of the sea, having seven heads and <u>ten horns, and upon his horns ten crowns</u>, and upon his heads the name of blasphemy. Revelation 13:1

And he shall <u>speak great words against the most High</u>, and shall wear out the saints of the most High, and think to change times and laws: and <u>they shall be</u> <u>given into his hand until a time and times and the dividing of time</u>. Daniel 7:25

And there was given unto him a mouth speaking great things and blasphemies; <u>and power was given unto him to continue forty and two</u> <u>months</u>. Revelation 13:5

In *Antichrist And His Ten Kingdoms* (1938), Albert Close says, *Futurists and Preterists overlook the fact that the antichrist is not to be an open and avowed antagonist of Christ, but one professing to be a Vice Christ, a rival Christ; one who would assume the character, occupy in the human heart the place, and fulfill the functions of Christ. He was to be a 'Mystery,' professing to be Divine, but really Satanic; the devil as an angel of light.*

106

CHAPTER 29 - THE LITTLE HORN OF DANIEL 7

Daniel 7:7 describes the Roman beast kingdom.

> *After this I saw in the night visions, and behold, a fourth beast, dreadful and terrible, exceedingly strong. It had huge iron teeth; it was devouring, breaking in pieces, and trampling the residue with its feet. It was different from all the beasts that were before it, and <u>it had ten horns</u>.*

John picks up the narrative of the *'dreadful, terrible, and exceedingly strong'* beast kingdom and describes it as a *'great red dragon'* in Revelation 12:3. Then the Western Roman Empire split into ten civil kingdoms after the Emperor was removed in power in 476.

Edward Gibbon says the ten kingdoms were: *The Alemanni, the Franks, the Burgundians, the Vandals, the Suevi, the Visigoths, the Saxons, the Ostrogoths, the Lombards, and the Heruli.*

The book *Paraphrase of the Revelation of Saint John According To E.B. Elliott* (1862) says, *For, by the time the Beast arose from out of the inundating flood, the ten Gothic kingdoms of Europe had been definitely formed – the Anglo-Saxons, the Franks of Central France, the Alleman Franks of Eastern, and the Burgundic Franks of Central France, the Visigoths, the Suevi, the Vandals, the Ostrogoths in Italy, the Bavarians and the Lombards – ten in all, each having its ruler wearing his diadem or kingly badge of power.*

It was within the century between 430 and 530 that the Papacy began to assume that principle of domination over the kingdoms of Western Christiandom. As well as of usurpation of Christ's place in the Church, blasphemy against God and hostility to God's saints, by which it was afterwards more fully characterized. This authority, claimed by the Roman Bishops, was legitimatized by the Roman Emperors, and shortly after being recognized and submitted to by barbarian Western Kings.

Daniel points to a *little horn*, the Roman Pope, rising among the ten kingdoms and demanding that the ten kings bow down to his authority

> *I considered the horns, and, behold, there came up among them another little horn, before whom there were three of the first horns plucked up by the roots: and, behold, in this horn were eyes like the eyes of man, and a mouth speaking great things.* Daniel 7:8

> *Thus he said, The fourth beast shall be the fourth kingdom upon earth, which shall be diverse from all kingdoms, and shall devour the whole earth, and shall tread it down, and break it in pieces. And the ten horns out of this kingdom are ten kings that shall arise: and another shall rise after them; and he shall be diverse from the first, and he shall subdue three kings.* Daniel 7:23-24

The three that were plucked out were from the invading armies sent against the Roman Empire during the trumpet judgments, because they weren't about to bow to a new leader's authority.

John Clark Ridpath (1840-1900), an American educator, historian, and editor, noted, *"The first kingdom established by the barbarians in Italy was that of the Heruli."* Ridpath gives the date of the overthrow of the Heruli as 493. They were overthrown by the Goths under Theodoric by what he called a divine commission from Eastern Roman Emperor Zeno. (2)

Nelson's Encyclopedia says, *"In 533 the Byzantine general, Belisarius, landed in Africa. The Vandals were several times defeated, and Carthage was entered on Sept. 15, 533. As a nation, the Vandals soon ceased to exist."* (3)

In *Outlines of Prophecy*, Dr. George Dawe, Professor Emeritus of Systematic Theology, Union Presbyterian Seminary, says, *Now concerning the little horn in verses 20-25, there is no question that it is a Roman power. If the fourth beast is Roman, so also are the ten horns and the 'little horn' likewise – the little horn with great pretensions. What diverse power arose out of the ten kingdoms after pagan Roman ceased? And what power has dominated the ten Roman kingdoms every since, down to the present time? None other than Papal Rome. The Papacy is Roman. Its seat is in Rome.*

Its very name, even today, is Roman Catholic (meaning universal). Did the Pope subdue three kings? Yes, the Heruli in 493, the Vandals in 534, and the Ostrogoths in 553.

The leaders of the three kingdoms were removed from power, but the Popes took control of the land and people in those areas. These ten kingdoms bowed their authority to the ACBP.

> *And the ten horns which thou saw are ten kings, which have received no kingdom as yet; but receive power as kings one hour with the beast. These have one mind, and shall give their power and strength unto the beast.* Revelation 17:12-13

Pope Pius IX declared their rise to power over the ten kingdoms, *"It is, therefore, by a particular decree of Divine Providence that, at the fall of the Roman Empire and its partition into separate kingdoms, the Roman Pontiff, whom Christ made the head and center of his entire Church, acquired civil power."*

Daniel is pointing to the ACBPs, who *speak* for the Roman beast and *harlot* RCC.

> *He shall speak pompous words against the Most High, Shall persecute the saints of the Most High, And shall intend to change times and law. Then the saints shall be given into his hand For a time and times and half a time.* Daniel 7:25

The office of the Papacy acts and speaks for the whole body, and the Popes have spoken pompous words, proclaiming to be God, to be Jesus Christ in the flesh, to forgive sins, and to provide salvation; all of which is blasphemous. The Popes of Rome caused tens of millions of saints to be killed during the *Dark Ages* and the *Inquisition*.

Catholics openly proclaim the power of the Pope to *'change the law.'* *The Pope has the power to change times, to abrogate laws, and to dispense with all things, even the precepts of Christ. The Pope has the authority and often exercised it, to dispense with the command of Christ.*

The Popes *changed the times* when they altered the Roman calendar to push the saints away from the Scriptural calendar and Sabbath. At the *Council of Nicaea* in 325, they changed the calendar to be based on the Sun, rather than the sun and moon as Yah ordained.

In 1582, Pope Gregory XIII re-established January 1st as New Year's Day; but the Scriptural new year starts in Spring. The Popes *changed the law* when they removed Elohim's 2nd Commandment, which forbids idol worship, and they divided the 10th commandment into two.

In *Romanism And The Reformation*, Henry Grattan Guinness says, *Its paramount influence depends, not on its mere material power, for it is small as a kingdom, a "little horn," but on its religious pretensions. Does not this exactly portray the Papacy? Was it not diverse or different from all the Gothic kingdoms amid which it existed? Was it a mere kingdom? Nay, but a spiritual reign over the hearts and minds as well as the bodies of men a reign established by means, not of material weapons, but of spiritual pretensions.*

Cyril of Jerusalem (about 300) foretold, *The predicted Antichrist will come when the times of the Roman Empire shall be fulfilled. . . . Ten kings of the Romans shall arise together. . . . Among these the eleventh is Antichrist, who, by magical and wicked artifices, shall seize the Roman power.* (7)

The Popes are the leader, the *little horn*, who rose to power out of the ten nations (*ten horns*) of the fallen Western Roman Empire. The papacy uprooted three nations when it rose to power because they would not bow to his authority. The Vatican is a diverse kind of nation. The office of the papacy is the man who speaks great words against Yah, as they claim to forgive sin and to be God, which is blasphemy. The papacy made war with the saints during the Dark Ages and the Inquisition. The papacy attempted to change the laws of Yah and changed the calendar. The papacy reigned exactly 1,260 years, from 538-1798.

The Popes of Rome fulfill the description in Daniel 7:24-25, as the *little horn*, proving that the fourth beast kingdom of Daniel 7 is the Roman beast kingdom.

CHAPTER 30 - THE SON OF PERDITION

Daniel points to the Popes of Rome in civil terms as the *little horn*. John points to them in civil and ecclesiastic terms as the *antichrist beast*, who leads the *harlot* church of Rome. And Paul points to them in ecclesiastic terms as the *man of sin*, the *son of perdition*. The early church saints no doubt wanted Messiah to return, so Paul tells them that before it takes place, there will be a great *falling away* from the Scriptural faith and that a deceiver would come in the name of Messiah.

Let no man deceive you by any means: for that day shall not come, except there come a falling away first, and that man of sin be revealed, the son of perdition; Who opposeth and exalteth himself above all that is called God, or that is worshipped; so that he as God sitteth in the temple of God, shewing himself that he is God. **2 Thessalonians 2:3-4**

When Emperor Constantine built on the foundation of what Simon the Sorcerer had started and joined the idol worship of pagan Rome with Scriptural faith, he created Romanism, the RCC's false religion. Many believers compromised their beliefs to be exalted in Rome after several centuries of severe persecution. The pure faith was *apostatized* into a religion with pagan theology, holidays, and idols.

Both of the times that the phrase *"son of perdition"* is used in the Bible refer to someone who claims to follow Messiah but is really *against* Him in their beliefs and actions. It's someone who pretends to be a part of the true Ekklesia but is a deceiver. Both Judas and the office of the Papacy have fulfilled this role.

The *grand mystery* of our redemption is that Messiah humbled Himself to become a man, and He did not esteem Himself but gave glory to His Father. The counter to this *mystery* is that a mortal, sinful man would claim to take Messiah's place and proclaim himself to be as God!

Keep in mind that when the Apostle Paul wrote 2 Thessalonians 2, the temple was still standing in Jerusalem, as the Romans didn't destroy it until 70 AD. Any reference to a physical temple would have been to that temple, not an end-times temple. Paul is pointing to the spiritual temple made up of followers of Messiah. Paul is saying that the *son of perdition* would sit in Yah's temple, that is, among the body of believers.

The Popes of Rome proclaim to lead Messiah's *'one-true church.'* Do you see the match? Paul is telling us that the *son of perdition* pretends to be a believer to deceive the world. Instead of being an infidel who doesn't believe in the Messiah of the Scriptures, the *son of perdition* feigns to be Messiah's key leader.

The Pope sits in his grandiose basilica, on an ornate throne, pretending to be the leader of Messiah's Ekklesia, which is the *temple* that Paul is describing. The Pope sits on the throne, pretending to be the *Vicar of Christ*, to replace Messiah, while teaching concepts contrary to Messiah.

In *The Approaching End Of The Age*, Henry Grattan Guinness says,
Further, he is called 'the son of perdition.' And this name, applied by our Lord to Judas Iscariot, the traitor, would prepare us to find the man of sin the antichrist, not in some openly and avowedly infidel power, but in a professedly Christian one. The 'son of perdition' was an apostate disciple, who betrayed his Lord with a kiss of seeming reverence and affection. This name would lead us to expect that a Judas character will attach to the great apostasy and its head, and lead us, therefore, to look for it in the professing Christian Church, the sphere in which Paul indeed distinctly states, that it will be revealed.

Remember ye not, that, when I was yet with you, I told you these things? And now ye know what withholds that he might be revealed in his time. For the mystery of lawlessness is already at work; only he who now restrains will do so until he is taken out of the way. 2 Thessalonians 2:5-7

Paul could not write that the Roman Emperors would be removed, as it would have invited even more persecution.

So Paul reminded the Thessalonians about what he told them in person, that it's the Roman Emperors who *withheld* the *son of perdition* from taking power. The Roman Popes and bishops were already drawing people away from the true faith, into the false religion of Romanism, in which the Pope takes the place of Messiah. Rome was a pagan city, and the Emperor was called the *Pontifex Maximus*, the high priest.

As long as the Western Roman Emperor was in power, the Roman bishop could not take power as Pontifex Maximus. The last Roman Emperor was removed in 476. Shortly after that, in 538, the Pope was given religious and civil power when Eastern Emperor Justinian issued a decree making the Pope head of all churches.

In *Romanism And The Reformation*, Henry Grattan Guinness says, *While the Caesars held imperial power, it was impossible for the predicted antichrist to arise. On the fall of the Caesars, he would arise. In the Catholic Douay Bible, issued under Romish authority and bearing the signatures of Cardinals Wiseman and Manning, the "man of sin" is interpreted as follows: 'He sitteth in the temple of God,' etc. By all these words is described to use the great antichrist… according to the unquestionable authority and consent of the ancient Fathers." The Catholic Church thus accepts our interpretation of the "man of sin," which Paul foresaw, "and admits that power to be the antichrist. I took them from Picart's description of the Roman ceremonial, a Roman Catholic authority. It is the Romanists themselves who use this significant phrase of the Papal pontiff: he "presides in the temple of the Lord."*

In *Horae Apocalypticae*, Edward Bishop Elliott says, *We have the consistent testimony of the early fathers, from Irenaeus, the disciples of St. John, down to Chrysostom and Jerome, to the effect that it (the restrainer) was understood to be the Imperial power ruling and residing at Rome.*

In *Key To The Apocalypse*, Henry Grattan Guinness says, *It is a remarkable fact, in relation to the "let" or hindrance to the manifestation of the "Man of Sin," that "we have the consenting testimony of the early Fathers, from Irenaeus, the disciple of the disciple of St. John, down to Chrysostom and Jerome, to the effect that it was understood to be the imperial power ruling and* *residing at Rome." Thus, commenting on the words, "Ye know what detaineth that he might be revealed in his time," Tertullian says: "What obstacle is there but the Roman state, the falling away of which by being scattered into ten kingdoms shall introduce Antichrist... that the Beast Antichrist, with his False Prophet, may wage war on the Church of God."*

In his work on the temporal power of the Popes, he says: "Now the abandonment of Rome was the liberation of the Pontiffs. What so ever claims to obedience the Emperors may have made, and what so ever compliance the Pontiff may have yielded, the whole previous relation, anomalous, and annulled again and again by the vices and outrages of the Emperors, was finally dissolved by a higher power. The providence of God permitted a succession of eruptions, Gothic, Lombard, and Hungarian, to desolate Italy, and to efface from it every remnant of the Empire. The Pontiffs found themselves alone, the sole fountains of order, peace, law, and safety. And from the hour of this providential liberation, when by a divine intervention the chains fell off from the hands of the successor of St. Peter, as once before from his own, no sovereign has ever reigned in Rome except the Vicar of Jesus Christ."

Theologian Jerome (347-420) declared, *If St. Paul had written openly and boldly that the man of sin would not come until the Roman Empire was destroyed, a just cause of persecution would then appear to have been afforded against the Church in her infancy. He shows that that which restrains is the Roman Empire; for unless it shall have been destroyed, and taken out of the midst, according to the prophet Daniel, Antichrist will not come before that. Let us, therefore, say what all ecclesiastical writers have delivered to us, that when the Roman Empire is destroyed, ten kings will divide the Roman world among themselves, and then will be revealed the man of sin.* (1)

Tertullian (155-240), an early Christian apologist said, *For the mystery of iniquity doth already work; only he who now hinders must hinder until he be taken out of the way. What obstacle is there but the Roman state, the falling away of which, by being scattered into ten kingdoms, shall introduce Antichrist upon (its own ruins).* (2)

Pope Pius IX proclaimed to take the place of the Roman Caesar, *"The Caesar who now addresses you, and to whom alone are obedience and fidelity due."* *"The Bishop of Rome mounted the throne whence the Emperors fell, and took, little by little, the position rendered vacant by the desertion of the successor of Augustus."*

Said of Pope Pius IX, *"The captain who gloriously fills the place of the ancient Caesars."*

Roman Cardinal Manning said, *"Now the abandonment of Rome [by Caesar] was the liberation of the Pontiffs. He was elevated to be, in his Divine Master's Name King of Kings and Lord of Lords. The abandonment of Rome left them free to become independent sovereigns, and to take up the sovereignty the Emperor had just laid down."*

Pope Innocent III declared, *"We may according to the fullness of our power, dispose of the law and dispense above the law. Those whom the Pope of Rome doth separate, it is not a man that separates them but God. For the Pope holdeth place on earth, not simply of a man but of the true God."*

Pope Nicholas said, *"I am in all and above all, so that God Himself and I, the vicar of God, hath both one consistory, and I am able to do almost all that God can do... wherefore, if those things that I do be said not to be done of man, but of God, what do you make of me but God? Again, if prelates of the Church be called of Constantine for gods, I then being above all prelates, seem by this reason to be above all gods. Wherefore, no marvel, if it be in my power to dispense with all things, yea with the precepts of Christ."*

Pope Pius V blasphemed, *"The Pope and God are the same, so he has all power in Heaven and earth."* **Pope Leo XIII said,** *"We hold upon this earth the place of God Almighty."*

Even St. Augustine of Hippo (345-430), who is highly revered by the Roman Catholic Church, in his work *City of God*, admitted, *"For what does he (Paul) mean by "For the mystery of iniquity doth already work: only he who now holdeth, let him hold until he be taken out of the way: and then shall the wicked be revealed?" I frankly confess I do not know what he means...*

However, it is not absurd to believe that these words of the apostle, refer to the Roman Empire." (11)

John Wycliffe, John Calvin, Martin Luther, John Knox, John Wesley, the Church of Scotland, the Church of Ireland, the Westminster Confession of Faith, the London Baptist Confession, and many more people, have proclaimed that the Popes fulfill Bible prophecy as the *man of sin,* the *son of perdition.*

In ***History Unveiling Prophecy,*** **Henry Grattan Guinness says,** *Paul said "you know" who it is, as I told you in person. If it was the Holy Spirit, he would have wrote that. He did not wish to expose the persecuted Christians to fresh dangers, by putting into the hand of the enemies, proof of what would by them have been considered a seditious creed. From Irenaeus, the disciple of Polycarp, the contemporary of St. John, we first hear that the hindrance mentioned by Paul when he was with the Thessalonians and alluded to in his second epistle was The Roman Empire; and from him downwards, the fathers are unanimous in this assertion.*

Human ambition could rise no higher. The Popes boldly laid claim to the attributes and prerogatives of Deity. He represented the Father, the Son, and the Holy Ghost. He claimed to rule in three worlds, Heaven, Earth, and Hell, and in token thereof was crowned with a triple crown. He paraded himself before the world as the infallible Teacher of faith and morals. Exalted above bishops, above councils, above kings, above conscience, from his decisions there was no appeal. He was the supreme Judge of mankind.

Lifted up to sit on the high altar of St. Peter's, the chiefest Church in Christendom, he was publicly adored, cardinals, the princes of the Church, kissing, in turn, his feet; bishops bending low before him in deepest reverence; and nations worshiping him as the visible representative of the Godhead, possessed of power to pardon sins on earth, to canonize saints in heaven, to loose souls from the pains of purgatory in the world beneath; to judge, to govern, to bless, to save mankind; whose sentences, clothed with the authority of God, were inherently irreversible, irrevocable, final and everlasting.

It only remained for the Popes to assume Divine honors. In the person of Boniface VIII, whose accession took place in 1294, the Pope sat "as God in the temple of God." Human ambition could rise no higher. The Pope boldly laid claim to the attributes and prerogatives of Deity. Jerome (a theologian and historian in the 4th century), in interpreting Paul's man of sin, declares that he is to sit in the temple, that is, in the Church. He adds, *It is only by assuming Christ's name that the simpler ones of believers can be seduced to go to Antichrist; for thus they will go to Antichrist while thinking to find Christ. Cyril of Jerusalem (a distinguished theologian in the 4th century) says of antichrist: This man will usurp the government of the Roman Empire, and will falsely call himself the Christ. He will sit in the temple of God: not that which is in Jerusalem, but in the Churches everywhere.*

Bishop of Salisbury (1522-57) wrote this commentary, proving the Pope is the *man of sin. He will come in the name of Christ, yet will he do all things against Christ and under pretense and color of serving Christ; he shall devour the sheep and people of Christ; he shall deface whatsoever Christ hath taught; he shall quench that fire which Christ hath kindled; those plants which Christ hath planted he shall root up; he shall undermine that house which Christ hath built; he shall be contrary to Christ, his faith contrary to the faith of Christ, and his life contrary to the life of Christ.*

In *What I Saw In Rome* **(1958), John F. Coltheart says,** *As each barbarian incursion took place [during the first four trumpet judgments], the position of the emperor declined, while the power of the bishop [of Rome], who became known as the pope, was enhanced.*

We've seen the *'mystery of iniquity'* by Simon the Sorcerer, the first Roman bishop, Pope. We've seen how Emperor Constantine codified the false doctrine of Romanism, as the *Pontifex Maximus*, the leader of church and state. And we see how the Popes fulfill prophecy as the *little horn* of Daniel 7, the *son of perdition* of 2 Thessalonians 2, and the *antichrist beast* of Revelation, who leads the *harlot* church of the *great city* of Rome. The *man of sin* is one who is lawless.

CHAPTER 31 - THE MAN OF SIN

Messiah warned us to beware of *false prophets (priests)* whose fruit reveals that they are *wolves* in disguise.

> *Beware of false prophets, which come to you in sheep's clothing, but inwardly they are ravening wolves. Ye shall know them by their fruits. Do men gather grapes of thorns, or figs of thistles?* Matthew 7:15-16

Paul described the Popes of Rome and their wicked works of Satan.

> *And then shall that Wicked be revealed, whom the Lord shall consume with the spirit of his mouth, and shall destroy with the brightness of his coming: Even him, whose coming is after the working of Satan with all power and signs and lying wonders.* 2 Thessalonians 2:8-9

The Apostle John declares this about keeping the commandments.

> *He that says, I know him, and keepeth not his commandments, is a liar, and the truth is not in him.* 1 John 2:4

> *By this we know that we love the children of God, when we love God, and keep his commandments.* 1 John 5:2

The *man of sin* is not an atheist; rather, he is someone who feigns to be a leader in Messiah's assembly of saints, a *false priest*, who himself is a liar who sins and misleads people to break the Father's commandments.

In *The Approaching End Of The Age*, Henry Grattan Guinness says, *Recognizing that no religion enjoining a high morality could ever be a popular one, in a world of sinners, who love sin, the Papacy presented a religion of ritual observance, instead of one of spiritual power; heaven could be secured by outward acts; obedience to the church, not a change of heart, was the great essential of salvation. Men naturally seek to earn heaven; Popery sets them to work to do so, teaching salvation by merit and denying salvation by faith.*

It provides convents for the ascetic and the mystic; carnivals for the gay; missions for the enthusiast; penances for the man suffering from remorse; sisterhoods of mercy for the benevolent; crusades for the chivalrous; secret mission for the man whose genius lies in intrigue; the Inquisition, with its racks and screws, for the cruel bigot; indulgences for the man of wealth and pleasure; purgatory to awe the refractory, and frighten the vulgar; and a subtle theology for the casuist and the dialectician.

Popes have proclaimed to be God, breaking the 1st Commandment. Pope Leo XIII (1878-1903) said, *"But the supreme teacher in the Church is the Roman Pontiff. Union of minds, therefore, requires, together with a perfect accord in the one faith, complete submission and obedience of will to the Church and to the Roman Pontiff, as to God Himself."*

The Heavenly Father declared that you shall have no other gods.

The Popes have used Catholics to murder the saints, causing them to break the 6th Commandment. Pope Innocent III (1198-1216) said, *"Anyone who attempts to construe a personal view of God which conflicts with (Catholic) church dogma must be burned without pity."*

Pope Gregory IX (1227-41) said, *"The lords of the districts shall carefully seek out the 'heretics' in dwellings, hovels, and forests, and even their underground retreats shall be entirely wiped out."*

They relentlessly tried to eliminate the *two witnesses* against them, the *Scriptures* and the *saints*. The Popes caused Catholics to torture and kill tens of millions of saints, whom they deemed heretics, during the Dark Ages and the Inquisition. The cruel torture devices that they used are the most barbaric made by man. Google '**catholic torture devices**' to see their horrendous inventions.

Catholic Cardinal Benno wrote descriptions of abuses committed by Gregory VII, including *necromancy, torture of a former friend upon a bed of nails, commissioning an attempted assassination, executions without trials.*

In *The Approaching End Of The Age*, Henry Grattan Guinness says, *Pope Clement XI promised complete exemption from the pains of purgatory to all who took up arms to exterminate the Protestants. This feature is so peculiar, so unlike the analogous features of the three first Beasts or Empires of Daniel, whose dominion was acquired by devouring, pushing, running furiously, smiting, breaking, stamping in pieces, in a word, by exercising physical force, instead of subtle spiritual influence, that it serves at once to indicate the power intended. The Papacy is the only great political power, which has ever held sway over all kindreds, tongues, and nations, without having to fight for it and with the consent of the subjected kingdoms.*

France was the scene of the greatest national crime which even the Papacy has ever instigated and approved, the Massacre of St. Bartholomew's Day, planned by the infamous Catherine de Medicis and ordered by her weak and wretched son, Charles IX. The horrible story of this unparalleled atrocity is too well known to need recounting here. In Paris alone, the blood of over ten thousand innocent Protestant citizens deluged the streets, and for a whole week, the shouts of "Kill, kill," resounded on every hand.

Vassals, were by the Popes absolved from allegiance to their superiors, should these latter refuse to join in the work of extermination; the lands and goods of heretics were given to their murderers; and plenary indulgence to the day of death was granted to every one taking part in the persecution. Pope Clement XI promised complete exemption from the pains of purgatory to all who took up arms to exterminate "the accursed and execrable race."

In his *Notes on Revelation* (1852), Albert Barnes points out the zeal of then Catholic monk Martin Luther, showing how mind-controlled the Popes have made Catholics. *"When I began the affair of the indulgences I was a monk and a most mad Papist. So intoxicated was I, and drenched in Papal dogmas, that I would have been most ready to murder, or to assist others in murdering, any person who would have uttered a syllable against the duty of obedience to the Pope."*

What would happen today if the ACBP told Catholics to kill the believers outside of their church, and he offered them forgiveness and salvation, and no purgatory for their seemingly righteous acts? That's what they've done in the past.

The Popes made themselves rich with the collection of indulgences, stealing the wealth of Catholics, which breaks the 8th commandment. They cause Catholics to believe that they can purchase forgiveness of sins and salvation, giving Catholics a license to sin. By this deception, the Popes have stolen the wealth of widows.

In *The Approaching End Of The Age*, Henry Grattan Guinness says, *Tetzel, the indulgence-monger, bearing the bull of Leo X on a velvet cushion, traveled in state from town to town in a gay equipage, took his station in the thronged church, and proclaimed to the credulous multitudes, "Indulgences are the most precious and sublime of God's gifts; this red cross has as much efficacy as the cross of Jesus Christ. Draw near, and I will give you letters duly sealed, by which even the sins you shall hereafter desire to commit, shall be all forgiven you. There is no sin so great that indulgence cannot remit. Pay, only pay largely, and you shall be forgiven.*

But more than all this, indulgences save not the living alone, they also save the dead. Ye priests, ye nobles, ye tradesmen, ye wives, ye maidens, ye young men, hearken to your departed parents and friends, who call to you from the bottomless abyss, "We are enduring horrible torment, a small alms would deliver us, you can give it, will you not?" The moment the money clinks at the bottom of the chest, the soul escapes purgatory and flies to heaven. With ten groschen, you can deliver your father from purgatory. Our Lord God no longer deals with us as God – he has given all power to the Pope."

The institution of indulgence, says Spanheim, was the mint which coined money, for the Roman Church; the gold mines for the profligate nephews and natural children of the Popes; the nerves of Papal wars; the means of liquidation debt; and the inexhaustible fountain of luxury to the Popes. The curse fell on Simon Magus for thinking that the gift of God might be purchased with money;

what shall we say of him, who pretends that he has divine authority to sell the grace of God for money?

Of him, who leads millions of immortal souls to incur the guilt and curse of Simon Magus, under the delusion that they are securing salvation? And who leads them to do this for his own wicked and selfish ends? Is it possible to find guilt of a deeper die, perfidy of a more atrociously cruel and satanic character?

The ACBPs have caused Catholics to steal the homes and goods of Protestants whom they killed.

The Popes have idols of Mary, the crucifix, Catholic saints, etc., which breaks the 2nd Commandment. Catholics have idols in their churches and their homes. Even the crucifix is an idol, and an evil one at that, as Messiah is not on the cross, He rose again. They bow to statues of Mary and pray to her. To cover this overt sin, the Popes caused the Catholic Church to remove the second commandment from their list and split the Ten Commandments in two.

> The second commandment says *You shall not make idols for yourselves; neither a carved image nor a sacred pillar shall you rear up for yourselves; nor shall you set up an engraved stone in your land, to bow down to it; for I am the LORD your God.* Leviticus 26:1
>
> *You shalt not make for yourself an idol in the form of anything in heaven above or on the earth beneath or in the waters below. You shall not bow down to them or worship them; for I, the LORD your God, am a jealous God.* Exodus 20:4-5

The Popes venerate skulls and bones in Cathedrals and crypts.
Saint Munditia's skull is found in a side altar at St. Peter's Church in Munich. Catholics revere her every year with a High Mass. *Capela dos Ossos, Chapel of Bones*, in Portugal, holds 5,000 skeletons, including two desiccated corpses, one of which is a child dangling from a chain.

They make prayers to dead saints, but Deuteronomy 18:10-11 forbids necromancy, communication with the dead.

The Popes have *born false witness* by proclaiming that people are heretics because they disagree with their false teachings, which breaks the 9th Commandment. The Pope's condemnations of the saints were false, as they were born out of their evil thoughts. Their false witness against the Scriptures was pure evil, and they tried to keep the saints from learning the truth.

The Popes heaped scornful epithets at the saints, accusing them of being *heretics, accursed, the children of the devil,* and *the spawn of hell.* Not a blasphemous term was there, which the Pope and his agents did not use against them.

The Popes have people call them the *'Holy Father,'* breaking the 3rd Commandment. Scripture says, *'You shall not take the name of the Lord your God in vain.'* Catholic priests are called *"Father,"* which also *takes the Father's name in vain.*

> Messiah said to call no religious leader by the title of Father, *And call no man your father upon the earth: for one is your Father, which is in heaven.* Matthew 23:9

Here's a list of other blasphemous titles which the Popes have assigned to themselves, which belong only to the Heavenly Father: *His Holiness, Most Blessed Father, Vicar of God, God on Earth,* and *the true God.*

The Popes banned and burned the Scriptures and prohibited lay people from reading them. They deny the Word of Yah, as they have repeatedly forbidden Bible reading, as it testifies to salvation by faith in Messiah, not by works through the Papal Church.

Pope Innocent III (1198-1216) declared, *"to be reproved are those who translate into French the Gospels, the letters of Paul, the psalter, etc. They are moved by a certain love of Scripture in order to explain them clandestinely and to preach them to one another. The mysteries of the faith are not to (be) explained rashly to anyone. Usually in fact, they cannot be understood by everyone but only by those who are qualified to understand them with informed intelligence.*

123

The depth of the divine Scriptures is such that not only the illiterate and uninitiated have difficulty understanding them, but also the educated and the gifted." (5)

Pope Innocent III decreed, *"We prohibit laymen possessing copies of the Old and New Testament. ...We forbid them most severely to have the above books in the popular vernacular."* They only allowed their priests to read the Scriptures in Latin. (6)

Pope Pius IV (1559-65) said, *"The Bible is not for the people; whosoever will be saved must renounce it. It is a forbidden book. Bible societies are satanic contrivances."* (7)

Pope Innocent III declared, *"As it has been clearly shown by experience that, if the Holy Bible in the vernacular is generally permitted without any distinction, more harm than utility is thereby caused."* (8)

They burned William Tyndale at the stake, and dug up Wycliffe's bones, and burned them. Why? Because Tyndale and Wycliffe translated the Scriptures into English so that people could read them.

Yah had the Bible written in Hebrew, Aramaic, and Greek. The Papal church only taught in Latin so that they could hide what Scripture is proclaiming. They don't forbid Bible reading now because Yah used the advent of the printing press and Bible societies to spread Bibles all over the world so that they can't stop it. Instead, they've been instrumental in creating modern Bibles that remove words and change the meaning to fit their teachings.

In *The Approaching End Of The Age,* **Henry Grattan Guinness says,** *Christ bids all men, for instance, "Search the Scriptures," "prove all things, and hold fast that which is good." On no one point are the Popes more resolved to enforce disobedience to the Divine will; in bull after bull, they have forbidden the use of the Scriptures in their own tongue to the people, saying, "Let it be lawful for no man whatever to infringe this declaration of our will and command, or to go against it with bold rashness."*

124

When Wycliffe published his translation, Pope Gregory sent a bull to the University of Oxford in 1378, condemning the translator as having "run into a detestable kind of wickedness." When Tyndale published his translation, it was condemned. In 1546, when Luther was preparing his German version, Leo X published a bull, couched in the most vile and opprobrious language.

The indignation of Pius VII (and other Popes) against Bible societies knows no bounds. He speaks of the Bible Society as a "crafty device by which the very foundations of religion are undermined," as "a pestilence dangerous to [Roman] Christianity;" "a defilement of the faith, eminently dangerous to souls;" "a nefarious scheme," etc., and strictly commands, that every version of Scriptures into a vulgar tongue, without the church's notes, should be placed in the Index among prohibited books.

Curses are freely bestowed on those who assert the liberty of the laity to read the Scriptures, and every possible impediment is thrown in the way of their circulation. Bible burning is a favorite ceremony with Papists; and their ignorance of the real contents of the book is almost incredible. The famous bull "Unigenitus," 1713, condemns the proposition that "the reading of the Scriptures is for everybody" as "false, shocking, scandalous, impious, and blasphemous."

The Popes condone the *stealing, killing, and destroying* of the SOJ. The SOJ has murdered kings and Presidents who oppose them. They have stolen the wealth of nations, and they have set up Rothschild central banks in almost every nation to control the money supply and steal the people's wealth.

In *The Approaching End Of The Age*, Henry Grattan Guinness says, *Its institution and patronage of the order of the Jesuits is another of the exceedingly sinful deeds of the Papacy. This Society, which has dared to appropriate to itself the Name which is above every name, by calling itself "the Order of Jesus" deserves rather, from the nature of its doctrines, and the work it has done in the world, to be called 'The Order of Satan.' Founded by Ignatius Loyola, a Spanish officer contemporary with Luther, its great object was to subjugate the whole human race to the power of the Papacy.*

The Catholic king of Portugal says: It cannot be, but that the licentiousness introduced by the Jesuits, of which the three leading features are falsehood, murder, and perjury, should give a new character to morals. Their doctrines render murder innocent, sanctify falsehood, authorize perjury, deprive the laws of their power, destroy the submission of subjects, allow individuals the liberty of killing, calumniating, lying, and forswearing themselves, as their advantage may dictate; they remove the fear of Divine and human laws, so that Christians and civil society could not exist, where they are paramount.

The Parliament of Paris, in 1762, used language quite as strong in a memorial to the king, accompanying a collection of extracts from 147 Jesuit authors, which they presented to him, "That he might be acquainted with the wickedness of the doctrine constantly held by the Jesuits, from the institution of their Society to the present moment – a doctrine authorizing robbery, lying, perjury, impurity; all passions, and all crimes; inculcating homicide, parricide, and regicide; overturning religion and sanctioning magic, blasphemy, irreligion and idolatry.

The book of "secret instructions" generally attributed to Lainez, the second Father-General of the Order, contains directions so unprincipled that on the first page it is ordained that, if the book fell into the hands of strangers, it was to be positively denied that these were the rules of the Society! Is this not the doctrine of devils, which is authorized by the Popes? Is it not he who patronizes such an order of Satan, the lawless one? Is he not, and does he not richly deserve to be, called the son of perdition?

The Popes teach a false Gospel which misleads billions of Catholics. What an evil strategy of Satan to cause the Popes to teach concepts that replace the true Scriptural faith with a false religion! They teach a false salvation message of works through the sacraments. Instead of being saved through Messiah alone, Catholics follow a false religion, which leaves them guilty of their sins and condemned.

They now cause 1.3 billion Catholics to *revere* (*mark* on the *forehead*) and *obey* (*mark* on the *right hand*, actions) the ACBP, so they have the *mark of the beast* on them.

The Popes cause Catholics to make repetitive prayers during Mass and while praying the Rosary. The liturgy of Roman Catholic services is repetitive recitations.

Pope Pius XII said, *"Every day, as the Church herself recommends, priests will recite the Holy Rosary, which, by proposing for our meditation the mysteries of the Redeemer, leads us to Jesus through Mary."*

Matthew 6:7 says, *But when ye pray, use not vain repetitions, as the heathen do: for they think that they shall be heard for their much speaking.*

The Popes have proclaimed that salvation is only through them.
Pope Pius XII said, *"We recognize the Holy, Catholic, Roman Church to be the only true Church of Jesus Christ, outside of which neither sanctity nor salvation can be found. Call them to the unity of the one fold, granting them the grace to believe every truth of our holy faith and to submit themselves to the Supreme Roman Pontiff, the Vicar of Jesus Christ on earth."*

Acts 4:12 says *Neither is there salvation in any other: for there is none other name under heaven given among men, whereby we must be saved.*

The Popes have proclaimed that Mary was sinless.
Pope John Paul II said, *"Preserved free from all guilt of original sin, the Immaculate Virgin was taken up body and soul into heavenly glory upon the completion of her earthly sojourn. She was exalted by the Lord as Queen of the Universe. For the Mother of Christ is glorified as 'Queen of the Universe."*

Pope Pius IX also said, *"The Blessed Virgin Mary to have been, from the first instant of her conception, by a singular grace and privilege of Almighty God, in view of the merits of Christ Jesus the Savior of Mankind, preserved free from all stain of original sin."*

Romans 3:23 says *For all men have sinned and fallen short of the glory of God.*

The Heavenly Father despises the worship of the Queen of Heaven, *The children gather wood, the fathers kindle the fire, and the women knead dough, to make cakes for the queen of heaven; and they pour out drink offerings to other gods, that they may provoke Me to anger.* Jeremiah 7:18

The Popes have proclaimed that Mary sits in heaven.
Pope Pius XI said, *"What will it cost you, oh Mary, to hear our prayer? What will it cost you to save us? Has not Jesus placed in your hands all the treasures of His grace and mercy? You sit crowned Queen at the right hand of your son: your dominion reaches as far as the heavens and to you are subject the earth and all creatures dwelling thereon. Your dominion reaches even down into the abyss of hell, and you alone, oh Mary, save us from the hands of Satan."* (13)

John 14:6 says *I am the way, the truth, and the life. No one comes to the Father except through Me.*

The Popes have proclaimed that Mary is the mediator to the Father.
Pope Leo XIII said, *"O Holy Mother of God; to thee we lift our prayers for thou, powerful and merciful, art the Mediatrix of our salvation."* (14)

"With equal truth it may be said that of the great treasury of all graces given to us by Our Lord—for grace and truth came by Jesus Christ—nothing comes to us except through Mary's mediation, for such is God's Will. Thus, as no man goes to the Father but by the Son, so no one goes to Christ except through his mother." (15)

1 Timothy 2:5-6 says, *For there is one God and one Mediator between God and men, the Man Christ Jesus, who gave Himself a ransom for all.*

They deny Messiah His rightful place by assigning His attributes of Mediator, Advocate, and Redeemer; to Mary; fulfilling 1 John 2:22.

The Popes have proclaimed that salvation is through Mary.
Pope Leo XIII said, *"O Virgin most holy, none abounds in the knowledge of God except through thee; none, O Mother of God, obtains salvation except through thee, none receives a gift from the throne of mercy except through thee."* (16)

Pope Pius IX (1846-78) said, *"God has committed to her the treasury of all good things, in order that everyone may know that through her are obtained every hope, every grace, and all salvation. For this is his will, that we obtain everything through Mary."*

Pope Pius X (1903-14) said, *"If it is impossible to separate what God has united, it is also certain that you cannot find Jesus except with Mary and through Mary."*

Pope Benedict XV (1914-22) said, *"To such extent did Mary suffer and almost die with her suffering and dying Son; to such extent did she surrender her maternal rights over her Son for man's salvation, that we may rightly say she redeemed the human race together with Christ."*

> Acts 4:12 says, *Neither is there salvation in any other: for there is none other name under heaven given among men, whereby we must be saved.*

The Popes have proclaimed that forgiveness is through them. Pope John Paul II said, *"Don't go to God for forgiveness of sins: come to me."*

> Hebrews 2:17 says, *Therefore, in all things He had to be made like His brethren, that He might be a merciful and faithful High Priest in things pertaining to God, to make propitiation for the sins of the people.*

The Popes prohibit priests and nuns from marrying.
This mandate has led to rampant homosexuality, rape of nuns, abortions, and pedophilia. 70% of Catholic priests are reportedly homosexual. Raping boys in Jesus' name accomplishes many things. First-born sons are set-apart for the Father, so violating them corrupts them. Many of these boys turn away from the Heavenly Father and Messiah because their supposed representative harmed them. Many of these boys become homosexuals, switch sexes, and commit suicide.

According to Jack and Diane Ruhl of the National Catholic Reporter, who decided to research this particular topic, since 1950, the Vatican has spent nearly $4 billion in payouts to victims of the sexual crimes of their priests. That number is conservative considering the amount of under the table dealings that have taken place. And many cases were never reported, nor were they taken to court, leaving their reality in the dark.

The priests corrupt the minds of the youth.

In the book *Fifty Years In The Church Of Rome*, former Catholic priest Charles Chiniquy said that during confessionals, the priests ask innocent children questions about things that they had never thought of before, such as about masturbation, sexual thoughts about the opposite sex, etc.; which then pervert their minds to think about those things.

In *The Approaching End Of The Age*, Henry Grattan Guinness says,
It has been by means of a counterfeit Christianity that Satan has, through the papacy, resisted the spread of true Christianity. The Papacy has its counterfeit high priest, the Pope; its counterfeit sacrifice, the mass; its counterfeit Bible, tradition; its counterfeit mediators, the Virgin, the saints, and angels; the forms have been copied, the realities set aside. Satan inaugurated and developed a system, not antagonistic to Christianity, but a counterfeit of it. In the selection of Rome as its seat of empire, the Papacy secured enormous prestige. "In no other spot would its gigantic schemes of dominion have been formed, or, if formed, realized. Sitting in the seat which the masters of the world had so long occupied, the Papacy appeared the rightful heir of their power. The Pontiffs also claimed to be successors of the Apostles: a more masterly stroke of policy still. As the successor of Peter, the Pope was greater than as the successor of Caesar. The one made him a king, the other made him king of kings; the one gave him the power of the sword, the other invested him with the still more sacred authority of the keys. The Papacy is the ghost of Peter crowned with the shadowy diadem of the old Caesars. Recognizing that no religion enjoining a high morality could ever be a popular one, in a world of sinners, who love sins, the Papacy presented a religion of ritual observance, instead of one of spiritual power: heaven could be secured by outward acts; obedience to the church, not a change of heart, was the great essential of salvation. Men naturally seek to earn heaven; Popery sets them to work to do so, teaching salvation by merit and denying salvation by faith.

The RCC has a counterfeit *high priest*, the Pope; a counterfeit *mediator*, Mary; a counterfeit *communion*, the Eucharist; a *counterfeit* ritualistic church service; and a counterfeit *Gospel* of works. How can all of these things not describe the *man of sin* that the Apostle Paul is describing?

CHAPTER 32 - MYSTERY, BABYLON THE GREAT

Revelation 17 is the key to understanding the fulfillment of the apocalyptic vision. People proclaim that *'Mystery, Babylon the Great'* is the USA, New York City, Jerusalem, etc., but you will see that the detailed description can only describe the *apostate* church of the ACBP.

And there came one of the seven angels which had the seven vials, and talked with me, saying unto me, Come hither; I will shew unto thee the judgment of the great whore that sitteth upon many waters. **Revelation 17:1**

The *seven angels* of the *seven bowls* are directly tied to this vision because the bowl judgments are poured out on the ACBP and the people of his *harlot* church. She is called a *great whore*, because she pretends to be Messiah's church, but she is full of idols, paganism, dead men's bones, and many teachings contrary to Scripture, including a false gospel.

The RCC has basilicas in the countries of the fallen Roman Empire and around the world; thus, she sits on many people groups. Recall that the word *'waters'* is pointing to people groups, so it's interesting that the RCC declares to be the *'Holy See.'* The *Holy See*, also called the *See of Rome*, is the Pope's jurisdiction, which includes the apostolic episcopal see of the Diocese of Rome <u>with universal ecclesiastical jurisdiction of the worldwide Catholic Church</u>.

Spiritual *whoredom* in Scripture points to idolatry, such as in Jeremiah 3:6-9, when the Israelites played the harlot when they worshiped false pagan gods. The Popes proclaim that the RCC is the *one true church* of Messiah, yet her fruit reveals that she's a *harlot*. The myriads of images before which Roman Catholics bow down, the Mass, the worship of the Host, the worship and prayers to saints and Mary, in the Church of Rome all reveal it as an *idolatrous whore*.

In *The Approaching End Of The Age*, **Henry Grattan Guinness says,** *The Babylonian harlot is represented as enthroned upon many waters, which are nations and peoples. She is not only a church, but a church ruling nations; that is, she claims a temporal as well as a spiritual sway. She claims two swords, she holds two keys, she crowns her Pontiff with two crowns, the one a mitre of universal bishopric; the other, a tiara of universal dominion. There is indeed a mystery on the forehead of the Church of Rome, in the union of these two supremacies, and it has often proved a mystery of iniquity. This word "abominations" designates, as is well known, idols. The literal ancient Babylon was the mother of almost all the literal idolatries that the earth has ever known.*

With whom the kings of the earth have committed fornication, and the inhabitants of the earth have been made drunk with the wine of her fornication. Revelation 17:2

'*Fornication*' is spiritual adultery by people who pretend to belong to Yah, but they disobey His commands and serve pagan gods. The RCC pretends to be Messiah's one true church, but the symbolism in her Eucharist ceremony reveals that they are really carrying out the *Babylonian Mystery Religion*.

In *The Book Of Revelation Explained*, **Joseph Benson says,** *National Israel is feminine. We can look at all of the passages in Jeremiah, Isaiah, Ezra, Hosea, etc., which proclaim the Israelites as "the daughter of Zion; the wife of Elohim; a comely delicate woman; a princess; the virgin of Israel; the sun-clothed woman," etc. And we see that Elohim called those who worshiped false gods, "a harlot; a backslidden daughter; an imperious whorish woman; backslidden daughter; a travailing woman; a wife of whoredom; a treacherous wife; an adulterous wife;" etc. In Revelation, Messiah speaks about two types of women: the pure bride, called Holy Jerusalem, and the harlot of Rome, called Babylon the Great.*

Many world leaders are Catholic and take part in her pagan-based ceremonies, which are contrary to Scripture, and steal glory away from the Heavenly Father and Messiah. They have been seduced into *revering* and *obeying* the ACBP and carrying out the persecution of the saints.

The Pope's blasphemous words, their sinful ways, their teachings contrary to Scripture, their giving Catholics a license to sin, their banning of the Scriptures, and their persecution of the saints; all prove that the RCC commits *fornication*.

No wine can more thoroughly intoxicate those who drink it than false zeal does the followers of the great whore. Catholics believe that they are part of the *one true church* and that others are heretics. They're programmed never to leave the Papal Church, lest they are damned.

So he carried me away in the spirit into the wilderness: and I saw a woman sit upon a scarlet colored beast, full of names of blasphemy, having seven heads and ten horns. **Revelation 17:3**

These verses show us that a woman in Scripture can represent an assembly of people:

For thy Maker is thine husband; the LORD of hosts is his name; and thy Redeemer the Holy One of Israel; The God of the whole earth shall he be called. For the LORD hath called thee as a woman forsaken and grieved in spirit, and a wife of youth, when thou was refused, said thy God. Isaiah 54:5-6

I have likened the daughter of Zion to a comely and delicate woman. Jeremiah 6:2

For I am jealous over you with godly jealousy: for I have espoused you to one husband, that I may present you as a chaste virgin to Christ. 2 Corinthians 11:2

There are two communities of women in Revelation, the pure bride of Messiah called *Holy Jerusalem*, and the *harlot* bride of the ACBP, called *Babylon the Great*. The feminine terms in Revelation 17 of *whore, her, woman,* and *mother of harlots*, are pointing to an apostate group of people led by the ACBP. The beast is the same as that in Revelation 13:1; the *antichrist beast* led Roman beast kingdom. The *scarlet* color represents the blood of the saints that they shed during the Dark Ages and Inquisition.

133

The *'seven heads and ten horns'* tell us who controls the woman, the ACBP of Rome, who rose to power out of the *sea* of people of the ten kingdoms of the fallen Roman Empire.

> *And I stood upon the sand of the sea, and saw a beast rise up out of the sea, <u>having seven heads and ten horns</u>, and upon his horns ten crowns, and upon his heads the name of blasphemy.* Revelation 13:1

Martin Luther had this woodcut drawing made about the fulfillment of the description in Revelation 17. The *great whore*, the RCC, is upon *many waters*, many people groups. She is on a *scarlet beast* with *seven heads and ten horns*, the Roman beast kingdom of the Popes. On her head is the Pope's mitre, pointing to him as her leader.

The *harlot* church has the *golden cup* of the Eucharist ceremony in her hand, once again confirming that it's pointing to the RCC. And the *kings* are kneeling before her, as they *give their power and strength unto the beast.*

The Popes proclaim the following blasphemous titles, which steal glory from the Heavenly Father and Messiah: *His Holiness, Holy Father, Vicar of Christ, Sovereign, Head of the Church, Supreme Pastor,* and *Universal Ruler.* Blasphemous titles that the Popes attribute to Mary are the *Great Mother,* the *Queen of Heaven,* the *Intercessor* to the Father, the *Co-Redeemer,* and the *Savior* of men.

And the woman was arrayed in purple and scarlet color, and decked with gold and precious stones and pearls, having a golden cup in her hand full of abominations and filthiness of her fornication. **Revelation 17:4**

The *harlot* church of the ACBP is *"arrayed in purple and scarlet color, and decked with gold and precious stones and pearls,"* which are worldly things, as she serves the god of mammon.

Google images of *'Pope mitres,'* and you see the dagon fish-god hats that the Roman popes and priests wear, decked with silver and gold and precious stones and pearls. Google images of *'Pope triple crowns,'* and you see their tiaras, which are decked with silver and gold and precious stones and pearls. She is the complete opposite of what Messiah's priests should look like.

The Catholic Encyclopedia identifies her. *"A cloak with a long train and a hooded shoulder cape, purple wool for bishops; for cardinals, it was <u>scarlet</u> watered silk (for Advent, Lent, Good Friday, and the conclave, <u>purple</u> wool); and rose watered silk for Gaudete and Laetare Sundays; and for the pope, it was red velvet for Christmas Matins, red serge at other times."* Cassock: *"The close-fitting, ankle-length robe worn by the Catholic clergy as their official garb. The color for bishops and other prelates is <u>purple</u>, for cardinals <u>scarlet</u>."*

The *harlot* Roman Catholic Church proclaims her official colors. *"The color for bishops and other prelates is <u>purple</u>, for cardinals <u>scarlet</u>... The pectoral cross should be made of <u>gold</u> and... decorated with <u>gems</u>..."*

When you read through the book of Exodus, you see Yah's instructions for the priests to wear *'blue, and purple, and scarlet.'* Rome's *harlot* church priests only wear purple and scarlet, so what are they missing in the color blue? In Numbers 15:38, you see that the priests of Yah were instructed to wear blue on the corners of their garments to remind them to remember His commandments and be holy.

The Popes have done the very opposite, as they've sinned greatly, and they've caused Catholics to violate Yah's commandments; thus, they are a *harlot* church.

The Popes' ecclesiastic and temporal power is foretold under the double symbol of a *woman* and a *beast*. We see the connection on medals that the Popes had minted, which point to the civil and ecclesiastical connection St. John is describing.

Here's a medal of Pope Innocent XI, with the *harlot* RCC represented on the back, standing on water, with the *great city* of Rome in the background. She's holding the Eucharist cup of abominations in one hand and the cross in the other. In Revelation 17:4, we see what Messiah thinks of the harlots' doctrine of transubstantiation; that '*it is full of abominations and filthiness of fornication.*'

The RCC openly portrays itself as a *woman* who holds the *golden cup*. This bronze papal medal of Pope Leo XII was minted in 1825 to commemorate his reign's second year. The inscription reads '*SEDET SUPER UNIVERSUM,*' declaring that *her seat of authority* is universal, over the entire earth. The Roman Catholic Popes and priests use the *golden cup* during the Eucharist ceremony.

Here's another medal from Pope Leo XII, with a woman holding a cross and the golden cup. Once again, she's sitting on a globe to show the RCC's authority over the kings of the world.

Here's an 1825 Papal States medal from Pope Leo XII showing the woman with sun god symbols above her head, as she's a *harlot* of paganism. She is pointing to the church, has the Pope's mitre beside her, and a cross in her hand.

Here's a medal from Pope Pius VIII, showing the common theme of the RCC being portrayed as a woman who holds the golden cup. The woman is continually associated with the Pope, reaffirming that the woman who sits on the beast in Revelation 17 is the RCC of the ACBP.

In *The Prophetic Outlook Today* (1918), E.P. Cachemaille says, *Purple, scarlet, gold, and gems. As said of the Romish Church, this is a truly characteristic picture, drawn from the life. The dress-color specified is distinctively that of the Romish ecclesiastical dignitaries, the scarlet being*

reserved by her to her Pontiffs and Cardinals. The ornaments are those with which she has been bedecked beyond any Church called Christian.

Babylon is not the Papacy, but the Romish Church, of which the Pope is the ecclesiastical head. The Pope has a twofold personality, represented by the Tiara and the Mitre. He claims to be Vicar of Christ and King of kings, ruler of the world—this is represented by the Tiara. He also claims to be head of the Christian Church, and in that capacity, wears the Mitre.

These are marks of identification of Babylon as the Romish Church. Widespread extension among the people of the world. "She sitteth upon many waters," and "waters are peoples, and multitudes, and nations, and tongues." She is "the mother of the harlots…of the earth," that is, of the Roman Catholic churches in other lands, which owe their origin to her. Rome's boasted "Catholicity" is thus one of the marks of her identification. Shedding the blood of Christ's saints and witnesses on a prodigious scale. This is writ large, in terrible characters of fire and blood, on the pages of History, and it cannot be wiped away.

Here's a medal of Pope Pius XI with a woman sitting in a catacomb. That's interesting because the Vatican is above a shrine to the pagan goddess Cybele. The *Temple of Cybele* is Rome's first and most important temple to the *Magna Mater* ("*Great Mother*"), known to the Greeks as Cybele. The Virgin Mary of the RCC is Cybele!

In *Notes on the Handbook of Revelation* (1852), Albert Barnes says, *Far as the design of striking this medal may have been from confirming this portion of the Book of Revelation, yet no one can fail to see that if this had been the design, no more happy illustration could have been adopted. Apostate churches, and guilty nations, often furnish the very proofs necessary to confirm the truth of the Scriptures.*

The Catholic Church points to the importance of her golden cups, *"The Eucharist chalice occupies the first place among sacred vessels. It is the most important of sacred vessels, which may be of gold or silver, and if the latter, then the inside must be surfaced with gold."* (3)

In *The Approaching End Of The Age*, Henry Grattan Guinness says, *Rome enjoins the worship of a bread-god – the wafer, or sacrament; and anathematizes all who refuse to render it. The Council of Trent plainly declares the doctrine of transubstantiation, that the bread and wine in the sacrament are "changed into Lord Jesus Christ, true God, and true man," and adds, "there is therefore now no room to doubt, that all the faithful in Christ, are bound to venerate this holy sacrament and to render thereto the worship of latria, which is due to the true God. If anyone shall say, that this holy sacrament should not be adored, nor carried about in processions, nor held up publically to the people, to adore it, or that its worshippers are idolaters, let him be accursed."*

Millions of martyrs have perished for protesting against this idolatry and asserting that it is blasphemy to say man can first make God and then eat him; a creed more degrading than any that the heathen hold. In the days when the "Corpus Christi" procession was a most imposing and dazzling ceremony, when friars, and monks, and priests, and pretends, and canons, and bishops, and archbishops, in varied and splendid costumes attended the bread-god through the streets of crowded cities, amid the clang of bells, bands of military music, choral hymns, and clouds of incense, it was no easy matter for a heretic to escape detection. From the moment the Host came in sight until it had passed right out of the range of vision, the multitudes were commanded to bow in profound adoration and awe! And woe to the man who dared to do otherwise, the Inquisition speedily became his home and the auto da fe his portion.

The following passage is from an encyclical letter from Pius IX, "But that our most merciful Lord may the more readily lend an ear to our prayers, and grant our petitions, let us ever call upon the most holy mother of God, the immaculate Virgin Mary, to intercede with him; for she is the fond mother of us all, our mediatrix, our advocate, our securest and greatest hope, than whole interposition with God, nothing can be stronger, nothing more influential!"

The "Te Deum" itself has been parodied in honor of Mary, "We praise thee, O Mother of God | we acknowledge thee, O Virgin Mary | All the earth doth worship thee, the spouse of the everlasting Father | Holy, holy, holy, Mary, Mother, and Virgin. The church throughout all the world joins in calling on thee, the Mother of the Divine Majesty | And the creeds, have in like manner been parodied.

Nor is it the Virgin alone who is worshipped, Images of her – mere dolls, are also adored; witness the degrading ceremony of the annual "coronation of the Virgin," in which the Pope himself takes part; witness the worship of the "Madonna of the Augustinians" and other Madonnas. Mariolatry, among the ignorant masses, is pure image worship, idolatry in its most sensual and childish form, the adoration of a doll.

We'll cover the Eucharist ceremony's evil symbolism in ***The Babylonian Priesthood Reborn*** chapter. Still, I'll summarize it by saying that they're symbolically carrying out the *Babylonian Mystery Religion*, which is *full of abominations and filthiness of her fornication.*

There's no mistaking who she is, as we see the RCC bishops and cardinals dressed in *purple* and *scarlet*; the Popes decked with mitres and tiaras of *gold*, *precious stones*, and *pearls*; and the priests using the *golden cup* in Eucharist ceremonies around the world.

***And upon her forehead was a name written, MYSTERY, BABYLON THE GREAT, THE MOTHER OF HARLOTS AND ABOMINATIONS OF THE EARTH.* Revelation 17:5**

The tribe of Judah was married to Yah but became a *harlot* as she committed spiritual adultery.

How is the faithful city become a harlot! It was full of judgment; righteousness lodged in it, but now murderers. Isaiah 1:21

Her title is prefaced here with the word *'Mystery'* for two reasons. First, because she pretends to be Messiah's church, but she teaches a false salvation message, and she persecutes the saints, which made John marvel. And second, because her symbolism is that of the *Babylonian Mystery Religion*, of the worship of the sun god and moon goddess.

John would have known that the saints spread around the Roman Empire, preaching the Gospel and that Paul helped set up a church in Rome. So he would have been shocked to see that the Roman church would apostatize, *fall away* from the true faith, and became the enemy of Messiah and the saints.

Thomas Newton (1704-1782), an English cleric and biblical scholar, said, *The title of mystery is in no respect proper to her more than any other city, and neither is there any mystery in substituting one heathen, idolatrous and persecuting city for another; but it is indeed a mystery that a city, called Christian, professing and boasting herself to be the city of God, should prove another Babylon in idolatry and cruelty to the people of God. She glories in the name of Roman Catholic, and well, therefore, may be called Babylon the great. She affects the style and title of our holy mother the church, but she is, in truth, the mother of fornications and abominations of the earth.* (4)

In the first century, Simon the Sorcerer caused the *'mystery of iniquity'* by going to Rome and combining the true faith with the pagan beliefs. This led to the formation of the RCC by Constantine, called *'Mystery, Babylon the Great'* as it symbolically carries out the *Babylonian Mystery Religion*.

The Catechism of the Catholic Church proclaims that they are the *'Mother,'* the author of salvation, the teacher in the faith, and the head of all believers: *169 Salvation comes from God alone; but because we receive the life of faith through the Church, she is our mother: "We believe the Church as the mother of our new birth, and not in the Church as if she were the author of our salvation." Because she is our mother, she is also our teacher in the faith.*

181 "Believing" is an ecclesial act. The Church's faith precedes, engenders, supports and nourishes our faith. The Church is the mother of all believers. "<u>No one can have God as Father who does not have the Church as Mother.</u>"

Here's a 1780 coin featuring Pope Pius V, with papal arms, proclaiming it to be the *'Holy Mother Church.'*

St. John Lateran is the Cathedral of the Bishop of Rome, the Pope. At the base of the columns on either side of the central entrance door, the inscription reads: *"Sacred Lateran Church, Universally for the City and the World, Supreme Mother of Churches,"* or *"Holy Lateran Church, Mother, and Head of all Churches in the City and the World."* They're telling you exactly who they are!

In 1564, Pope Pius IV proclaimed in the *Council of Trent*, twelve decrees that he charged all men that would be saved to own and swear unto. The eleventh one states: *"<u>I do acknowledge that holy Catholic and apostolic Roman Church to be the mother and mistress of all churches</u>: And I do promise to swear true allegiance to the Bishop of Rome, the successor of St. Peter, the prince of the apostles, and Vicar of Jesus Christ."*

In his induction for a universal jubilee, Pope Benedict XIII, in 1725, said: *"It is most deservedly called the city of priests and kings, built for the pride of ages, the city of the Lord, the Sion of the Holy of Israel… Inasmuch as this very*

143

Catholic and Apostolic Roman Church, constituted the head of the world by the sacred seat of the blessed Peter, is <u>the mother of all believers</u>, the faithful interpreter of the Divinity, and the mistress of all churches." (7)

She proudly proclaims that she is the *'Supreme Mother of Churches.'* This cannot be clearer!

Most Catholics have no clue about the Babylonian pagan symbolism used in the Catholic churches and ceremonies, but that's no excuse because they should be reading the Scriptures to see that what the Catholic Church teaches is contrary to Scripture.

Since the RCC's creation, they have helped create many false religions, which are their *daughters*. The Orthodox Church split away from the RCC in 1054, so they're a daughter. Orthodox Churches revere Mary as their Intercessor and teach that salvation is through the sacraments. They are basically the same as the *harlot* church; only they don't revere the Pope as their leader… yet.

Mormonism, Jehovah's Witnesses, etc., were created by Freemasons, no doubt by the influence of Rome's Jesuits. Sadly, though Yah inspired the Protestant Reformers to come out of the control of the RCC; and though the church denominations which were created by their influence initially separated themselves from Rome and protested against the ACBPs; the SOJ's counter-reformation tactics have brought them back into partnership with the Pope, and they're mere *daughters of the harlot* church now.

The word *'abominations'* designates idols. Literal Babylon was the mother of almost all the idolatries that the earth has ever known. John was foretelling that the Church of Rome would be idolatrous. When you see images of *St. John Lateran Cathedral, St. Peter's Square* and *Basilica*, and the many Roman Catholic basilicas around the world, you see countless images of idols, most of which represent pagan gods but have been given Christian names.

And I saw the woman drunken with the blood of the saints, and with the blood of the martyrs of Jesus: and when I saw her, I wondered with great admiration. **Revelation 17:6**

We don't have to look far to find an apostate Christian church that has historically shed the saints' blood; for any person who reads history knows that the RCC persecuted the saints during the Dark Ages and the Inquisition.

Historians estimate that the RCC used its priests and Catholics to kill over fifty million saints who dared to own a Bible (which the Church forbid) or proclaim the Gospel of Messiah. The Pope acts in Messiah's name to deceive billions with a false salvation message and uses his influence over these people to make war with Messiah and His saints. That is anti-Christ.

In *The Book Of Revelation Explained*, Joseph Benson says, *St. John's admiration also plainly evinces that Christian Rome was intended: for it could be no matter of surprise to him that a heathen city should persecute the Christians when he himself had seen and suffered the persecution under Nero: but that a city, professedly Christian, should wanton and riot in the blood of Christians, was a subject of astonishment indeed; and well might he, as it is emphatically expressed, wonder with great wonder.*

In *The Approaching End Of The Age*, Henry Grattan Guinness says, *But that Rome should not only become a Christian church, but, being such, should be also a bitter persecutor of Christians than even heathen Rome had been, this was indeed astonishing, and John might will wonder! That the Church of Rome deserves pre-eminently to be stigmatized as "drunk with the blood of saints" cannot be disputed. What other church ever established an Inquisition, instigated a St. Bartholomew, and gloried in her shame in having done so? What other Christian church has slain fifty millions of Christians for no crime but Christianity, as she has done?*

145

And the angel said unto me, Wherefore didst thou marvel? I will tell thee the mystery of the woman, and of the beast that carrieth her, which hath the seven heads and ten horns. **Revelation 17:7**

John was stunned that a proclaimed church of Messiah is led by His arch-enemy, the *antichrist beast*, who teaches a false Gospel to mislead billions of people and uses its people to persecute Messiah's true saints. Because John marveled so much and couldn't comprehend it all, he was given more explanation to show him how the ACBP and their *harlot* church rose to power over the Roman beast kingdom.

The beast that thou sawest was, and is not; and shall ascend out of the bottomless pit, and go into perdition: and they that dwell on the earth shall wonder, whose names were not written in the book of life from the foundation of the world, when they behold the beast that was, and is not, and yet is. **Revelation 17:8**

Daniel's first beast kingdom <u>was</u> Babylon, out of which came Satan's pagan *Babylonian Mystery Religion*, which exalted Satan and stole praise from the Father. In John's day, the Babylon priesthood <u>was not</u>. Then out of the bottomless pit of Satan's lies came the priest of the *harlot* church of Rome, the Pope of Rome, who carries out the *Babylonian Mystery Religion*, just like Nimrod. He will be captured and cast into *perdition*, into *destruction*, into *a lake of fire burning with brimstone.*

In *The Book Of Revelation Explained*, Joseph Benson says, *It is the same idolatrous power revived again; but only in another form; and all the corrupt part of mankind, whose names were not enrolled as good citizens in the registers of heaven, are pleased at the revival of it; but in this last form it shall go into perdition — It shall not, as it did before, cease for a time and revive again, but shall be destroyed forever.*

And here is the mind which hath wisdom. The seven heads are seven mountains, on which the woman sitteth. **Revelation 17:9**

We're looking for a city that is home to an apostate, idolatrous church. Some people point to Jerusalem as having seven hills, but Jerusalem does not fit the description given throughout Revelation 17. The great city of John's day was Rome, which was famous for its seven hills. Some people say that Rome's seven hills aren't mountains, but Strong's Greek word 3735 *oros* means; *a mountain (as lifting itself above the plain): - hill, mount(-ain);* so it's pointing to a hill or a mountain. Rome was the great power of John's day, known for its seven hills: Aventine, Caelian, Capitoline, Esquiline, Palatine, Quirinal, and Viminal.

In *Notes on the Handbook of Revelation* (1852), Albert Barnes says, *Tertullian said: "I appeal to the citizens of Rome, the populace that dwell on the seven hills" (Apol. 35). And again, Jerome to Marcella, when urging her to quit Rome for Bethlehem, said: "Read what is said in the Apocalypse of the seven hills," etc. In so common a book as Adam's Roman Antiquities, a description may be found of the forms of Roman administration that corresponds almost precisely with this. In confirmation of the same thing, I may refer to the authority of Bellarmine, a distinguished Roman Catholic writer. In his work De Pontiff, he thus enumerates the changes which the Roman government had experienced or the forms of administration that had existed there.*

In *The Book Of Revelation Explained*, Joseph Benson says, *It is evident, therefore, that the city seated on seven mountains must be Rome; and a plainer description could not be given of it without expressing the name, which there might be several wise reasons for concealing. A new form of government was not erected till Rome fell under the obedience of the eastern emperor, and the emperor's lieutenant, the exarch of Ravenna, dissolved all the former magistracies, and constituted a duke of Rome, to govern the people, and to pay tribute to the exarchate of Ravenna.*

In *The Seventh Vial* (1848), James Aitken Wylie says, *This, as Elliot remarks, "is a character as important as it is obvious. It binds the power symbolized, through all its various mutations, from its earliest beginning to its end, to that same seven-hilled locality." This leads us at once to the city of Rome. The seven heads symbolize seven kings, i.e., seven forms of government.*

147

Here's a coin made of Emperor Vespasian, who reigned from 69-79 AD. On it, we see a *woman* sitting on the *seven hills* of Rome. It doesn't get any clearer; John is pointing to Rome!

Seven hills is a well-known feature of the city of Rome. All the Latin poets for five hundred years speak of Rome as the *seven-hilled city*. Early Church Father Victorinus, who suffered martyrdom in 303 under Diocletian, wrote the earliest commentary on the Apocalypse. It says in Revelation 17: *"The seven heads are the seven hills on which the woman sitteth – that is, the city of Rome."*

The Catholic Encyclopedia states, *"It is within the city of Rome, called the city of seven hills, that the entire area of Vatican States proper is now confined."* (8)

In *The Approaching End Of The Age*, Henry Grattan Guinness says,
The last words of the angel to John, seem to leave no possibility of mistake as to the city. 'The seven heads are seven mountains on which the woman sitteth... and the woman which thou sawest is that great city which reigneth over the kings of the earth.' There was but one great city, which in John's day reigned over the kings of the earth. It was ROME; and Rome is the only city which was great then, has been great, in one way or other, ever since, and is so still.

And Rome was seated on seven hills, 'the seven mountains on which the woman sitteth.' <u>Her common name with the classic writers of St. John's age is 'the seven-hilled city.'</u> The medals and coins of the day represent Rome as a

148

woman sitting on seven hills; and her titles show with sufficient clearness how thoroughly she reigned. She was styled 'the royal Rome,' 'the mistress of the world,' 'the queen of nations.'

Her sway was all but universal. She was the metropolis of that fourth great empire which Daniel foretold would break in pieces and subdue all things, 'dreadful and terrible and strong exceedingly,' and at the time of the Apocalyptic visions, her power was at its height.

We previously saw that she must represent a church, now we know what church. The harlot is the Church of Rome; for simple minds, there seems no escape from this conclusion. <u>And it is a singular and notable fact that no other city but Rome has ever given its name to a church, which has embraced many kindreds and nations</u>.

These have one mind, and shall give their power and strength unto the beast. Revelation 17:13

In *Notes on the Handbook of Revelation* **(1852), Albert Barnes says,** *In 496 A.D., Clovis, the king of the Franks, on occasion of his victory over the Allemanni, embraced the Catholic faith, and so received the title, transmitted downward through nearly thirteen hundred years to the French kings as his successors, of "the oldest son of the church"; in the course of the sixth century, the kings of Burgundy, Bavaria, Spain, Portugal, England, embraced the same religion, and became the defenders of the papacy.*

In *Key To The Apocalypse,* **Henry Grattan Guinness says,** *The ten horns are interpreted as ten kingdoms, then future, into which the empire should be divided. These horns or kingdoms first submit to the Harlot City, and then rise against her, and" make her desolate and naked, and eat her -flesh, and burn her with fire." Their futurity at that early date is indicated in the words, they "have received no kingdom as yet" (ver. 12).*

It is a notorious matter of history that the Western Roman Empire was thus divided into the Gothic kingdoms, whose average number has been ten for the last twelve or thirteen centuries; and that these Gothic kingdoms have

149

overthrown the city of Rome, and laid it waste, after having been subject to it for centuries as the city of the Popes.

These shall make war with the Lamb, and the Lamb shall overcome them: for he is Lord of lords, and King of kings: and they that are with him are called, and chosen, and faithful. Revelation 17:14

Making war with the Lamb means they attack His followers. These ten kingdoms acted as the ACBP's military power. They were used to systematically persecute the saints, seeking to eliminate the witnesses against the Popes. Countries such as France and Spain obeyed the Popes and followed his orders to persecute the saints.

> Revelation 13:7 says about the Popes of Rome, *And it was given unto him to make war with the saints, and to overcome them: and power was given him over all kindred, and tongues, and nations.*

And he said unto me, the waters which thou sawest, where the whore sitteth, are peoples, and multitudes, and nations, and tongues. Revelation 17:15

Such was certainly the position of Rome. The nations of the world were then, and for centuries after, subject to her sway. The Popes of Rome rose to great power in the 12th century, when they commanded the kings of the earth and all those in their domain.

Joseph Benson's Commentary on Revelation (1847) says, *So many words in the plural number fitly denote the great extensiveness of her power and jurisdiction; and it is a remarkable peculiarity of Rome, different from all other governments in the world, that her authority is not limited to her own immediate subjects, and confined within the bounds of her own dominions, but extends over all kingdoms and countries professing the same religion.*

And the ten horns which thou saw upon the beast, these shall hate the whore, and shall make her desolate and naked, and shall eat her flesh, and burn her with fire. For God hath put in their hearts to fulfil his will, and to agree, and give their kingdom unto the beast, until the words of God shall be fulfilled. **Revelation 17:16-17**

The Popes have historically ruled over the ten countries that occupy the area controlled by the Roman Empire. I'll cover verses 16-17 more in the *Mystery, Babylon The Great Destroyed* chapter.

In *The Approaching End Of The Age*, Henry Grattan Guinness says, *From its rise to the fourth century, it was one an undivided; since its decline and fall as an empire, it has been broken up into many independent sovereignties, held together by a common submission to the Popes of Rome. The number of distinct kingdoms into which the Roman Empire in Europe has been divided has always been about ten, at times exactly ten, sinking at other times to eight or nine, and rising occasionally to twelve or thirteen, but averaging on the whole ten.*

And the woman which thou sawest is that great city, which reigns over the kings of the earth. **Revelation 17:18**

John is being told that the *harlot* church would be based out of the *great city* that reigns over the earth at his time, which is Rome. The Popes reigned in power as the leader of the *sea* beast phase of the Roman beast kingdom for 1,260 years, from 538-1798, and they still have worldwide civil and ecclesiastic influence.

In his *Lectures on the Revelation* (1878), William J. Reid says, *"This part of the angel's explanation (seven mountains) is of great clearness and importance. It describes and fixes the locality of the civil power symbolized by the beast in such a way as precludes the possibility of mistake. There is a city builded upon seven hills, which has long been known as the seven-hilled city of Rome. This name is well known to every student of history."*

Here's a coin featuring Pope Saint John XXIII. It was made in 1961, and it has the words 'CITTA' DEL VATICANO.'

The word *Vaticanus* refers to Vatican Hill (in Latin, *Vaticanus Mons*). The etymology of the word *anus* can point to an *'old woman.'* Putting them together, we see that *'CITTA' DEL VATICANO'* is pointing to the *'city of an old woman of prophecy.'*

Waldensian Reincrius Saccho (1254) asserted, *"that the Romish church is not the church of Jesus Christ, but a church of malignants and that it apostatized under Sylvester—and that the Church of Rome is the harlot in the apocalypse."* (10)

Michal of Cesena declared the Church of Rome to be the Whore of Babylon. Michal (1270-1342), who came out of the Franciscan Order of the Catholic Church, declared the Pope *"to be Antichrist, and the church of Rome to be the whore of Babylon, drunk with the blood of the saints."* (11)

In his farewell letter before being burned to death by order of the Pope, Nicholas Ridley said, *"The see of Rome is the seat of Satan, and the bishop of the same, that maintaineth the abominations thereof, is Antichrist himself indeed. And for the same causes, this see at this day is the same which St. John calls, in his Revelation, Babylon, or the whore of Babylon, and spiritually, Sodom and Egypt, the mother of fornications and abominations* upon earth." Again, in his *Lamentation for the Change of Religion*, he said: *"What city is there in the whole world that, when John wrote, ruled over the kings of the earth? or what city can be read of, in any time, that, of the city itself, challenged the empire over the kings of the earth, but only the city of Rome, and that since the usurpation of that see, has grown to her full strength?"*

Commenting on the RCC in his *History of Redemption*, Jonathan Edwards stated, *"So that antichrist has proved the greatest and most cruel enemy the church of Christ ever had, agreeable to the description given of the church of Rome, [Rev. xvii. 6.] 'And I saw the woman drunken with the blood of the saints, and with the blood of the martyrs of Jesus.'" "Thus did the devil, and his great minister antichrist, rage with violence and cruelty against the church of Christ! And thus did the whore of Babylon make herself drunk with the blood of the saints and martyrs of Jesus!"*

Joseph Benson's Commentary on Revelation (1847) says, *Little doubt can remain after this, what idolatrous church was meant by the whore of Babylon; but for the greater assuredness, it is added by the angel, Revelation 17:18, the woman which thou sawest is that great city, &c. — He hath explained the mystery of the beast, and of his seven heads and ten horns; and his explanation of the mystery of the woman is, that great city, which reigneth over the kings of the earth — And what city, at the time of the vision, reigned over the kings of the earth, but Rome? She hath, too, ever since reigned over the kings of the earth, if not with temporal, yet at least with spiritual authority. Rome, therefore, is evidently and undeniably this great city; and that Christian, and not heathen, Papal, and not imperial Rome was meant, hath appeared in several instances, and will appear in several more.*

In *Key To The Apocalypse*, Henry Grattan Guinness says, *Five principal points are dealt with in the explanation under the expressions: "the beast that thou sawest" (ver. 8); "the seven heads" (ver. 9); "the ten horns which thou sawest" (ver. 12); "the waters which thou sawest" (ver. 15); "the woman which thou sawest" (ver. 18). Every point interpreted fixes the application of the vision to Rome.*

153

[1] The Woman is interpreted as signifying the city of Rome. "The woman which thou sawest is that great city which reigneth over the kings of the earth." At the date when the Apocalypse was written Rome governed the world.

[2] The City is represented as sitting on "seven hills." This is a well-known feature of the city of Rome. All the Latin poets for five hundred years speak of Rome as the seven-hilled city. Rome is depicted on her imperial coins as sitting on seven hills. Among the early Fathers, Tertullian and Jerome may be cited as referring to this feature. "I appeal," says Tertullian, "to the citizens of Rome, the populace that dwell on the seven hills."

Jerome, when urging Marcella to quit Rome for Bethlehem, writes: "Read what is said in the Apocalypse of the seven hills." The names of the seven hills of Rome are the Palatine, Quirinal, Aventine, Coelian, Viminal, Esquiline, and Janiculan.

[3] The Harlot City is represented as seated "upon many waters" (Rev. 17:1), which are interpreted to mean "peoples, and multitudes, and nations, and tongues" (ver. 15). Such was certainly the position of Rome. The nations of the world were then, and for centuries after, subject to her sway.

[4] The Harlot City is represented as seated upon the seven-headed, ten-horned Beast. In the prophecies of Daniel, the ten-horned Wild Beast is the fourth Gentile empire or the Roman. No city ruled the Roman Empire but Rome.

[5] The sixth head of the Wild Beast power, which carried the Harlot, is stated to have been in existence at the time when the Apocalypse was written. Of the seven heads of the Wild Beast, the angel says, "five are fallen, and one is, and the other is not yet come." These seven heads are interpreted to be ruling powers. Five of these were past, the sixth in existence, the seventh in the future. Hence the Wild Beast under its sixth head represented the Roman Empire as governed by the then existing Roman Emperors, and consequently, the Harlot City borne by that Beast must have represented Rome itself.

[6] The ten horns are interpreted as ten kingdoms, then future, into which the empire should be divided. These horns or kingdoms first submit to the Harlot City, and then rise against her, and "make her desolate and naked, and eat her

flesh, and burn her with fire." Their futurity at that early date is indicated in the words, they "have received no kingdom as yet" (ver. 12). It is a notorious matter of history that the Western Roman Empire was thus divided into the Gothic kingdoms, whose average number has been ten for the last twelve or thirteen centuries; and that these Gothic kingdoms have overthrown the city of Rome, and laid it waste, after having been subject to it for centuries as the city of the Popes.

[7] The attire, character, and persecuting action of the Harlot City identify her with Rome. The view that the Babylon of the Apocalypse represents Rome has prevailed in the Christian Church, both Eastern and Western, from the earliest times. "Tell me, blessed John," says Hippolytus, "what didst thou see and hear concerning Babylon? Arise and speak, for it sent thee also into banishment." Victorinus, the author of the earliest known commentary on the Apocalypse, says: "The seven heads are the seven hills on which the Woman sitteth — that is, the city of Rome."

Augustine writes of "Rome the second Babylon, and the daughter of the first, to which it pleased God to subject the whole world, and bring it all under one sovereignty." Protestant interpreters maintain while Roman Catholic interpreters admit that the Babylon of the Apocalypse is Rome. Cardinal Bellarmine says: "Rome is signified in the Apocalypse by the name of Babylon."

Pagan Rome was no "Mystery" in Christian eyes. Her idolatry was open and confessed. The Christian Church was never deceived by her. Heathen Rome never claimed to be other than she was. But this Harlot "Babylon" deceives the nations by professing to be Christian, while in reality, she is anti-Christian. What is this "Mystery" but the development of that "MYSTERY OF INIQUITY" which began to work in the Christian Church in apostolic times?

Take note of the contrasted features of the *Whore* of the RCC and the *Bride* of Messiah.

Here's a comparison of the two women of Revelation, which I adapted from *Antichrist And His Ten Kingdoms* (1938) by Albert Close.

155

These prophecies present two broadly contrasted women and cities. They're not two disconnected visions, but a pair associated, not by likeness, but by contrast.

The Church of Rome, the bride of the ACBP, is called *"Babylon the Great."*

The Ekklesia of Messiah, the bride of the Lamb, is called *"Holy Jerusalem."*

And there came one of the seven angels which had the seven vials, and talked with me, saying unto me, Come hither; I will shew unto thee the judgment of the great whore that sitteth upon many waters. 17:1

And there came unto me one of the seven angels which had the seven vials full of the seven last plagues, and talked with me, saying, Come hither, I will shew thee the bride, the Lamb's wife. 21:9

So he carried me away in the spirit into the wilderness: and I saw a woman sit upon a scarlet colored beast, full of names of blasphemy, having seven heads and ten horns. 17:3

And he carried me away in the spirit to a great and high mountain, and shewed me that great city, the holy Jerusalem, descending out of heaven from God. 21:10

And the woman was arrayed in purple and scarlet color, and decked with gold and precious stones and pearls, having a golden cup in her hand full of abominations and filthiness of her <u>fornication</u>. 17:4

And to her was granted that she should be arrayed in fine linen, clean and white: for the fine linen is the <u>righteousness</u> of saints. 19:8

And upon her forehead was a name written, MYSTERY, BABYLON THE GREAT, THE MOTHER OF HARLOTS AND ABOMINATIONS OF THE EARTH. 17:5

And I John saw the holy city, new Jerusalem, coming down from God out of heaven, prepared as a bride adorned for her husband. 21:2

And I saw the woman drunken with the blood of the saints, and with the blood of the martyrs of Jesus. 17:6

> *And I saw the souls of them that were beheaded for the witness of Jesus, and for the word of God, and which had not worshipped the beast, neither his image, neither had received his mark upon their foreheads, or in their hands; and they lived and reigned with Christ a thousand years. 20:4*

The seven heads are seven mountains, on which the woman sitteth. And the woman which thou sawest is that great city, which reigneth over the kings of the earth. 17:9,18

The church of the ACBP had her origin at the *seven-hilled* city of Rome, and from there, it branched forth into all the world. She is called the *'great city.'*

> The Ekklesia of Messiah had her origin in the city of Jerusalem, and from there, it spread forth unto all the world. She is called *'heavenly Jerusalem.'*

The church of the RCC is the *tares*, and Messiah's Ekklesia is the *wheat*.

> *Let both grow together until the harvest: and in the time of harvest, I will say to the reapers, Gather ye together first the tares, and bind them in bundles to burn them: but gather the wheat into my barn. Matthew 13:30*

The dual-narrative of the Ekklesia of Messiah and the Church of the ACBP validates that *Babylon the Great* is the RCC.

In *Antichrist And His Ten Kingdoms* (1938), Albert Close says, *Our Lord in His Revelation to St. John, in chapter 17, foretold that a great apostate church would arise in the world, that she would endure for centuries, exert a subtle and world-wide influence, and be guilty of exceeding iniquity and cruelty, which she would practice in the name of Christianity. He further revealed that her seat of power would be at a great city which was seated on seven mountains and reigning over the kings of the earth in St. John's day. Now what great church, with her seat of power at a city seated on seven hills,* *has fulfilled all these predictions? There can be but one reply— THE CHURCH OF ROME.*

Another important identification of the church of Rome with 'Babylon,' is the fact that the High Priest of the old Babylonian religion was the original Pontifex Maximus. When Xerxes the Persian conquered Babylon in 487, the Babylonian priests were expelled. They removed and settled in the Western city of Pergamos, in Asia Minor, where they fixed the Central College. The last Pontifex of the original Babylonian priests, King Attalus II, Pontiff king of Pergamos, bequeathed the title and his dominions to the Roman. Julius Caesar accepted the title about 68 BC, and the Roman Emperor from that time was Pontifex Maximus, up to the year 375 AD, when Emperor Gratian renounced it, and the Bishop of Rome (the Pope) took it up, and, to the present time styles himself Pontifex Maximus. Here, therefore, we have a direct connection between the ancient heathen Babylonian religion and the Church of Rome, which has adopted the Babylonian rites and titles.

The office of the papacy, the Popes of Rome, fulfill Bible prophecy as the *little horn* of Daniel 7, the *son of perdition* of 2 Thessalonians 2 and the *antichrist beast* of Revelation, who leads the *harlot* church of Rome, which is called *'Mystery, Babylon the Great.'*

When you consider the detailed description in Revelation 17 and the whole narrative of the book of Revelation, there's no mistaking the *harlot* woman called *'Mystery, Babylon the Great,'* and who leads her. She has proclaimed that she is a church based in the city of prophecy, Rome, the great city of *seven hills*. In her hand is the *golden cup* of her abominations, which represents her symbolically carrying out the *Babylonian Mystery Religion*. She is an apostate church used by the ACBPs to mislead the world with a false gospel and persecute the saints of Messiah's Ekklesia.

CHAPTER 33 - THE EIGHTH KING OF REVELATION 17

And there are seven kings: five are fallen, and one is, and the other is not yet come; and when he cometh, he must continue a short space. **Revelation 17:10**

People try to apply this verse to the current day, saying that it's about the modern-day Popes, Presidents, etc. But Revelation is from John's perspective so that we have an absolute reference point.

> *Write the things which thou hast seen (past), and the things which are (present), and the things which shall be hereafter (future).* Revelation 1:19

The angel shows John how the ACBP and his *harlot* church rose to power out of the fallen Roman Empire. The *'seven kings'* is pointing to seven forms of government of the Roman beast kingdom. We see this in Revelation 12:3, where the *seven heads* are *crowned*, telling us that the Roman beast kingdom is in power.

> *And there appeared another wonder in heaven; and behold a great red dragon, having seven heads and ten horns, and seven crowns upon his heads.*

Two great Roman historians, Livy in his *The History of Rome Complete* books 1:60, 3:33, 4:7, and 6:1; and Tacitus in his *Annals* 1:1, documented the first seven forms of government of the Roman Empire.

At the time that John wrote Revelation, five forms of the Roman kingdom had come and gone. 1) Kings, 2) Consuls, 3) Dictators, 4) Decemvirs, and 5) Military Tribunes.

The sixth form of the Roman government was the Imperial head, commencing with Octavian, better known as Augustus Caesar or the Emperors. This form of government existed in John's day and was in power until the last Western Emperor was removed in 476, during the fourth trumpet judgment.

During the *"short space"* until the *eighth king* would arrive, the seventh form of government of the Roman beast was the *Dukedom of Rome*. Renowned historian Edward Gibbons tells us that Italy was divided unequally between the kingdom of the Lombards and the Exarchate of Ravenna.

John was being told that the *eighth king*, the ACBP, would rise to power after the seven forms of government of the Roman Empire had passed.

Eastern Emperor Justinian empowered the Popes of Rome in 538, a *'short space'* after the last Western Roman Emperor was removed in 476. Daniel gave this same message in Daniel 7 when he said that the *little horn* would rise to power out of the ten kingdoms of the fallen Roman Empire. This is the same message that Paul gave in 2 Thessalonians 2 when he said that the *son of perdition* would rise to power when the *'restrainer,'* the Western Roman Emperor, is removed.

And we see it in the *sea beast* narrative of Revelation 13:1.

> *And I stood upon the sand of the sea, and saw a beast rise up out of the sea, having seven heads and ten horns, and upon his horns ten crowns, and upon his heads the name of blasphemy.*

The *crowns* are now off of the *seven heads*, off of the pagan Roman Empire, and on the *ten horns* of the ten kingdoms of the fallen Roman Empire who gave their authority to the ACBP.

Remember, Paul and John had to hide their message, as they couldn't write that the Roman Empire would be destroyed, as that would have invited more persecution from Rome.

And the beast that was, and is not, even he is the eighth, and is of the seven, and goeth into perdition. Revelation 17:11

John is being told that the *eighth king*, the Popes of Rome, would rise to power out of the fallen Roman Empire. The Popes fulfill Bible prophecy

160

as the *son of perdition* and will be captured by Messiah and thrown into the fiery pit of *perdition*.

In *Key To The Apocalypse*, **Henry Grattan Guinness says,** *The sixth head of the Wild Beast power 'which carried the Harlot, is stated to have been in existence at the time when the Apocalypse was written. Of the seven heads of the Wild Beast, the angel says, "five are fallen, and one is, and the other is not yet come." These seven heads are interpreted to be ruling powers. Five of these were past, the sixth in existence, the seventh in the future. Hence the Wild Beast under its sixth head represented the Roman Empire as governed by the then existing Roman Emperors, and consequently, the Harlot City borne by the Beast must have represented Rome itself.*

The European kingdoms which arose at the dissolution of the Roman Empire did surrender themselves to the dominion of the Church of Rome. Italy, Switzerland, Germany, Poland, Hungary, France, Belgium, Spain, Portugal, and our own England, for many centuries, were subject to the Papacy. Such are her claims declared at the coronation of every Pontiff. 'Know thyself the father of kings and princes, ruler of the world.' These are the words with which he is addressed when the tiara is placed on his brow.

In *The Seventh Vial* (1848), **James Aitken Wylie says,** *When the beast (Pope) found himself on the throne of the dragon, and the world prostrate before him, his heart was lifted up within him, like that of the king of Babylon of old. He imagined himself to be God, and the pride of his heart found vent in the dreadfully blasphemous words of his mouth.*

Though the prophecy is pointing to the ACBP rising to civil power after *seven forms of government* of the Roman Empire, there's an interesting secondary ecclesiastic fulfillment. In 313, Constantine gave the *Lateran Palace* on Caelian Hill to the Bishop of Rome, the Pope. The palace was the popes' principal residence from the fourth century and continued for about a thousand years. The palace is adjacent to the *Archbasilica of St. John Lateran*, the cathedral church of Rome, built under Pope Melchiade (311-314).

The *St. John Lateran Palace* and *Basilica of Saint John* are located on the side of the Tiber River that has *seven hills*.

Interestingly, the Popes' ecclesiastical residence moved temporarily from Rome to Avignon, France, because of political conditions in the 14th century. And when they moved back to Italy, Vatican Hill became the papacy's ecclesiastical headquarters. It was the Roman temple site to the *Great Mother Goddess Cybele*, which houses secret tunnels underneath where the Vatican is located, where the secret worship ceremonies of Cybele, including child sacrifice, occurred. I suspect that these sacrifice ceremonies still take place under the Vatican, as the leaders serve Satan. And it's rumored that an image of the dragon is in the catacombs of the Temple of Cybele.

Vatican Hill is located across the Tiber River from the traditional *seven hills* of Rome; thus, *the eighth is of the seven*.

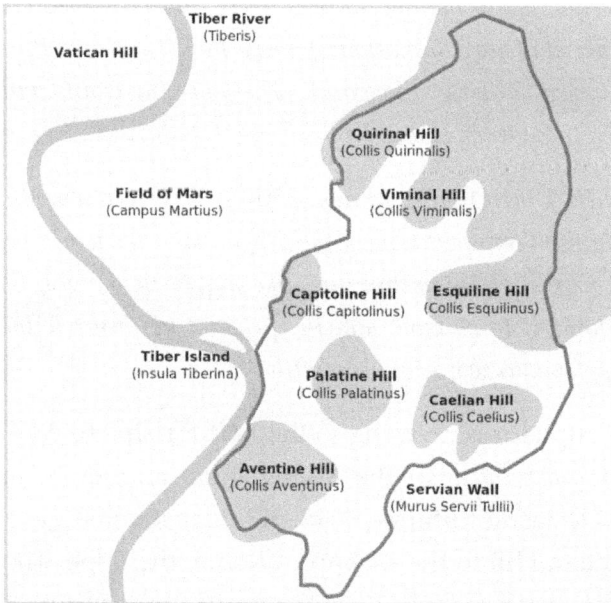

Amazingly, the *eighth king* of Revelation 17:10 is the Popes of Rome, who rose to power over the fallen Roman Empire. They lived in Rome's great city, where there are seven hills, but now they reign from an *eighth hill* across from the seven hills.

CHAPTER 34 - ROME IS BABYLON

And the beast that was, and is not, even he is the eighth, and is of the seven, and goeth into perdition. **Revelation 17:11**

I believe that the *'beast that was'* refers to the Babylonian beast kingdom, in which Nimrod acted as the leader of church and state, to war against the Heavenly Father and steal praise from Him. That beast kingdom <u>is not</u> alive when John wrote Revelation.

The Babylonian beast kingdom has come back to life with the *eighth* king, the Popes of Rome, who proclaim the title of *Pontifex Maximus*, the leader of church and state. His role is to make war against the Heavenly Father to steal praise from Him. And in the future, the ACBP will lead the One World Government, which Nimrod sought to build.

The Popes are the High Priest of the false religion of Romanism, who symbolically carry out the *Babylonian Mystery Religion*, of the worship of the sun god (Nimrod), the moon goddess (Semiramis), and the incarnate christ-child Tammuz.

Martin Luther said: *"Nothing else than the kingdom of Babylon and of very Antichrist. For who is the man of sin and the son of perdition, but he who by his teaching and his ordinances increases the sin and perdition of souls in the church; while he yet sits in the church as if he were God? All these conditions have now for many ages been fulfilled by the papal tyranny."*

These early church saints proclaimed that Rome is Babylon.

Tertullian (155-240), *"Babylon, in our John, is a figure of the city Rome, as being equally great and proud of her sway, and triumphant over the saints."*

Eusebius Pamphilius (303), *"It is said that Peter's first epistle... was composed at Rome itself; and that he himself indicates this by referring to that city, figuratively as Babylon."*

Roman Catholic theologians have admitted that Rome is Babylon.

163

A top apologist for the RCC, Karl Keating (1950), emphatically states: *"Babylon is a code word for Rome. It is used that way six times in the last book of the Bible."* (3)

Revered Cardinal Gibbons (1834-1921), an American prelate of the Catholic Church and Archbishop of Baltimore, stated: *"The penetration of the religion of Babylon became so general and well known that Rome was called the New Babylon."* (4)

RCC Saint Augustine of Hippo (354-430), in his book on the apocalypse called *The City of God*, said: *"Rome, the second Babylon, and the daughter of the first, to which it pleased God to subject the whole world, and bring it all under the sovereignty, was not founded."* (5)

SOJ educator Sylvester J. Hunter (1829-1896) said: *"There is no room for doubt that by the Babylon of the Apocalypse is meant the city of Rome. And down to the time of the Reformation, it was the unanimous judgment of all writers… that the Babylon of St. Peter's Epistle is the same Rome."* (6)

Roman Cardinal Baronius (1538-1607) said: *"By Babylon is to be understood Rome."* *"Rome is signified by Babylon; it is confessed of all* (7)

Cardinal Bellarmine (1542-1621), an Italian Jesuit and a Cardinal, and one of the most important figures in the counter-reformation, said: *"John, in the Apocalypse, calls Rome Babylon."* (8)

These esteemed theologians, who wrote whole Bible commentaries, proclaimed that Rome is Babylon:

Matthew Poole's Commentary on the Holy Bible (1684) says, *Most judicious interpreters, by the great city here, understand Rome, which is seven or eight times (under the name of Babylon) so-called in this book, Revelation 14:8; 16:19; 18:10,16,18-19,21; nor is any other city but that so-called.*

In *Notes on the Handbook of Revelation* (1852), Albert Barnes says, *Babylon the great. Papal Rome, the nominal head of the Christian world, as Babylon had been of the heathen world.*

In *Verse Expositions of the Bible,* **Charles Haddon Spurgeon says,** *May the Spirit of God take away the veil from our eyes while we read what was revealed to the beloved apostle John! Here we have the prophecy of the destruction of the great anti-Christian system of Babylon, which, being interpreted, is and can be none other than the apostate church of Rome. We have no difficulty in knowing to what city this great Babylon refers, for the Church of Rome, in the plenitude of its wisdom, has taken the title to itself in attempting to claim that Peter was the first bishop of Rome. They quote the text, "The church that is in Babylon saluteth thee" that church, they say, being the church in Rome. Therefore, Rome is Babylon. Besides, the whole of the eighteenth chapter gives such a description as can only apply to her, and she must, and shall, come to her end.*

John Gill's Exposition of the Entire Bible (1748) says, *"Babylon the great"; that is, the great city, by which name the church of Rome may well be called, because of the signification of it, confusion, its doctrine and worship being a confused mixture of Paganism, Judaism, and Christianity; and because of the pride and haughtiness of it, its tyranny and cruelty, and its sorceries and idolatry.*

In *History Unveiling Prophecy,* **Henry Grattan Guinness says,** *The character and history of the Church of Rome, her proud position as seated on "the seven hills" of the Imperial city, and "reigning over the kings" and peoples of the earth, her gorgeous self-adornment, her fabulous wealth and luxury, her adulterous association with kings and princes of the Roman Empire, her multiplied idolatries, and cruel persecutions of the saints, and her judgment as finally hated and cast off, stripped and torn by the ten-horned wild beast power which had previously carried her, and done her bidding; all this has been recognized as marvelously portrayed in the Apocalyptic vision of the harlot "Babylon the Great," drunken with "the blood of the saints and of the martyrs of Jesus."*

Revelation 17 is clearly describing the *harlot* church of Rome, *Babylon the Great,* which is led by the *eighth king,* the ACBP.

CHAPTER 35 - THE BABYLONIAN PRIESTHOOD REBORN

The ACBP of Rome has taken the role of the High Priest of Rome's *harlot* church, which teaches a false Gospel, and many concepts contrary to Scripture. But the truth gets much more sinister than that. The symbols that are used during their Eucharist ceremony tell the real story that they're the priests of the *Babylonian Mystery Religion*. This is why she is called *'Mystery, Babylon the Great.'*

The word *'Mystery'* is not part of her title; it's part of her description. She's a *mystery* because she feigns to be Messiah's Church, but is really a Babylonian church of sun god worship. The evil ones communicate their message through symbolism while they deceive with their words.

The *Babylonian Mystery Religion* is based on Nimrod, the *sun* god, Semiramis, the *moon* and fertility goddess, and their incarnate *christ* child Tammuz.

Jasher 27:7 says that Esau killed Nimrod by cutting off his head when he was out hunting. The pagan legend of Nimrod is that he was killed and cut into thirteen parts, which were scattered to different areas. His wife Semiramis found twelve parts but could not find his reproductive organ. So she fashioned a phallic symbol to put on his body, and by the magic of her sorcerer, she claims to have become pregnant with his incarnate son Tammuz. We can only surmise that she engaged in sexual rituals with the sorcerer, which caused her to become pregnant.

In Egypt, the same story was told about Osiris, the *sun* god, Isis the moon goddess, and their incarnate *christ*-child Horus. To honor Osiris, the Egyptians created obelisks, which are phallic symbols that represent his missing member. They were prominent in the ancient Egyptians' architecture, and when placed at the entrance of a temple, it designates it as a place of *sun*-god worship.

An obelisk is also called *Baal's Shaft*.

The disobedient Israelites worshipped the sun god and moon goddess of the pagans, Baal and Asherah.

> *The sons of Israel did what was evil in the sight of the LORD, and forgot the LORD their God and served the Baals and the Asheroth.* Judges 3:7

> *But ye shall destroy their altars, break their images, and cut down their Asherim.* Exodus 34:13

When you look at pictures of St. Peter's Square at the Vatican, doesn't it seem odd that a *supposed* church of Messiah would have an Egyptian obelisk in the courtyard of its main temple? This well-known Egyptian obelisk was *erected* in front of St. Peter's Basilica in 1586. It's surrounded by a sun wheel, with the points lining up with the Vernal Equinox, the Summer Solstice, and the Winter Solstice.

On top of the obelisk is a cross. Do we think that Messiah is honored with a cross, representing His one-time sacrifice for our sins, being placed on top of an Egyptian sun god worship phallic symbol? Surely not! What seems to be a cross to Catholics is the symbol of the god that the Popes are worshiping, Tammuz, the incarnate sun god.

But the symbolism of the obelisk in St. Peter's Square gets even more twisted. It's designed so that the street to the east of St. Peter's Basilica allows the rising sun to align perfectly on the Spring Equinox (3/21). The sun strikes the phallic symbol of the *sun god* and causes a shadow to fall onto the dome of St. Peter's Basilica, which represents the *womb* of the *moon goddess*. This represents their annual sexual union.

Nine months later, on 12/21, when the sun is at its furthest point from the earth, the pagans believe that their sun god dies. They believe that he's dead for three days and then is reborn, so they celebrate the pagan sun god's birth on 12/25.

It's the worst day to have been selected to celebrate Messiah's birth, but it was specifically chosen because they're symbolically revering their christ child, Tammuz, who is symbolically born nine months after his conception on 3/21. Messiah was born in the fall, on the Feast Day of Tabernacles, as He came to *dwell* among us.

Even more sinister is that the RCC plays out the sexual union of the sun god and moon goddess at their churches worldwide.

That is what takes place during their Eucharist ceremony. Catholic Popes and priests hold up the round Eucharist wafer to revere it, and they cause Catholics to do the same. Most priests and Catholics believe that it represents Messiah's body, but it represents the Babylonian sun god Nimrod. On the wafer are the sun wheel lines, which point to the spring and fall equinoxes, summer and winter solstices, once again pointing to the sun god being especially revered on those days.

Then the Popes and priests place the sun god wafer in a monstrance, which has sun rays emanating from it, an overt symbol of the sun god. The round wafer is held in place by a crescent moon shaped holder, called a *lunette*, representing the moon goddess, Semiramis.

Do a Google image search '*Catholic monstrance*' to see the many sun rays and the crescent moon holder. This act symbolizes their sexual union, which produces their '*christ in the flesh,*' Tammuz, the incarnate sun god. Then Catholics are given a wafer to eat, which they are told represents the body of Christ, but it really represents the incarnate christ Tammuz.

You see this played out visually on Ash Wednesday when Catholics think that they are getting a cross on their forehead, but it's a 't' for Tammuz. Catholics believe that it represents the true faith, but it really is contrary to the true faith of Scripture, and it symbolically represents pagan gods.

Do you now see the Satanic pagan god worship being played out all over the world in plain sight?

Semiramis was used to help create the *Babylonian Mystery Religion.*

A wild boar reportedly killed her son Tammuz at age 40, so she started observing forty days of fasting for Tammuz to remember his forty years of his life. Yah chastised the House of Judah for weeping for Tammuz.

> *He said also unto me, Turn thee yet again, and thou shalt see greater abominations that they do. Then he brought me to the door of the gate of the LORD'S house which was toward the north; and, behold, there sat women weeping for Tammuz.* Ezekiel 8:13-14

This lines up with the Catholics' *forty days of lent*, after which ham is traditionally served during the pagan holiday of Easter (Ishtar, Semiramis). The ham points back to the wild boar that killed Tammuz. Interestingly, the Babylonians may have started this tradition to spite Yah. He commanded His followers not to eat the flesh of swine, as they're unclean animals due to their eating habits, digestive system, and inability to get rid of toxins effectively.

Semiramis was the fertility goddess who supposedly became pregnant by immaculate conception. This is why pagan-based Easter features symbols of fertility, with rabbits and eggs. Hot-crossed buns with a Tammuz cross on them are eaten on Good Friday by Catholics, marking the end of their forty days of Lent. The House of Judah was chastised for making cakes for the *Queen of heaven.*

> *The children gather wood, and the fathers kindle the fire, and the women knead their dough, to make cakes to the queen of heaven, and to pour out drink offerings unto other gods, that they may provoke me to anger.* Jeremiah 7:18

Semiramis, the moon goddess, was symbolized by her standing above a crescent moon. Do a Google image search for '**Mary crescent moon**,' and you'll see images of Catholic Mary standing on a crescent moon. Just as Semiramis proclaimed to be the *Queen of Heaven*, the Roman Church calls Mary the *Queen of Heaven.*

The Popes wear the mitre of Nimrod.

The Babylonians worshiped *Dagan*, the god of agriculture, plenty, and good fortune. The Babylonian priests wore a headdress with an open fish mouth on the head, with the rest of the fish body forming a cloak. Do a Google search for images of **'dagon fish-god.'** The Pope's mitre is shaped like an open fish mouth, symbolizing Dagan.

The Popes and his priests wear the Zuccheto to honor the sun god.

The Zucchetto, worn by Catholic priests, cardinals, and the Pope, represents *'respect, fear, and submission'* to Cybele, the *Mother Goddess* of Rome. The *Cap of Cybele* is one of the oldest and most sacred pagan religious symbols of humanity, dating back to 2,000 BC. The sun priests of Egypt wore the skull cap. The thin, slightly rounded skullcap is known by various titles, the Yarmulke (Jewish) and Kufi (Muslims).

> The Bible declares, *Every man praying or prophesying, having his head covered, dishonors his head.* 1 Corinthians 11:4

Catholic Popes and priests cover their heads in reverence to the sun god, which dishonors Messiah, the *head* of the true Ekklesia.

The Popes wear the same cross on their chest as the Babylonian deity.

The *Maltese Cross* represents Shamash, a native Mesopotamian deity, the god of the *'Sun and Justice'* in the Akkadian, Assyrian, and Babylonian pantheons. This cross was identified with a Sun god eight centuries before Messiah and long before it was called the Maltese Cross by the Knights of Malta. It's also called the *Iron Cross*. Roman Catholic Adolph Hitler used the Iron Cross and superimposed the Nazi swastika in its center. Catholic Popes, Cardinals, and Bishops wear this sun god cross prominently on their 'priestly' vestments.

Pine cones symbolize the worship of the solar god Osiris.

Pine cones were associated with spiritual enlightenment by ancient Babylonians, Egyptians, and Greeks. They represent the mysterious link between the physical and the spiritual worlds, which can be found in the human brain in the pineal gland. The pine cone staff symbolizes the solar god Osiris, the Egyptian 'messiah' who supposedly died for his people and whose mother, Isis, was worshiped as the Virgin Mother. The Popes use a staff with a pine cone on it, showing their reverence to the sun god. Search Google for images of '**pope pine cone staff**.'

The Popes have placed Egyptian obelisks in front of their temples.

You've already seen the sun god obelisk in St. Peter's Square, which designates the Vatican as a temple of sun god worship. But their symbolism is even more telling with the Catholic Church Sancta Maria ad Martyrs, which interestingly means *'St. Mary and the Martyrs.'* This RCC used to be the Roman *Pantheon*, built by Emperor Hadrian in 126 and dedicated to *pan theos*, meaning *"all the gods."* One would think that a church of Messiah would destroy such a pagan temple, but the Popes made it into a Catholic Church. To proclaim their true religion, the Popes had an Egyptian obelisk placed in front of the Pantheon, once again designating it as a temple of sun god worship.

The Popes revere images of dragons, which point to Satan.

Revelation 13:4 tells us the *dragon* empowers the *antichrist beast* to deceive the world. Search Google for images of '**Vatican dragons**.' Dragons are seen in the Coat of Arms of Pope Paul V and Pope Gregory XIII, along with Janus and Cybele's mystical keys. They were the pagan god and goddess representing Nimrod and Semiramis, respectively. In the Sistine Hall of the Vatican Library, a column fresco features a harlot-looking woman, whose gown is white and red, holding a cross in one hand, and has a dragon by her side. There's a mosaic on the Round Room floor, which has a pagan god with two dragons. There's a sea monster in the *Otricoli Floor Mosaic* in the *Sala Rotunda*.

Can you see how the Popes of Rome are the priests of the *Babylonian Mystery Religion*, who carry out their pagan religious rites with symbols under the guise of the Scriptural faith?

CHAPTER 36 - 1,260 YEAR REIGN OF POWER

Revelation 13:5 says that the ACBP is given power for *forty-two months*. In Revelation 11:2, he uses the same terminology, but, interestingly, John wrote down the time frame in two other formats; *'a thousand two hundred and threescore days;'* and *'a time, and times, and half a time;'*

John may be pointing to different times of the Pope's civil authority and his ecclesiastic authority. In defining the 1,260-year reign of the ACBP, we have to look at the beginning and ending points. You will see that the Pope was taken captive in 1798 as part of the fifth bowl judgment, which removed their civil power. So we have to look back to 538 to see if it matches up with his being given authority, and it does.

In 533, Eastern Roman Emperor Justinian acknowledged the Pope as head of the Roman Church, thus the head of all of Christendom, which conferred on him a title belonging only to Messiah. But it took until 538 for the opposers to be uprooted and eliminated.

In *The Last Prophecy*, Edward Bishop Elliott says, *Eastern Roman Emperor Justinian's decree, although promulgated about 533, could not be given effect immediately, because several groups warred against the bishop of Rome still, including the Ostrogoths, the Vandals, and the Heruli. After the first two were dealt with, the Ostrogoths besieged Rome in 537 with the pope inside the city walls. Thus, the pope was effectively imprisoned by the Ostrogoths, who were certainly intent on overthrowing him. But in 538, Belisarius lifted the siege of Rome, and the pope was rescued. In that year, also, Justinian replaced the deposed Silverius with Vigilius as the new pope and gave him military protection. Napoleon's General Berthier was left in charge of the army after the Treaty of Campo Formio. He was in this post in 1798 when he entered Italy, invaded the Vatican, organized the Roman republic, and took Pope Pius VI as prisoner back to Valence, France, where, after a torturous journey under Berthier's supervision, the pope died, thus dealing a major blow to the Vatican's political power.*

Henry Grattan Guinness, Martin Luther, and other theologians point to the 1,260 years starting in 606, when Emperor Phocas confirmed Justinian's grant and conferred on him the title of *'Universal Bishop.'* What events took place in 1866 to mark the end of the 1260 years?

The Italian government declared war on the Papal States, which were under the sovereign rule of the Pope from the 8th century until 1870. But they couldn't take possession of Rome, because Napoleon III kept a French garrison there to protect the Pope. The opportunity to eliminate the Papal States came when the Franco-Prussian War began in July 1870, and Napoleon III had to recall his garrison from Rome. The Italian Army captured Rome, which was annexed to the Kingdom of Italy.

Others point to him gaining temporal power in 755-756 when Pepin, King of France, gave Pope Stephen II power, and Charlemagne afterward confirmed it. That would put the end-point in 2015-2016.

We know that the ABCP's civil power was removed in 1798 during the fifth bowl judgment, so I use the 538 starting point in my explanations. Look at the Revelation Fulfillment Chart. On the 1ˢᵗ Layer in the middle, we see the narrative of the ACBPs who now control the Roman beast kingdom. They rose to power over the ten kingdoms of the fallen Roman Empire, fulfilling the prophecy of the *little horn* of Daniel 7.

On the 2ⁿᵈ Layer, you see the saints of the two church eras of Thyatira and Sardis, who witnessed against the ACBPs during their 1,260-year reign of power from 538-1798. On the 3ʳᵈ Layer, you see the rise of Islam and the Muslim armies to carry out judgment on the Roman Empire. And you see the Turks attacking the Eastern Roman Empire, to capture Constantinople.

And we see the *little book* of Revelation 10, the printed Bible, which was badly needed after the ACBP's banned and burned the Scriptures and only taught in Latin during the Dark Ages. During this time, the ACBP's *harlot* RCC gains influence to deceive people with a false gospel, which effectively hides the pure Gospel of Messiah.

CHAPTER 37 - THE THYATIRA CHURCH ERA
538-1514 AD

The Thyatira Church era is described in Revelation 2:18-29.

Looking at the Revelation Fulfillment Chart, we see the church era of Thyatira begins. It is one of the two *lampstands*, the two church eras, which *witnessed* against the ACBP, who took power in 538.

> *The mystery of the seven stars which thou sawest in my right hand, and the seven golden candlesticks. The seven stars are the angels of the seven churches: and <u>the seven candlesticks which thou sawest are the seven churches</u>.* Revelation 1:20

Thyatira reportedly means *'ruled by a woman,'* which is the perfect name because Rome's *harlot* church ruled this era. King Ahab's wife, Jezebel, deceived her husband into idolatry. The Popes deceive Catholics into idolatry. Jezebel fed the prophets of Baal from her table. The Popes provide for their Cardinals and Bishops, the priests who are knowing or unknowing are carrying out the idolatry of the *Babylonian Mystery Religion.* Jezebel killed the prophets of Yah. The Popes use Catholics to kill the saints of Messiah.

Jezebel taught Israel to worship idols and to burn incense to Ashtoreth, the *Queen of Heaven*. Rome's *harlot* church teaches Catholics to revere idols and burns candles and incense to the Virgin Mary, who the RCC calls the *Queen of Heaven*. Jezebel had 850 false prophets of *Ashtoreth and Baal*. Papal Rome employs a large priesthood teaching the worship of *mother and child*.

Jezebel used King Ahab over the *ten northern tribes* to carry out her evil plotting. The papal church controls the *ten kingdoms* of the fallen Roman Empire to carry out their evil plans. Jezebel slew the prophets. Papal Rome slew millions of saints. The striking figure of Jezebel perfectly describes the abominations of the ACBP and their influence.

Catholics proclaim that the Protestant Churches came after the Popes, thus proclaiming that the Papal Church is the *one true church*, but the saints were *protesting* long before the Protestant Reformation.

As the Popes rose to power, so did people groups who opposed them. Persecution strengthened the saints and their resolve and bonded them together into a community where they served one another.

Berengar of Tours (999-1088) disputed with the Popes over the doctrine of Eucharist transubstantiation. People who followed his teachings and protested against the Popes and their *harlot* church were called the Berengarians, who numbered 800,000 according to historian Bellarmine.

Peter Waldo (1140 –1205) proclaimed the Gospel of Messiah. He sold all he had in the year 1170 and distributed it to the poor, and became the leader to certain missionary bands known thenceforth under the name of Waldenses, as well as *'the Poor Men of Lyons.'* Some of these people groups fled to the wilderness, just as Revelation 12 foretold, to escape persecution. The Waldenses took refuge in the valleys of the neighboring Alps, where they maintained, in opposition to the church of Rome, their witness to New Testament teachings.

These people groups were the *candlestick* who *preached* the Scriptures to expose Rome's deceptions and *light* the way for people during the Dark Ages. The astounding development of papal ambition in Innocent III, and the papal war of extermination which followed against the Albigenses and Waldenses, led the latter, early in the thirteenth century, to accept as an article of their creed the doctrine, *"That the papacy and Church of Rome were to be regarded as the Apocalyptic Harlot Babylon, and by consequence Antichrist."* (1)

In 1167, the Albigenses held a council at Toulouse. *"All agreed in regarding the Church of Rome as having absolutely perverted Christianity, and in maintaining that it was she who was designated in the Apocalypse by the name of the whore of Babylon."* (2) The *Albigensian Crusade (Cathar Crusade)* was a twenty-year military campaign initiated by Pope Innocent III to eliminate the Albigenses in southern France.

Jan Hus, aka John Huss, was a former Czech Roman Catholic priest, philosopher, master, dean, and rector. He was a well-educated man from Bohemia, who came upon Wycliffe's writings, which caused him to break with Rome's church. Hus became a Reformer, an inspirer of Hussitism, a key predecessor to Protestantism, and a seminal figure in the Bohemian Reformation. He vigorously opposed auricular confession, papal indulgences, corruption, masses for the dead, etc.

Under guaranteed *'safe passage,'* he attended the Catholic *Council of Constance* to defend his beliefs. However, his safe passage was revoked, and he was condemned and executed without getting a fair chance to present a defense of his beliefs. He said, *"The Pope is ... the true Antichrist, of whom it is written, that he sitteth in the temple of God, among the people where Christ is worshiped."* (1)

He was burned at the stake for heresy against the RCC doctrines, including those on ecclesiology, the Eucharist, and other theological topics. After Hus was executed in 1415, the followers of his religious teachings (known as Hussites) rebelled against their Catholic rulers. They defeated five consecutive papal crusades between 1420 and 1431 in what became known as the *Hussite Wars*.

The year following that of Huss and Jerome's martyrdom in 1416, witnessed the burning of Lord Cobham, at Smithfield. When brought before King Henry V and admonished to submit himself to the Pope as an obedient child, this was his answer, *"As touching the Pope, and his spirituality, I owe him neither suit nor service, forasmuch as I know him by the Scriptures to be the great Antichrist, the son of perdition, the adversary of God, and an abomination standing in the Holy Place."* (3)

For his testimony, Lord Cobham was taken to *St. Giles Field* and hanged there in chains of iron and so consumed alive in the fire, praising the name of Yah as long as his life lasted.

176

In His letter, Messiah is not just speaking to the people in Thyatira, but to the saints who were spread around the Roman Empire, who faced persecution and the corrupted teachings of the Popes. Messiah's promise of the *"rod of iron"* points to the Scriptures, as Messiah told them that even though they faced persecution because they held the Scriptures dear, they would come alive again and rule the nations.

In *The Seventh Vial* (1848), James Aitken Wylie says, *Mr. Elliot has traced their history from the close of the sixth century till the era of the Reformation. Here, amid these alpine regions, they kept alive the lamp of truth, while darkness covered the rest of Europe. They were renowned for the purity of their faith, the simplicity of the life, and the constancy with which they testified against the Roman doctrines, resisting even unto blood.*

A *"morning star"* was promised to this church era, and it was fulfilled with John Wycliffe (1330-1384), who is called *'the Morning Star of the Reformation.'* John taught at Oxford University and was extraordinarily gifted in theology. He proclaimed, *"We suppose that Antichrist, the head of all these evil men, is the pope of Rome."*

He fought against the enemy by *illuminating* people's minds with the *light* of the Scriptures when he translated the Latin Vulgate Bible into English. Wycliffe's teachings were the means of the enlightenment of John Huss, who, in turn, influenced Martin Luther, who sparked the Protestant Reformation. People who followed and taught the teachings of Wycliffe were called *Wycliffites* or *Lollards*. The Pope condemned them at the *Council of Constance*, and the remains of the Reformer, by the Pope's command, were taken up and burned. His ashes were cast into the brook of Lutterworth, whence they were conveyed to the Avon, the Severn, and the sea. What hate the ACBP's have for Scriptures of Yah!

Here are some quotes from John Wycliffe, *"All Christian life is to be measured by Scripture; by every word thereof." "Holy Scripture is the highest authority for every believer, the standard of faith and the foundation for reform." "I am ready to defend my convictions even unto death. I have followed the Sacred Scriptures and the holy doctors."*

CHAPTER 38 - WHAT IS ANTICHRIST?

The word *'antichristos'* has several meanings and even numeric and symbolic representations. The basic meaning is *an opponent of Messiah,* but the deeper meaning is someone who *comes in place* of Messiah as a *substitute.*

Messiah told us, *Beware of false prophets (priests), which come to you in sheep's clothing, but inwardly they are ravening wolves.* Matthew 7:15

The Popes teach concepts that are unscriptural and anti-Messiah.

John told us, *Who is a liar but he that denies that Jesus is the Christ? He is antichrist, that denieth the Father and the Son.* 1 John 2:22.

How does the ACBP deny Messiah? They proclaim to be the leader, the high priest of Messiah's church, which denies Messiah as our sole High Priest. They teach a false Gospel of works, denying salvation through Messiah alone. They carry out the *Babylonian Mystery Religion,* denying the pure faith of Messiah.

They teach that Mary is the mediator to the Father, which denies Messiah. They teach that Mary was sinless, which denies Messiah. They have proclaimed that salvation is only through them and the Catholic Church, denying that it's through Messiah alone. They teach that their Popes and priests can forgive sins, which denies Messiah.

The Popes have used their priests and Catholics to torture and kill tens of millions of Messiah's saints; thus, they are anti-Messiah. The Popes deny the Father by proclaiming that they are God on earth, and they have taken the title of *Holy Father,* which denies the Heavenly Father.

In *Romanism And The Reformation*, Henry Grattan Guinness says, *We must, therefore, inquire whether self-exalting utterances of a peculiarly impious nature have been a characteristic of the Papacy. We turn to the public documents, issued by various Popes, and find that they have marvelously* *fulfilled this prediction; the pretensions they have made are blasphemies, the claims they have put forth, are, to be equal, if not superior to God Himself; no power on earth has ever advanced similar pretensions.*

Henry Grattan Guinness records this quote from William Tyndale, *"Though the Bishop of Rome and his sects give Christ these names (His rightful names), yet in that they rob Him of the effect, and take the signification of His names unto themselves, and make of Him but a hypocrite, as they themselves be, they be the right antichrists and deny both the Father and the Son; for they deny the witness that the Father bore unto His Son, and deprive the Son of all the power and glory that His Father gave Him."*

The Popes *take the place* **of Christ, which is** *anti-Christ.*

Webster's 1828 Dictionary, which is based on the King James, defines *'anti'* as: *A preposition signifying against, opposite, contrary, or in place of.*

Since the fifth century, the Popes of Rome have proclaimed the title of *'Vicar of Christ,'* which means *'in place of Christ,'* therefore he is proclaiming that he's antichrist. The word *'Vicarius'* is a legal term with means *'substituting for'* and *'in place of,'* so they are legally declaring to take Messiah's place. *Antichrist* doesn't just mean *'against Christ'* but also *'in place of Christ,'* and that's exactly what the title *'Vicar of Christ'* means.

Vicarius Filii Dei (Latin: *Vicar or Representative of the Son of God*) is a phrase first used in the forged medieval *Donation of Constantine* to refer to Saint Peter, who they proclaim is the first Catholic Church Pope. The *Donation of Constantine* is a forged Roman imperial decree by which the 4th century Emperor Constantine the Great supposedly transferred authority over the western part of the Roman Empire to the Pope. Composed probably in the 8th century, it was used, especially in the 13th century, to support the papacy's political authority claims.

Pope Boniface VIII said, *"We declare, assert, define and pronounce to be subject to the Roman Pontiff is to every creature altogether necessary for salvation... I have the authority of the King of Kings. I am all in all, and above all, so that God Himself and I, the Vicar of Christ, have but one consistory, and*

I am able to do almost all that God can do. What, therefore, can you make of me but God?" (1)

Pope Pius IX said, *"I alone... am the successor of the apostles, the vicar of Jesus Christ. I am the way, the truth, and the life."* (2)

Pope Pius X declared, *"The Pope is not simply the representative of Jesus Christ. On the contrary, he is Jesus Christ Himself, under the veil of the flesh. Does the Pope speak? It is Jesus Christ who is speaking; hence, when anyone speaks of the Pope, it is not necessary to examine but to obey."* (3)

Pope Pius XI proclaimed in the Vatican Throne Room before kneeling Cardinals, Bishops, priests, and nuns; *"You know that I am the Holy Father, the representative of God on earth, the vicar of Christ, which means that I am God on the earth."* (4)

These blasphemous Papal proclamations oppose Messiah, who is our sole intercessor to the Father, *'the way, the truth, and the life.'* We can see that the ACBP fulfills both definitions of *antichrist, in place of,* and *contrary to,* Messiah.

Pope Gregory I wrote to the Byzantine Emperor Maurice in 597, concerning the titles of bishops, *"I say with confidence that whoever calls or desires to call himself 'universal priest' in self-exaltation of himself is a precursor of the Antichrist."* (5)

The Greek roots of the term *'Catholic'* mean *'according to (kata-) the whole (holos),'* or more colloquially, *'universal.'* By that, we can see that the bishop of Rome, the Pope, is the *universal priest,* and thus, the *antichrist.*

In *Romanism And The Reformation*, Henry Grattan Guinness says,
Thus Christ is eclipsed, salvation is stolen; the Papal priest is substituted for the Savior of sinners, the mystery of iniquity for the mystery of godliness, the proud pope of Rome for the holy Prince of Peace, poison for food; and Satan himself is palmed upon the Church of Jesus Christ as her head and husband.

Babylon, in the Apocalypse, is a city and a harlot. Jerusalem, in the same book, is a city and a bride. The former is the corrupt associate of earthly kings;

the latter, the chaste bride of the heavenly King. But the latter is a Church; the former then is no mere heathen metropolis. The contrast is between Church and Church; the faithful Church and the apostate Church.

It has its own Savior – the church. It has its own sacrifice – the mass. It has its own mediator – the clergy. It has its own salvation – the sacrament. It has its own justification – self-righteousness. It has its own forgiveness – the confession. And in heaven, it has its own infallible, all-powerful advocate – the Mother of God, Mary (a representative unknown to the Gospel).

In *The Rise and Fall of the Papacy* (1701, Robert Fleming says, *That the great enemy of Christ and his church, represented in the book of Revelation under the figurative names of Babylon, and the Woman who sits on the scarlet-colored Beast, is Rome Antichristian, or the Papal Church, we thought to be a position beyond all doubt among Protestants. The prophecy cannot admit of an application to any other: the whole description answers to an ecclesiastic power, supporting a system of idolatry, superstition, corrupt doctrine, and tyranny; a power which has managed a stated opposition to the followers of Christ and the true religion, not for a short time, but during a succession of many ages.*

The Popes fulfill the number 666.

Here is wisdom. Let him that hath understanding count the number of the beast: for it is the number of a man; and his number is Six hundred threescore and six. Revelation 13:18

Rome is the Latin kingdom, and the word *Lateinos*, the Latin man, identifies the *antichrist beast*. No name appears more proper and suitable than that the one mentioned by Irenaeus, who lived not long after St. John's time and was the disciple of Polycarp. He said that *"the name Lateinos contains the number of six hundred and sixty-six; and it is very likely because the last kingdom is so-called, for they are Latins <u>who now reign</u>."*

In *Treatise on Christ and Antichrist* (230), Hippolytus of Portus says, *"It is manifest to all, that those who at present still hold the power, are Latins.*

If then, we take the name (or number) '666' as the name of a single man – it becomes Latinus." (6)

In *The Papal System: From Its Origin to the Present Time* **(1872), William Cathcart says,** *<u>It is also a notable fact that Pope Vitalian was the first to ordain public worship should be celebrated in the Latin tongue, in the year 666, the year with the same number as the antichrist beast</u>. The Council of Trent declared that "the Mass must be celebrated in Latin." The 'Latin Church' is one of the proper names of the mighty papal sect, just as the 'Greek Church' describes the Eastern Orthodox denomination. The documents of the popes and of the Roman court, intended for the ecclesiastical authorities of all lands, have been written in Latin from the earliest times; and are still communicated in the same grand old tongue.* (7)

The *People's New Testament* **by Barton Johnson (1891) says,** *The Greeks did not express numbers by figures, but by letters, just as among the Romans, X stood for ten and C for one hundred. Six hundred and sixty-six could be expressed by spelling out the words in the Greek language or by using the letters which were symbols for various quantities.*

Greek Lateinos = 666. *L = 30, A = 1, T = 300, E = 5, I = 10, N = 50, O = 70, S = 200*

And what is this name? The number of a man; the Greek method of spelling the name of Latinus, the reputed founder of the Latin race. The Romans were a Latin race and spoke the Latin language. The Romish Church is continually officially called the Latin Church, to distinguish it from the Greek Church, the other branch of the great ancient schism; the Catholic sacred books are written in the Latin tongue; the worship is conducted in every country in the Latin alone, and when a Catholic council convenes, all its conferences are conducted in the tongue of the ancient Latins.

There is, then, a Latin Church, whose official and sacred speech is the Latin language, which has for its seat the ancient Latin capital. That Church is the great Apostate Church, upon whose head the names of blasphemy have been written, which has claimed universal dominion upon the earth and has slain the saints of the Most High.

Its name is the number of the beast, and that name, Lateinos, the name or number of a man, is 666. It does not destroy the force of this that these numerals and letters can be so combined as to spell out other names. This name is one that at once points to a power which has displayed every mark which is assigned to the beast.

Revelation 13:18 says that 666 is the number of a man. The Pope's title is *'Vicar of Christ,'* which in Latin is *'Vicarius Filii Dei,'* equates numerically to the number 666 in Latin.

The crucifix is the evil *image* of 666 of the ACBP.

The New Testament was written in Greek, so we have to look at the Greek representation of 'Six hundred threescore and six.' The Strong's Greek Dictionary words are *'chi xi stigma.'*

Chi has a numerical value of 600, and it's an abbreviation for *Christ. Xi* has a numerical value of 60, and it's an abbreviation letter for *Xulon: a beam from which anyone is suspended, a cross.* Stigma is a ligature of the Greek letters *sigma* (Σ) and *tau* (T). *Stigma* has a numerical value of 6, and it means *a hole, or mark, pierced with a pointed instrument, on the hands.* The plural is *stigmata,* pointing to the nails that affix Messiah to the cross.

666, *Chi-Xi-Stigma,* points to the crucifix of the ACBP and their *harlot* church. But it has a more sinister meaning. We celebrate that Messiah died on the cross and then rose again.

> Galatians 3:13 says, *Christ hath redeemed us from the curse of the law, being made a curse for us: for it is written, Cursed is every one that hangs on a tree.*

The Pope keeps Him on the cross, which openly curses and mocks Him. They removed the second commandment about making graven images and bowing to them, and they split the tenth commandment into two.

The *666* crucifix is displayed in Catholic churches worldwide, where they carry out their *Babylonian Mystery Religion* during the blasphemous Eucharist ceremony, in front of a crucifix that mocks our Messiah.

Popes, including Francis I, use the *bent cross*, which features a repulsive and distorted figure of Messiah hanging on it, mocking Messiah even more. Google '**pope bent cross**'. Do you see what the term *'antichrist'* and the number *'666'* mean? It's all hidden in plain sight!

In *The Approaching End Of The Age*, Henry Grattan Guinness says,
At the coronation of Pope Innocent X, Cardinal Colonna on his knees, in his own name and that of the clergy of St. Peter's, address the following words to the Popes: "Most holy and blessed father, head of the church, ruler of the world, to whom the keys of the kingdom of heaven are committed, whom the angels in heaven revere, and the gates of hell fear, and all the world adores, we specially venerate, worship, and adore thee."

This feature of the Little Horn of Daniel 7, the Son of Perdition of 2 Thessalonians 2, and the antichrist beast; is marvelously fulfilled in the Papacy. What a mouth has that Latin ruler! What a talker! What a teacher! What a thunderer! How has he boasted himself and magnified himself, and excommunicated and anathematized all who have resisted him! Has the world ever seen his equal in this respect? All the Gothic kings were his humble servants. He was, by his own account, and is, the representative of Christ, of God, ruler of the world, armed with all the powers of Christ in heaven, earth, and hell. He is infallible; his decrees are irreformable. A mouth indeed is his, a mouth speaking great things!

In *The Papacy is the Antichrist* (1852), Rev. James Aitken Wylie says,
The man of sin is a priest who is the opposite of Messiah who was without sin. If antichrist signifies a Vice-Christ - that is, one who comes in the room of Christ - deception, dissimulation, counterfeit must be an essential element in his character. The antichrist has to fit all of the description, not just some of it. An open enemy, an atheist, is not pretending to be Christ. Romanism alone meets all the requirements of prophecy, and exhibits all the features of the Vice-Christ; and it does so with a completeness and a truthfulness which enable the

man who permits himself to be guided by the statements of the Word of God on the one hand, and the facts of history on the other, to say at once, "This is the antichrist."

Daniel called him a little horn. Paul called him the man of sin, the son of perdition. John called him the beast. Why just the beast? Because he is the primary leader of the Roman beast, who is the adversary of Messiah. John said, "Who is a liar but he that denies that Jesus is the Christ? He is antichrist, that denies the Father and the Son."

If he comes boldly and truthfully avowing himself the enemy of Christ, how is he a liar? "Without controversy, great is the mystery of godliness: God was manifest in the flesh." From the beginning, Satan had made the line of error to run parallel with the line of truth. Beginning his career in the days of Paul, it was not till the thirteenth century that the "man of sin" reached his maturity and stood before the world full-grown. During all these ages, he kept stretching himself higher and higher, piling assumption upon assumption, and prerogative upon prerogative, till at last, he raised himself to a height from which he looked down not only upon all churches but upon all kings and kingdoms.

In *The Approaching End Of The Age*, Henry Grattan Guinness says, *The fact is that the things which John foresaw have come to pass. Their fulfillment is written on the page of history in letters of blood and flame. There has arisen in the sphere of the Roman Empire, and there has reigned in and from the city of Rome, the seven-hilled city of the Caesars, just such a power as is predicted in the Apocalypse. Translate the symbolic language of the prophecy into plain non-figurative terms, and it becomes the history of the last twelve to fourteen centuries.*

As its head is an aged Pontiff, claiming the highest authority in the world as the visible representative of Deity, the Vicar of Jesus Christ, the Head of the Church of Christ on earth, God's Vicegerent, the Infallible Teacher of Faith and Morals, whose doctrines and decrees are irreformable; having power to bind and loose the souls of men in heaven, earth, and hell; canonizing souls in heaven, pardoning sins on earth, and remitting the pains of purgatory in the world

185

beneath; reigning thus in three worlds, and wearing in token of the fact a triple crown; a crown grafted on a miter; a miter within as the great High Priest in the Church of God; and a crown without as the highest monarch; crown above crown in three-fold splendor, encircling and glorifying his miter with the incomparable symbol of celestial, terrestrial, and infernal dignity.

At his feet, as he sits on the day of his coronation on the high altar of St. Peter's, kneel seventy cardinals, attired in long scarlet robes, princes of the Catholic Church, constituting her highest conclave; they kneel at his feet in the presence of assembled awestruck thousands, and one by one they kiss his feet, worshiping him as the representative of Deity. "They adore his Holiness on their knees, kissing his feet and his right hand."

He lifts up his right hand, extending two fingers and the thumb, symbolizing his authority as the representative of the three Persons of the Trinity, the Father, the Son, and the Holy Ghost; thus, he blesses the assembled kneeling multitudes in the vast and solemn sanctuary, who form a visible part of the two hundred millions of Christendom owning his spiritual sway.

The Popes of Rome proclaim to lead Messiah's *one-true church*, but they deceive Catholics with a false gospel of works and that Mary is the intercessor to the Father, which denies Messiah. Their teachings are against Messiah. The Popes have proclaimed themselves to be the '*vicar of Christ*,' to take His place; thus, they are anti-Christ. The Popes have taken the title of '*Holy Father*' and have proclaimed to forgive sins and provide salvation; thus, they deny the Heavenly Father. The Popes have changed the law and the times; thus, they pretend to be god on earth.

The Popes have tortured and persecuted Messiah's saints and banned and burned the Scriptures, revealing their hatred for the Heavenly Father and Messiah. They use the wicked crucifix, which corresponds to 666, as they keep Messiah on the cross in churches and Catholics' homes worldwide, putting Him to open shame. The enemy is *hidden in plain sight*, yet most people can't see how the Popes of Rome fulfill Bible prophecy as the *antichrist beast*, which leads the *harlot* church of Rome.

CHAPTER 39 - ANTICHRIST BEAST VERSUS MESSIAH

The *'beast'* is the main character of Revelation, and we know that the *'beast'* is the Popes of Rome because Daniel pointed to his rise to power as the *'little horn,'* and the Apostle Paul pointed to him rising to power as the *'son of perdition.'* Though John doesn't call him the *antichrist* in Revelation, just the *'beast,'* we'll prove out that the *'he'* in Revelation 13:1-10 is describing the office of the papacy, the Popes of Rome.

Let's look at what the word *'beast'* means in Greek and apply it. The Strong's Greek Dictionary word for *beast* is 2342 *therion,* which means; *a dangerous animal:—(venomous, wild) beast.*

> This word is used in Titus 1:10-12. *For there are many unruly and vain talkers and deceivers, specially they of the circumcision: Whose mouths must be stopped, who subvert whole houses, teaching things which they ought not, for filthy lucre's sake. One of themselves, even a prophet of their own, said, The Cretians are alway liars, evil beasts, slow bellies.*

Now let's apply it to the Popes of Rome, the *'beast'* in Revelation. They have a track record of being *liars, vain talkers* who teach concepts contrary to Scripture, who steal the wealth of Catholics with promises of reduced time in purgatory and salvation, for a price.

> In 1 Corinthians 15:32, the Apostle Paul mentions fighting with *beastly* men. *If after the manner of men I have fought with beasts at Ephesus, what advantageth it me, if the dead rise not? Let us eat and drink; for tomorrow we die.*

The phrase *'fought with beasts'* in Strong's Greek Dictionary is 2341 *theriomacheo* from a compound of 2342 and 3164; which means *to be a beast-fighter (in the gladiatorial show), i.e. (figuratively) to encounter (furious men):—fight with wild beasts*

He's saying that he has contended with *furious men* who should be regarded as *wild beasts.*

Peter pointed to *'false prophets.'* *But there were false prophets also among the people, even as there shall be false teachers among you, who privily shall bring in damnable heresies, even denying the Lord that bought them, and bring upon themselves swift destruction. And many shall follow their pernicious ways; by reason of whom the way of truth shall be evil spoken of. And through covetousness shall they with feigned words make merchandise of you: whose judgment now of a long time lingeth not, and their damnation slumbeth not.* 2 Peter 2:1-3

Peter calls them *'brute beasts.'* *But these, as natural brute beasts, made to be taken and destroyed, speak evil of the things that they understand not; and shall utterly perish in their own corruption; And shall receive the reward of unrighteousness, as they that count it pleasure to riot in the day time. Spots they are and blemishes, sporting themselves with their own deceivings while they feast with you; Having eyes full of adultery, and that cannot cease from sin; beguiling unstable souls: an heart they have exercised with covetous practices; cursed children. Which have forsaken the right way, and are gone astray, following the way of Balaam the son of Bosor, who loved the wages of unrighteousness.* 2 Peter 2:12-15

The book of Jude also points to ungodly men, *brute beasts*, creeping into the church.

For there are certain men crept in unawares, who were before of old ordained to this condemnation, ungodly men, turning the grace of our God into lasciviousness, and denying the only Lord God, and our Lord Jesus Christ. Jude 1:4

But these speak evil of those things which they know not: but what they know naturally, as brute beasts, in those things they corrupt themselves. Jude 1:10

The word *'beast'* in Greek can point to a *'lying, vain talking deceiver,'* and to a *'false prophet.'* We see how it applies to the Pope of Rome, a *false priest* who pretends to serve Messiah to better make war with His saints.

John was prompted to refer to the Popes as *'the beast'* because they have been the primary focus of the Roman beast kingdom. The Pope is a major player in the world today and will lead the One World Government of the future. Indeed, he is a *beast*!

The Satan-empowered ACBP leads the *harlot* church of Rome while proclaiming that it's the *'one true church'* of Messiah.

What the Popes proclaim is contrary to what Messiah taught. They have used Catholics to burn the Scriptures, which testify about Messiah and kill Messiah's saints; thus, they are *against Christ.*

The Popes proclaim the title of the *'Vicar of Christ,'* and they have proclaimed to be *Christ in the flesh,* to stand in place of Christ; thus, they are the *substitute Christ.* The Pope wears a crown at his coronation called the *Triple Crowns*, or the *Triple Tiaras.* It bears the inscription, *'Vicarius Filii Dei,'* which in English means *'Vicarius Son of God.'* A vicarious person is one who stands in the place of another, his substitute. By asserting to be the *vicar of Christ,* the Pope claims to act *in place of* Christ.

The Popes proclaim to forgive sins and provide salvation, and they proclaim that Mary is the sinless intercessor to the Father; thus, they *deny Christ* His rightful place. So we can see that the Roman Popes have fulfilled all three definitions of *antichrist.*

As Messiah acts for His Father, so the ACBP acts for Satan, who indeed empowered him for this very purpose, as his coming is *"after the working of Satan."* Messiah and the ACBP are antagonistic powers of *light* and *darkness*, the majesty of heaven and the might of hell. The Son of Yah humbled Himself, the *man of sin* exalts himself.

Seeing then it is certain that the Roman Pontiff has impudently transferred to himself the most peculiar properties of Yah and Messiah, there cannot be a doubt that he is the leader and standard-bearer of an impious and abominable kingdom. The Popes have become the king over the *Babylonian* religious, political, and economic system of the

189

earth, while Messiah is the rightful king over the *House of Israel*, *Holy Jerusalem*, made up of the saints.

Revelation presents two broadly contrasted women, identified with two broadly contrasted cities; the *harlot* and *Babylon* are one; the *bride* and *heavenly Jerusalem* are one. The two women are contrasted in every particular that is mentioned about them; the one is pure as she has *"made herself ready"* and fit for heaven's unsullied holiness; the other, foul as corruption could make her fit only for the *fires of destruction*.

The one belongs to the Lamb, who loves her as the bridegroom loves the bride; the other is associated with a wild beast and the kings of the earth, who ultimately divorce her and destroy her. The one is clothed with *fine linen*, and in another place is said to be clothed with the sun and crowned with a coronet of stars: that is, robed in divine righteousness, and resplendent with heavenly glory. The other is attired in *scarlet* and gold, in jewels and pearls, gorgeous indeed, but only with earthly splendor.

The one is persecuted and worn-out, to the point of being *as dead*, but was lifted back up to power and authority by Messiah; the other is *drunk with martyr blood* and seated on a beast which has received its powers from the persecuting dragon, Satan. The one is represented as a *chaste virgin*, espoused to Messiah; the other is the *mother of harlots* and *abominations of the earth*, married to the *antichrist*. The one goes in with the Lamb to the marriage supper, amid the glad HalleluYahs of heaven; the other will be *burned and desolated*.

You can see the clear contrast between the character, the actions, and the destiny; of the ACBP's *harlot* church and Messiah's Ekklesia of saints. The heart-breaking part is that Satan has convinced Catholics that they are a part of the *'one true church.'* Even more heart-breaking is that Christians, even those who call themselves *'Protestants'* aren't *protesting* against Rome anymore. They aren't actively exposing the ACBP and his *harlot* church to remove their power over people's minds, to set the RCC captives free.

CHAPTER 40 - THE CHURCH OF SATAN

Recall the story of Satan tempting Messiah.

> *Again, the devil took him up into an exceeding high mountain, and showed him all the kingdoms of the world, and the glory of them; And said unto him, All these things will I give thee, if thou wilt fall down and worship me. Then said Jesus unto him, Get thee hence, Satan: for it is written, Thou shall worship the Lord thy God, and him only shall thou serve.* Matthew 4:8-10

Revelation 13:4 proclaimed this about the ACBPs.

> *And they worshipped the dragon which gave power unto the beast: and they worshipped the beast, saying, Who is like unto the beast? Who is able to make war with him?*

The ACBPs took Satan up on his offer. They mimic Messiah as the High Priest. They offer a false salvation message in the name of Messiah. They kill Messiah's saints under the banner of the cross. They worship the *dragon*, Satan, and bow before him, and they've been rewarded with having control of the kingdoms of the world.

Emmanuel Milingo was an exorcist who wrote the book *Face to Face with the Devil*. He gave a speech at the *Fatima 2000 International Congress on World Peace*, entitled, "*Satanists at work in the Vatican.*" To an audience of Catholic bishops, priests, nuns, and laity, he said, "*The Devil in the Catholic Church is so protected not that he is like an animal protected by the government; put on a game preserve that outlaws anyone, especially hunters, from trying to capture or kill it. The Devil within the Church today is actually protected by certain Church authorities.*"

Malachi Martin is quoted as saying, "*Archbishop Milingo is a good bishop and his contention that there are Satanists in Rome is completely correct. Anybody who is acquainted with the state of affairs in the Vatican in the last thirty-five years is well aware that the prince of darkness has had and still has his surrogates in the court of St. Peter in Rome.*"

Let's hear from two of the most respected Catholic Cardinals to see their view of the RCC, which is very telling.

Cardinal and Archbishop of Westminster, Henry Edward Manning (1808-1892), gave this assessment of his church. *"… a system like this is so unlike anything human, it has upon it notes, tokens, marks so altogether supernatural, that men now acknowledge it to be either Christ or Antichrist. There is no alternative between these extremes. <u>The Catholic Church is either the masterpiece of Satan or the Kingdom of the Son of God</u>."* (3)

Manning also proclaimed, *"But the Church of Jesus Christ (he is pointing to the Roman Catholic Church), within the sphere of revelation, of faith and morals. Is all this, or is nothing, or worse than nothing – an imposture and a usurpation – that is, it is Christ or Antichrist!"* (4)

Cardinal John Henry Newman (1801-1890) put it even more bluntly, *"Another serious question is this, whether… a branch of Christ's Church, not merely has evil extensively prevailing within it, but is actually the kingdom of evil, the kingdom of God's enemy… The question really lies, be it observed, between those two alternatives, <u>either the Church of Rome is the house of God or the house of Satan; there is no middle ground between them</u>."* (5)

Those statements are quite astounding! The Apostle St. Paul warned us in 2 Corinthians 11:14-15.

> *And no marvel; for Satan himself is transformed into an angel of light. Therefore it is no great thing if his ministers also be transformed as the ministers of righteousness; whose end shall be according to their works.*

The Vatican is located on top of the catacombs of the pagan *Temple of Cybele*. There's a phallic symbol of the Egyptian sun god in the middle of a sun wheel in front of *St. Peter's Basilica*, which designates it as a temple of sun god worship. Inside, we see a massive sunburst symbol, statues of pagan gods, the 666 crucifix, and an extravagant throne. The RCC is the masterpiece of Satan, designed to hide the true faith and subvert Messiah. It's the *tares* church, which was planted by the enemy.

In *Romanism And The Reformation*, Henry Grattan Guinness says,

Even the Romanists themselves shame you in their clear-sighted comprehension of the issues of this question. Cardinal Manning says: "The Catholic Church is either the masterpiece of Satan or the kingdom of the Son of God." Cardinal Newman says: "A sacerdotal order is historically the essence of the Church of Rome; if not divinely appointed, it is doctrinally the essence of antichrist."

In both these statements, the issue is clear, and it is the same. Rome herself admits, openly admits, that if she is not the very kingdom of Christ, she is that of antichrist. Rome declares she is one or the other. She herself propounds and urges this solemn alternative. You shrink from it, do you? I accept it. Conscience constrains me.

Recall that Satan caused Emperor Constantine and the Roman bishops to create Romanism, Roman Christianity, which has the veneer of the Scriptural faith but is symbolically worshipping false gods, which brings Satan honor and glory.

Satan has done much more damage to the true faith by creating Romanism and the *harlot* RCC than he did with the pagan Roman Emperors who persecuted the saints. In the name of Messiah, the RCC has carried out atrocious acts, which have turned people away from the true faith of Scripture because of the association.

Catholic children are traumatized by nuns' harsh treatment in school, and they run away from the Heavenly Father. Young boys who are sexually violated by priests turn away from the true faith. Nuns and priests who commit these crimes may be chastised, but they rarely face criminal prosecution because the RCC-controlled system is designed to protect its own.

It's not an exaggeration to call the RCC of the ACBPs, the Church of Satan, for her Cardinals have openly declared it. This is why Messiah commanded His saints to *'come out of her!'*

193

CHAPTER 41 - THE POPES BLASPHEME

And he opened his mouth in blasphemy against God, to blaspheme his name, and his tabernacle, and them that dwell in heaven.
Revelation 13:6

Once again, we can see that John picked up the narrative about the fourth beast kingdom, in that he declares that the ACBP will *blaspheme*.

> *And there, in this horn, were eyes like the eyes of a man, and a mouth speaking pompous words.* Daniel 7:8

> *And he shall speak great words against the most High, and shall wear out the saints of the Most High, and think to change times and laws: and they shall be given into his hand until a time and times and the dividing of time.* Daniel 7:25

Paul, too described the blasphemy of the Popes of Rome.

> *Who opposeth and exalteth himself above all that is called God or that is worshiped, so that he sitteth as God in the temple of God, shewing himself that he is God.* 2 Thessalonians 2:4

The Popes proclaim that salvation is ONLY through them.

Pope Innocent III (1198-1216), *"We believe, and with our lips, we confess but one Church, not that of the heretics, but the Holy Roman Catholic and Apostolic Church, outside which we believe that no one is saved."* (1)

Pope Boniface VIII (1294-1303), *"We are compelled, our faith urging us, to believe and to hold – and we do firmly believe and simply confess – that there is one holy Catholic Apostolic Church, outside of which there is neither salvation nor remission of sins."* (2)

"We declare, say, define, and pronounce that it is absolutely necessary for the salvation of every human creature to be subject to the Roman Pontiff." (3)

Pope Eugene IV (1431-47), *"No one, let his alms giving be as great as it may, no one, even if he pour out his blood for the Name of Jesus Christ, can be saved unless they abide within the bosom and unity of the Catholic Church*

Pope Gregory XVI (1831-46), *"It is not possible to worship God truly except in Her; all who are outside Her will not be saved."*

Pope Pius IX (1846-78), *"It must be held by faith that outside the Apostolic Roman Church, no one can be saved; that this is the only ark of salvation; that he who shall not have entered therein will perish in the flood."*

Pope Clement VI (1342-52), *"No man outside obedience to the Pope of Rome can ultimately be saved. All who have raised themselves against the faith of the Roman Church, and died in final impenitence have been damned, and gone down to Hell."*

Pope Leo XII (1823-29) said, *"We profess that there is no salvation outside the (Catholic) Church. For the Church is the pillar and ground of the truth. With reference to those words, Augustine says: `If any man be outside the Church he will be excluded from the number of sons, and will not have God for Father since he has not the Church for mother."*

Pope Leo XIII (1878-1903), *"Remember and understand well that where Peter is, there is the Church; that those who refuse to associate in communion with the Chair of Peter belong to Antichrist, not to Christ. He who would separate himself from the Roman Pontiff has no further bond with Christ."* *"This is our last lesson to you; receive it, engrave it in your minds, all of you: by God's commandment salvation is to be found nowhere but in the Church."*

Pope Pius X (1903-14), *"It is our duty to recall to everyone great and small, as the Holy Pontiff Gregory did in ages past, the absolute necessity which is ours, to have recourse to this Church to effect our eternal salvation."*

Pope Pius XII (1939-58), *"O Mary Mother of Mercy and Refuge of Sinners! We beseech thee to look with pitying eyes on poor heretics and schismatics. Do thou, who art the Seat of Wisdom, enlighten the minds wretchedly enfolded in the darkness of ignorance and sin, that they may clearly recognize the Holy,*

Catholic, Roman Church to be the only true Church of Jesus Christ, outside of which neither sanctity nor salvation can be found." (12)

Pope Pius XII (1939-58), *"It is absolutely necessary that the Christian community be subject in all things to the Sovereign Pontiff if it wishes to be a part of the divinely-established society founded by our Redeemer."* (13) *"By divine mandate the interpreter and guardian of the Scriptures, and the depository of Sacred Tradition living within her, the Church alone is the entrance to salvation: She alone, by herself, and under the protection and guidance of the Holy Spirit, is the source of truth."* (14)

Pope Benedict XV (1914-22), *"Such is the nature of the Catholic faith that it does not admit of more or less, but must be held as a whole, or as a whole rejected: This is the Catholic faith, which unless a man believe faithfully and firmly, he cannot be saved."* (15)

Pope Pius XI (1922-39), *"The Catholic Church alone is keeping the true worship. This is the font of truth, this is the house of faith, this is the temple of God; if any man enter not here, or if any man go forth from it, he is a stranger to the hope of life and salvation. Furthermore, in this one Church of Christ, no man can be or remain who does not accept, recognize and obey the authority and supremacy of Peter and his legitimate successors."* (16)

Pope John XXIII (1958-63), *"Into this fold of Jesus Christ no man may enter unless he be led by the Sovereign Pontiff and only if they be united to him can men be saved."* (17)

Acts 4:12 proclaims that salvation is only through Messiah. *Nor is there salvation in any other, for there is no other name under heaven given among men by which we must be saved.* Messiah, the true High Priest, says: *I am the way, the truth, and the life. No one comes to the Father except through Me.* John 14:6

Can you see how the Popes blasphemed and spoke great things against Yah and Messiah? Amazingly, the Popes have falsely proclaimed these things, yet people today don't know that they're the *antichrist beast* of Revelation!

CHAPTER 42 - THE POPES PERSECUTED THE SAINTS

As the popes gained more power, they persecuted the saints with more vigor. Daniel, John pointed to this.

I beheld, and the same horn made war with the saints, and prevailed against them. Daniel 7:21

And he shall speak great words against the most High, and shall wear out the saints of the most High, and think to change times and laws: and they shall be given into his hand until a time and times and the dividing of time. Daniel 7:25

And it was given unto him to make war with the saints, and to overcome them: and power was given him over all kindred, and tongues, and nations. Revelation 13:7

And I saw the woman drunken with the blood of the saints, and with the blood of the martyrs of Jesus: and when I saw her, I wondered with great admiration. Revelation 17:6

And in her was found the blood of prophets, and of saints, and of all that were slain upon the earth. Revelation 18:24

The Popes of Rome were given power over the ten kingdoms of the fallen Roman Empire, who were used to make war with the saints.

And the ten horns which thou saw are ten kings, which have received no kingdom as yet; but receive power as kings one hour with the beast. These have one mind, and shall give their power and strength unto the beast. These shall make war with the Lamb, and the Lamb shall overcome them: for he is Lord of lords, and King of kings: and they that are with him are called, and chosen, and faithful. And he said unto me, The waters which thou saw, where the whore sits, are peoples, and multitudes, and nations, and tongues. Revelation 17:12-15

In *The Seventh Vial* (1848), James Aitken Wylie says, *There is not one of the ten horns (the ten kingdoms of the fallen Roman Empire, who were subservient to the antichrist beast Popes) which has not at some period of history persecuted the saints; nor is there a spot of Europe, which was not sprinkled with their blood.*

The Papal Church relentlessly sought to eliminate the dual witness of the Scriptures and the saints, and as this happened, the world became a very dark place where evil prevailed, called the *Dark Ages*.

In *Key To The Apocalypse*, Henry Grattan Guinness says, *But more than this, more than by any other mark, we recognize Papal Rome by the last, the most marvelous characteristic, which is given us in the sacred prediction — her strange and terrible inebriation with the blood of saints and martyrs! Old Heathen Rome persecuted for a brief period the early Church, but Papal Rome through long centuries has held the preeminence as the persecutor of those faithful to the teachings of the Gospel of Christ. She has been all along in her essential and unalterable character a persecuting Church.*

Persecution has occupied a prominent place in her excommunications, doctrines, decrees, canons, tribunals, trials, condemnations, imprisonments, executions, and exterminating wars. Centuries of persecuting action witness against her. Her laws for the persecution and extermination of heretics have increased in malignity from their first rise down to modern times. Plainly and openly she has declared herself to be a persecuting Church. She has gloried in her intolerance. Her avowed doctrine is "that heretics ought to be visited by the secular powers with temporal punishments, and even with death itself."

Bellarmine, her great cardinal, who wrote those words, said of the saints of God who protested against her iniquity: "If you shut them in prison or send them into exile, they corrupt those near them with their words and those at a distance with their books; therefore the only remedy is to send them be times into their own place." Under these maxims Rome has always acted. What a long roll of bloody persecutions is her record!

The extirpation of the Albigenses, the massacre of the Waldenses, the martyrdoms of the Lollards, the slaughter of the Bohemians, the burning of Huss, Jerome, Savonarola, Frith, Tyndale, Ridley, Hooper, Cranmer, Latimer, and thousands of others as godly and faithful as they, have been her acts; the demoniacal cruelties of the Inquisition were invented by her mind and inflicted by her hand — that Inquisition which was for centuries the mighty instrument of her warfare against devoted men and women whose crime was only this, that they "kept the commandments of God and the faith of Jesus."

The ferocious cruelties of the Duke of Alva in the Netherlands; the bloody martyrdoms of Queen Mary's reign; the extinction by fire and sword of the Reformation in Spain and Italy, in Portugal and Poland; the massacre of St. Bartholomew; the long and cruel persecutions of the Huguenots, and all the infamies and barbarities of the Revocation of the Edict of Nantes, which flung its refugees on every shore of Europe, were perpetrated by Papal Rome. Her victims have been innumerable.

In Spain alone, Llorente reckons as the sufferers of the Inquisition, 31,912 burnt alive, and 291,450 so-called penitents forced into submission 'by water, weights, fire, pulleys, and screws, and all the apparatus by which the sinews could be strained without cracking, and the bones bruised without breaking, and the body racked exquisitely without giving up the ghost. A million perished in the massacre of the Albigenses.

In the thirty years which followed the first institution of the Jesuits, nine hundred thousand faithful Christians were slain; Thirty-six thousand were dispatched by the common executioner in the Netherlands, by the direction of the Duke of Alva, who boasted of the deed. Fifty thousand Flemings and Germans were hanged, burnt, or buried alive under Charles V. And when we have added to this the bloodshed of the Thirty Years' War in Germany, and the long agony of other and repeated massacres of Protestants in England, Ireland, Scotland, France, Spain, Italy, and the Netherlands, we have to remember that for all this "no word of censure ever issued from the Vatican, except in the brief interval when statesmen and soldiers grew weary of bloodshed and looked for means to admit the heretics to grace.

In *The Approaching End Of The Age*, **Henry Grattan Guinness says** that the following is one of the authorized curses, published in the Romish Pontifical, to be pronounced on heretics by Romish priests: *"May God Almighty and all his saints curse them, with the curse with which the devil and his angels are cursed. Let them be destroyed out of the land of the living. Let the vilest of deaths come upon them, and let them descend alive into the pit. Let their seed be destroyed from the earth; by hunger, and thirst, and nakedness, and all distress, let them perish. May they have all misery, and pestilence, and torment. Let all they have be cursed. Always and everywhere, let them be cursed. Speaking and silent, let them be cursed. Within and without, let them be cursed. By land and by sea, let them be cursed. From the crown of the head to the sole of the foot, let them be cursed. Let their eyes become blind, let their ears become deaf, let their mouth become dumb, let their tongue cleave to their jaws, let not their hands handle, let not their feet walk. Let all the members of the body be cursed. Cursed let them be standing, lying, from this time forth forever; and this let their candle be extinguished in the presence of God, at the day of judgment. Let their burial be with dogs and asses. Let hungry wolves devour their corpses. Let the devil and his angels be their companions forever. Amen, amen; so be it, so let it be."*

At the commands of the Popes, priests and Catholics tortured and killed the saints, whom the Popes deemed as heretics since they opposed the teachings of the antichrist Popes. The saints were shot, stabbed, stoned, drowned, beheaded, hanged, drawn, quartered, impaled, burnt, buried alive, roasted on spits, baked in ovens, thrown into furnaces, tumbled over precipices, cast from the tops of towers, sunk in mire and pits,, starved with hunger and cold, hung on tenterhooks, suspended by the hair of the head, by the hands or feet, stuffed and blow up with gunpowder, ripped with swords and sickles, tied to the tails of horses, dragged over streets and sharp flints, broken on the wheel, beaten on anvils with hammers, blown with bellow, bored with hot irons, torn piecemeal by red-hot pincers, slashed with knives, hacked with axes, hewed with chisels, planed with planes, pricked with forks, stuck from head to foot with pins, choked with water, lime, rages, urine, excrement, or mangled pieces of their own bodies crammed down their throats, shut up in caves and dungeons, tied to stakes, nailed to trees, tormented with lighted matches, scalding oil, burning pitch, melted lead.

They have been flayed alive, had their flesh scalped and torn from their bones; they have been trampled and danced upon, till their bowels have been forced out, their guts have been tied to trees and pulled forth by degrees; their heads twisted with cords till the blood or even their eyes started out; strings have been drawn through their noses, and they led about like swine and butchered like sheep. To dig out eyes, tear off nails, cut off ears, lips, tongues, arms, breasts, etc., has been but an ordinary sport with Rome's converters and holy butchers. Catholics have been compelled to lay violent hands on their dearest friends, to kill or to cast into the fire their parents, husbands, wives, children, etc., or to look on while they have been most cruelly and shamefully abused. Women and young maids have also suffered such barbarities, accompanied with all the imaginable indignities, insults, shame, and pungent pains, to which their sex could expose them. Tender babes have been whipped, starved, drowned, stabbed, and burnt to death, dashed against trees and stones, torn limb from limb, carried about on the point of spikes and spears, and thrown to the dogs and swine.

In *Romanism And The Reformation*, Henry Grattan Guinness says, *Under these bloody maxims, those persecutions were carried on, from the eleventh and twelfth centuries almost to the present day, which stand out on the page of history. After a signal of open martyrdom had been given in the canons of Orleans, there followed the extirpation of the Albigenses under the form of a crusade, the establishment of the Inquisition, the cruel attempts to extinguish the Waldenses, the martyrdom of the Lollards, the cruel wars to exterminate the Bohemians, the burning of Huss and Jerome, and multitudes of other confessors, before the Reformation; and afterward, the ferocious cruelties practiced in the Netherlands, the martyrdom of Queen Mary's reign, the extinction, by fire and sword, of the Reformation in Spain and Italy, by fraud and open persecution in Poland, the massacre of Bartholemew, the persecutions of the Huguenots by the League, the extirpation of the Vaudois, and all the cruelties and perjuries connected with the revocation of the Edict of Nantes. These are the more open and conspicuous facts which explain* *the prophecy, besides the slow and secret murders of the holy tribunal of the Inquisition.*

Wow! I can't describe the crimes of the ACBP's and their *harlot* church of Rome better than Henry Grattan Guinness, which is why I feature his commentaries so prevalently in this book.

What clearer evidence is there than a professed church of Messiah killing the saints? Messiah would never condone creating torture devices to convert people to the faith. Messiah would never advocate murdering those who oppose the Gospel.

The irony is that the Popes proclaim that their church is built on the foundation of Peter as the first Pope, citing Matthew 16:18.

> *And I say also unto thee, that thou art Peter, and upon this rock I will build my church; and the gates of hell shall not prevail against it.*

But it's the very opposite, as the *gates of hell* were unleashed by the Satan-empowered ACBPs who persecute Messiah's Ekklesia.

People today envision a one-man antichrist who will kill tens of millions of saints, but they ignore that the Popes of Rome have already carried out those evil deeds. They ignore the suffering of the saints who have gone before them and think that all of Revelation is about the end times saints. We live in a sad state of ignorance and self-absorption.

Messiah's Ekklesia is called to expose false teachings by those who proclaim His name, but we are certainly not called to kill those who teach wrong doctrine. Our sword is the Scriptures, and our power is the authority of the name of Messiah and the power of the Spirit of Yah.

> *And have no fellowship with the unfruitful works of darkness, but rather reprove them.* Ephesians 5:11

CHAPTER 43 - THE IRON-CLAY FEET OF DANIEL 2

In this chapter, we'll look at the *'iron/clay feet'* of the statue in Daniel 2. Here's the narrative in Daniel 2:41-43.

> *And whereas thou saw the feet and toes, part of potters' clay, and part of iron, the kingdom shall be divided; but there shall be in it of the strength of the iron, forasmuch as thou saw the iron mixed with miry clay. And as the toes of the feet were part of iron, and part of clay, so the kingdom shall be partly strong, and partly broken. And whereas thou saw iron mixed with miry clay, they shall mingle themselves with the seed of men: but they shall not cleave one to another, even as iron is not mixed with clay.*

The *'iron legs'* of the statue in Daniel 2 point to the Western and Eastern divisions. We've seen how the first four trumpet judgments were against the Western part of the Empire, which led to the ACBP taking civil and ecclesiastic power over the Roman beast kingdom. Since they didn't have a standing army to conquer their enemies, they hired mercenary armies to do their dirty work.

The *iron* in the feet still points to the Roman beast kingdom, but they join with another people group referred to as *'miry clay.'* The key words to focus on are *mixed* and *mingle*. The Bible gives us the definition, so we need not speculate about the meanings.

The Strong's Aramaic word for both *'mixed'* and *'mingle'* is 6151 **arab**. That word is not found anywhere else, as this passage was originally written in Aramaic, which is closely related to Hebrew. When we do a word study, we see that the Aramaic 6151 *'arab'* corresponds to Hebrew words that describe the mixing of the Arab race. Aramaic word 6151 corresponds to Hebrew word 6148 `**arab**: which means; *to braid, i.e., **intermix**; to **mingle***.

Is that not what the *iron* and *clay* are doing? *Intermixing, mingling* together?

Hebrew word 6150 `arab is a primitive root identical with 6148, which signifies *dusk, to be darkened.*

Hebrew word 6152 `**Arab** is derived from 6150, and it signifies **an Arab**, *Arabia.*

Hebrew word 6154 `ereb is derived from 6148. It signifies *a 'web of cloth,'* also *a mixture (or mongrel race),* and **especially the people of Arabia**, *a 'mingled people'* or *'mixed multitude.'*

Hebrew word 6163 `**Arabiy** is derived from 6152 and signifies *'an Arabian or inhabitant of Arabia.'*

We can see a clear link of the words *mixed* and *mingled* with the Arab people. Now let's look at the story of the words *'miry clay.'* When I think of the *'potters clay,'* I think of Jeremiah 18:6, when the Father is talking to the tribes of the House of Israel.

> *O house of Israel, cannot I do with you as this potter? Saith the LORD. Behold, as the clay is in the potter's hand, so are ye in mine hand, O house of Israel.*

When I think of *'miry clay,'* I think of the Ishmaelites who were born of Abraham's seed when he **mixed** with a foreigner, an Egyptian bondwoman named Hagar.

Two great nations were made through Abraham, that of the twelve tribes of Israel, through Jacob/Israel who had twelve sons. *And I will make of thee a great nation, and I will bless thee, and make thy name great; and thou shalt be a blessing.* Genesis 12:2

And that of Ishmael, who also had twelve sons. *And as for Ishmael, I have heard thee: Behold, I have blessed him, and will make him fruitful, and will multiply him exceedingly; twelve princes shall he beget, and I will make him a great nation.* Genesis 17:20

The twelve tribes of Israel are the *'clay,'* and the descendants of Ishmael's twelve sons are the *'miry clay.'* The Strong's Hebrew word for *'nation'* is 1471 *gowy: rarely (shortened) goy {go'-ee}; a foreign nation; hence, a Gentile; also (figuratively) a troop of animals, or a flight of locusts:—Gentile, heathen, nation, people.*

Though the word *gowy* is used in pointing to the nation of Israel and the nation of Ishmael, we can see that it can point to a *flight of locusts by a heathen people.* That will come into play in the fifth trumpet judgment, which is about locust and scorpions, which come from Arabia.

The *'iron/clay feet'* represent the enemy of Messiah, which He will desolate. Today, the false religions of Romanism and Islam hide the true Gospel from over three billion people.

Let's look at some Scriptures which use the word *'mingled'* regarding the Arabs.

> Ezekiel 30:5 points to the hired soldiers of Arabia. *Ethiopia, and Libya, and Lydia, and <u>all the mingled people</u>, and Chub, and the men of the land that is in league, shall fall with them by the sword.*
>
> Jeremiah 25:24 points to the Arabs. *And all the kings of Arabia, and all the kings of the <u>mingled people</u> that dwell in the desert.*
>
> Jeremiah 50:37 also points to the Arabs, the mercenaries of the Chaldeans. *A sword is upon their horses, and upon their chariots, and upon all the <u>mingled people</u> that are in the midst of her; and they shall become as women: a sword is upon her treasures; and they shall be robbed.*

Scripture is identifying Arabs as a *"mingled people"* who are used by kingdoms as hired soldiers. And that is what the *iron-clay feet* are describing, the Roman Popes (the *iron*) using Arabs (the *miry clay*) as their mercenary army. You'll see this play out in the fifth trumpet when the Islamic Muslims are released to attack the middle and eastern Roman Empire. And then in the sixth trumpet when Turkish armies attack the Eastern Roman Empire and conquer Constantinople.

205

The RCC didn't just hijack Islam; they helped create it. Augustine, the bishop of North Africa, effectively won Arabs to Catholicism, but many did not convert. At the same time, Messiah's missionaries were preaching the pure Gospel in North Africa, Asia Minor, and other places. Satan didn't want the Arabs to know the true path of salvation, so he had the Augustinians create the false religion of Islam to deceive them. The Qur'an gives Muslims a religious cause so that they don't read the Gospel and become saved.

Before we answer the question *"why was Islam created,"* let's go back to the story of Abraham and Sarah, who in their old age were promised that they would have a son. Sarah scoffed and had Abraham sleep with her Egyptian handmaiden Hagar, who bore Abraham's first son Ishmael. Sarah then bore Isaac, and when she found Ishmael mocking Isaac, she kicked Hagar and Ishmael out.

An angel of Yah came to Hagar when she was crying, and he promised her, *Arise, lift up the lad, and hold him in thine hand; for I will make him a great nation.* Genesis 21:18. Note that Genesis 21:20 says that Ishmael became a great archer, as you will see that his descendants, the Saracens were great archers too. *And God was with the lad, and he grew, and dwelt in the wilderness, and became an archer.*

So what does this have to do with Mohammed and the creation of the false religion of Islam? Isaac bore Jacob, who was renamed *Israel* when he came into a covenant relationship with Yah. He had twelve sons who became the twelve tribes of Israel. Ishmael also had twelve sons, through which the great nation of Arabs was born.

Yah's Son was born from the tribe of Judah. Malachi 3:1 calls Him the messenger of His everlasting covenant.

> *Behold, I will send my messenger, and he shall prepare the way before me: and the Lord, whom ye seek, shall suddenly come to his temple, even the messenger of the covenant, whom ye delight in: behold, he shall come, says the LORD of hosts.*

Mohammed came from the lineage of Ishmael, Abraham's first-born son, and he became Satan's *messenger*. Through Mohammed and Islam, Satan took control of the other great nation that descended from Abraham to blind them and use them for his glory. Muslims repeat the mantra of *"There is no God but Allah, and Mohammed is his messenger."*

Satan has taken the rejected nation of Ishmael and has hidden the Gospel from them, and he is praised when they worship Allah because he is Allah; he is *Abaddon, Apollyon.*

> *And they had a king over them, which is the angel of the bottomless pit, whose name in the Hebrew tongue is Abaddon, but in the Greek tongue hath his name Apollyon.* Revelation 9:11

There is way too much information to cover to explain how the Roman bishops created Islam, so I will summarize here to give you the big picture of why they did it. And then you can read the whole story on this website. **www.IronClayFeet.com**

Romanism and Islam are the two masterpieces of Satan.

Qur'an 1:1 states that Allah is the god (lord) of this world, *"The praise be to Allah, the lord of the worlds."* 2 Corinthians 4:4 foretold Satan's strategy.

> *In whom the god of this world hath blinded the minds of them which believe not, lest the light of the glorious gospel of Christ, who is the image of God, should shine unto them.*

That is exactly what Satan has done, *blind* the minds of people with Romanism and Islam so that they can't see the truth of the Gospel.

Both Qur'an 3:54 and 8:30 state that Allah deceives, *"And they deceived, and Allah deceived. And Allah is the best deceiver."*

> Revelation 20:10 identifies the deceiver, *And the devil that deceived them was cast into the lake of fire and brimstone, where the beast and the false prophet are and shall be tormented day and night for ever and ever.*

Romanism has 1.3 billion Catholics, and Islam has 1.9 billion Muslims. 40% of the world's population are deceived by the two primary false religions that Satan helped create. Are your eyes opening up?

The enemy is the master of using *'controlled opposition.'* Islam is *Romanism for Arabs.* Revelation 17 calls the Roman Church the *Mother of Harlots,* and Islam is one of the *daughter* religions that they created.

Mohammed was the perfect person to prop up as a prophet.

Mohammed was born in 570, but his father died before his birth. His grandfather possessed the authority of the house of Koreish, the governors of Mecca. Then his grandfather died when Mohammed was age 8, causing Mecca's governorship to be passed onto someone else. He could have been a *'star'* in the house of Koreish; instead, it passed him over. No doubt this disturbed Mohammed greatly, and he still desired to take control of Mecca, which set up his mindset to be misled by Satan, who proclaimed him as a prophet of god for the people of Mecca and all Muslims.

Mohammed married a Catholic woman named Khadijah in 595. He was 25; she was 40. They had two sons (Qasim and Tahir, who died as infants) and four daughters (Ruqiyah, Zaynab, Umm Kulthum, and Fatima, the most prominent and honored of them all.) Khadijah was rich, so Mohammed didn't have to work, which gave him too much time on his hands, including spending time in the *Cave of Hera,* where he received visions.

The Augustinians used Khadijah's Catholic cousin Waraquah to help interpret Mohammed's visions, from which came the Qur'an. We see a clear connection to Islam being created through Mohammed and all of his Catholic influences.

The Augustinians exalted Mohammed as a prophet to unite Arabs, and they used the Qur'an to give them a mission.

Islam was designed to mimic Roman Catholicism to kill the same people groups they deem as heretics. Islam means *'submission'* or *'surrender,'* defining their mission from the Catholic Church, to make war against heretics. Mohammedism borrows from both Judaism and Christianity so that it appears to be a religion that points to the same god; but has Arabian superstition mixed in to draw in the Arabs. They revere Abraham, Moses, and Messiah as prophets of Allah (god). Roman Catholicism and Islam both believe in forced conversions by the sword and killing heretics.

They both teach the concept of the Immaculate Conception of Mary. Mary is for the Moslems the true Sayyida or Lady. After Fatima's death, Mohammed wrote: *"Thou shalt be the most blessed of all the women in Paradise, after Mary."* These similarities with Mary and Fatima are designed to draw Muslims to the Pope.

Both Roman Catholicism and Islam revere the moon god and sun god. Many Catholic Virgin Mary images show her with a sun symbol behind her head, and she's standing over a crescent moon. And there are many sun worship images through the Catholic Church, including at St. Peter's Basilica at the Vatican. Islamic mosques have the crescent moon representing the *moon* goddess and a *star* for the sun god. You often see pictures with the sun cradled in the Islamic crescent moon symbol, representing their sexual union. We can see that they both use the same Babylonian symbolism of pagan god worship.

Roman Catholicism and Islam both use prayer beads. They're used to mark the repetitions of prayers and chants, forbidden in Scripture.

> *But when ye pray, use not vain repetitions, as the heathen do: for they think that they shall be heard for their much speaking.* Matthew 6:7.

In Roman Catholicism, they're used to pray the rosary to the Virgin Mary. In Islam, the beads are used to keep count while saying the prayer known as the *"Tasbih of Fatimah,"* a form of prayer offered as a gift by Muhammad to his daughter, Fatimah.

Roman Catholicism and Islam both have pilgrimages. Roman Catholics flock to the Vatican to visit St. Peter's Basilica. The Hajj is an Islamic pilgrimage to Mecca and a mandatory religious duty for Muslims that must be carried out at least once in their lifetime by all adult Muslims who are physically and financially capable of undertaking the journey.

Islam appears to fulfill Bible prophecy about the *antichrist*. The Qur'an was written in such a way as to mimic the description of the *antichrist beast*, to fool undiscerning people. It teaches that the Mahdi will be a powerful political, military, and religious leader who will emerge in the last days. They say that Muslim Jesus will be a secondary figure who will support the Mahdi during the last days. The Mahdi will supposedly make an Israel peace treaty for seven years through a Levite Jew and will rule for approximately three years and establish an Islamic caliphate from Jerusalem.

We see a direct connection between Islam and the false teachings of the SOJ, who both point to a futuristic 70th week of Daniel 9 and a one-man antichrist. And no doubt the SOJ will position someone to seem to fulfill the role to deflect blame away from the ACBP.

Roman Catholicism and Islam both have Holy wars. Both religions are designed to kill their enemies. Catholics have primarily targeted the saints. Islam historically has been used to target Orthodox Christians, who have similar beliefs as the Catholic Church but don't acknowledge the Pope as their leader.

Islam and Jesuitism teach that deception is acceptable if it's for the *'glory of god.'* Islam practices deceit as one of its tools to assist its ascendancy. It has a specific doctrine that allows and even calls for deception to achieve its desired end. The SOJ manta is *'by way of deception though shalt do war.'* Islam is Romanism with a Babylonian Judaism twist. It's a false religion that has *darkened* this world.

The Vatican helped to finance the building of these massive Islamic armies in exchange for these favors. The ACBPs use Muslim mercenary armies to attack people who oppose them, such as Jews and the saints; protect the Augustinian monks and Roman Catholics; conquer additional territory controlled by their enemies; and capture Jerusalem for the Pope as he coveted the Holy City. History shows that they obtained most of their goals.

Muslims and RCC have battled against each other. Daniel said that the *iron-clay feet* would *mix*, but not *cleave* to another, just as iron does not *mix with clay*. In other words, they would be similar enough to respect each other and get along most of the time, but different enough that they would sometimes battle against each other.

Muslims and Catholics have battled each other over territory as the Muslims pressed forward to expand their control of the world. During the *Holy Land Crusades*, the Roman Popes battled to take back control of Palestine, as the Muslims sought to keep possession.

Romanism and Islam are designed to be different enough to deceive two huge people groups, but similar enough that they'll join together with the ACBP in the One World Government.

It's heartbreaking to see how Satan has used Romanism and Islam to deceive so many people. Pray for Catholics and Muslims to have an encounter with the living Messiah so that they have a covenant relationship with the Heavenly Father.

Interestingly, after the fifth and sixth trumpet judgments, the Western Roman Empire is controlled by the Popes of Rome, the *iron*. And the Eastern Roman Empire is controlled by Islam, the *clay*, headquartered in Istanbul, formerly Constantinople. So we see how the *iron/clay feet* control the land of the former Roman Empire.

Next, we'll see how the '*miry clay*,' the Arabs, are used by the ACBP's to carry out Yah's judgments. What the Popes do out of spite is used by Yah to make a judgment on apostate people.

211

CHAPTER 44 - THE WOE JUDGMENTS

The first four trumpet judgments in Revelation 8 were against the Western Roman Empire, but now a shift occurs as we approach the remaining trumpet judgments. In Revelation 8:13, Messiah declares that three *'woe judgments'* are coming.

If you search for the word *'woe'* in Scripture, you see that it can point to judgment against people who proclaim to follow the true faith but are practicing false religion. An example of this is in Matthew 23, when Messiah cast woes upon the Jewish leaders because they continued in their rebellion against the Father and they sought to deliver Him up to be killed. Their judgment came when the Roman army was sent to desolate their nation in 70 AD.

These woe judgments in Revelation are the same, as they are poured out primarily on Orthodox Christians, who have very similar beliefs as the RCC, in their observance of the sacraments for salvation and their reverence of Mary as their supposed Intercessor. After Constantine took power, he relocated to the Eastern Roman Empire, centered in Constantinople. He took his false Romanism beliefs with him, and the Eastern Orthodox Church was polluted with idol worship, so it was ripe for judgment.

Smaller schisms between the Orthodox Christians and the Pope led to the *East-West Schism*, also called *The Great Schism*, in 1054. This divorce was the incentive for the Popes to exact vengeance against the Orthodox Christians. If he did it openly, that would be too obvious; so he covertly used the Islamic mercenary army to do his dirty work.

The takeaway is that we can't lump all people called *'Christians'* into one group. Most Catholics and Orthodox Christians are steeped in man's traditions, such as revering Mary as the intercessor to the Father. The Father uses foreign armies, including the Muslims, to carry out His righteous judgment against these apostate people.

The Fall Of The Eastern Roman Empire

CHAPTER 45 - THE FIFTH TRUMPET JUDGMENT
632-782 AD

It only took 76 years for the Goths, Huns, Vandals, and Heruli of the first four trumpets; to conquer the Western Roman Empire, which is why only seven verses were used to describe those attacks. The fifth and sixth trumpets give much more detailed information as the fulfillment timeframes were much longer, 150 and 391 years, respectively.

One-third of the Roman Empire was lost to the barbarian invasions during the first four trumpets. One third will be attacked during the fifth trumpet starting in 612. The last third of the Roman Empire will be attacked during the sixth trumpet.

And the fifth angel sounded, and I saw a star fall from heaven unto the earth: and to him was given the key of the bottomless pit. And he opened the bottomless pit; and there arose a smoke out of the pit, as the smoke of a great furnace; and the sun and the air were darkened by reason of the smoke of the pit. **Revelation 9:1-2**

Pagan superstition holds that caves serve *'as the seats of oracles and sources of inspiration.'* Mohammed opened the *bottomless pit* of Satan's lies when he spent time in the *Cave of Hira* every year. In 610, it's said that Mohammed received his first revelation from the archangel Gabriel, which consisted of the first five ayats (verses) of *Surah Al-Alaq*. The angel was no doubt a fallen angel or Satan himself.

2 Corinthians 11:14 tells us, *And no wonder! For Satan himself transforms himself into an angel of light.*

Scripture records the angel Gabriel's interaction with people, and he starts by reassuring them to remove their fear. He did this with Daniel (8:16-18,10:12), Zechariah (1:13), and Mary (Luke 1:30).

But that's not what happened with Mohammed. While sleeping, he had a dream where he was pressed hard by an entity and commanded to read and recite what he had read. Muhammad's description of experiencing forcible pressure from an angel, commanding him to recite, is a graphic description of demonic oppression.

Obviously, it was not Gabriel because he would not teach concepts that directly oppose Yah's Word, such as *'The son of Mary was a messenger of Allah.'* The Qur'an denies the deity of Messiah and says that He was just a prophet. It denies that He died on the cross and shed his blood for redemption. It says that He fainted or went unconscious on the cross and was brought around later. And it denies the inerrancy of Scripture.

The *'falling star'* points to Mohammed, who lost his place as the leader of Mecca. It also points to Satan, who fell from heaven, who, out of his *bottomless pit* of lies, created Islam's false religion to deceive billions of people.

In *Vision Of The Ages* (1881), **Barton Johnson says,** *The "star," or ruler of Mecca, held the key of the Caaba, a kind of idol shrine, and the possession of that key in a family was significant of its princely power. The loss of the key had made Muhomet a fallen star. The key of the bottomless pit now given him, not only restores him to the position of ruler of his own countrymen but makes him a prince among the kings of the earth.*

The Gospel of the *Sun of Righteousness* (Messiah) was *darkened* (hidden) from the Arabs, as Islam's smoke blinded them from seeing the truth. Islamic nations have been held in bondage by the false doctrine of Islam for 1,400 years, and to leave the religion to become a follower of Messiah is to be condemned to death.

Their caliphs' battle-cry was *"Before you is paradise; behind you are death and hell."* That's sadly ironic, as Islam's false religion rose from the *bottomless pit* of hell, and belief in Islam condemns people to the second death in the fiery pit.

In *The Last Prophecy*, Edward Bishop Elliott says, *To see how Mahomet was a fallen star, we must trace his history back to his birth. His origin was princely, being descended from one of the noblest families in Arabia. Gibbon says: "The grandfather of Mahomet and his lineal ancestors appeared in foreign and domestic transactions as the princes of their country." Then the governorship of Mecca and the keys of the Caaba (or holy place of religion amongst the Arabians) attached to the office passed into another branch of the family. Thus Mahomet became a star fallen from power. Mahomet, however, was imbued with a spirit calculated to struggle against and triumph over misfortune. That was already stiffing in his mind, which was to raise him far above a mere prince of Mecca, the scheme of reascending to the station he had lost by introducing a new system of superstition.*

The revelation Mohammed received that night was the first of many over the next twenty-three years that became the Qur'an, which means the *recitation*, as he merely recited what was given to him. Each year during the month of Ramadan, he would withdraw from the world and …in the cave of Hera, three miles from Mecca, he consulted the spirit of fraud or enthusiasm whose abode is not in the heaven, but in the mind of the prophet.

The cave is called *Jabal an-Nour* in Arabic, which means the *'Mountain of the Light'* or *'Hill of the Illumination.'* It's near Mecca in Saudi Arabia. It was a *'Mountain of Darkness'* as the blinding smoke of Islam's religion rose out of it, as a dark angel spoke the vision to Mohammed.

This cave has aptly suggested to interpreters the idea of the *pit of the abyss*, whence the pestilential fumes and darkness were seen to issue. The *smoke* that rose is the false doctrine of the Qur'an, which covers the Gospel of Messiah from the eyes of Arabs.

The phrase *'and to him was given the key of the bottomless pit'* points to Mohammed, who said, "I have been granted the keys of (all) treasures on earth."

215

215

The term *'bottomless'* is Strong's Greek Dictionary word *abussos*, the source of our English word *abyss*. Where does Satan, the god of this earth, reside? In a cave, in an abyss where light doesn't shine.

Mohammed's family had the *key*, as guardians of the sacred, black Kaaba stone in Mecca. But that key was given to another because Mohammed was too young to receive it when his grandfather died. Satan then offered him the *key* as the leader of Islam.

The Qur'an says that Mohammed was given the power of heaven and the fire below, *'I have been given the keys of all the treasures of the earth.'*

In *Horae Apocalypticae*, **Edward Bishop Elliott says,** *The Koran continually speaks of the key of God which opened to them the gates of the world and of religion. So in the Koran, 'Did not God give to his legate (Mohammed) the power of heaven which is above and fire which is beneath? With the key, did he not give him the title and power of a porter, that he may open to those whom he shall have chosen?'*

In a book called *Towards Understanding Islam,* **written to introduce English-speaking people to the basics of Islam, author Sayyid Abul Ala Maududi says,** *In that benighted era, there was a territory where darkness lay even heavier than elsewhere. They did not have a single educational institution or library. No one seemed interested in the cultivation and advancement of knowledge. A study of the remnants of their literature reveals how limited was their knowledge, how low was their standard of culture and civilization, how saturated were their minds with superstitions, how barbarous and ferocious were their thoughts and customs, and how decadent were their moral standards.*

There was no law except the law of the strongest. Loot, arson, and murder of innocent and weak people was the order of the day. Whatever notions they had of morals, culture, and civilization were primitive in the extreme. They could hardly discriminate between pure and impure, lawful and unlawful. Their lives were barbaric. They reveled in adultery, gambling, and drinking.

Looting and murder were part of their everyday existence. As regards their religious beliefs, they worshipped stones, trees, idols, stars, and spirits.

Regarding Mohammed, Maududi said, *He is completely illiterate and unschooled. He never gets a chance to sit in the company of learned men, for such men were non-existent in Arabia.*

Maududi tells his readers that Mohammed and his message came out of *"Arabia – out of the Abyss of Darkness."*

From that description, we see the environment that Mohammed lived in, as it was a *bottomless pit* of barbarianism; and we see that he was completely uneducated and ripe to be misled by knowledgeable people. What a perfect person to use, as he no doubt wanted to control Mecca very badly. Satan gave it back to him, and he became the great prophet that came out of the *dark abyss of Arabia.*

Hebrew word 5150 *'Arab'* means *to be darkened,* and we can see how Islam, which rose from the *abyss,* has *darkened* the world. In Scripture, *error* and *evil* are symbolized by *darkness, truth* by *light.*

Islam fosters all of the carnal human heart's wicked passions, such as war, murder, slavery, and lust. Indeed, it's from the *bottomless pit* of Satan's wicked mind. The Bishops of Rome created the perfect way to deceive many people with false religion and use their beliefs to carry out the Pope's agenda.

In *The Last Prophecy,* **Edward Bishop Elliott says,** *As the natural light of the sun is a fit emblem of the spiritual illumination that comes down from God and Father of lights, so may we infer that whatever is described as darkening the atmosphere, even as smoke from a pit, must be meant in the opposite sense of a moral or spiritual pollution. The deadly evil of Mohammed and his Qur'an came out from Arabia at the very time we speak of, with a creed the invention of fanaticism and fraud. In its system, the blessed God is described as cruel and unholy; and in its morals, pride, ferocity, superstition, and sensuality are held up for admiration and show palpably whence it had its origin.*

In *A Short History of the Near East,* **William S. Davis said about Mohammed,** *At that juncture, however, like a meteorite from the blue came into the world a new religion, a religion primarily of power and not of love, a militant fanaticism appealing to the evil which lies in men, and only partly to the good.* (4)

Edward Gibbon pointed to how Islam gave the Arabs a great cause, *The Arabs had languished in poverty and contempt, till Mohammed breathed into those savage hordes the soul of enthusiasm. Mohammed was alike instructed to preach and to fight, and the union of these opposite qualities contributed to his success: his voice invited the Arabs to freedom and victory, to arms and rapine, to the indulgence of their darling passions, in this world and the next.* (5) *The temper of a people thus armed against mankind was doubly inflamed by the domestic license of rapine, murder, and revenge.* (6)

The book *Paraphrase of the Revelation of Saint John According To E.B. Elliott* (1862) says, *And by the invention of a false religion, of hellish origin — from beginning to end a lie; in its pretensions superseding the gospel of the Lord Jesus; in its doctrines inculcating views of the blessed God dark, cruel, and unholy; and in its morals a system of pride, ferocity, superstition, and sensualism — he opened the bottomless pit; and his false religion rose suddenly into eminence, and was seen as if there arose a pestilential smoke out of the pit, as the smoke of a great furnace: and the imperial sun and the air or moral atmosphere were darkened by reason of the smoke of the pit.*

And there came out of the smoke locusts upon the earth: and unto them was given power, as the scorpions of the earth have power. Revelation 9:3

Literal locusts came from the east, from Arabia.

And Moses stretched forth his rod over the land of Egypt, and the LORD brought an east wind upon the land all that day, and all that night; and when it was morning, the east wind brought the locusts. Exodus 10:13

218

Scripture also defines that *locusts* represent Arabians.

> *For they came up with their cattle and their tents, and they came as grasshoppers (Hebrew word arbeh, locust) for multitude; for both they and their camels were without number: and they entered into the land to destroy it.* Judges 6:5

> *Now the Midianites and Amalekites, all the people of the East, were lying in the valley as numerous as locusts; and their camels were without number, as the sand by the seashore in multitude.* Judges 7:12

In describing the Ninevites, Nahum 3:15 refers to them as locusts. *There shall the fire devour thee; the sword shall cut thee off, it shall eat thee up like the cankerworm: make thyself many as the cankerworm, make thyself many as the locusts.*

The scorpion is of the same native locality, as we see Moses reminding the Israelites of Yah's goodness to them throughout their forty-year wanderings.

> *Who led thee through that great and terrible wilderness wherein were fiery serpents and scorpions.* Deuteronomy 8:15

Recall that the Strong's Hebrew word for 'nation' is 1471 *gowy*: which means *a Gentile, heathen, nation, people.* The nation of Islam is a *heathen troop of animals*, a *flight of locusts.*

In the Arabian romance *The Romance of Antar*, *locusts* are introduced as the national emblem of the Ishmaelites, *"I shall command these armies, numerous as the locusts, to assault you, and to grind you like grain, and to ride you like lions."* Mohammedan tradition speaks of *locust* having dropped into the hands of Mohammed, bearing on their wings this inscription, *"We are the army of the Great God."*

Niebuhr, a famous traveler of the nineteenth century, journeying through Arabia, described the appearance of the swarms of locusts that afflicted that region: *The swarms of these insects darken the air and appear at a distance like clouds of smoke*

Nothing would better represent the numbers of the Saracenic hordes that came out of Arabia, who spread over Egypt, Libya, Mauritania, Spain, and that threatened to spread over Europe — than such an army of locusts. The religion of Islam became the motivating force that inspired the Arabs to go on their mission of devastation.

In *The Caliphate: Its Rise, Decline, and Fall* (1891), William Muir says, *<u>Like swarms from a beehive or like locusts darkening the air</u>, the one Arabian tribe after the other emerged and rolled into the North, and then spread out in great hordes to the East and the West." Thus the Arab Moslems then almost totally wiped out the Christian Church – all the way from Northern India to Northwest Africa. Onward and still onward like swarms from the hive, or <u>flights of locusts darkening the land</u>, tribe after tribe issued forth and hastening northward spread in great masses to the east and to the west.* (9)

In *The Ottoman Empire* (1829), Edward Upham says, *The Persian Empire soon attracted the arms of 'these locusts' as the swarms of the Saracens were not inaptly called.* (10)

In *Essay on Language* (1825), William Samuel Cardell says, *In the seventh century, an extra-ordinary individual founded a religious system, which was overspreading the fairest portion of the earth. The Mahometan banners were everywhere displayed, and the Saracens, like the <u>locust</u> of a former age, over-spread the land.* (11)

In *History of Latin Christianity* (1854), Henry Hart Milman says, *In a passage in a later letter to Count Boso, <u>the Pope describes the Saracens as an army of locusts</u>, turning the whole land into a wilderness: extensive regions were so desolate as to be inhabited only by wild beasts.* (12)

***And it was commanded them that they should not hurt the grass of the earth, neither any green thing, neither any tree; but only those men which have not the seal of God in their foreheads.* Revelation 9:4**

When real locusts invade a land, all vegetation is devoured, so obviously, these locusts aren't literal but symbolic. During his life, Muhammad gave various injunctions to his forces and adopted Islamic military jurisprudence practices toward war. Abu Bakr, Mohammed's companion, and the first Caliph declared, *"Bring no harm to the trees, nor burn them with fire, especially those which are fruitful."*

That is a perfect match! Unlike the Goths of the previous trumpet judgment, who had a *scorched earth policy* of burning everything up, Mohammedans were commanded not to harm the trees or the fields so that they could take them over and prosper from them.

In *The Last Prophecy*, Edward Bishop Elliott says, *The command to not destroy the palm trees, or fields of corn, of fruit trees; was a dictate of policy, not of mercy; for by following this plan the Saracens had, soon after their conquest, formed flourishing countries round them. It was a marked peculiarity, for in other invasions, as the Gothic, fire, sword, and devastation tracked the invader's progress, and was accordingly prefigured in the Apocalyptic imagery; but with the Saracens, it was the very reverse, and this reverse still more connects it with the prediction now before us.*

Abu-Bakr, Muhammed's successor, declared: *You will meet religious people, living in recluse cloisters… Leave them alone, do not kill them. You shall meet another sort of people who belong to the school of Satan, who have their heads shorn as a crown (tonsure); split their skulls without mercy, unless they become Muslims or pay tribute. They wore their hair long and disheveled and shaved their heads when they were ordained priests. The circular tonsure was sacred and mysterious; it was the crown of thorns, but it was likewise a royal diadem and every priest was a king.*

And here we have another match, as the command is to leave Catholic monks alone but to attack Orthodox Christians. A tonsure is a practice of cutting or shaving some or all of the hair on the scalp as a sign of religious devotion or humility. The Muslims encountered tonsured Orthodox Christians, the idolaters and saint worshipers of the Eastern Roman Empire, who were not sealed with the Holy Spirit.

This was done out of vengeance from the ACBP of Rome against people who proclaimed that he is not their leader. The bigger picture is that

Yah used the Muslims of Islam as a scourge and punishment upon those who did not have His seal on their foreheads.

And to them it was given that they should not kill them, but that they should be tormented five months: and their torment was as the torment of a scorpion, when he striketh a man. Revelation 9:5

Literal locusts come out for five months, from April to September. Using the year-for-a-day principle, five months points to 150 years. (five months x 30 days = 150 years). In 632, Mohammed died, and the Arabs moved out of Arabia to conquer other lands. This was the time of the supremacy of Islamic power, and for one hundred fifty years, they conquered Arabia, Palestine, Syria, Egypt, Spain, and North Africa.

They moved north, east, and west; to Armenia, Cypress, Crete, Syria, Persia, Kazakstan, Babylonia, Sardinia, Corsica, and France. The great Charles Martel, called the *'Hammer,'* finally stopped them in 732 at the *Battle of Tours* in Northern France.

In *Horae Apocalypticae*, Edward Bishop Elliott says, *In ten years (634– 644), the Saracens had reduced to his obedience 36,000 cities or castles, destroyed 4000 churches, and built 1400 mosques for the exercise of the religion of Mohamet.*

In 762, caliph Almansor built Bagdad as his empire's future seat and called it the *City of Peace*. The Saracens no longer made rapid conquests but only engaged in ordinary wars like other nations. In 782, they signed the *Treaty of Constantinople*, which brought peace. The five months, 150 prophetic years, were fulfilled from 632-782.

In *The Book Of Revelation Explained* (1847), Joseph Benson says, *As often as they besieged Constantinople, they were repulsed and defeated. They attempted it in the reign of Constantine Pogonatus, A.D. 672, but their men and ships were miserably destroyed by the sea-fire invented by Callinicus, and after seven years fruitless pains, they were compelled to raise the siege and to conclude a peace. They attempted it again in the reign of Leo Isauricus, A.D. 718; but they were forced to desist by famine and pestilence, and losses of* various kinds. In this attempt, they exceeded their commission, and therefore they were not crowned with their usual success. The taking of this city, and the putting an end to this empire, was a work reserved for another power, as we shall see under the next trumpet.

In *Notes on the Handbook of Revelation* (1852), Albert Barnes says, *It should be added, also, that in the year 762, Almanzor, the caliph, built Bagdad and made it the capital of the Saracen Empire. Henceforward that became the seat of Arabic learning, luxury, and power, and the wealth and talent of the Saracen Empire were gradually drawn to that capital, and they ceased to vex and annoy the Christian world.*

And in those days shall men seek death, and shall not find it; and shall desire to die, and death shall flee from them. Revelation 9:6

The Mohammedans were not allowed to eradicate the apostate Christians. They gave them a choice; convert to become a Muslim, be killed if they decided to challenge them, or agree to be second-class citizens and pay tax to the Muslims. If a Muslim came to their door, they had to bring them in and feed them. Many didn't have the spirit of Yah to accept martyrdom for their faith. They chose to become second class citizens who were subservient to the Muslims. They sought death but couldn't find it because they had not the nerve to fight.

And the shapes of the locusts were like unto horses prepared unto battle; and on their heads were as it were crowns like gold, and their faces were as the faces of men. Revelation 9:7

The nomadic Bedouin people prized the Arabian horse, often being brought inside the family tent for shelter and theft protection. More than any other people group, the horse fills up their poetry, art, and romantic legends. The Arabian breed has great capacity in sustaining speed over great distances while requiring less food and water than other horses, making it the perfect *'war horse'* for the Arabs in the desert.

The Arab warriors issuing from Arabia with their great speed, far-ranging, and irresistible progress; were fittingly symbolized by locust swarms, likened to *horses prepared for battle.*

This self-portrait of Antar, who was a contemporary of Mohammed, gives us a visual of the fulfillment. He's on a *horse that is prepared for battle.* The *crowns of gold* represent the gold and yellow saffron-colored turbans that they wore. They had *faces were as the faces of men* because they had beards, which is a sign of their masculinity. Romans and other races shaved their faces, so this would have stood out to John.

In the Arabian tale *Antar,* it's written that God intended for the Arabs *"that their turbans should be unto them instead of diadems (crowns)."* (15)

Ezekiel 23:42 says, *And a voice of a multitude being at ease was with her: and with the men of the common sort were brought Sabeans (Arabs) from the wilderness, which put bracelets upon their hands, and <u>beautiful crowns upon their heads</u>.*

And they had hair as the hair of women, and their teeth were as the teeth of lions. **Revelation 9:8**

Antar also refers to shoulder-length hair and turbans on Arab men. *He adjusted himself properly, twisted his whiskers, and folded up his hair under his turban, drawing it off his shoulders.*

In *Natural History*, Pliny the Elder (23-79), the Apostle John's contemporary, spoke of *"the turbaned Arabs with their uncut hair."*

The Muslim warriors had long hair like women, which when they were preparing for battle, they would tie it up under the turbans. *'And their teeth were as the teeth of lion's* means that they were savage and ferocious.

> Joel 1:6 points to the Assyrians, who were fierce as a great lion: *For a nation is come up upon my land, strong, and without number, whose teeth are the teeth of a lion, and he hath the cheek teeth of a great lion.*

> In describing Arabia, Isaiah 30:6, says: *the land of trouble and anguish, from whence come the young and old lion, the viper and fiery flying serpent, they will carry their riches upon the shoulders of young asses, and their treasures upon the bunches of camels, to a people that shall not profit them.*

***Antar: A Bedoueen Romance* says,** *But I must assail you without further preparation, and I shall command these armies, numerous as the locusts, to assault you and to grind you like grain, and to ride you like lions.*

Roman Empire historian Edward Gibbon documented, *The intrepid souls of the Arabs were fired with enthusiasm; the death which they had always despised became an object of hope and desire. The first companions of Mohamet advanced to the battle with a fearless confidence; there is no danger where there is no chance: they were ordained to perish in their beds; or they were safe and invulnerable amidst the darts of the enemy. Eutychius, the Patriarch of Constantinople, observed that the Saracens fought with the courage of lions.*

"The sword," says Mahomet, *"is the key of heaven and of hell; a drop of blood shed in the cause of God, a night spent in arms, is of more avail than two months of fasting and prayer: whosoever falls in battle, his sins are forgiven."*

Seventy-two Houris, or black-eyed girls, of resplendent beauty, blooming youth, virgin purity, and exquisite sensibility, will be created for the use of the meanest believer; a moment of pleasure will be prolonged to a thousand years; and his faculties will be increased a hundred fold, to render him worthy of his felicity. (16)

In *Horae Apocalypticae*, **Edward Bishop Elliott records,** *"Who,"* said Mahomet, after announcing his mission, *"will be my Vizier and Lieutenant?" "O prophet,"* replied Ali (who Mahomet <u>named Lion of God</u>), *"I am the man. Whoever rises against thee, I will dash out his teeth, tear out his eyes, break his legs, rip open his belly. O Prophet, I will be thy Vizier."*

And they had breastplates, as it were breastplates of iron; and the sound of their wings was as the sound of chariots of many horses. Revelation 9:9

The Arab army wore chain-mail (*breastplates of iron*) as they went into battle. Mohammed, in the Qur'an, says: *"God has given you coats of mail to defend you in your wars."* (17) In the *Battle of Ohud*, the second battle that Mohammed fought, with the Koreish of Mecca (624), seven hundred were armed with cuirasses. (18)

In *Notes on the Handbook of Revelation* **(1852), Albert Barnes says,** *In the poem Antar, the steel and iron cuirasses of the Arab warriors are frequently noticed: 'A warrior immersed in steel armor.' 'Fifteen thousand men armed with cuirasses, and well accoutred for war.' 'They were clothed in iron armor and brilliant cuirasses.' 'Out of the dust appeared horsemen clad in iron.'* (19)

The *'sounds of their wings'* represent the rapid conquests of the Saracens, as they moved over countries as swiftly as locust, their many horses causing a great sound.

Adam Clarke noted that the horse and rider were as one being. *The Arabs are the most expert horsemen in the world: they lived so much on horseback that the horse and his rider seem to make but one animal.*

226

And they had tails like unto scorpions, and there were stings in their tails: and their power was to hurt men five months. **Revelation 9:10**

The Bible notes the Ishmael was an *archer*, and his descendants mastered the skill. The Saracens were excellent horsemen and archers, and they had the unique ability to fight rearwards, shooting arrows backward with precision while at full gallop; thus, *there were stings in their tails*.

Edward Gibbon says, *I shall here observe what I must often repeat, that the charge of the Arabs was not like that of the Greeks and Romans, the effort of a firm and compact infantry: their military force was chiefly formed of cavalry and archers.*

And they had a king over them, which is the angel of the bottomless pit, whose name in the Hebrew tongue is Abaddon, but in the Greek tongue hath his name Apollyon. **Revelation 9:11**

Proverbs 30:27 says, *The locusts have no king, yet go they forth all of them by bands.* Mohammed has not been referred to as a *king*. The *fallen angel of the bottomless pit* is Satan. *Abaddon* and *Apollyon* are words that essentially mean *destroyer* or *one who exterminates*, which is what Satan does. Allah, Satan, the *destroying angel,* is the king over Islam.

One woe is past; and, behold, there come two woes more hereafter. **Revelation 9:12**

The fulfillment of the fifth trumpet prophecy is one of the most vivid in Revelation, as we can see that all of the Arabian references were pointing to the rise of Islam and the Mohammedan army, who were sent to attack apostate Christians.

The fifth trumpet effectively ends in 762, and the sixth trumpet starts in 1062, which is a 300-year time gap. In the 9th century, Arabian caliphs began employing Turkish soldiers as mercenaries. The Turkish leaders gained authority, and before long, they took control of the territory where the caliph reigned.

CHAPTER 46 – THE ANTICHRIST HEIGHT OF POWER

And all that dwell upon the earth shall worship him, whose names are not written in the book of life of the Lamb slain from the foundation of the world. **Revelation 13:8**

The word *'earth'* is Greek *'ge,'* which points to the *land* of the Roman Empire. Though the ACBPs were given civil and ecclesiastic authority over the Roman beast kingdom in 538, it took centuries for them to ascend to full power. The Popes of the 11th-12th century's issued bulls and declarations of their authority, and most kings *revered* the ACBP.

In *Romanism And The Reformation*, Henry Grattan Guinness says, *The pontificate of Gregory VII (1073-85) was the era of the Papacy unveiled. At this date, the pope dropped the mask of the shepherd and exchanged the crook for the scepter and the sword. The accession of Gregory VII, or Hildebrand, as he was called, created, as we have before stated, the Papal theocracy. Do you know what this means? He claimed for himself, in the name of God, absolute and unlimited dominion over all the states of Christendom, as the successor of St. Peter, and vicar of Christ upon earth. The popes who came after him pushed these claims to their utmost extent. At the end of the thirteenth century, they assumed the proud title of masters of the world.*

When the papacy was at its height of power, the kings of countries bowed to his authority, literally and figuratively. Nicholas I, who was Pope from 858-867, said: *"Fear, then, our wrath and the thunders of our vengeance; for Jesus Christ has appointed us [the popes] with his own mouth absolute judges of all men; and kings themselves are submitted to our authority."* (1)

Pope Innocent III (1198-1216) was the *'most powerful of all the Popes.'* He proclaimed himself to be the *'Vicar of God,' 'Vicar of Christ,'* and *'Supreme Sovereign over the Church and the World.'* He claimed the right to depose kings and princes; and that *"All things on earth and in Heaven and in Hell — are subject to the Vicar of Christ."*

The ACBP proclaimed that he led the one true church and that those who are are outside of it are not saved; that the Scriptures were for priests only, and he prohibited laymen from possessing them, even issuing a decree that those who read the Scriptures should be *'put to death,'* and that anyone who disagrees with the Papal church dogma must be *'burned without pity.'*

He decreed the confession of sins to priests, the blasphemous teaching of transubstantiation, papal infallibility, and instituted the Inquisition and the extermination of heretics, including the massacre of the Albigenses. He declared, *"We may according to the fullness of our power, dispose of the law and dispense above the law. Those whom the Pope of Rome doth separate, it is not a man that separates them but God. For the Pope holdeth place on earth, not simply of a man but of the true God."*

In *The Approaching End Of The Age*, Henry Grattan Guinness says, *Every utterance of the tiara-crowned monarch was heard with awe, every command was implicitly obeyed. Men trembled under his curse and gloried in his benediction as if they had been those of Deity. The thunders of his interdicts shook the nations, and the fires of his excommunications spread death and destruction abroad. No wonder the sentence is addressed to every pope on his coronation, "Know thou art the father of princes and kings, and the governor of the world;" no wonder that he is worshipped by cardinals and archbishops and bishops, by priests and monks and nuns innumerable, by all the millions of Catholics throughout the world; no wonder that he has dethroned monarchs and given away kingdoms, dispensed pardons and bestowed indulgences, canonized saints, remitted purgatorial pains, promulgated dogmas, and issued bulls and laws and extravagants, laid empires under interdicts, bestowed benedictions, and uttered anathemas!*

Who is like unto him on earth? What are great men, philosophers, statesmen, conquerors, princes, kings, and even emperors, of the earth compared to HIM? Their glory is of the earth, earthy; his is from above, it is Divine! He is the representative of Christ, the Creator, and Redeemer, the Lord of all.

He is as Christ; he takes the place of Christ. He is as God, as God on earth. This blasphemous notion is the keystone of the entire Papal arch; it is the stupendous axis on which the whole Papal world has rotated for ages, and is rotating at this hour.

In *Romanism And The Reformation*, Henry Grattan Guinness says, *It must never be forgotten that the Roman Papacy was for long ages an absolute, unlimited, tyrannical monarchy, a worldly, secular government. It had its territorial dominions, its provinces, cities, and towns; it had its court, its nobles, its ambassadors, its army, its police, its legislature, its jurisprudence, its laws, its advocates, its prisons, its revenues, its taxes, its exchequer, its mint, its arsenals, its forts, its foreign treaties, and its ambitious, selfish plans and policy, just as much as any mere secular kingdom. But it was also something very different it was the head of the Latin Church; it was a great ecclesiastical power; it was a religion as well as a government. As such, it had its dioceses and parishes, its spiritual hierarchy of archbishops, bishops, priests, and deacons, its theological schools and colleges and professors, its abbots and deans, its councils and synods and chapters, its monasteries and convents, its orders of mendicant and other friars, its services and sacraments, its creeds and confessions, its doctrines and discipline, and its penances and punishments.*

Joseph Benson's Commentary on Revelation (1847) says, *The power of this new Roman government became so great, by divine permission, that it prevailed against the worshippers of God, either to force them to a compliance with the corruptions established by its authority, or to persecute them for their constancy; and this oppressive power was extended far and wide, even over all, or many, kindreds, and tongues, and nations.*

Billions of Catholics have *revered (worshiped)* the Pope. It's heartbreaking that the Popes have convinced them that they're in the *'one true church,'* but it is the ACBP's *apostate church.* Civil and ecclesiastic leaders bowed to the Popes throughout history, kissed their rings, and *revered* them. Even today, we see that with the leaders of countries visiting Vatican City to bow to the Pope.

CHAPTER 47 - THE SIXTH TRUMPET JUDGMENT
1062-1453 AD

The Western third of the Roman Empire fell to the barbarians during the first-fourth trumpet judgments. During the fifth trumpet, the Muslims attacked the middle third and the Eastern Roman Empire. And the sixth trumpet judgment leads to Constantinople's fall.

In *History Unveiling Prophecy*, Henry Grattan Guinness says, *There is perhaps no point on which historical interpreters of the Apocalypse from Mede to Goodwin onwards are more agreed than in the application of the fifth and sixth trumpets to the overthrow of the corrupt and apostate Eastern Empire by the Saracens and Turks.*

Recall that the word *'woe'* is pointing to Yah executing judgment against an apostate people group. That's what is taking place during the fifth and sixth trumpet judgments. This gives a very different perspective to those who point to Muslims killing millions of *'Christians.'*

And the sixth angel sounded, and I heard a voice from the four horns of the golden altar which is before God, Saying to the sixth angel which had the trumpet, Loose the four angels which are bound in the great river Euphrates. Revelation 9:13-14

The *'golden altar'* is the place of intercession, mediation, and atonement; by Messiah, our High Priest. The Eastern Orthodox Church teaches that Mary is the intercessor to the Father. They esteem Mary as the *Queen of Heaven* and pray to icons, relics, and dead saints, so they were deserving of judgment. Google images of '**orthodox church Mary**.'

The Old Testament points to the Euphrates River area as the place where the great kingdoms of Assyria, Babylon, and Persia, arose to be used to carry out judgments against pagan people groups. Now the Turks have been gathered into this area, to be released to attack the apostate Orthodox Christians.

The historical rise of the Turks was recorded by Edward Gibbon, who documented that by the 11th century, the Turks (also known as the *Tartars* and *Turkomans*) controlled the area near the Euphrates River; but that they did not cross the river to make conquests on the other side until the 11th century. According to Dr. Strong, the word '*Euphrates*' means '*to break forth - rushing*.' It seems that this meaning was based on the fact that when the snows of Mr. Ararat melted, the Euphrates became a roaring, raging torrent that often overflowed its banks.

Isaiah 8:7-8 points to a *river* of people, the Assyrians, who were sent in judgment of the House of Israel.

> *Now therefore, behold the Lord brings up upon them, the waters of the river, strong and many, even the king of Assyria, and all his glory: and he shall come up over all his channels, and go over all his banks: And he shall pass through Judah; he shall overflow and go over, he shall reach even to the neck; and the stretching out of his wings shall fill the breadth of thy land, O Immanuel* (Israel).

Isaiah was likening the Assyrian power to the Euphrates' overflowing when it's flooding, thus the Euphrates River represents a rushing, invading power. The Turks of the Ottoman Empire soon overflowed the Eastern Roman Empire.

In *The Rise And Fall Of The Papacy* (1701), Robert Fleming says, *They were bound at the river Euphrates for a time, but are now let loose to pass that river, and make their inroads into the Roman Empire, and to erect themselves into a monarchy upon the ruins of it. For at their remarkable passing the river Euphrates, they were under the command of Solyman Shahum and his three sons; and when he was drowned in the passage, they brought themselves under four other captains, viz. Ostrogules and his three sons; of whom was the famous Ottoman, who a little after laid the foundations of that great empire, over which his family keeps the sceptre to this day.*

In his *Exposition of the Apocalypse,* **Thomas Goodwin (1639) says of the sixth trumpet, or Euphratean woe,** *No prophecy doth or can more punctually describe any nation or event than this doth the Turks, and their irruption upon Eastern Europe, who when they came first out of their native country, about the year 1040 after Christ, did seat themselves first by the River Euphrates, and were divided into four several governments or kingdoms, etc., and completed their conquest of the Roman Empire in the year 1453, which is 186 years since, who possess that whole Eastern Empire unto this day.*

And the four angels were loosed, which were prepared for an hour, and a day, and a month, and a year, for to slay the third part of men.
Revelation 9:15

The Turks lived near the Euphrates, but the river prevented (*bound them*) them there. In 1055, the Caliph of Bagdad asked Togral Beg to be his protector, and he was given the title of Sultan. When he died, the charge was given to his son, Alp Arslan.

In 1062, leader Alp crossed the Euphrates to wage a holy war against Greek '*Christendom.*' He died in battle and was succeeded by Malek Shah, who divided the kingdom under his four sons, who represent the '*four angels,*' as they were the leaders who were released from the Euphrates River to execute Yah's will.

The People's New Testament by Barton Johnson (1891) says,
There were four angels. This would imply, in some way, four powers. It is remarkable that these people were divided into four bodies, which formed four kingdoms, under the four grandsons of the leader who established the empire of the Turks in western Asia. The prince who was commissioned by the Caliph to attack the Greek Empire was named Togrul, but dying, his son, Alp Arslan, led the Turks across the Euphrates, and when he was slain in battle, he was succeeded by Malek Shah. If the reader will open at the 532nd page of Gibbon, Vol. V., he will find that the mighty empire of Malek Shah was divided into four principalities, under his four sons, which are described by the historian under the names of Persia, Kerman or India, Syria, Roum or Asia Minor, extending

from the shores of the Indian Ocean to the Mediterranean. There are then four angels or messengers of destruction.

When you apply the *'day for a year principle'* of prophecy, one year = 360 years, one month = 30 years, one day = one year, an hour = approx two months, for a total of just over 391 years. Bible prophecy is based on a 360-day year, as that used to be the astronomical design before the 8th century BC. But that's a story for another day.

In 1062, the Turks moved out of the Euphrates Valley to conquer. For 391 years, they conquered the remaining third part of the Roman Empire. By 1391, the Turks had captured most of the Byzantium Empire area. Then in 1453, they captured the prized capital city of Constantinople, the headquarters of the Eastern Roman Empire. That's a perfect fulfillment of the period that John gave us, as it's 391 years.

The *'third part of men'* is not saying that one-third of the earth's population would die. It's saying that the Eastern Roman Empire would be conquered, and their leadership effectively ended. On May 16th, 1453, the Byzantine Empire ceased to exist; and its capital became the seat of the Ottoman Empire.

Joseph Benson's Commentary on Revelation (1847) says, *That is, as before, the men of the Roman Empire, and especially in Europe, the third part of the world. The Latin or western empire was broken to pieces under the four first trumpets; the Greek or eastern empire was cruelly hurt and tormented under the fifth trumpet; and here, under the sixth trumpet, it is to be slain and utterly destroyed. The third part of men, or the Roman Empire then represented by the Constantinople monarchy, is to be slain, and not merely tormented.*

In *History Unveiling Prophecy*, Henry Grattan Guinness says,
The story of the Turks in Eastern Europe is that of a succession of dreadful massacres without a parallel in the history of the world. With the capture of Constantinople, when Constantine XIV, the last Emperor of the East, fell and was "buried under a mountain of the slain."

And the number of the army of the horsemen were two hundred thousand thousand: and I heard the number of them. **Revelation 9:16**

Messiah is telling us how the troops of the horsemen would be organized. Instead of being translated as '*two hundred thousand thousand*' or '*two hundred million,*' the language should read '*two myriads of myriads.*' The Strong's Greek word for *thousand* is 3461 *murias*: which means *a ten-thousand; by extension, a myriad or indefinite number:—ten thousand.* John's vision represented groups of *ten thousand*, which the Turks fulfilled as they organized their armies into units of ten thousand.

Roman Empire historian Edward Gibbon documented that 200,000 horsemen were available for battle: *As the subject nations marched under the standard of the Turks, their cavalry, both men and horses, were proudly computed by millions; one of the effective armies consisted of four hundred thousand soldiers. Gaznevide, a sultan, had inquired what supply of men he (a chief of the Seljuks) could furnish for military service. "If you send," replied Ismael, "one of these arrows into our camp, fifty thousand of your servants will mount on horseback. And if that number should not be sufficient, send this second arrow to the horde of Balik, and you will find fifty thousand more.""But," Gaznevide, disassembling his anxiety, "if I should stand in need of the whole force of your kindred tribes?" Islam replied "Dispatch my bow, and as it is circulated around, the summons will be obeyed by two hundred thousand horse." The myriads of Turkish horse overspread a frontier of 600 miles from Tauris to Erzeroum, and the blood of 130,000 (Orthodox) Christians was a grateful sacrifice to the Arabian prophet.*

Joseph Benson's Commentary on Revelation (1847) says, *When Mohammed the Second besieged Constantinople, he had about four hundred thousand men in his army, besides a powerful fleet of thirty larger and two hundred lesser ships.*

In *The Art of War in the Middle Ages,* **Oman says,** *The Turkish invasion was a scourge far heavier than that of the Saracens. While the latter when bent on permanent conquest offered the tribute as an alternative to the 'Koran or the sword,' the Seljouks were mere savages who slew for the pleasure of slaying.*

And thus I saw the horses in the vision, and them that sat on them, having breastplates of fire, and of jacinth, and brimstone: and the heads of the horses were as the heads of lions; and out of their mouths issued fire and smoke and brimstone. **Revelation 9:17**

The Turks, like the Saracens, rode horses, and their uniforms were red (*fire*), blue (*jacinth*), and yellow (*brimstone*).

In *Horae Apocalypticae*, Edward Bishop Elliott quotes Daubuz, an English scholar, writing of this time, said, *From their first appearance the Ottomans have affected to wear warlike apparel of scarlet, blue and yellow: a descriptive trait the more marked from its contrast to the military appearance of Greeks, Franks or Saracens (Arabs) who were contemporary.* (4)

In *The Last Prophecy*, Edward Bishop Elliott says, *It needs but to see the Turkish cavalry to be struck with their rich and varied coloring. The word hyacinthine or jacinth fixes the meaning of the other two words, fire-like, sulphur-like, necessarily to color; these words, fire, and sulphur, having no indistinct bearing on other characteristics of the Turkish armies. The heads of the horses, being unnatural, are clearly symbolical; the symbol being constantly used to designate the leaders of the people, and that of lions we take to signify the lion-like haughtiness of their characters and bearing.*

The adoption of the Turk's weapons was so rapid that they preceded both their European and Middle Eastern adversaries in establishing centralized and permanent troops specialized in the manufacturing and handling of firearms. *'Fire, smoke, and brimstone'* is the perfect symbolic representation of gunpowder.

Messiah is telling us that the army's destroying power would appear to issue out of the horses' mouths. Turkish horsemen were able to fire muskets while charging on horseback into battle, which would have put the end of the rifle near the horse's head, making the *fire, smoke, and brimstone* appear to come out of the horse's mouths. During the rule of

Sultan Mehmed II, they were drilled with firearms and became perhaps the first standing infantry force equipped with firearms in the world.

The Turkish tribes carried a *horse*-tail, instead of banners, as they rode into battle. They wore them on their Fez's (hats). The more horsetails, the more important you were. This is seen with the modern-day Shriners, who wear red Fez's that have a scimitar, a Muslim sword on it, with their symbol of the crescent moon and the five-pointed star. The red color represents the blood of those who the Turks killed.

The phrase '*the heads of the horses were like the heads of lions*' points to the Turkish leaders. It's no coincidence that the leaders, who began the 391-year attack on the Eastern Roman Empire, had Arslan's name, a Turkic masculine surname, which is translated as '*lion*.' Alp Arslan, whose real name was Muhammad bin Dawud Chaghr, was known as the *Heroic Lion*. Edward Gibbon noted that Alp Arslan passed the Euphrates as the '*head*' of the Turkish cavalry. The *head*, the horsemen leader, was like a *lion*, just like Revelation 9:17 proclaimed.

Alp's successor was named Kilidge Arslan, which means the *Noble Lion*. Other Turkish leaders had names like *the brace lion*, *the heroic lion*, etc. The Turks compare their king to the *lion* and other kings to little dogs. The *lion-head* was then, and is now, a notable ensign among the Turks. Here's a silver dirham of Kaykhusraw II from 1240 AD, featuring a *lion* and the *sun*, representing the lion leader.

In *The Slave Kings & the Islamic Conquest*, **Andre Wink says,**
All authors of adab (Islamic etiquette) works, manuals of war, and mirror for princes, agree on the military superiority of the Turks, their hardiness, their skill with horses and the bow and arrow, as well as their 'lion-like' qualities and pride. Ultimately the 'lion-like' Turk was linked to the climate of his country of origin, which predisposed him to a certain robustness and military valor. (5)

Interestingly, C. S. Lewis may have created the name *Aslan*, the lion in *The Chronicles of Narnia* series, based on Arslan's Turkish name.

By these three was the third part of men killed, by the fire, and by the smoke, and by the brimstone, which issued out of their mouths. **Revelation 9:18**

It's not saying that all of the men in the Eastern Roman Empire would be killed, but rather that the kingdom was killed politically and religiously. This attack ended the Eastern Roman Empire, and Constantinople, the home of Orthodox Christians, became the Turks' home and was renamed Istanbul.

Mehmed II took over the Turkish throne in the early 15th century, and he proclaimed the title of *Hunkiar*, which means *'Slayer of men.'* Roman Empire historian Edward Gibbon documented Mehmed II's unrelenting resolve to capture Constantinople: *"I ask a present far more valuable and important – Constantinople."* (6)

The *'fire, smoke, and brimstone'* describe the large cannons that the Turks used in this battle. Constantinople was an almost impregnable fortress because of her strong walls. In preparation for his attack, Mahomet II researched the latest weapons that might aid him in penetrating the city, including the newly developed use of gunpowder in artillery. Instrumental to this Ottoman advancement in arms production was a somewhat mysterious figure named Orban, a master founder who initially tried to sell his services to the Byzantines, but they could not secure the funds needed to hire him.

Orban then left Constantinople and approached Mehmed II, claiming that his weapon could blast *'the walls of Babylon itself.'* Given abundant funds and materials, the Hungarian engineer established a foundry. Within a few months, they produced a 27-foot long cannon that could hurl a 600-pound missile over a mile.   This photo is of the *Dardanelles Gun,* which was cast in 1464 and based on the Orban bombard used for the Ottoman besiegers of Constantinople in 1453.

In *The Book Of Revelation Explained* **(1847), Joseph Benson says,**
By these, the Othmans made such havoc and destruction in the Greek or eastern empire. Amurath the Second broke into Peloponnesus and took several strong places by means of his artillery. But his son Mohammed, at the siege of Constantinople, employed such great guns as were never made before. One is described to have been of such a monstrous size that it was drawn by seventy yoke of oxen and by two thousand men. Two more discharged a stone of the weight of two talents. Others emitted a stone of the weight of half a talent. But the greatest of all discharged a ball of the weight of three talents or about three hundred pounds; and the report of this cannon is said to have been so great, that all the country round about was shaken to the distance of forty furlongs. For forty days, the wall was battered by these guns, and so many breaches were made that the city was taken by assault, and an end put to the Grecian empire.

In *Diadem of Histories*, **Ottoman Empire historian Sa'd Al-Dīn says,**
The Moslems placed their cannon in an effective position and threw up their entrenchments. The gates and ramparts of Constantinople were pierced in a thousand places. The flames which issued from the mouths of these instruments

239

of warfare, of brazen bodies, and fiery jaws, cast grief and dismay among the miscreants. The smoke, which spread itself in the air, and ascended towards the heavens, rendered the brightness of day somber as night; and the face of the world soon became as dark as the black fortune of the unhappy infidels. (8)

Roman Empire historian Edward Gibbon documented, *For the conveyance of this destructive engine, a frame or carriage of thirty wagons was linked together and drawn long by a team of sixty oxen; two hundred men on both sides were stationed to poise and support the rolling weight; two hundred and fifty workmen marched before to smooth the way and repair the bridges; and near two months were employed in a laborious journey of one hundred and fifty miles. The great cannon of Mahomet has been separately noticed, an important and visible object in the history of the times; but that enormous engine was flanked by two fellows almost of equal magnitude; the long order of the Turkish artillery was pointed against the walls; fourteen batteries thundered at once on the most accessible places, and of one of these it is ambiguously expressed, that it was mounted with one hundred and thirty guns, or that it discharged on hundred and thirty bullets. From the lines, the galleys, and the bridge, the Ottoman artillery thundered on all sides; and the camp and city, were involved in a cloud of smoke which could only be dispelled by the final deliverance or destruction of the Roman Empire.* (9)

For their power is in their mouth, and in their tails: for their tails were like unto serpents, and had heads, and with them they do hurt. Revelation 9:19

This was the first recorded time that a city fell because of superior artillery. It's pointing to cannons, pulled by horses, and then swung around to aim at their victims. They lit the fuse at the cannon's *'tail'* to ignite the *brimstone* (gunpowder), which is the *power* that propelled the huge balls from the *mouth* of the cannon. The cannons shot forth with *'fire and smoke'* to take down the battle fortified walls.

In *The Byzantine Achievement: An Historical Perspective*, **Robert Byron says,** *This was the first event of historic importance engineered with the* *most important weapon of modern warfare: gunpowder. If it was not for gunpowder, the siege would have failed.*

The name *"basilisks"* was given to the Turkish cannons of the 15ᵗʰ century, named after the famous *serpent* who *'breathed fire and brimstone.'* They were long and relatively thin compared to the larger cannons; so they looked like a serpent. These cannons launched metal balls out of the lion's mouth, which hissed as they shot through the air.

Gibbon documented, *The volleys of lances and arrows were accompanied with the smoke, the sound, and the fire of the musketry and cannon ... the long order of the Turkish artillery was pointed against the walls; fourteen batteries thundering at once on the most accessible places ... the fortifications which had stood for ages against hostile violence, were dismantled on all sides by the Ottoman cannon, many breaches opened, and near the gate of St. Romanus, four towers leveled with the ground ... from the lines, the galleys and the bridge, the Ottoman artillery thundered on all sides, the camp and city, the Greeks and the Turks, were involved in a cloud of smoke, which could only be dispelled by the final deliverance or destruction of the Greek Empire ... the double walls were reduced by the cannon to a heap of ruins' ... the Turks at length ... rushing through the breaches ... Constantinople was subdued, her empire subverted, and her religion trampled in the dust by the Muslim conquerors"*

Constantinople's walls stood for eleven hundred years, and it repelled Goths, Huns, Avars, Persians, Bulgarians, and the Saracens; one after another, its walls remaining impregnable. On April 6, 1453, Mahomet II assembled 258,000 men to commence the attack.

There's no mistaking the exacting fulfillment of the *serpent*-like cannons, shooting heavy balls out of their *mouths*, emitting *fire and smoke* from the *brimstone*, to knock down the once-impregnable walls of Constantinople, which brought judgment on apostate Christians.

And the rest of the men which were not killed by these plagues yet repented not of the works of their hands, that they should not worship devils, and idols of gold, and silver, and brass, and stone, and of wood:

241

which neither can see, nor hear, nor walk. Neither repented they of their murders, nor of their sorceries, nor of their fornication, nor of their thefts. **Revelation 9:20-21**

This verse declares the reason for the attacks on Constantinople. The ACBP used the *'clay'* of the Turkish army to carry out vengeance against the Orthodox Christians, as they had denounced the Pope as their leader. But the bigger picture is that it served as a judgment by the Heavenly Father against apostate people who proclaim to follow Him. During the attack, they prayed to the Virgin Mary to deliver them, ironically pointing to the very reason they were being attacked, because of their idol worship. Ironically, Emperor Constantine helped create pagan Romanism, and the Eastern Empire capital that he founded was destroyed as part of Yah's judgment against apostate Christians.

In ***Constantinople: The Last Great Siege*, 1453, Roger Crowley says,**
The Virgin was the protector of the city; her icons were paraded along the walls at time of crisis and were considered to have saved the city during the siege of 717. The common people spent their days listening to the Orthodox priests, drinking unwatered wine in the taverns, and praying to the icon of the Virgin. Huge belief was placed in the supernatural powers of the Mother of God. Her most holy icon, the Hodegetria, 'the one who shows the way,' was a talisman credited with miraculous powers. Accordingly, a huge crowd gathered at the icon's shrine, the church of St Saviour in Chora near the city walls, to seek protection from the Virgin. (12)

Interestingly, the last Eastern Roman Emperor was named *Constantine XIV,* named after Emperor *Constantine,* who established the Eastern Roman Empire in Constantinople. It's very significant that Edward Gibbon's six-volume work, *The History of the Decline and Fall of the Roman Empire,* essentially terminates with Constantinople being captured in 1453. His epic historical work lines up with the period from when the Roman Empire was at its height of power in conquering nations during the first seal until the Empire's fall during the sixth trumpet judgment. History unveils prophecy, and it's amazing to behold!

CHAPTER 48 - SECONDARY LITERAL FULFILLMENTS

The trumpet judgments use *symbolic* terms to point to a *literal* fulfillment, but you may have noticed that there was a secondary, literal fulfillment as well. This chapter summarizes the symbolism, the primary literal fulfillment, and secondary literal fulfillment; to help you see how amazing Yah is in causing these events to line up perfectly.

In the first trumpet judgment, the symbolism of *'hail'* points to a military attack from the north by Alaric and the Goths.

The secondary, literal fulfillment was that eight-pound *hailstones* fell on the Roman Empire during that period.

In the second trumpet judgment, the symbolism of a *'burning mountain'* points to the *kingdom* of Vandals attacking Rome's coastlines and *burning* their ships.

The secondary, literal fulfillment was that Mount Vesuvius in Naples, Italy erupted in 472. The *burning mountain* caused the night sky to light up as if it was daytime, and Southern Europe was blanketed by ash. Ashfalls were reported as far away as Constantinople, perhaps pointing to its pending doom during the sixth trumpet.

In the third trumpet, the symbolism of a *'great burning star'* points to Attila the Hun attacking the Roman Empire.

The secondary, literal fulfillment was that Halley's Comet *blazed* overhead in 451, before Attila the Hun's defeat at the *Battle of Chalons*. Not long after that battle, Attila was drunk on his wedding night when an artery burst, and he drowned in his blood. He *flashed* onto the scene and faded away quickly, just like Halley's Comet.

In the fourth trumpet, the symbolism of the *'sun being darkened'* pointed to the last Western Roman Emperor (the *sun*) being removed from power in 476.

The secondary, literal fulfillment is that a solar eclipse occurred on July 7, 476, perhaps as a sign.

In the fifth trumpet, the symbolism of a *'star falling from heaven'* points to Satan using Mohammed to create the false religion of Islam.

One of the secondary, literal fulfillments is that Halley's Comet *blazed* overhead in 607 when Mohammed was given visions from Satan or one of his fallen angels. Lucifer was once a leader in heaven, but he *fell* into apostasy; thus, he was a *fallen star*. Another secondary fulfillment is that there's a black stone at the Kaaba in Mecca that reportedly contains a meteorite, *'a star that fell from heaven.'*

In the sixth trumpet, the symbolism of *'tails were like unto serpents'* points to the Turks attacking the Eastern Roman Empire.

The secondary literal fulfillment is that Halley's Comet *blazed* overhead in 1066, which is at the beginning of the Turks attacks. The comet was described as looking like a dragon (*serpent*) with multiple tails, which matches the sixth trumpet description, which points to their *'tails, which were like unto serpents.'*

In 1456, a few years after the Turks conquered Constantinople, Halley's Comet blazed overhead again. It reportedly resembled a Turkish *Scimitar* (a curved sword). How amazing is that?

The trumpet judgments' primary fulfillment is amazing, but the secondary fulfillments leave me in awe. Our Heavenly Father orchestrates the perfect timing of events on earth and in the heavens. HalleluYah!

CHAPTER 49 - 1514 AD TIMELINE ANALYSIS

1514 AD is one of the most important years in the history of Messiah's Ekklesia, yet Pastors don't teach about it. It changed the world, but historians don't write about it. The next few chapters will show you why it is so important to Messiah and His saints.

Look at the Revelation Fulfillment Chart to see the 1514 year mark on the bottom of the timeline. At this point, the ACBP has been in power for almost one thousand years. And the saints had been protesting against the Popes for over five hundred years. To counter the testimony of the Scriptures and the saints, the ACBP relentlessly worked to eliminate the two witnesses against them. The Popes banned and burned the Scriptures and only taught in Latin during the Dark Ages to control all of Christendom.

Pope Innocent III (1198-1216) declared: *"To be reproved are those who translate into French the Gospels, the letters of Paul, the psalter, etc. They are moved by a certain love of Scripture in order to explain them clandestinely and to preach them to one another. The mysteries of the faith are not to (be) explained rashly to anyone. Usually in fact, they cannot be understood by everyone but only by those who are qualified to understand them with informed intelligence. The depth of the divine Scriptures is such that not only the illiterate and uninitiated have difficulty understanding them, but also the educated and the gifted."*

In 1229, at the Catholic *Synod of Toulouse*, it was proclaimed: *We prohibit also that the laity should be permitted to have the books of the Old and New Testament; but we most strictly forbid their having any translation of these books.*

In 1234, at the Catholic *Council of Tarragona*, they declared: *No one may possess the books of the Old and New Testaments in the Romance language (such as French, Italian, Spanish, etc.), and if anyone possesses them he must turn them over to the local bishop within eight days after the promulgation of this decree, so that they may be burned.* (3)

In 1408, at the *Third Synod of Oxford*, they proclaimed this regarding John Wycliffe's translation in the late 14th century: *It is dangerous, as St. Jerome declares, to translate the text of Holy Scriptures out of one idiom into another, since it is not easy in translations to preserve exactly the same meaning in all things. We therefore command and ordain that henceforth no one translate the text of Holy Scripture into English or any other language as a book, booklet, or tract, of this kind lately made in the time of the said John Wyclif or since, or that hereafter may be made, either in part or wholly, either publicly or privately, under pain of ex-communication, until such translation shall have been approved and allowed by the Provincial Council. He who shall act otherwise let him be punished as an abettor of heresy and error.* (4)

What kind of leader proclaims to represent Messiah, but bans and burns the Scriptures? The one that was empowered by the enemy to steal glory away from the Heavenly Father and Messiah, the *antichrist beast*. The ACBPs declared war against the saints, causing Catholics to persecute them in an attempt to wipe out their witness.

Messiah declares that the seven church eras are seven candlesticks (*lampstands*), as the saints shine as a *light* in this world.

> *The mystery of the seven stars which thou saw in my right hand, and the seven golden candlesticks. The seven stars are the angels of the seven churches: and the seven candlesticks which thou saw are the seven churches.* Revelation 1:20

The Scriptures are the *olive trees* that provide *oil* for the *lampstands*, the saints. Without the Scriptures and the saints, this world becomes very dark. Messiah gave the saints of the church era of Thyatira this promise.

> *And he that overcomes, and keeps my works unto the end, to him will I give power over the nations: And he shall rule them with a rod of iron; as the vessels of a potter shall they be broken to shivers: even as I received of my Father.* Revelation 2:26-27

He is telling them that those things are dark right now, that by the power of the *rod of iron*, the Scriptures, the saints will take back control of the nations over which the ACBP held power.

The ACBP's were so effective at wiping out the Scriptures and the saints who testified against them that at the *Fifth Lateran Council* in May 1514, it was declared that *'all of Christendom was under their authority and that there were no witnesses against them.'*

In 1514, the ACBP proclaimed that the Two Witnesses against them, the Scriptures and the saints were as *'good as dead.'*

That's a profound declaration! At this point, the Popes had silenced the witness of the Scriptures, which describe them as the *son of perdition* and the *antichrist beast*. And they had caused any remaining saints to cease protesting against them. The two witnesses against the ACBPs, the Scriptures and the saints were *as good as dead*.

Many movies depict a hero who has been so tormented by the enemy that they seemed to be dead, and then they came back to life to defeat the enemy. Are you ready to hear that come back story?

Messiah foretold what the seven church eras would face. The church era of Thyatira faced the ACBP from 538 until this point in 1514. Now the church era of Sardis begins, and they were used to counter the enemy, to take back the nations for the glory of their King.

Look at what Messiah says to the saints of the church era of Sardis.

> *And unto the angel of the church in Sardis write; These things says he that hath the seven Spirits of God, and the seven stars; <u>I know thy works, that thou hast a name that thou lives, and art dead</u>*. Revelation 3:1

At this point in May 1514, we have a perfect match. The ACBP proclaimed that the saints were as good *as dead*, as they weren't witnessing against them anymore. And Messiah is proclaiming the very same thing! Can you see the synchronicity?

Then Messiah gives the church era of Sardis saints commands to help them come back to life, proving that they weren't physically dead.

Be watchful, and strengthen the things which remain, that are ready to die: for I have not found thy works perfect before God. Revelation 3:2

The hero is being empowered to come back to life to *overcome* the enemy! And what does a hero need to carry out their mission? They need a powerful weapon. The saints were given the *rod of iron*, the Scriptures, which had been taken away by the enemy. Messiah has protected the Scriptures during the Dark Ages, and He's moving to put them into the saint's hands. HalleluYah!

To the saints of Thyatira's previous church era, Messiah gave an amazing promise of a future leader, a *'star,'* who would help the saints be *overcomers*.

And I will give him the morning star. Revelation 2:28

Messiah is pointing to John Wycliffe, who translated the Latin Scriptures into English so that everyone could read them again. He was called the *'morning star of the Reformation.'* Once again, you can see the synchronicity of the prophecies in Revelation. HalleluYah!

Here are a few quotes from John Wycliffe, a hero of the faith.

"All Christian life is to be measured by Scripture; by every word thereof."

"Holy Scripture is the highest authority for every believer, the standard of faith and the foundation for reform."

Now let's look at how the saints came back to life by the power of the Scripture, the Word of life.

The Revival Of The True Faith
CHAPTER 50 - THE LITTLE BOOK OF REVELATION 10

And the voice which I heard from heaven spoke unto me again, and said, Go and take the little book which is open in the hand of the angel which standeth upon the sea and upon the earth. And I went unto the angel, and said unto him, Give me the little book. And he said unto me, Take it, and eat it up; and it shall make thy belly bitter, but it shall be in thy mouth sweet as honey. And I took the little book out of the angel's hand, and ate it up; and it was in my mouth sweet as honey: and as soon as I had eaten it, my belly was bitter. **Revelation 10:8-10**

The New Testament was written in Aramaic and Greek, but the ACBP chose to translate them into Latin to control the message and hide the truth. Latin is the language of the powerful, the rich, the learned, and the clergy, and not of the ordinary man. Jerome (340-420), the Bishop of Rome, was tasked with creating the *Latin Vulgate Bible* to hide the message from the saints.

The witness of the Scriptures had been *sealed up*, closed, by the ACBPs who banned it and burned it and only taught in Latin. Now Messiah would *open it up* to the saints to take back control of the nations. Knowing that the Latin Vulgate Bible that Wycliffe used wasn't the best foundation to translate the Scriptures, our beloved Messiah preserved the Greek manuscripts, which would be used for purer translations.

The Orthodox Christians of Constantinople initially used Latin from 395-610, but from 610-1453, the common language was Greek. They had copies of the Greek Scriptures in Constantinople during the Dark Ages, while the Popes were banning and burning the Scriptures in Western Europe. Messiah protected them until the perfect time. When the Turks were sent to attack the Eastern Roman Empire, the priests in Constantinople took the Scriptures and other Greek writings and fled to Western Europe.

Not only did priests flee Constantinople, but so did scholars who brought their knowledge of the Greek language to Western European universities. During the Dark Ages, this type of study had been suppressed, but this revival of the study of Greek led to the Renaissance and the Reformation.

Shortly after the Greek manuscripts were taken to Western Europe, German Johannes Gutenberg invented the movable type printing press in 1454; and then in 1476, Caxton introduced printing in England. The printing press's timely advent took place in the 15th century, and the Gutenberg Bible was the first book that was printed. Though it was an edition of the Latin Vulgate, which originated with Jerome in the 4th century, it was still a momentous event. The printing press would play a major role in Greek and English Bibles, which were forthcoming.

Then Erasmus, a Catholic that wrote in pure Latin, was inspired to write the Scriptures in the original Greek. He wanted the Scriptures to be available for everyone, not just the elite. The preface of his Bible reads: *Would that these were translated into each and every language. Would that the farmer might sing snatches of Scripture at his plough and that the weaver might hum phrases of Scripture to the tune of his shuttle, that the traveler might lighten with stories from Scripture the weariness of his journey.*

His *Novum Instrumentum omne* Greek New Testament was published in 1516. Accompanying it were study notes, which corrected 600 errors in Jerome's Latin Vulgate. Erasmus's second edition (1519) was the basis for Martin Luther's German translation of the New Testament. After he posted his 95 Thesis, the Popes sought Luther's life, so he took refuge at the castle of Wartburg and invested his time translating the New Testament, which brought the message of Messiah and His disciples to the hearts of Germans, and many were saved. HalleluYah!

In *History Of The Christian Church* (1819-93), Philip Schaff says, *The richest fruit of Luther's rest time in the castle of Wartburg, and the most important and most significant work of his entire life, was the translation of the New Testament, through which he brought the teachings and example of Christ* *and the apostles to the mind and hearts of the Germans in a reproduction similar to real life…. he made the Bible the book of the people in church, school, and the home.*

In *Notes on the Handbook of Revelation* (1852), Albert Barnes says, *It would be difficult to imagine now a more striking symbol of the art of printing or to suggest a better device for it than to represent an angel giving an open volume to mankind. The leading doctrine of the Reformers was that the Bible is the source of all authority in matters of religion and, consequently, is to be accessible to all the people.*

William Tyndale spent much time studying Erasmus's New Testament. When Catholic John Walsh opposed him, Tyndale said, *"I defy the Pope and all his laws. If God spare my life ere many years, I will cause a boy that driveth the plow, shall know more of the Scripture than thou dost."*

Tyndale said, *"The preaching of God's word is hateful and contrary unto them. Why? For it is impossible to preach Christ, except thou preach against antichrist; that is to say, them which with their false doctrine and violence of sword enforce to quench the true doctrine of Christ."*

William Tyndale used Erasmus's third edition (1522) to translate into English. In 1526, he began smuggling English Bibles into England, with the first run of three thousand. Many copied editions were printed as well. The Papal Church hated him for his Bible translation and captured him to kill him. Before he was strangled and his body burned at the stake, he cried out, *"Lord, open the King of England's eyes."*

One year after Tyndale's execution in October of 1536, Tyndale's friend John Rogers, operating under the assumed name *Thomas Matthew*, produced the 1537 *Matthew-Tyndale Bible*. This was the very first printing of a complete English Bible to be translated directly from the original language of Hebrew and Greek. It was reprinted once again in a more practical size in 1549.

Yah answered Tyndale's prayer by having King Henry VIII of England authorize *The Great Bible* by Miles Coverdale in 1540, which was read aloud in church services of the Church of England. That may not seem remarkable now, but back then, it was very significant. The *Geneva Bible* was published in 1560, and it became the primary Bible of 16th century Protestantism. This version of the Holy Bible is significant because, for the very first time, a mechanically printed, mass-produced Bible was made available directly to the general public. Over a million copies were printed between 1560 and 1640. It has lots of notes from the Protestant Reformers, which explained the historical fulfillment of prophecy, pointing to the Popes as the *antichrist beast* and the *son of perdition*, and the RCC as the *harlot* church of Revelation 17.

In *A History of England* (1828), Henry Walter says, *As Queen Elizabeth passed under a triumphal arch erected in Cheapside, a Bible was let down into her hands by a white-robed child called "Truth." The queen received it, kissed it, and pressed it to her heart, replying that this present was more acceptable to her than any of the more costly ones the city had to give her that day of the accession.* (4)

The ACBPs responded to this turn of events with angry declarations. At the *Council of Toulouse*, they declared, *"We prohibit laymen possessing copies of the Old and New Testament. ...We forbid them most severely to have the above books in the popular vernacular."* (5)

Pope Innocent III (1198-1216) declared, *"To be reproved are those who translate into French the Gospels, the letters of Paul, the psalter, etc. They are moved by a certain love of Scripture in order to explain them clandestinely and to preach them to one another. The mysteries of the faith are not to (be) explained rashly to anyone. Usually in fact, they cannot be understood by everyone but only by those who are qualified to understand them with informed intelligence. The depth of the divine Scriptures is such that not only the illiterate and uninitiated have difficulty understanding them, but also the educated and the gifted."* (6)

Pope Pius IV (1559-65) said, *"The Bible is not for the people; whosoever will be saved must renounce it. It is a forbidden book. Bible societies are satanic contrivances."* (7)

Pope Leo XIII declared, *"As it has been clearly shown by experience that, if the Holy Bible in the vernacular is generally permitted without any distinction, more harm than utility is thereby caused."*

Popes who proclaim to represent the Heavenly Father and Messiah condemned Scripture being read. If this is not the antichrist, who is?

The *Bishop's Bible* was published in 1568. Then in 1604, King James commissioned a team of scholars to create the *King James Bible*, which was completed in 1611. One of the KJV losses is that all of the study notes included in the Geneva Bible were not included in the KJV. This is significant because as the KJV became more popular, the readers did not see the truth about the fulfillment of the 70th week of Daniel 9 and Revelation.

I don't think that there's one printed Bible version in particular that the *'little book'* of Revelation 10 prophecy was pointing to, just the printed Bible of the 16th century. The large hand-written scrolls were replaced with smaller printed Bibles. To John, the printed Bible would be a *little book*, compared to the long scrolls of his day.

With the advent of the printing press and the Word of Yah translated, millions of people were finally able to read the Gospel. The Scriptures are alive. When we *eat* the Word, it gives us the strength to live victorious lives for Yah. Studying Scripture is more important to our life than our daily bread. After the famine of the Dark Ages, the printed Bible became the most treasured thing in the world. It was diligently read by millions, who hungered for the *bread of life*. They carried it with them, studied it, and committed it to memory.

So indeed, the *little book* of Revelation 10, the printed New Testament, was *sweet* on the mouths of the saints, who had hungered for it.

In *Romanism And The Reformation*, Henry Grattan Guinness says, *And not Luther only, but all the reformers – like the apostles – held up the Word of God alone for light, just as they held up the sacrifice of Christ alone for salvation. They gave to the world the book which Christ had given to them,* *which they had found sweet to their souls, though it subsequently brought on them bitter trouble.*

The *little book* was *'bitter'* because it brought the Reformers at once into conflict with all the power of the Papacy and the priesthood, exposing them to persecution; aroused against them a host of enemies among the princes and rulers of the earth. Many saints were burned alive with their printed Bible hung around their necks. The SOJ military army was empowered to counter the Reformation, which they did by torturing and murdering saints during the Inquisition.

In *Notes on the Handbook of Revelation* (1852), Albert Barnes says, *From the year 1540 to the year 1570, comprehending a space of only thirty years, no fewer than nine hundred thousand Protestants were put to death by the papists in different countries of Europe. During the short pontificate of Paul the Fourth, which lasted only four years (1555-1559 A.D.), the Inquisition alone, on the testimony of Vergerius, destroyed a hundred and fifty thousand!*

The *'seven thunders'* mentioned in Revelation 10 may have been from the Popes who were angry that the Bible was being translated and printed, and they issued Papal bulls which *thundered* from Rome. Historians often refer to *Papal Edicts* and *Bulls* as *'thunders.'* At the *Council of Trent*, the Papal Church declared that preserved Bibles are on the *"Index of Forbidden Books,"* and the writings of William Wycliffe, Jan Hus, John Calvin, and other reformers were condemned.

***And he said unto me, Thou must prophesy again before many peoples, and nations, and tongues, and kings.* Revelation 10:11**

In *The Last Prophecy*, Edward Bishop Elliott says, *As Wickliffe in England, so Huss in Bohemia. Both Hussite and Wickliffite preachers were soon excommunicated as heretics and nearly suppressed by the terrors of the sword. And so this most important part of the Christian minister's duty – the addressing the hearts and consciences of the people from the Word of life, the setting forth God's grace and love through a dying, risen, and interceding Savior, - was again neglected, and all but unknown, until the close of the* *fifteenth century, and until Luther began the Reformation. At this very period, the word went forth, as from the Angel to St. John, "Thou must prophecy again," etc.*

When Luther had proclaimed the Papal oracle to be the voice of the antichrist and persisted at Worms before the Emperor in rejecting it, the severest condemnatory decrees were issued against him and his fellow laborers. By these, they were excommunicated from the Church and downgraded from their ministry in it; and on pain of confiscation of their goods, imprisonment, and even death, they were interdicted from preaching the Gospel. Luther was outlawed, and his friend, the Elector of Saxony, to save his life, hid him in a lonesome castle in the forest of Wartburg.

"The voice said, Go, take the little book out of the Angel's hand." Luther's chief occupation in his year of exile was the translation of the New Testament into German. He felt this was needed to spread the light of truth among ministers and people, for the overthrow of Papal superstitions. No sooner was the translation of the New Testament finished than he himself felt he could no longer remain silent. A crisis had arrived, which seemed to call for his assistance. Persecution had begun against his fellow laborers in Germany; besides which, a sect called Anabaptists had arisen, styling themselves Christians, but in truth bringing discredit on the name they professed.

Melancthon urged his return, with a view to heading the little body of Reformers in the fulfillment of their ministerial, it might be said their apostolic, commission. At the risk of his proscribed life, as if impelled by a voice from above, he returned to Wittenberg. In excuse, he wrote to his patron, the Elector, "The Divine will is plain, and leaves me no choice; the Gospel is oppressed and begins to labor." Again, "It is not from men, I have received my commission, but from the Lord Jesus Christ. Henceforth I wish to reckon myself his servant and to take the title of Evangelist."

It was in 1522 that Luther arrived at Wittenberg; and within the two or three years the message of salvation was heard by princes and people, not in Germany only, but in Sweden, Denmark, Pomerania, Livonia; in France, Belgium, Spain, and Italy also, though the less general acceptance, and, last

255

mentioned but not least, in England. Preachers were raised up on every side, and translations of the Scriptures were multiplied. The prediction was in course of fulfillment. "Thou must prophesy again before many people, and nations, and languages, and kings."

With the *little book*, the printed New Testament, in their hands, Revelation 10:11 is the command to preach the Gospel in the Roman Empire. Millions of Catholics heard the pure Gospel and were redeemed for the kingdom, and they came out of the *harlot* church and formed the Protestant Churches. The power of the Roman beast kingdom had to be broken with the *rod of iron*, the Scriptures. They had sealed it up in the dead language of Latin. In his hands, the radiant angel had an open book for the Reformers to present the Gospel to the nations again.

It's been translated into all languages after being locked up in Latin. It became very affordable after handwritten copies were so expensive. It's the all-time best-selling book, after almost being extinguished. And it has *prophesied*, it has proclaimed the Gospel, for the last five centuries, redeeming many for the kingdom. HalleluYah!

Fervent prayer and the Scriptures are a powerful weapon against the enemy, for truth prevails over the enemy's deceptions.

Put on the whole armor of God, that ye may be able to stand against the wiles of the devil. For we wrestle not against flesh and blood, but against principalities, against powers, against the rulers of the darkness of this world, against spiritual wickedness in high places. Wherefore take unto you the whole armor of God, that ye may be able to withstand in the evil day, and having done all, to stand. Stand therefore, having your loins girt about with truth, and having on the breastplate of righteousness; And your feet shod with the preparation of the gospel of peace; Above all, taking the shield of faith, wherewith ye shall be able to quench all the fiery darts of the wicked. And take the helmet of salvation, and the sword of the Spirit, which is the word of God. Ephesians 6:11-17

CHAPTER 51 - THE SARDIS CHURCH ERA
1514-1798 AD

The Sardis Church era is described in Revelation 3:1-6.

Looking at the Revelation Fulfillment Chart, we see the church era of Sardis begins. It's the second of two *lampstands*, the two church eras, which *witnessed* against the ACBP during the 1,260-year reign of power.

This church era spans from when the ACBP proclaimed that the witnesses against them were *'as dead'* in 1514 to when the Popes were taken captive in 1798, ending their 1,260-year reign of power.

The meaning of the word *"Sardis"* is the *"escaping one,"* or those who *"come out,"* so it's an excellent symbol of the church era during the Reformation period when the Protestants preached the Gospel and millions were saved and *came out* of the *harlot* church of Rome. They didn't shed all of the Roman church's false teachings, but they addressed the Popes' main deceptions, and they were heroes of the faith who boldly stood up against the ACBP.

Many of them were brutally tortured and burned at the stake for their witness against the ACBPs and the *harlot* church. They are heroes of the faith, who understood who is the enemy of Messiah and His saints, and boldly stood up against them.

Our generation should not sit as their judge just because we have access to more information than them. They acted on what they were shown, and they battled against the enemy, often paying for the testimony with their lives.

In a sad irony, most people called *'Protestants'* today don't heed the command given to them in witnessing against the teachings of the ACBP to help Catholics see the errors of Romanism so that they have a covenant relationship with the Heavenly Father through Messiah.

CHAPTER 52 - MEASURING THE TEMPLE
1514-1517 AD

And there was given me a reed like unto a rod: and the angel stood, saying, Rise, and measure the temple of God, and the altar, and them that worship therein. **Revelation 11:1**

It's not telling them to measure a physical temple. Ephesians 2:19-22 tells us that the *'holy temple'* is the Ekklesia, the body of Messiah's saints.

> *Now, therefore, you are no longer strangers and foreigners, but fellow citizens with the saints and members of the household of God, having been built on the foundation of the apostles and prophets, Jesus Christ Himself being the chief corner stone, in whom the whole building, being joined together, grows into a holy temple (naos) in the Lord, in whom you also are being built together for a dwelling place of God in the Spirit.*

The saints now have the Scriptures in their hands, to compare what the Popes teach against the *'reed like a rod.'* This is how we know who is teaching truth and is a part of Yah's true temple; and who is teaching concepts that are contrary to Scripture.

In *Notes on the Handbook of Revelation* (1852), Albert Barnes says, *The command to 'measure the Temple of God' was a direction to take an estimate of what constituted the True Church – the very work which it was necessary to do in the Reformation! For this was the first point which was settled, whether the Papacy was the (leader of the) True Church, or was the Antichrist. This was true not only in the pomp and splendor of worship, and in the processionals and imposing ceremonials, but in the worship of images, in the homage rendered to the dead, in the number of festival-days, in the fact that the statues reared in heaven Rome to the honor of the gods had been reconsecrated in the services of Christian devotion to the apostles, saints, and martyrs; and in the robes of the Christian priesthood, derived from those in use in the ancient heathen worship. To determine this, and to separate the true church from it, was no small part of the work of the Reformation.*

There were, therefore, three things, as indicated by this verse, which John was directed to do, so far as the use of the measuring-rod was concerned: (a) to take a just estimate of what constitutes the true church, as distinguished from all other associations of people; to institute a careful examination into the opinions in the church on the subject of sacrifice or atonement — involving the whole question about the method of justification before God; and to take a correct estimate of what constitutes true membership in the church, or to investigate with care the prevailing opinions about the qualifications for membership.

This, as we have seen, would relate to the prevailing opinions on the subject of sacrifice and atonement, on the true method of a sinner's acceptance with God, and, consequently, on the whole subject of justification. As a matter of fact, it need not be said that this was one of the first questions which came before the Reformers and was one which it was indispensable to settle, in order to a just notion of the church and of the way of salvation.

The papacy had exalted the Lord's supper into a real sacrifice; had made it a grand and essential point that the bread and wine were changed into the real body and blood of the Lord, and that a real offering of that sacrifice was made every time that ordinance was celebrated; had changed the office of the ministers of the New Testament from preachers to that of priests; had become familiar with the terms altar, and sacrifice, and priesthood, as founded on the notion that a real sacrifice was made in the "mass;" and had fundamentally changed the whole doctrine respecting the justification of a sinner before God.

The altar in the Roman Catholic communion had almost displaced the pulpit; and the doctrine of justification by the merits of the great sacrifice made by the death of our Lord had been superseded by the doctrine of justification by good works, and by the merits of the saints. It became necessary, therefore, to restore the true doctrine respecting sacrifice for sin and the way of justification before God, and this would be appropriately represented by a direction to "measure the altar."

Messiah is telling His people to use the Scriptures to determine who is the true Ekklesia, the temple of Yah, and who is a false church.

In *The Last Prophecy,* **Edward Bishop Elliott says,** *Martin Luther found a Bible hid in the shelves of the University library. It was at this time he met with Staupitz, Vicar-general of the Augustines. Staupitz told Luther, "It is from the love of God alone that true repentance has its origin. Seek it not in those macerations and mortifications of the body! Seek it in contemplating God's love in Christ Jesus! Love him who has thus first loved you!"*

Through much study, Luther was inwardly prepared to enter upon the work designed for him, as God's chose minister, of showing to others what he had himself experienced. And the way was soon opened. He was nominated by Staupitz to a professorship in the University at Wittenberg, recently founded by the Elector of Saxony. Then in 1512, being appointed doctor of divinity ad Biblia and having to vow on his appointment to defend the Bible doctrines, he received his vocation as a Reformer.

He posted his celebrated 95 theses against indulgences, affixing them, as was customary, on the door of the principal church, and offering to maintain them against all opposed. The truths put forward most prominently were – the Pope's insufficiency, and the true penitent's participation by God's free gift now merely in the blessing of forgiveness, but in all the riches of Christ, irrespective of Papal absolution or indulgence.

To these, he added other declarations also, as to the Gospel of the grace of God, and not the merits of saints, being the true treasure of the Church, and against the avarice of the priestly traffickers in indulgences; and, moreover, an exhortation to real Christians.

Writing to Staupitz the next year, he says: "The abominations of the Pope, with his whole kingdom, must be destroyed; and the Lord does this without hand, by his word alone. The Scriptures understood by and by, lead to an army of people preaching against the Papal tyranny from the Word of God, until this 'man of sin' is deserted by all his adherents, and dies of himself."

When Martin Luther and others measured the RCC teachings against Yah's Word, they saw that it's a false church. They found no justification for a Pope or hierarchy of Archbishops and Bishops, just the early church's five-fold ministry. They found salvation by repentance and faith in the Father who sent Messiah, not in works, and not through the Catholic Church. They found no place of purgatory, where people could be refined so that they could go to heaven. They didn't have to go to a confession box with a priest because they have direct access to Messiah, the High Priest.

They found that bowing down to statues is forbidden. They didn't have to count rosary beads or pray to anyone like Mary, but only to the Father in Messiah's name. They learned the simplicity of the Holy Communion to remember Messiah's death on Passover, but no Eucharist mass ceremony and no wafer that supposedly becomes the body of Messiah. They learned that all of these things were strange and alien to the Word of Yah, and they testified that the RCC was not part of Messiah's true Ekklesia.

The five *solae* (in Latin, sola means *'alone'*) of the Protestant Reformation are **Sola Scripture**: The Bible is our highest authority. **Sola Fide**: We are saved through faith in Messiah. **Sola Gratia**: We are saved by the grace of Yah alone. **Solus Messiah**: Messiah is our Intercessor and our High Priest. **Soli Deo Gloria**: We live for the glory of Yah alone.

We're told to *'measure the altar.'* Messiah, our High Priest, serves from the altar, interceding for the saints. The ACBP of Rome proclaims to be the High Priest and that Mary is the intercessor to the Father. By that, we know that the RCC is not part of the true assembly of saints, the true temple, but that they are an apostate gentile church.

We're told to *'measure those who worship there,'* so we are to judge righteously those who proclaim to be Messiah's saints, to see who is following Scripture and who is not. Measuring what leaders teach, exposing their falsehood, is not being judgmental. We're called to expose the deceptions of the enemy, to help set the captives free.

In *Visions of the Ages*, **B.W. Johnson says,** *It evidently then means that the worship of the Church shall be measured. Those that worship at the altar shall be measured also. By this divine reed the apostles shall measure the Church, the modes of worship, and the character of the worshipers. After this explanation of the meaning of terms, the significance becomes plain. This prediction will be fulfilled if, under the sixth trumpet, before the seventh is blown, a corrupted Church, corrupted during long ages of apostasy, shall be compared with some divine standard. Or, in other words, after 1453, there ought to be an effort to reform the Church and to conform it to the New Testament.*

Not the traditions of men, not the decisions of councils, not the decrees of synods, or conferences, not the creeds of any uninspired body that ever met on the face of the earth, but the standard measure, is the New Testament. It was held by the papacy, which then lorded over Christendom, that the writings of the fathers, tradition, and the decrees of the councils were not only an additional measure but might even set aside the Word of God. The great Reformation planted itself upon the principles maintained by Martin Luther, and the corner-stone of Protestantism is that the Bible is the only rule of faith and practice of the Christian Church. Protestantism has not always been true to its principles, but it has always conceded that the final standard of measurement is the Word of God.

Martin Luther said, *"Let us believe the Gospel, let us believe St. Paul, and not the letters and decretals of the Pope."* Luther was asked by a Roman archbishop, *"Are you the man that undertakes to reform the papacy?"* Luther replied, *"Yes, I am the man. I confide in Almighty God, whose Word I have before me."* When the archbishop tried to persuade him to retract his writings, he said, *"Sooner sacrifice my body and my life, better allow my arms and legs to be cut off, than abandon the clear and genuine Word of God."* (1)

But leave out the court which is outside the temple, and do not measure it, for it has been given to the Gentiles. And they will tread the holy city underfoot for forty-two months. Revelation 11:2

The physical temple didn't originally have an outer court of Gentiles; it was added to accommodate people who desired to worship. It's not part of the temple, though it has the appearance of being so. To the eye of an observer, the RCC would seem to belong to Messiah's Ekklesia, His assembly of saints, as much as the outer court seemed to pertain to the temple. But when you examine the Popes and Catholic Church's teachings, you realize that they're proclaiming a false gospel and a false messiah; thus, they are not part of the true temple.

The word *'leave'* has a strong meaning in the Greek word *ekballo*, which means: *to eject (literally or figuratively): to bring forth, cast (forth, out), drive (out), expel, leave, pluck (pull, take, thrust) out, put forth (out), send away (forth, out)*. It's saying to *cast out, drive out, expel,* the *harlot* church.

Messiah was instructing the Protestant Reformers to witness against the teachings of the RCC so that people can understand they can only be saved through Him. They proclaimed that RCC is not part of Messiah's true Ekklesia. While Rome excommunicated the Reformers, the Reformers excommunicated Rome in obedience to the command in Revelation 11. The Pope of Rome was resisted and condemned as *'the man of sin,' 'the antichrist, the 'standard-bearer'* as John Calvin calls him, *'of an abominable apostasy.'*

In *Romanism And The Reformation*, Henry Grattan Guinness says, about Luther separating from the Roman church: *If we reform not, I and all that worship Christ do account your seat to be possessed and oppressed by Satan himself, to be the damned seat of antichrist, which we will not be subject to nor incorporate with, but do detest and abhor the same.*

Today, believers proclaim that there are 1.5 billion Christians globally, but that number includes Catholic and Orthodox Christians, who believe in salvation via the sacraments and that Mary is the intercessor to the Father. It also includes Christian cults such as the Mormons and Jehovah's Witnesses. Revelation 11:1-2 commands us to compare what they teach against Scripture to determine who is part of Messiah's true assembly of saints; and who is in a false religion.

It's not judgment or hate to declare that what the Popes teach and Catholics believe is contrary to Scripture. It's our mandate which needs to be carried out with diligence and love! Catholics have been programmed to believe that the RCC is the *'one true church,'* appointed by Messiah when the truth is that it's the *harlot* church of the *antichrist beast* and Satan. We're called to share Scriptural truth with them, to help them come out of false teachings.

Revelation 11:2 is not talking about physical gentiles, but *spiritual* ones. *Spiritual Israel* consists of those who have a covenant relationship with the Father through the Son. Spiritual gentiles are those who don't. The *'holy city'* is not Jerusalem, as some people teach. Remember, Messiah is speaking *symbolically*. The ACBP led RCC *'tread underfoot'* Messiah's assembly of saints, *Holy Jerusalem*, for 1,260 years (42 prophetic months), from 538-1798. Revelation 21:2 declares that the *holy city* is the bride of Messiah, the saints.

Then I, John, saw the holy city, New Jerusalem, coming down out of heaven from God, prepared as a bride adorned for her husband.

Messiah's bride is called the holy temple.

Know ye not that ye are the temple of God and that the Spirit of God dwelleth in you? If any man defile the temple of God, him shall God destroy; for the temple of God is holy, which temple ye are. 1 Corinthians 3:16-17

In *Notes on the Handbook of Revelation* (1852), Albert Barnes says, *The "holy city," Jerusalem, was regarded as sacred to God — as his dwelling-place on earth, and as the abode of his people, and nothing was more natural than to use the term as representing the church.*

The *'measuring of the temple'* in Revelation 11 describes the time when the RCC was revealed to be a gentile church, an *apostate* church, and not part of the true Ekklesia of Messiah.

CHAPTER 53 - THE TWO WITNESSES OF REVELATION 11
538-1798 AD

The concept of two men being the two witnesses is based on the futuristic explanations of Revelation, in which the supposed one-man antichrist reigns in power for 3 ½ years. But we know that's a false premise, as the ACBP reigned in power for 1,260 years, so we know that the two witnesses are not just two men.

In *Romanism And The Reformation*, Henry Grattan Guinness says, *The two witnesses of Revelation 11 are symbolic and do not represent two actual men from whose mouth literal fire proceeds, and who literally shut heaven, and literally turn waters to blood, and smite the earth with literal plagues, and who are slain and lie dead for three and a half literal days, and then literally rise from the dead, and literally and visibly ascend to heaven in a cloud; nor is their ascension followed by a literal earthquake and a literal fall of the tenth part of a literal city, and by literal lightnings, voices, thunderings, and hail. All these are symbols of other things, and their literal interpretation is an absurdity. It forms a leading element in the testimony of martyrs and reformers. Like the prophets of old, these holy men bore a double testimony a testimony for the truth of God and a testimony against the apostasy of His professing people. The providential position which they occupied, the work they accomplished, gave singular and special importance to their testimony; and this was their testimony, and nothing less, that Papal Rome is the Babylon of prophecy, drunken with the blood of saints and martyrs; and that its head, the Roman pontiff is the predicted "man of sin," or antichrist.*

Given where we're at in the timeline, who has been the target of the ACBPs? Is it not the Scriptures, which testify about faith in Messiah alone, and describe them as the enemy of Messiah? Is it not the saints, who have testified against their false teachings, and have witnessed against them, proclaiming that they are the *son of perdition* and the *antichrist beast* which leads the *harlot* church of Rome?

I can show you who the *two witnesses* are, with one picture. This is JSG Ignatius Loyola stepping on a saint who is holding the Scriptures, both of which testify against Rome's ACBP. This shows the ACBP's hatred of the Scriptures and the saints.

The book that Ignatius is holding says, *"To the greater glory of God, Constitutions of the Society of Jesus,"* which lays out their plans to bring Protestants back to the Catholic Church so that they revere the Pope. Their *'god'* is Satan, as the JSGs work for the glory of the *prince of this world*, Satan. You can see a smiling serpent crawling underneath Luther, which shows you who they serve.

My friend, it's as simple as that! It's the Scriptures which describe the *little horn* of Daniel 7, the *son of perdition* of 2 Thessalonians 2, and the *antichrist beast* of Revelation who leads the *harlot church* of Rome; all of which describe the office of the papacy, the Popes of Rome. So the Popes sought to eliminate the Scriptures by banning and burning them.

It's the saints of the two church ages of Thyatira and Sardis, who witnessed against the ACBPs during their 1,260-year reign of power from 538-1798. The Popes sought to eliminate the saints by causing Catholics to kill them.

***And I will give power unto my two witnesses, and they shall prophesy a thousand two hundred and threescore days, clothed in sackcloth. These are the two olive trees, and the two candlesticks standing before the God of the earth.* Revelation 11:3-4**

Messiah proclaimed that the Scriptures *testify* about Him and His Gospel. The Greek word for *'testify'* is *'martureo,'* which means <u>*to be a witness*</u>, *to give evidence, to bear record, to give testimony.*

> *You search the Scriptures, for in them you think you have eternal life; and these are they which testify of Me.* John 5:39

Messiah told us that His saints are His witnesses. The Greek word for *'witnesses'* is *'martus,'* which can mean <u>*a martyr, a record, a witness*</u>.

> *But you shall receive power when the Holy Spirit has come upon you, and you shall be witnesses to Me in Jerusalem, and in all Judea and Samaria, and to the end of the earth.* Acts 1:8

'Witnesses' is the same word that John used when he spoke of martyrs.

> *And they overcame him by the blood of the Lamb and by the word of their <u>testimony</u>, and they did not love their lives to the death.* Revelation 12:11

> *And the dragon was enraged with the woman, and he went to make war with the rest of her offspring, who keep the commandments of God and have the <u>testimony</u> of Jesus Christ.* Revelation 12:17

> *I saw the woman, drunk with the blood of the saints and with the blood of the <u>martyrs</u> of Jesus. And when I saw her, I marveled with great amazement.* Revelation 17:6

Is that not what the saints did, die *witnessing* against the enemy of Messiah and His saints? The power that Messiah gave the saints is the Scriptures, the *rod of iron*, which we use to *testify* about the pure Gospel of Messiah and to identify the *antichrist beast* and *witness* against him.

Joseph Benson's Commentary on Revelation (1847) says, *Our Saviour himself sent forth his disciples, (Luke 10:1,) two and two; and it hath been also observed that the principal reformers have usually appeared, as it were, in pairs; as the Waldenses and Albigenses, John Huss and Jerome of Prague, Luther and Calvin, Cranmer and Ridley, and their followers. Not that I conceive that any two particular men, or two particular churches, were intended by this prophecy; but only that there should be some in every age, though but a few in number, who should bear witness to the truth, and declare against the iniquity and idolatry of their times.*

In *Horae Apocalypticae,* Edward Bishop Elliott says, *Tichonius in the 4th century saw "the sackcloth-robed witnesses as either the two Testaments or the light-giving Church fed by the oil of those two Testaments."*

Even though the prophecy about the *two witnesses* of Revelation has a specific context in time, it applies to all saints, especially our Laodicean Church era, as the FPJSG has greatly deceived us. Our mandate is to preach the pure Gospel of Messiah and witness against the ACBP and their *harlot* church, expose their deceptions, and set captives free!

The *'two olive trees'* are the Scriptures, the *Tanach* (Old Testament) and *Brit HaHadashah* (New Testament), which provide *oil* for the saints. Messiah was pointing back to Zechariah 4:11-14, which says that two olive trees supply oil to the candlestick.

The word *'anointed'* is Hebrew 3323 *Yishar*, which means *oil (as producing light); figurately, anointing: anointed oil.* The *'oil'* of the Scriptures provides fuel for the *'lampstands'* of the saints, to be able to see in this dark world.

When interpreting prophecy, we need to look to see how Scripture defines the terms. In Revelation 1:20, Messiah told us,

The mystery of the seven stars which you saw in My right hand, and the seven golden lampstands: The seven stars are the angels of the seven churches, and <u>the seven lampstands which you saw are the seven churches</u>.

The Greek word for *'candlesticks'* is 3087 *luchnia*, which means *a lamp-stand (literally or figuratively)*. If seven candlesticks (*lampstands*) represent the seven church eras, then two *lampstands* represent two church eras. Using Messiah's definition, we know that the *two candlesticks* in Revelation 11:4 are pointing to the two church eras of Thyatira and Sardis, which existed during the reign of the ACBP, from 538-1798.

We are called to be the *'light of the world,'* but we can only shine when we're filled with the Scriptures and the Spirit. The Popes banned and burned the Scriptures and only taught in Latin during the Dark Ages. It became so dim that the saints were *as dead*, with no *light* emanating from them. They were not exposing the dark works of the ACBPs and their *harlot* church.

In Messiah's *'parable of the foolish virgins,'* they don't have *oil* for their lamps. He's proclaiming that they don't have Scriptural truth, so they'll be caught by surprise at His return. That describes a lot of people right now, as they don't understand Revelation. Pray for an awakening! The enemy has deceived them with false explanations because they believed pastors without searching the Scriptures to prove it.

In *The Seventh Vial* (1848), James Aitken Wylie says, *There is an evident allusion here to the vision exhibited to Zechariah, at a period of great depression in the history of the Old Testament Church. The prophet was shown a candlestick, all of gold, with seven lamps burning on its branches. Beside the candlestick stood two olive-trees, whose oil flowed into the seven lamps and kept them alive. The prophet had the vision interpreted to him, and was given to understand that the candlestick was the symbol of the Old Testament Church, the lamp of divine truth preserved by God in the midst of heathenism; and that the two olive-trees which supplied that candlestick with oil were "the two anointed ones (sons of oil) that stand by the Lord of the whole earth," meaning the prophets and priests who communicated the truth to the Church of old.*

And if any man will hurt them, fire proceeds out of their mouth, and devoureth their enemies: and if any man will hurt them, he must in this manner be killed. These have power to shut heaven, that it rain not in the days of their prophecy: and have power over waters to turn them to blood, and to smite the earth with all plagues, as often as they will. **Revelation 11:5-6**

It's not speaking of literal *fire*, but symbolically talking about the power of the Scriptures, which is the context of the *little book* of Revelation 10 and the *measuring of the temple* in Revelation 11.

> *Therefore thus says the LORD God of hosts: "Because you speak this word, <u>Behold, I will make My words in your mouth fire, And this people wood, And it shall devour them.</u>* Jeremiah 5:14

> <u>*Is not My word like a fire?*</u>*" says the Lord, "And like a hammer that breaks the rock in pieces?* Jeremiah 23:29

Jeremiah knew about being *'clothed in sackcloth'* as he proclaimed the Scriptures amid persecution. The same was true of the saints who faced persecution and martyrdom for their witness. Messiah's saints prophesied judgment against the ACBPs, which distressed them, and caused them to be full of fiery indignation. Messiah's saints will not overcome the ACBP by the physical sword, but only by the *sword of Scripture*, by prayer, and by exposing their many deceptions.

Joseph Benson's Commentary on Revelation (1847) says, *that is, they are like unto Moses and Elijah, who called for fire upon their adversaries. But their fire was real, this is symbolical, and proceedeth out of the mouth of the witnesses, denouncing the divine vengeance on the corrupters and opposers of true religion; much in the same manner as it was said to Jeremiah, (Jeremiah 5:14,) I will make my words in thy mouth fire, and this people wood, and it shall devour them. During this time, the divine protection and blessing shall be withheld from those men who neglect and despise their preaching and doctrine.*

That is, they are like Moses and Aaron, who inflicted these plagues on Egypt, and they may be said to smite the earth with the plagues which they denounce;

270

for, in Scripture language, the prophets are often said to do those things which they declare and foretell. But it is most highly probable that these particulars will receive a more literal accomplishment when the plagues of God and the vials of his wrath (chap. 16.) shall be fully poured out upon men, in consequence of their having so long resisted the testimony of the witnesses. Their cause and the cause of truth will finally be avenged on all their enemies.

Obviously, it didn't literally stop raining for 1,260 years. Again, it's speaking symbolically of spiritual matters. Messiah's saints possess the keys of the kingdom of heaven, and whatever they bind or loose on earth is bound or loosed in heaven. This has been shown to mean that they would have the power to cause blessings to be withheld from people as if the rain were withheld.

> *My doctrine shall drop as the rain, and my speech shall distill as the dew, as the small rain upon the tender herb, and as the showers upon the grass.* Deuteronomy 32:2

> *For as the rain cometh down, and the snow from heaven, and returneth not thither, but watereth the earth, and maketh it bring forth and bud, that it may give seed to the sower, and bread to the eater: So shall my word be that goeth forth out of my mouth: it shall not return unto me void, but it shall accomplish that which I please, and it shall prosper in the thing whereto I sent it.* Isaiah 55:10-11

Isaiah 6:10 shows the utter condemnation of an apostate people in praying that the *rain* of Scriptural truth would be withheld from them so that they're unable to see the truth.

> *Make the heart of this people dull, And their ears heavy, And shut their eyes; Lest they see with their eyes, And hear with their ears, And understand with their heart, And return and be healed.*

No doubt the saints who were tortured and killed by Catholics cried out to Yah for His vengeance.

271

And when they shall have finished their testimony, the beast that ascendeth out of the bottomless pit shall make war against them, and shall overcome them, and kill them. And their dead bodies shall lie in the street of the great city, which spiritually is called Sodom and Egypt, where also our Lord was crucified. **Revelation 11:7-8**

The beast out of the *bottomless pit* is Satan, who empowered the Popes of Rome. He used the Roman Emperors to kill millions of saints, but Messiah's assembly just grew faster.

> *And the dragon was wroth with the woman, and went to make war with the remnant of her seed, which keep the commandments of God, and have the testimony of Jesus Christ.* Revelation 12:17

Then he used the Roman Popes to try to wipe out Messiah's assembly, and he was very close to being successful, as the saints were *worn out* and *overcome*. Without the Scriptures, Messiah saints became powerless, and their protests had ceased. They had *'finished their testimony,'* and at this point, they were *'as dead.'*

Millions of saints were physically dead, but the context of the *two witnesses* is that they are *dead* in their protests against Rome. The saints of the church of Thyatira were persecuted so severely that they were *'as dead'* by 1514. They had been silenced, banished to the corners of the world, unable to stand against the ACBP.

Messiah also said that the saints were *as good as dead* in His message to the saints of the church era of Sardis.

> *And unto the angel of the church in Sardis write; These things saith he that hath the seven Spirits of God, and the seven stars; I know thy works, that thou hast a name that thou lives, and art dead.* Revelation 3:1

But then Messiah commands them to take action, so being called *'dead'* symbolizes their lack of actions.

> *Be watchful, and strengthen the things which remain, that are ready to die: for I have not found thy works perfect before God.* Revelation 3:2

Ephesians 5:14-16 gives us another example of people who are called '*dead*,' but then told to take action to come alive again.

> *Wherefore he said, <u>Awake thou that sleeps and arise from the dead</u>, and Christ shall give thee light. See then that ye walk circumspectly, not as fools, but as wise, redeeming the time, because the days are evil.*

1 Peter 4:6 describes the Gospel being proclaimed to spiritually dead people, *the gospel preached also to them that are dead, that they might be judged according to men in the flesh.*

The Protestant Reformers proclaimed that the *harlot* Papal church is *spiritual* Sodom and Egypt, as she is an impure church, whose priests have sodomized many boys. She is full of idolatry with her many idols and pagan gods, including the Virgin Mary. The saints condemned the blasphemous Eucharist ceremony. The RCC pretends to practice a Scriptural faith, but it's symbolically the old religion of Babylon, sun worship, and ultimately, Satan worship.

It's saying that the Popes who controlled '*the great city*' of Rome caused the saints to be *as dead*. Jerusalem is called '*the holy city*' and was never called '*the great city*.' But in Revelation 18:9-10, Messiah called Babylon *the great city*, and you've already seen that Babylon is Rome, and *the great city* is the name of the Roman beast.

Messiah did not die in the streets of Jerusalem. He died outside the city gates, on a hill called Golgotha, and Judea was a Roman province when Messiah died. If it was pointing to literal Jerusalem, there's no reason that John wouldn't have just said that. Instead, it's pointing to His saints being killed in the Roman Empire, called the *great city*.

In Acts 22:7-8, Messiah confronts Saul about persecuting the saints.

> *And I fell unto the ground, and heard a voice saying unto me, Saul, Saul, why persecutest thou me? And I answered, Who art thou, Lord? And he said unto me, I am Jesus of Nazareth, whom thou persecutest.*

He's saying that persecuting the saints is the same as persecuting Him. The treatment of His saints was such that it might be said that He was *'crucified afresh'* there, for what is done to His saints may be said to be done to him. The Scriptures were burned in the streets, often hung around the saints' necks, as they were burned to death in the city plaza.

The translators render the text as *'where our Lord was crucified,'* but the word *'was'* is inserted as there's no Greek word in the manuscripts for it. This implies that it occurred in the past. But it could also be rendered as *'where our Lord is crucified,'* which points directly at the Popes, as Messiah is crucified afresh every day by the *great city*, the Roman beast kingdom of the ACBP, during their Eucharist ceremony.

The book *Paraphrase of the Revelation of Saint John According To E.B. Elliott* (1862) says, *Martin Luther wrote to Spalatin in 1519, "I have been reading the Papal Decrees, and would whisper into your ears, that I know not whether the Pope be not Antichrist. To such an extent is Christ dishonored in them, and crucified."*

In *Notes on the Handbook of Revelation* (1852), Albert Barnes says, *It is to be understood as meaning that He was practically crucified there; that is, that the treatment of His friends – His church – was such that it might be said that he was 'crucified afresh' there; for what is done to His church may be said to be done to Him.*

It is to be assumed; therefore, that Revelation 9:20-21 refers to the state of the ecclesiastical world after the conquest of Constantinople by the Turks, and previous to the Reformation; that Revelation 10 refers to the Reformation itself; that Revelation 11:1-2 refers to the necessity, at the time of the Reformation, of ascertaining what was the true church, of reviving the Scripture doctrine respecting the atonement and justification, and of drawing correct lines as to membership in the church. All this has reference, according to this interpretation, to the state of the church while the papacy would have the ascendency, or during the twelve hundred and sixty years in which it would trample down the church as if the holy city were in the hands of the Gentiles.

If this be so, then what is here stated (Revelation 11:3-13) must be supposed to occur during the ascendency of the papacy and must mean, in general, that during that long period of apostasy, darkness, corruption, and sin, there would be faithful witnesses for the truth, who, though they were few in number, would be sufficient to keep up the knowledge of the truth on the earth, and to bear testimony against the prevailing errors and abominations.

The sixteenth-century opened with a prospect of all others the most gloomy, in the eyes of every true Christian. Corruption both in doctrine and in practice had exceeded all bounds, and the general face of Europe, though the name of Christ was everywhere professed, presented nothing that was properly evangelical. The Waldenses were too feeble to molest the popedom; and the Hussites, divided among themselves, and worn out by a long series of contentions, were reduced to silence.

The language of Mr. Cunninghame may here be adopted as describing the state of things at the beginning of the sixteenth century: "At the commencement of the sixteenth century, Europe reposed in the deep sleep of spiritual death, under the iron yoke of the papacy. The meaning is not that he would send two witnesses to prophesy, but rather that these were, in fact, such "witnesses," and that he would during that time permit them to exercise their prophetic gifts or give them the privilege and the strength to enunciate the truth which they were commissioned to communicate as his "witnesses" to mankind. Some word, then, like "power, privilege, opportunity, or boldness," is necessary to supply in order to complete the sense.

Then it came to be employed in the sense in which the word "martyr" is now — to denote one who, amidst great sufferings or by his death, bears witness to the truth; that is, one who is so confident of the truth, and so upright, that he will rather lay down his life than deny the truth of what he has seen and known. The sense here is that they would, in some public manner, hold up or maintain the truth before the world.

That is, an effect would be produced as if they were put to death. They would be overcome; would be silenced; would be apparently dead. Any event that would cause them to cease to bear testimony as if they were dead would be properly

275

represented by this. It would not be necessary to suppose that there would be literally death in the ease, but that there would be some event which would be well represented by death — such as an entire suspension of their prophesying in consequence of force.

This must mean when they should have borne full or ample testimony; that is, when they had borne their testimony on all the great points on which they were appointed to bear witness. This, then, must not be understood as referring to the time of the completion of the twelve hundred and sixty years, but to any time during that period when it could be said that they had borne a full and ample testimony for the truths of the gospel, and against the abominations and errors that prevailed.

Edward Bishop Elliott believed that Revelation 11:7 would be better translated as *when the witnesses had perfected their testimony'* rather than *'when they had finished their testimony.'* This meant the death of the witnesses was during their prophetic period, not at the end. This fits into the description, as in 1514, the Popes proclaimed that there were no witnesses left against them.

In *A Dissertation On Prophecies* (1806), George Stanley Faber says, *In an age of the worst corruptions of Popery, the Waldenses and the Hussites carefully preserved the precious Word of God as their best treasure, made it the sole standard of their faith, and uniformly appealed to it in all their controversies with their enemies. This was a light to the feet of the two witnesses, during their prophesying in sackcloth; and this, when translated into the vulgar tongues of Europe, was the most powerful weapon in the hands of the reformers. (It is sharper than any two-edged sword, it is a rod of iron).*

In *The Last Prophecy*, Edward Bishop Elliott says, *The 1215 fourth Lateran General Council revived all former plans of extirpation, and gave new powers and privileges to the Crusaders against heretics, the same as to those who joined in the crusades against the Holy Land. The Councils of Narbonne and of Toulouse followed, in which besides other methods of detection, even children were compelled to inform against heretics; and besides other methods of suppression, the Holy Scriptures were strictly forbidden by laity.*

Continuing throughout the thirteenth and fourteenth centuries, the same papal cause continued without cessation. Bulls, councils, inquisitions, crusades, Dominicans, and Franciscans everywhere pursued and tracked with bloodhound spirit these faithful martyrs of Jesus. Not in Piedmont and Dauphiny alone, but in Spain and Calabria, in Germany, France, and Flanders. Not the Waldenses only, but the Wickliffites and Lollards in England, and Hussites in Bohemia.

And yet, in spite of the racks and prisons, of the sword and of the flame, their voice was still raised in protestation against the lies of Popery, and for the truth, as it is in Jesus. At length, however, towards the close of the fifteenth century, after a furious crusade against the Waldenses and Hussites, the Papal object seemed almost attained and its triumph complete.

There is, by the common consent of historians, but one period in European history in which the voice of anti-Papal testimony was wholly suppressed, and the symbol of death might be properly taken to describe the complete stillness that prevailed. It was the opening of the sixteenth century, just before the Reformation. In vain, Bohemian Churches sent deputies to search through Europe for any of kindred feeling whom they might hail as brethren. The deputies returned unsuccessful.

Campegius Vitringa (1669-1722), a Dutch Protestant theologian, says, Rome is said to be Babylon on account of idolatry; is said to be Egypt, because tyrannizing the People of God; is said to be Sodom, on account of the corruption of morals; but is spiritually said to be Jerusalem, because in her the Lord is said to be crucified in a mystical way, during the Romish Mass.

And they of the people and kindreds and tongues and nations shall see their dead bodies three days and an half, and shall not suffer their dead bodies to be put in graves. And they that dwell upon the earth shall rejoice over them, and make merry, and shall send gifts one to another; because these two prophets tormented them that dwelt on the earth. Revelation 11:9-10

The Popes controlled the ten kingdoms of the fallen Roman Empire and caused them to persecute the saints, so people of different ethnicities and languages all saw the saints' dead bodies. Many of the martyrs who were killed by the Papal Church were not buried or given the blessing of a priest, which Rome deemed to signify that they were condemned to hell. The canon law of the Papal church prohibits the burial of 'heretics.' At the Lateran Council in 1179, they declared, *we forbid under pain of anathema that anyone should keep or support them in their houses or lands or should trade with them. If anyone died in this sin, then neither under cover of our privileges granted to anyone, nor for any other reason, is mass to be offered for them or are they to receive burial among Christians.* (2)

Pope Innocent III in the *Fourth Lateran Council* (1215) forbade clerics under pain of losing their ecclesiastical offices to grant burial to heretics or to those who had been excommunicated or placed under *interdict nominatim*. By a decree of Pope Alexander IV (1254), ex-communication was incurred *ipso facto* by those who knowingly gave a proper burial to heretics or those who believe, receive, defend or favor heretics, absolution from the censure being denied until the delinquent had publically and with his own hands removed the body unlawfully buried. In the *Council of Vienne* (1312), Pope Clement V enacted the same censure for those who knowingly bury persons publicly ex-communicated, interdicted by name, or manifest usurers. (3)

To leave a body unburied is to treat it with contempt, and among the ancients, nothing was regarded as more dishonorable than such treatment. They left the bodies out in the open, to be a reminder of the consequences of speaking against the Popes of Rome. Being dead for *'three days and an half'* is an odd statement, but 3 ½ years makes perfect sense, which you will see in the next few verses.

In *Notes on the Handbook of Revelation* (1852), Albert Barnes says, *Now this not only expresses what was, in fact, the general feeling among the papists in respect to those whom they regarded as heretics, but it had a literal fulfillment in numerous cases where the rites of Christian burial were denied* *them. One of the punishments most constantly decreed and constantly enforced in reference to those who were called "heretics" was their exclusion from burial as persons excommunicated and without the pale of the church.*

In *Horae Apocalypticae*, Edward Bishop Elliott says, *A Papal bull was issued on December 16, 1513, summoning the dissidents in question (the remaining Bohemian brethren who had opposed the antichrist Popes and their church) to appear and plead before the Council at the Ninth Session of the Fifth Lateran Council to be held on May 5, 1514. Thus was the crisis come which was to try the faith of this bleeding remnant of witnesses, and exhibit its vitality or death. Would they face their Lord's enemies? Would they brave the terrors of death, and plead his cause before the lordly Legate or the antichristian Council; like the Waldenses at Albi and at Pamiers, like Wycliffe and Cobham in England, like Huss and Jerome at the Constance Council, or Luther afterward at Augsburg and at Worms? Alas! No.*

No Protestant showed, and this was hailed this as a great victory. This is the time that you read about in the ***1514 AD Timeline Analysis*** chapter when the ACBP declared that the witnesses against them are *as dead.* This caused the Pope and the countries that supported him to rejoice, and they held great feasts to celebrate the end of the saints' witness against them. The truth of Yah gives evil men pain and fills them with vexation and wrath. The people groups of the Waldenses, Albigenses, Bohemian Brethren, Vaudois, and Wycliffites; all testified against the Catholic Church, which tormented them. The Catholic leaders celebrated that they didn't have to hear the testimony against them; about their false doctrine, their impure lives, their idol worship, and their coming judgment at the hand of Yah.

Joseph Benson's Commentary on Revelation (1847) says, *One of the greatest cities of Europe; for they were not suffered to be buried, being the bodies of heretics; but were dragged through the street, or thrown into the river, or hung upon gibbets, and exposed to public infamy. Great rejoicings too were made in the courts of France, Rome, and Spain; they went in procession to the churches, they returned public thanks to God, they sang Te Deums, they* *celebrated jubilees, they struck medals, and it was enacted that St. Bartholomew's day should ever afterward be kept with double pomp and solemnity.*

Vassals, were by the Pope absolved from allegiance to their superiors, should these latter refuse to join in the work of exterminations; the lands and goods of heretics were given to their murderers; and plenary indulgence to the day of death was granted to everyone taking part in the persecution.

In Ireland, in 1641, the Romanist Bishops proclaimed a 'war of religion' and incited the people by every means in their power to massacre the Protestants. North, south, east, and west, throughout the island, Protestant blood flowed in rivers; houses were reduced to ashes, villages and towns all but destroyed in the deadly strife; the only burial allowed to the martyrs was the burial of the living, and their persecutors took a fiendish delight in hearing their cries and groans, issuing from the earth.

In *Romanism And The Reformation*, Henry Grattan Guinness says, *As the sixteenth century opened, no danger seemed to threaten the Roman pontiffs. The agitations excited in former centuries by the Waldenses, Albigenses, Beghards, and others, afterwards by the Bohemians, had been suppressed and extinguished by council and by the sword. The surviving remnant of Waldenses hardly lived, pent up in the narrow limits of Piedmontese valleys, and those of the Bohemians, through their weakness and ignorance, could attempt nothing, and thus were an object of contempt rather than fear.*

In *Horae Apocalypticae*, Edward Bishop Elliott says, *Throughout the length and breadth of Christendom Christ's witnessing servants were silenced; they appeared as dead. The orator of the Session ascended the pulpit; and, amidst the applause of the assembled Council, uttered that memorable exclamation of triumph - an exclamation notwithstanding the long multiplied anti-heretical decrees of Popes and Councils, notwithstanding the yet more multiplied anti-heretical crusades and inquisitorial fires, was never, I believe, pronounced before, and certainly never since.*

"There is an end of resistance to the papal rule and religion: opposers there exist no more" and again, "The whole body of Christendom is now seen to be subjected to its Head, i.e., to Thee: (the Pope). For it seems scarcely possible that we can be mistaken in regarding it as the precise commencing date of the predicted three and half years, during which Christ's witnesses were to appear as mere dead corpses in the face of Christendom. It was May 5, 1514.

We find that an edict was issued from Pope and Council, that same day, just after the Preacher's oration of triumph; that declared punishments imposed on heretics by former Bulls and Councils that affected the heretic when dead; the exclusion of his corpse from burial. An indignity borrowed from those inflicted by the Roman Pagan persecutors on the early Christian martyrs, but of which the force and terrors were under the Papal regime tenfold great in general estimation; forasmuch as it was supposed to involve the eternal damnation of the wretch unburied.

At the Lateran Council a strict enforcement of this punishment, this mark of reprobation on the corpses of such as might then be lying dead, convict of heresy, in any part of Christendom. So that it was the fulfillment to the very letter of what was predicted: "They from the kindreds and tongues and people shall not suffer their dead bodies to be put into graves."

The splendor of the dinners and celebrations given by Pope Leo X and the Roman Cardinals on the triumphant close of the Fifth Lateran Council – a splendor unequaled since the days of Pagan Rome's greatness - is made the subject of special record by the Historian of Leo the Xth.

At the commencement of the sixteenth century, Europe reposed in the deep sleep of spiritual death, under the iron yoke of the Papacy. There was none that 'move the wing or opened the mouth, or peeped' – when suddenly, in one on the universities of Germany the voice of an obscure monk was heard, the sound of which rapidly filled Saxony, Germany, and Europe itself; shaking the very foundations of the Papal power, and arousing men from the lethargy of ages. The fire, ill-smothered says he (by Pope Leo and his Legate's measures of conciliation and repression) at the close of 1513 and of 1514, was blown up again by Luther's bellows, and spread its flames far and wide, more than ever before.

William Cuninghame of Lainshaw (1775–1849), a writer on biblical prophecy, says, *At the commencement of the 16th century, Europe reposed in the deep sleep of spiritual death, under the iron yoke of the papacy. There was none that moved the wing, or opened the mouth, or peeped: when, suddenly, in one of the universities in Germany the voice of an obscure monk was heard, the sound of which rapidly filled Saxony, Germany, and Europe itself, shaking the very foundations of the Papal power, and arousing men from the lethargy of ages.* (4)

And after three days and an half the Spirit of life from God entered into them, and they stood upon their feet, and great fear fell upon them which saw them. And they heard a great voice from heaven saying unto them, Come up hither. And they ascended up to heaven in a cloud, and their enemies beheld them. **Revelation 11:11-12**

From the public declaration of the *antichrist beast* Pope on May 5, 1514, to the public declaration of Martin Luther on October 31, 1517, when he posted his 95 Thesis on the door of the Church of Wittenberg, in Germany, was exactly three and a half years.

Luther's act was the defining moment that the Ekklesia of Messiah came alive again, as it ignited the Protestant Reformation. HalleluYah!

In *Notes on the Handbook of Revelation* (1852), Albert Barnes says, *Now it happens that there was a point of time, just previous to the Reformation when it was supposed that a complete victory was gained for over those who were regarded as "heretics," but who were, in fact, the true witnesses for Christ. That point of time was during the session of the council of Lateran, which was assembled 1513 A.D., and which continued its sessions to May 16, 1517. In the ninth session of this council, a remarkable proclamation was made, indicating that all opposition to the papal power had now ceased. The scene is thus described by Mr. Elliott (ii. 396,397).*

"The orator of the session ascended the pulpit; and, amidst the applause of the assembled council, uttered that memorable exclamation of triumph — an exclamation which, notwithstanding the long multiplied anti-heretical decrees of popes and councils, notwithstanding the yet more multiplied anti-heretical crusades and inquisitorial fires, was never, I believe, pronounced before, and certainly never since — 'Jam nemo reclamat, nullus obsistit' — 'There is an end of resistance to the papal rule and religion; opposers there exist no more:' and again, 'The whole body of Christendom is now seen to be subjected to its Head, that is, to Thee.'"

This occurred on May 5, 1514. It is, probably, from this "time" that the three days and a half, or the three years and a half, during which the "dead bodies of the witnesses remained unburied," and were exposed to public gaze and derision, are to be reckoned.

In *Horae Apocalypticae*, **Edward Bishop Elliott says,** "Now, from May 5, 1514, to May 5, 1517, are three years; and from May 5, 1517, to October 31 of the same year, 1517, the reckoning in days is as follows: May 5-31, 27 days. August 31 days. June 30 days. September 30 days. July 31 days. October 31 days. In all, 180 days, or half of 360 days, that is, half a year; so that the whole interval is precisely, to a day, three and a half years"

Not in the compass of the whole ecclesiastic history of Christendom, save and except in the case of the death and resurrection of Christ Himself, is there any such example of the sudden, mighty, and triumphant resuscitation of his cause and Church from a state of deep depression, as was just after the separation of the Lateran Council exhibited, in the protesting voice of Luther, and burst force of the glorious Reformation. So that whole interval is precise, to a day, three and a half years; precisely to a day, the period predicted in the apocalyptic prophecy! – Or wonderful prophecy is the explanation that again forces itself on my mind!

Everything was quiet; every heretic exterminated, and the whole Christian world supinely acquiescing in the enormous absurdities inculpated on them when, in 1517, the empire of superstition received its first attack from Martin Luther.

Luther connected the Gospel of the New Testament with protesting against the enemy of Messiah, saying, *We are not the first ones who applied the Antichristian kingdom to the Papacy: this many great men have dared to do many years before us and that frankly and openly under the greatest persecution. The old divinely-ordained witnesses confirm our doctrine, and the bodies of these saints arise as it were among us with the newly–vilified Gospel, and awaken much confidence.* (7)

Luther became an enemy of the Popes, so the Spirit caused German Prince Frederick to dream about a monk who used a 100-year old goose quill to poke the Pope's ears. One hundred years before Luther, the martyr, John Huss, had a dream while in his dungeon at Constance, a few nights before he was burned to death at the stake.

In *Horae Apocalypticae*, Edward Bishop Elliott says that Huss wrote, *It seemed as if some pictures of Christ, that he had been painting on the walls of his oratory, were effaced by the Pope and the Bishops. The dream afflicted him. But the next night he dreamed again and seemed to see painters more in number, and with more effect, restoring the pictures of Jesus. He told the dream to friends, saying I am no vain dreamer; but hold for certain that the image of Christ shall never be effaced. They wish to destroy it: but it shall be painted afresh in the hearts of gospel-preachers better than myself.*

Huss, which means '*a goose*', foretold the reformation of Martin Luther, *"They will roast a goose now, but after a hundred years they will hear a swan sing, and him they will endure. In one hundred years, God will raise up a man whose calls for reform cannot be suppressed."*

The Popes killed John Huss and Jerome of Prague because they proclaimed that the saints should regard the Scriptures, not the Papal church, as their authority. They both proclaimed that the office of the papacy fulfills prophecy as the *son of perdition* and the *antichrist beast*. The Popes persecuted the followers of John Huss and Jerome of Prague, seeking to extinguish their witness. And now, in Martin Luther, their witness was *alive* again.

284

In *Notes on the Handbook of Revelation* (1852), Albert Barnes says, *John Huss said, speaking of the gospel-preachers who should appear after he had suffered at the stake, "and I, awaking as it were from the dead, and rising from the grave, shall rejoice with exceeding great joy."* HalleluYah!

Martin Luther not only protested against the Popes and their church, but he translated the Scriptures into German, which led to many people being saved. Are you seeing how the Scriptures and saints came back to life after being proclaimed as *dead*?

Martin Luther had this woodcut made to accompany the Revelation 11 passage in his 1522 Bible. The setting is Rome, *the great city*. It depicts him and another Reformer speaking the Word *as fire coming out of their mouth* against a dragon with the triple-crown its head, pointing to the ACBP who is empowered by Satan. On the left, you can see two dead witnesses laying on the street, not buried.

It's amazing to see that Luther understands his role in the *two witnesses* prophecy. He brought the saints back to life when he posted his 95 Thesis in opposition to the ACBP. I pray that this Revelation Timeline Decoded book does the same thing in waking the saints up out of their slumber in these end times.

In Messiah's message to the Sardis Church era, which started in 1514, Messiah said, *"Be watchful and strengthen the things which remain, that are ready to die."* He had called them *'dead,'* but He admonished them to take action to proclaim the Gospel, to proclaim the truth of Scriptures, to witness against the ACBP and their apostate *harlot* church. The Popes thought that they had killed the witnesses against them, but now the Bible was being printed in English, and much to their dismay, millions of copies were being spread worldwide, and the saints preached the Gospel throughout their Roman kingdom.

In *Horae Apocalypticae,* **Edward Bishop Elliott says,** *In turning from John Huss to Pope Adrian, Leo Xth's successor, we find a commentator, such as Huss might have little expected, both on the martyr's dream and on the apocalyptic prophecy. In 1523, he wrote in a brief addressed to the Diet of Nuremberg, "The heretics Huss and Jerome seem now to be alive again in the person of Luther."*

How amazing is it that the ACBP, who proclaimed that the *two witnesses* against them were *dead*, now declares that the witnesses have come back to life? HalleluYah!

I've included some commentaries that have redundant information, so you can see that the saints did not believe that the two witnesses' narrative is about two men in the end times. That said, we are called to carry out the ministry of the saints who have gone before us, to proclaim the Gospel, to witness against the ACPBs and their false teachings, to set the captives free.

Millions of people heeded the Reformers' call, they were saved by the pure Gospel of Messiah, and they came out of the *harlot* RCC. Messiah's saints were stronger than ever; they proclaimed salvation through Messiah, not through the Pope; and they boldly testified against the ACBP. With the Scriptures, Messiah's saints re-assumed their former station, to be in a position and a state of readiness to serve Messiah, defend His truths, and discharge their duty with boldness and courage, fearing the face of none.

The ACBP's RCC controlled the nations, but now the saints took back control with the *'rod of iron,'* the Scriptures. The Pope's deeds were exposed. They lost a lot of power over the nations during the Protestant Reformation, and they knew that more judgment was coming.

The *two witnesses* didn't literally ascend to heaven, but symbolically they had been raised into heavenly places in Messiah. It points to them being exalted in power and glory, in prevailing over the enemy.

> *Blessed be the God and Father of our Lord Jesus Christ, who hath blessed us with all spiritual blessings in heavenly places in Christ.* Ephesians 1:3

> *(Christ) raised us up together, and made us sit together in the heavenly places in Christ Jesus.* Ephesians 2:6

The Protestant Reformers were winning the spiritual battle with the Scriptures and by the power of the Spirit. The Popes saw them enter into a purer and more glorious spiritual state than before.

Satan used the Roman Emperors to try to wipe out the saints and the Scriptures through persecution, but the Scriptures were preserved, and Messiah's Ekklesia grew supernaturally. Then Satan used the Roman Popes to try to wipe out the two witnesses of the saints and the Scriptures. Our Messiah said that *the gates of hell shall not prevail against it,* and His saints preached the Gospel and took back power over the nations.

In *Notes on the Handbook of Revelation* (1852), Albert Barnes says, *The meaning is that they would triumph as if they should ascend to heaven, and he received into the presence of God. The sense of the whole is that these* witnesses, after bearing a faithful testimony against prevailing errors and sins, would be persecuted and silenced; that for a considerable period their voice of faithful testimony would be hushed as if they were dead; that during that period they would be treated with contempt and scorn as if their unburied bodies should be exposed to the public gaze; that there would be general exultation and joy that they were thus silenced; that they would again revive, as if the dead were restored to life, and bear a faithful testimony to the truth again; and that they would have the divine attestation in their favor, its if they were raised up visibly and publicly to heaven.

Amazingly, in 1528, Martin Luther wrote: *We are not the first ones who applied the anti-Christian kingdom of the papacy; this, many great men have dared to do many years before us and that, frankly and openly, under the greatest persecution. The old divinely-ordained witnesses confirm our doctrine, and the bodies of the saints arise as it were among us with the newly vivified Gospel, and awaken much confidence.* (8)

And the same hour was there a great earthquake, and the tenth part of the city fell, and in the earthquake were slain of men seven thousand: and the remnant were affrighted, and gave glory to the God of heaven. Revelation 11:13

An '*earthquake*' symbolically represents a great commotion in the civil affairs of kingdoms. In the sixth seal, we saw that the *earthquake* symbolized the political upheaval taking place in the Roman Empire as it was declining. Now there is upheaval in the Roman beast kingdom, as the ACBP was losing power over the nations.

England was the first nation to break away from the RCC, calling it *Babylon the great city.* In 1534, Parliament's *Act of Supremacy* separated the English Church from the RCC, which was a '*tenth part*' of their influence. In 1537, the *Irish Supremacy Act* was passed by the Parliament of Ireland, establishing Henry VIII as the supreme head of the Church of Ireland, instead of the Pope. At length, in England, during King William's reign, the *Society for the Propagation of the Gospel in Foreign Parts* was the first Protestant Missionary Society.

Edward Bishop Elliott notes that the word *'thousand'* is properly translated as *'chiliads,'* meaning *provinces* or *countries*. We can look to history to see how seven provinces *died* in regard to supporting the Pope. In 1579, the seven provinces of the Netherlands signed the *Union of Utrecht* and later formally declared independence from Catholic Spain in 1581, during *The Dutch Revolt*. The seven childiads/provinces that separated from the Roman Catholic Church were Holland, Zealand, Utrecht, Freiseland, Groningen, Overyssel, and Guilderland.

In *Notes on the Handbook of Revelation* (1852), Albert Barnes says, *There can be little difficulty in applying this to the shock produced throughout Europe by the boldness of Luther and his fellow-laborers in the Reformation. No events have ever taken place in history that would be better compared with the shock of an earthquake than those which occurred when the long-established governments of Europe, and especially the domination of the papacy, so long consolidated and confirmed, were shaken by the Reformation. In the suddenness of the attack made on the existing state of things, in the commotions which were produced, in the overthrow of so many governments, there was a striking resemblance to the convulsions caused by an earthquake. So Dr. Lingard speaks of the Reformation: "That religious revolution which astonished and convulsed the nations of Europe." Nothing would better represent the convulsions caused in Germany, Switzerland, Prussia, Saxony, Sweden, Denmark, and England by the Reformation than an earthquake.*

The Bible was translated into English, German, French, etc., and millions of Bibles were printed and spread worldwide. Millions of people were saved by the pure Gospel, and they came out of the RCC. This formed the Protestant Churches, which led to worldwide missions, and many were redeemed for the kingdom. The Popes feared losing their power, and they beheld the hand of Yah. They convened at the *Council of Trent* to map out a strategy to bring the Protestant Churches back under them, and in fact, to bring the whole world under their control.

The book *Paraphrase of the Revelation of Saint John According To E.B. Elliott* **(1862) says,** *The 16th century opened with a prospect of all others most gloomy in the eyes of every true Christian. Corruption, both in doctrine and in practice, had exceeded all bounds: and the general face of Europe, though Christ's name was everywhere professed, presented nothing that was properly evangelical. The Roman Pontiffs were the uncontrolled patrons of impiety. The Waldenses were too feeble to molest the Popedom: and the Hussites, divided among themselves, and worn out by a long series of contentions, were at length reduced to silence. The Witnesses were persecuted and overcome by the "beast from the abyss," and they triumphed over their death proclaimed it to the world at the Ninth Session of the Great Lateran Council, May 5th, A.D. 1514. Their resurrection after "three days and a half," i.e., 3 1/2 years, on the 31st of October, A.D. 1517, upon the memorable occasion of Luther's public protest in posting up his theses at Wittenberg, the well-known epoch of the Reformation.*

The epic tale of the *two witnesses*, the Scriptures, and the saints, being persecuted by the enemy so relentlessly that they were '*as good as dead*,' and then coming back to life to proclaim the Gospel so that millions of people were saved, should be the story that pastors love to tell. But I've never heard a pastor proclaim it.

Because the enemy has caused the end-times saints not to understand who is the ACBP who leads the *harlot* RCC, they have neglected their calling to help Catholics see how what the Popes teach is contrary to Scripture, so that they enter into a covenant relationship with the Father through the Son. Because the enemy has been so effective and believers have been so lax in pursuing Scriptural truth, the witness of the glorious fulfillment of the prophecies in Revelation has remained hidden. They've not been proclaimed to the world so that people can see how they validate the Bible's authority and the deity of Messiah.

What a sad statement about our end-times generation! This is why Messiah called the end-times church era of Laodicea *"wretched, miserable, naked, poor and blind."* I pray that this book is *"eye salve,"* which *"anoints your eyes that thou may see."*

CHAPTER 54 - THE HISTORICAL WITNESSES

Though the ACBP was given civil and ecclesiastic authority in 538, it took several centuries to gain power over the leaders. When they started issuing decrees which are contrary to Scripture, the saints began to protest against them.

There are many more witnesses than what I've included here, no doubt many millions of them. I've listed the most significant quotes to reinforce that proclaiming that the office of the papacy, the Popes of Rome, fulfill Bible prophecy as the *little horn of Daniel 7*, the *son of perdition* of 2 Thessalonians 2, and the *antichrist beast* of Revelation; is not just my interpretation, but the belief of the saints for over 1,000 years, many of whom paid for their testimony with their blood.

Here are some declarations from whole church bodies, as the Protestant Reformers took back control of the nations where the Pope's false Gospel had misled people.

The Church of England *Book of Homilies* **(1547, 1562, 1571).**
The Bishop of Rome teaches that they that are under him are free from all burdens and charges of the commonwealth, and obedience towards their prince; most clearly against Christ's doctrine and St. Peter's. He ought therefore rather to be called antichrist, and the successor of the scribes and pharisees, than Christ's vicar, or St. Peter's successor; seeing that, not only on this point, but also in other weighty matters of Christian religion, in matters of remission and forgiveness of sins, and of salvation, he teacheth so directly against both St. Peter, and against our savior Christ.'

After this ambition (to be head of all the church and lord of all kingdoms,) the Bishop of Rome became at once the spoiler and destroyer both of the church, which is the kingdom of our Saviour Christ, and of the Christian empire, and all Christian kingdoms, as an universal tyrant over all.

The Church of Scotland Confession of Faith in 1560.

There is no other Head of the Church than the Lord Jesus Christ, nor can the Pope of Rome be in any sense the Head thereof ; but is that antichrist, that man of sin and son of perdition, that exalteth himself in the church against Christ, and all that is called God. (2)

The Lutheran confession of faith in 1603.

The Pope is the very Antichrist, who exalteth himself above, and opposeth himself against Christ, because he will not permit Christians to be saved without his power, which, nevertheless, is nothing, and is neither ordained nor commanded by God. (3) *Since the Bishop of Rome has erected a monarchy in Christendom, claiming for himself dominion over all churches and pastors, exalting himself to be called God, wishing to be adored, boasting to have all power in heaven and upon earth, to dispose of all ecclesiastical matters, to decide upon articles of faith, to authorize and interpret at his pleasure the Scriptures, to make a traffic of souls, to disregard vows and oaths, to appoint new divine services; and in respect to the civil government, to trample underfoot the lawful authority of magistrates, by taking away, giving, and exchanging kingdoms, we believe and maintain that it is the very Antichrist and the son of perdition, predicted in the Word of God under the emblem of a harlot clothed in scarlet, seated upon the seven hills of the great city, which has dominion over the kings of the earth; and we expect that the Lord will consume it with the spirit of his mouth, and finally destroy it with the brightness of his coming, as he has promised.* (4)

The Irish Articles of Religion of 1615.

The Bishop of Rome is so far from being the supreme head of the universal Church of Christ, that his works and doctrines do plainly discover him to be that man of sin, foretold in the Holy Scriptures, whom the Lord shall consume with the spirit of His mouth, and abolish with the brightness of His coming. (5)

The Westminster Confession of Faith of 1644.

There is no other head of the church but the Lord Jesus Christ, nor can the Pope of Rome in any sense be head thereof, but is that antichrist, that man of sin, and son of perdition, that exalteth himself in the church against Christ, and all that is called God." An act of Parliament ratified this statement in 1649.

The London Baptist Confession of 1689.
The Lord Jesus Christ is the Head of the church, by the appointment of the Father, all power for the calling, institution, order or government of the church, is invested in a supreme and sovereign manner; neither can the Pope of Rome in any sense be head thereof, but is that antichrist, that man of sin, and son of perdition, that exalteth himself in the church against Christ, and all that is called God; whom the Lord shall destroy with the brightness of his coming.

Keep the following testimonies in mind when persecution strikes; for we have a great cloud of witnesses who have gone before us, who have run the race, who stayed true to Messiah and exposed the enemy.

Arnulf (991) was the Bishop of Orleans.
Arnulf disagreed with the policies and morals of Pope John XV. At the *Council of Reims*, which was called by the King of France in 991, Arnulf declared that *the pontiff, clad in purple and gold, was "Antichrist, sitting in the temple of God, and showing himself as God."*

Berengar of Tours (1088) was a gifted teacher and brilliant theologian.
For he called Pope Leo IX, not pontifex but pompifex and pulpifex; the Roman Church a council of vanity, the church of the malignant; and the Apostolic See the seat of Satan.

Eberhard II von Truchsees (1240) was the archbishop of Salzburg. He denounced Pope Gregory IX at the *Council of Regensburg.*
Stated at a synod of bishops held at Regensburg in 1240 that the people of his day were "accustomed" to calling the pope Antichrist.

John Wycliffe translated the Latin Vulgate Bible into English and placed it in the hands of the people. *We suppose that antichrist, the head of all these evil men, is the pope of Rome.*

Matthias of Janow was a fourteenth-century Bohemian ecclesiastical writer. His writings paved the way for the Hussite movement.

The Antichrist has already come. He is neither Jew, pagan Saracen nor worldly tyrant, but the 'man who opposes Christian truth and the Christian life by way of deception;—he is, and will be, the most wicked Christian (the Pope), falsely styling himself by that name, assuming the highest station in the church, and possessing the highest consideration, arrogating dominion over all ecclesiastics and laymen;' one who, by the working of Satan, assumes to himself power and wealth and honor, and makes the church, with its goods and sacraments, subservient to his own carnal ends. (12)

Sir John Oldcastle (1417) was an English Lollard leader.

But as touching the Pope and his Spirituality, I owe them neither suit nor service, for so much as I know him by the Scriptures to be the great Antichrist, the Son of Perdition, the open Adversary of God, and the Abomination standing in the holy place. (13) *I know him (the Pope) by the scriptures to be the great Antichrist, the son of Perdition... Rome is the very nest of Antichrist, and out of that nest come all the disciples of him* (14)

William White, a well-spoken priest and follower of John Wycliffe.

That the wicked living of the pope, and his holiness is nothing else but a devilish estate and heavy yoke of antichrist, and therefore he is an enemy unto Christ's truth. (15)

William Tyndale translated the Scriptures into English.

The preaching of God's word is hateful and contrary unto them. Why? For it is impossible to preach Christ, except thou preach against antichrist (Pope); that is to say, them which with their false doctrine and violence of sword enforce to quench the true doctrine of Christ.' (16)

Tyndale was arrested, tried, and sentenced to death.

Huldreich Zwingli (1484-1531) was a great Swiss Reformer.

I know that in it works the might and power of the Devil, that is, of the Antichrist... the Papacy has to be abolished... But by no other means can it be more thoroughly routed than by the word of God, because as soon as the world receives this in the right way, it will turn away from the Pope without compulsion.

John Calvin (1509-1564) was an influential French theologian.

I deny him to be the vicar of Christ, who, in furiously persecuting the gospel, demonstrates by his conduct that he is Antichrist – I deny him to be the successor of Peter. I deny him to be the head of the church." "Some persons think us too severe and censorious when we call the Roman pontiff Antichrist.

Daniel and Paul had predicted that Antichrist would sit in the temple of God…we affirm him to be the Pope. Some persons think us too severe and censorious when we call the Roman pontiff Antichrist. But those who are of this opinion do not consider that they bring the same charge of presumption against Paul himself, after whom we speak.

Martin Luther (1483-1546) sparked the Protestant Reformation

Nothing else than the kingdom of Babylon and of very Antichrist. For who is the man of sin and the son of perdition, but he who by his teaching and his ordinances increases the sin and perdition of souls in the church; while he (the Pope) yet sits in the church as if he were God? All these conditions have now for many ages been fulfilled by the papal tyranny. I know that the pope is Antichrist and that his throne is that of Satan himself.

Nicolaus von Amsdorf (1483-1565) was a colleague of Luther.

He will be revealed and come to naught before the last day so that every man shall comprehend and recognize that the pope is the real, true Antichrist and not the vicar of Christ. Therefore those who consider the pope and his bishops as Christian shepherds and bishops are deeply in error, but even more are those who believe the Turk is the Antichrist. Because the Turk rules outside of the church and does not sit in the holy place, nor does he seek to bear the name of Christ but is an open antagonist of Christ and His church. This does not need to be revealed, but it is clear and evident because he persecutes Christians openly and not as the pope does, secretly under the form of godliness.

Philipp Melanchthon (1497-1560) was a German Reformer.
Since it is certain that the pontiffs and the monks have forbidden marriage, it is most manifest, and true without any doubt, that the Roman Pontiff, with his whole order and kingdom, is very Antichrist. Likewise in II Thes. 2, Paul clearly says that the man of sin will rule in the church, exalting himself above the worship of God, etc. But it is certain that the popes do rule in the church and under the title of the church in defending idols. Wherefore I affirm that no heresy hath risen, nor indeed shall be, with which these descriptions of Paul can more truly and certainly accord and agree than with this pontifical kingdom. (23)

Ulriucus Zuinglius (1487-1531) was a Swiss Protestant Reformer.
Let our doctrine be examined, and it will appear that they are false. We preach Jesus Christ and him crucified, and that he is the only Reconciler, and the only succor of man, but the Papists preach the Pope, the Antichrist, whom here Paul so accurately describes. (24)

John Hooper was the Bishop of Gloucester from 1551-1554, an English Reformer who was martyred during the Queen Mary persecutions.
Because God hath given this light unto my countrymen, which be all persuaded that the Bishop of Rome, nor none other is Christ's vicar upon the earth, it is no need to use any long or copious oration: it is so plain that it needeth no probation: the very properties of Antichrist, I mean of Christ's great and principal enemy, are so openly known to all men that are not blinded with the smoke of Rome, that they know him to be the beast that John describeth in the Apocalypse. (25)

In 1555, Master John Bradford, a faithful minister, valiantly and cheerfully gave his blood testifying against the ACBP. *The usurped authority of the supremacy of the bishop of Rome is undoubtedly that great Antichrist, of whom the apostles do so much admonish us. Wherefore I now am condemned and shall be burned as a heretic. For, because I will not grant the antichrist of Rome to be Christ's vicar-general and supreme head of his church here and everywhere upon earth, by God's ordinance.* (26)

296

Hugh Latimer, the Bishop of Worcester, was burned to death for his witness against the Pope, next to John Bradford and Nicholas Ridley.
What fellowship hath Christ with Antichrist? Therefore it is not lawful to bear the yoke with the Papists. Come forth from among them, and separate yourselves from them, saith the Lord.

Nicholas Ridley was the English Bishop of London.
The see of Rome is the seat of Satan, and the bishop of the same, that maintaineth the abominations thereof, is Antichrist himself indeed. And for the same causes, this see at this day is the same which St. John calls, in his Revelation, Babylon, or the whore of Babylon, and spiritually, Sodom and Egypt, the mother of fornications and abominations upon earth.

Thomas Cranmer (1489-1556) was the Archbishop of Canterbury.
He was responsible for establishing the first doctrinal and liturgical structures of the Reformed Church of England. He was tried for treason and heresy, imprisoned for two years. He was set in a tower and forced to watch the execution of Hugh Latimer and Nicholas Ridley. He fainted at the sight of the burnings, and under pressure, he renounced his faith. On March 21, 1556, he withdrew his forced confession, proclaimed the truth about the true faith, and testified against the Pope.

Christ biddeth us to obey the king. The bishop of Rome biddeth us to obey himself: therefore unless he be Antichrist, I cannot tell what to make of him. Wherefore if I should obey him, I cannot obey Christ. Whereof it followeth Rome to be the seat of antichrist, and the pope to be very antichrist himself. I could prove the same by many other scriptures, old writers, and strong reasons.   As for the Pope, I refuse him as Christ's enemy and the Antichrist, with all his false doctrine.

He was taken to where Latimer and Ridley had been burnt six months before and set on fire. He placed his hand in the fire, the one with which he had falsely signed the renouncement of his beliefs, and said, *"This hath offended!" He held his hand in the fire never pulling it out until the fire took all of him.*   Wow, what a hero of the faith!

John Hullie (1520-1556) was a Cambridge King's College minister. *Mark well here, good Christians, who is this beast, and worshippers that shall be partakers of that unspeakable torment. The beast is none other but the carnal and fleshly kingdom of antichrist, the pope with his rabble of false prophets and ministers, as it is most manifest; which, to maintain their high titles, worldly promotions, and dignities, do with much cruelty, daily more and more set forth and establish their own traditions, decrees, decretals, contrary to God's holy ordinances, statutes, laws, and commandments, and wholly repugnant to his sincere and pure religion and true worshipping.* (32)

John Knox (1505-1572), a great leader of the Reformation in Scotland. *First, then, not only are all the impious traditions and ceremonies of the papists taken away, but also that tyranny which the pope himself has for so many ages exercised over the church, is altogether abolished; and it is provided that all persons shall in the future acknowledge him to be the very antichrist, and son of perdition, of whom Paul speaks. The mass is abolished, as being an accursed abomination and a diabolical profanation of the Lord's Supper; and it is forbidden to all persons in the whole kingdom of Scotland either to celebrate or hear it. As for your Roman Church, as it is now corrupted. I no more doubt but that it is the synagogue of Satan, and the head thereof, called the Pope, to be the man of sin of whom the apostle speaketh.* (33)

William Fulke (1538-1589) was an English Puritan who disputed with SOJ priests about their false teachings. *The see being found, it is easy to find the person by St. Paul's description; and this note especially, that excludeth the heathen tyrants, 'He shall sit in the temple of God': which when we see to be fulfilled in the Pope although none of the eldest Fathers could see it, because it was performed after their death, we nothing doubt to say and affirm still, that the Pope is that 'Man of Sin,' and 'Son of Perdition,' the adversary that lifteth up himself 'above all that is called God'; and shall be destroyed by the spirit of the Lord's mouth, and by the glory of His coming.* (34)

Roger William (1603-1683) was the first Baptist Pastor in America.
He spoke of the Pope as *"the pretended Vicar of Christ on earth, who sits as God over the Temple of God, exalting himself not only above all that is called God, but over the souls and consciences of all his vassals, yea over the Spirit of Christ, over the Holy Spirit, yea, and God himself, speaking against the God of heaven, thinking to change times and laws; but he is the son of perdition.*

In *Fall of Babylon*, Cotton Mather (1663-1728) said, *Is the Pope of Rome to be looked upon as The Antichrist, whose coming and reigning was foretold in the ancient oracles? The oracles of God foretold the rising of an Antichrist in the Christian church; and in the Pope of Rome, all the characteristics of that Antichrist are so marvelously answered that if any who read the Scriptures do not see it, there is a marvelous blindness upon them.*

In *A Discourse on the Man of Sin*, Samuel Cooper (1725-1783) said, *If Antichrist is not to be found in the chair of St. Peter, he is nowhere to be found.*

Sir Isaac Newton (1643-1727) was a faithful expositor of prophecy.
But it [the little horn] was a kingdom of a different kind from the other ten kingdoms. By its eyes it was a Seer; and by its mouth speaking great things and changing times and laws, it was a Prophet as well as a King. And such a Seer, a Prophet and a King, is the Church of Rome. With his mouth he gives laws to kings and nations as an Oracle; and pretends to Infallibility, and that his dictates are binding to the whole world; which is to be a Prophet in the highest degree.

Jonathan Edwards (1703-1758) was an American Gospel preacher.
So that antichrist has proved the greatest and most cruel enemy the church of Christ ever had, agreeable to the description given of the church of Rome, (Rev. 17:6) 'And I saw the woman drunken with the blood of the saints, and with the blood of the martyrs of Jesus.' Thus did the devil, and his great minister antichrist, rage with violence and cruelty against the church of Christ! And thus did the whore of Babylon make herself drunk with the blood of the saints and martyrs of Jesus!

John Wesley (1703-1791) was an Anglican cleric and theologian.
He (the Pope) is in an emphatical sense, the Man of Sin, as he increases all manner of sin above measure. And he is, too, properly styled the Son of Perdition, as he has caused the death of numberless multitudes, both of his opposers and followers. He it I that exalteth himself above all that is called God, or that is worshipped, claiming the highest power and highest honor, claiming the prerogatives which belong to God alone. <u>The whole succession of Popes from Gregory VII are undoubtedly Antichrist</u>. Yet this hinders not, but that the last pope in this succession will be more eminently the Antichrist, The man of sin, adding to that of his predecessors, a peculiar degree of wickedness from the bottomless pit." (40)

Rev. J. A. Wylie (1808-1890), Scottish historian of religion, minister.
The same line of proof which establishes that Christ is the promised Messiah, conversely applied, establishes that the Roman system is the predicted Apostacy. In the life of Christ we behold the converse of what the Antichrist must be; and in the prophecy of the Antichrist, we are shown the converse of what Christ must be, and was. And when we place the Papacy between the two, and compare it with each, we find, on the one hand, that it is the perfect converse of Christ as seen in his life; and on the other, that it is the perfect image of the Antichrist, as shown in the prophecy of him. We conclude, therefore, that if Jesus of Nazareth be the Christ, the Roman Papacy is the Antichrist. (41)

Charles Haddon Spurgeon (1834-1892), Reformed Baptist preacher.
Her idolatries are the scorn of reason and the abhorrence of faith! The iniquities of her practice and the enormities of her doctrine almost surpass belief! Popery is as much the masterpiece of Satan as the Gospel is the masterpiece of God! There can scarcely be imagined anything of devilish craftiness or Satanic wickedness which could be compared with her—she is unparalleled as the queen of iniquity. Behold upon her forehead the name, MYSTERY, BABYLON THE GREAT, THE MOTHER OF HARLOTS AND ABOMINATIONS OF THE EARTH. The Church of Rome and her teachings are a vast mountain of rubbish covering the Truth of God! For weary years good men could not get at the Foundation because of this very much rubbish.

300

It is the bounden duty of every Christian to pray against Antichrist, and as to what Antichrist is no sane man ought to raise a question. If it be not the popery in the Church of Rome there is nothing in the world that can be called by that name. If there were to be issued a hue and cry for Antichrist, we should certainly take up this church on suspicion, and it would certainly not be let loose again, for it so exactly answers the description.

Popery is contrary to Christ's Gospel, and is the Antichrist, and we ought to pray against it. It should be the daily prayer of every believer that Antichrist might be hurled like a millstone into the flood and for Christ, because it wounds Christ, because it robs Christ of His glory, because it puts sacramental efficacy in the place of His atonement, and lifts a piece of bread into the place of the Saviour, and a few drops of water into the place of the Holy Ghost, and puts a mere fallible man like ourselves up as the vicar of Christ on earth; if we pray against it because it is against Him, we shall love the persons though we hate their errors: we shall love their souls though we loath and detest their dogmas, and so the breath of our prayers will be sweetened because we turn our faces towards Christ when we pray.

I am ashamed that sons of the Reformers should bow themselves before the beast and give so much as a single farthing to the shrine of the devil's firstborn son. Take heed to yourselves, ye Protestants, lest ye be partakers of her plagues; touch her not, lest ye be defiled. Give a drachma to her, or a grain of incense to her censors, ye shall be partakers of her adulteries and partakers of her plagues. Every time you pass the house of Popery let a curse light upon her head: Thus saith the Lord:—'Come out of her, my people, that ye be not partakers of her sins and that ye receive not of her plagues. For her sins have reached unto heaven, and God hath remembered her iniquities.

These are battles with sin, and battles with false doctrines, and battles with war. Fight these battles Christian and you will have enough to do. We must have no truce, no treaty with Rome. War! War! War! with her!

There cannot be peace. She cannot have peace with us – we cannot have peace with her. She hates the true Church, and we can only say that the hatred is reciprocated. We would not lay a hand on her priests; we would not touch a hair of their heads. Let them be free; but we will attempt to destroy their doctrine from the face of the earth because it is the doctrine of demons. (42)

The *Wisconsin Evangelical Lutheran Synod*, founded in 1850, stated this about the Pope and the Catholic Church. *There are two principles that mark the papacy as the Antichrist. One is that the pope takes to himself the right to rule the church that belongs only to Christ. He can make laws forbidding the marriage of priests, eating or not eating meat on Friday, birth control, divorce, and remarriage, even where there are no such laws in the Bible. The second is that he teaches that salvation is not by faith alone but by faith and works. The present pope upholds and practices these principles. This marks his rule as antichristian rule in the church. All popes hold the same office over the church and promote the same antichristian belief, so they all are part of the reign of the Antichrist. The Bible does not present the Antichrist as one man for one short time, but as an office held by a man through successive generations. It is a title like King of England.* (43)

In *Romanism And The Reformation*, Henry Grattan Guinness says, *The rule of Rome revived in a new form, and was as real under the popes of the thirteenth century as it had been under the Caesars of the first. It was as oppressive, cruel, and bloody under Innocent III. as it had been under Nero and Domitian. The reality was the same, though the forms had changed. The Caesars did not persecute the witnesses of Jesus more severely and bitterly than did the popes; Diocletian did not destroy the saints or oppose the gospel more than did the Inquisition of Papal days. Rome is one and the same all through, both locally and morally. One dreadful wild beast represents her, though the symbol, like the history it prefigures, has two parts. There was the undivided stage, and there has been the tenfold stage. The one is Rome pagan, the other Rome Papal; the one is the old empire, the other the modern pontificate; the one is the empire of the Caesars, the other is the Roman Papacy.*

You shrink from it, do you? I accept it. Conscience constrains me. History compels me. The past, the awful past rises before me. I see THE GREAT APOSTASY, I see the desolation of Christendom, I see the smoking ruins, I see the reign of monsters; I see those vicegods, that Gregory VIII, that Innocent III, that Boniface VIII, that Alexander VI, that Gregory XIII, that Pius IX; I see their long succession, I see their abominable lives; I see them worshipped by blinded generations, bestowing hollow benedictions, bartering lying indulgences, creating a paganized Christianity! I see their liveried slaves, their shaven priests, their celibate confessors; I see the infamous confessional, the ruined women, the murdered innocents; I hear the lying absolutions, the dying groans; I hear the cries of the victims; I hear the anathemas, the curses, the thunders of the interdicts; I see the racks, the dungeons, the stakes; I see that inhuman Inquisition, those fires of Smithfield, those butcheries of St. Bartholomew, that Spanish Armada, those unspeakable massacres. I see it all, and in the name of the ruin it has wrought in the Church and in the world, in the name of the truth it has denied, the temple it has defiled, the God it has blasphemed, the souls it has destroyed; in the name of the millions it has deluded, the millions it has slaughtered, the millions it has damned; with holy confessors, with noble reformers, with innumerable martyrs, with the saints of ages, I denounce it as the masterpiece of Satan as the body and soul and essence of antichrist.

The saints who have gone before us have told us who is the *son of perdition* and the *antichrist beast*, but the enemy has pushed their witness aside. We are called to expose the enemy's deceptions, cast down their power over people, and help set the captives free. We may pay a price for our witness, maybe even our life, but the heavenly rewards for those who wage war against the enemy are priceless.

> *Who will rise up for me against the evildoers? or who will stand up for me against the workers of iniquity?* Psalm 94:16

CHAPTER 55 - THE SEVENTH TRUMPET

The seventh trumpet in Revelation 11 represents the Protestant Reformation, when Messiah saints took back control of the nations, the Word of Yah was spread around the world, and the Gospel was preached. It foretold His coming bowl judgments upon those who obeyed the ACBP in killing the saints.

The first four trumpet judgments point to armies being sent against the pagan Roman Empire. The first *woe* judgment was fulfilled during the fifth trumpet when the Muslims were sent to attack apostate Orthodox Christians in the Roman Empire. The second *woe* judgment was fulfilled during the sixth trumpet when the Turks were sent to attack the apostate Orthodox Christians in the Eastern Roman Empire.

The third *woe* judgment is fulfilled during the seventh trumpet, starting a sequence of seven bowl judgments, which are poured out against the ACBP and Catholics. The Popes used Catholics to kill tens of millions of saints, and they still practice apostate Roman Christianity and have not repented, so judgment awaits them.

"The kingdoms of this world are become the kingdoms of our Lord, and of his Christ" may be better translated as *"are becoming,"* as it's a process. Protestant saints led the kingdoms that the Popes had controlled, so the Father and Messiah are glorified in this victory! The saints are supposed to keep protesting against the *antichrist beast* and the false salvation of his church, to set the captives free.

The Catholic nations saw the *two witnesses*, the Scriptures and the saints, come back to life and take back control of the nations. Catholics had obeyed the ACBP in killing the saints and burning the Scriptures, and they could sense that their judgment was at hand.

Revelation 9 foretold the Turks attacking Constantinople, which caused Greek priests to take the Scriptures to Western Europe. Revelation 11 told the saints to *measure* what the Popes taught against the Scriptures, and they determined that the RCC is an *apostate* church that is not part of the true Ekklesia, and they came out of her.

Revelation 10 told the saints that they would enter a time of proclaiming the Gospel again, as they had been given the Scriptures, the *little book*. The Reformation was, effectively, *the republication of the gospel*. Revelation 11 proclaimed that the saints would come back to life after being deemed as *dead*, and they were called to witness against the ACBP and their false gospel message. Messiah heralded the Reformation, as it could only have been by the direct intervention of Divine Providence because nothing could have been less likely to succeed by human agency alone because the ACBP's were effective at silencing the saints.

Look at the Revelation Fulfillment Chart. The 1st layer describes the three different phases of the Roman beast and its leaders. The 2nd layer is the chronological narrative of the seven church eras. And the 3rd layer is made up of the various prophecies in Revelation, which overlay the other two layers.

Revelation 12-13 is about the different phases of the Roman beast kingdom, so Revelation 14 picks up the chronological narrative after chapter 11. After the *little book* of Revelation 10, *measuring the temple* in Revelation 11, and the *two witnesses* of Revelation 11, comes the narrative of the *harvests* of Revelation 14, which are about the Protestant Reformation and the bowl judgments against those who persecuted the saints.

Joseph Benson's Commentary on Revelation (1847) says, *The same select number that was mentioned Revelation 7:4, the genuine followers of the twelve apostles, apostolically multiplied, and therefore the number of the church, as six* *hundred and sixty-six is the number of the beast; Or rather, the meaning is, that they had kept themselves pure from the stains and pollutions of spiritual whoredom, or idolatry, with which the other parts of the world were miserably debauched and corrupted. 144,000 refers to a type of people, rather than the numerical sum. It represents the Israel of Elohim, a Set-Apart people; who are not a part of the harlot system. It represents the first fruits of the Protestant Reformation. They are not literally before the throne of Elohim.*

In *The Last Prophecy*, Edward Bishop Elliott says, *While the antichrist beast, the usurper of Christ's supremacy, had been exalting himself against God and blaspheming, - with clergy and councils aiding and abetting, with Rome for his capital, and the world wondering after him, worshiping him, and receiving his mark – there were all the while in existence, though trampled on and oppressed, another city and another people, the followers of the Lamb, with their Father's name upon their foreheads.*

They had been, on the commencement of the Apostasy, depicted as the subjects of divine grace, elected out of the symbolic Israel, and sealed as the 144,000. Preserved against the judgments of false Christendom and witnessing against the evils that increased around them, they yet remained indestructible and were ultimately triumphant. These 144,000 are now again pictured to St. John, presenting a beautiful and animating contrast to the visions of the Antichristian beast and his people.

Most people associate the *'harvest of the earth'* in Revelation 14 with Messiah's return. But when you understand the proper context, you see that it's pointing to the harvest of the Protestant Reformation and the judgment of those who *revered* and *obeyed* the ACBP.

In reading Revelation 14:6-7, recall that the word *'angel'* can point to an earthly messenger, a Pastor. This passage describes the Protestant Reformers who proclaimed the Gospel of the *little book* of Revelation 10. The Protestant Reformation reaped a great harvest for Yah's kingdom, as millions of people came out of Rome's *harlot* church. This led to the witness of worldwide missions, and Bible societies and millions of people were redeemed for the kingdom. HalleluYah!

"Every nation, and kindred, and tongue, and people" is the domain of the ACBP. We see that proved out in Revelation 13:7.

> *And it was given unto him to make war with the saints, and to overcome them: and power was given him over all kindreds, and tongues, and nations.*

It's pointing to the Gospel being preached again in the European countries of the Popes' domain. Since the Protestant Reformation, the everlasting Gospel has been broadcast and published throughout the world.

Revelation 14:8-11 is pointing to the Catholic countries who *revered* and *obeyed* the ACBP's command to kill the saints. They are judged as part of the great winepress of the wrath of Yah during the bowl judgments.

The Protestant Reformers proclaimed that the office of the papacy, the Popes of Rome, fulfill prophecy as the *little horn* of Daniel 7, the *son of perdition* of 2 Thessalonians 2 and the *antichrist beast* of Revelation. They proclaimed that the Popes' *harlot* church was *Mystery, Babylon the Great,* who had made the nations drunk with her sorcery.

The RCC responded with the *Council of Trent* in the 16th century, when they empowered the SOJ to bring the Protestants back under their control. They implemented the Inquisition to torture and kill the Protestants. The Popes caused the leaders of countries, such as France and Spain, to persecute the saints.

In Revelation, there are two separate contexts to the *'mark of the beast.'* The first is referenced in Revelation 14-16, which applied to the people in the ACBP-controlled countries of France, Spain, etc., who *revered* (*mark* on *forehead*) and *obeyed* (*mark* on the *right hand,* actions) the ACBP, and killed the saints. They felt the wrath of Yah during the bowl judgments, which were poured out on those countries.

The second fulfillment is referenced in Revelation 13 and 19, and it applies to the end-times One World Government, which we'll cover in another chapter.

Joseph Benson's Commentary on Revelation (1847) says, *By Babylon is meant Rome, including the antichristian kingdom, the papal hierarchy seated there. Her fornication is her idolatry, invocation of saints and angels, worship of images, human traditions, with all that outward pomp, yea, and that fierce and bloody zeal, wherewith she pretends to serve God. But, as Bishop Newton observes, though Rome, with the antichristian power above described, was evidently here intended, it would not have been prudent to predict and denounce its destruction in open and direct terms; it was for many wise reasons done thus covertly under the name of Babylon, the great idolatress of the earth, and enemy of the people of God in former times. If any man worship the beast — That is, embrace and profess the religion of the beast; or, what is the same, the religion of the Papal hierarchy.*

Revelation 14:12-13 is describing the saints who are killed during the Inquisition. This directly relates to the *little book* bringing *bitterness*, as the ACBPs were in a rage because the Scriptures were being proclaimed to the masses, so they empowered the SOJ army to counter the Reformation. Even when faced with persecution, torture, and death, the set-apart saints kept the faith. They didn't follow the teachings of the Popes of Rome, but rather they followed the commands of Scripture.

France was known as the *'eldest son'* of the Papacy, who had the mark of the beast as they *revered* (*mark* on forehead) the Pope and *obeyed* (*mark* on hand, action) his commands to persecute and kill the saints. From 1540-1570, Papal Rome sent army after army of Roman Catholic soldiers into Southern France and surrounding areas to try to exterminate the Waldensian Bible-believing Christians. These Roman Catholic armies butchered up to 900,000 Waldensian Christians – men, women, and children – during those thirty years. Monks and priests, dressed in holy garments — directed, with heartless cruelty and inhuman brutality — the work of torturing and burning alive innocent men and women, and doing it in the name of Christ — by the direct order of the *'Vicar of Christ!'*

In 1572, Roman Catholic soldiers butchered upwards of 100,000 French Protestants (Huguenots) during the *St. Bartholomew's Day Massacre* that started in Paris. The (Roman Catholic) king of France had cleverly arranged a marriage between his sister and Admiral Coligny, the chief Protestant leader. There was a great feast with much celebrating. After four days of feasting, the soldiers were given a signal.

At midnight, all the houses of the Protestants in the city were forced open at once. The admiral was killed, his body thrown out of a window into the street where his head was cut off and sent first to the Roman Catholic Cardinal of Lorraine and then on to the ACBP. In the first three days, over ten thousand were killed. The bodies were thrown into the river, and blood ran through the streets into the river until it appeared like a stream of blood. From Paris, the destruction spread to all parts of the country. Very few Protestants escaped the fury of the RCC persecutors.

At Orleans, a thousand were slain of men, women, and children, and six thousand at Rouen. At Meldith, two hundred were put into prison, and later brought out by units and cruelly murdered. At Lyons, eight hundred were massacred. At Augustobona, on the people hearing of the massacre at Paris, they shut their gates that no Protestants might escape. They searched diligently for every individual of the Reformed Church, imprisoned and then barbarously murdered them.

Upon hearing of the bloodshed in Paris, Pope Gregory XIII celebrated by declaring a jubilee day of public thanksgiving. He had a coin made to commemorate the *St. Bartholomew's Day Massacre*, which shows an angel (symbolizing the *harlot* RCC) holding a cross and a sword slaying the Huguenot saints.

It represents the RCC as an avenging angel slaying the '*heretics*,' offering them the alternative of the crucifix or the sword. The dead lie all around the feet of the blood-drunk slayer.

Subsequently, Pope Gregory XIII commissioned a mural by Giorgio Vasari to hang in the Vatican depicting the wondrous St. Bartholomew's Day Massacre. The king also commanded the day to be kept with every demonstration of joy, concluding that the Huguenots' whole race was extinct. Google images of '**St. Bartholomew's Day Massacre**'.

In 1685, the Roman Catholic French King Louis XIV, at the urging of his father-confessor, Jesuit priest Pere La Chaise, revoked the '*Edict of Nantes*' that had granted religious liberty to the Protestants. The King then ordered his murderous dragoons to persecute the French Protestant Huguenots. They took their children and put them in Catholic schools. They confiscated their property. They demolished their churches. The French Soldiers lodged in the Huguenot houses and used them as horse stables. They raped the women and imprisoned them in convents. They made the men be galley slaves. They burned their Bibles. Five hundred thousand innocent Protestants were killed! The Huguenot's prayers cried out for vengeance!

Here's a coin that King Louis XIV had struck, which says '*Extinguish Heresies*,' marking his revocation of the *Edict of Nantes* (1685), causing the saints to be persecuted. It features a lady, the *harlot* church of Rome, seeking to eliminate the *witnesses* against them.

Here's a 1686 French medal marking the Huguenots' destruction, in which the Pope is wearing his three-tiered tiara. He's holding two keys in his left hand, declaring his authority in heaven and earth, and three arrows in his right hand, signifying his thunderbolt bulls. An SOJ priest is holding a scroll, no doubt their *Constitutions*, which lay out their plan to bring the Protestants back under the pope's power.

There is a French horseman with a sword, leading saints to their death; a woman hanging from a scaffold; dead saints on the ground with animals eating their bodies, and a crowd of priests looking on. There's no mistaking who is the *antichrist beast*!

In each parish, the Popish French governors declared that the king would no longer suffer any Huguenots (French Protestants) in his kingdom, that they had to change their religion and become Catholic, either freely or by force. The Protestants replied that they *'were ready to sacrifice their lives and estates to the king, but their consciences being God's they could not so dispose of them.'*

Instantly the troops seized the gates and avenues of the cities, and placing guards in all the passages, entered with sword in hand, crying, *"Die, or be Catholics!"* And they practiced every wickedness and horror they could devise to force them to change their religion. There are many more stories of the saints being killed, which you can read in *Foxes' Book of Martyrs.*

In *History Unveiling Prophecy*, Henry Grattan Guinness says, *Meanwhile, back in Paris, the King of France and his Court spent their time drinking, reveling, and carousing. The Court spiritual adviser—a Jesuit priest—urged them to massacre the Protestants—as penance for their many sins! To catch the Christians off-guard, every token of peace, friendship, and ecumenical goodwill was offered.*

Suddenly—and without warning—the devilish work commenced. Beginning at Paris, the French soldiers and the Roman Catholic clergy fell upon the unarmed people, and blood flowed like a river throughout the entire country. Men, women, and children fell in heaps before the mobs and the bloodthirsty troops. In one week, almost 100,000 Protestants perished. The rivers of France were so filled with corpses that for many months no fish were eaten. In the valley of the Loire, wolves came down from the hills to feel upon the decaying bodies of Frenchmen. The list of massacres was as endless as the list of the dead!

Many were imprisoned—many sent as slaves to row the King's ships—and some were able to escape to other countries. The massacres continued for centuries. The best and brightest people fled to Germany, Switzerland, England, Ireland, and eventually America and brought their incomparable manufacturing skills with them. France was ruined.

You can see why judgment was warranted against the Catholics who *revered* and *obeyed* the ACBP in killing the saints. This all points back to the profound importance of 1514. Recall that the *ACBP* had been so effective at eliminating the *two witnesses* against them that they proclaimed that all of Christendom was under their authority, and that there was no witness left against them, that they were *as good as dead*.

Recall that Messiah put the Scriptures into the saints' hands during this time so that they could see who is the *son of perdition*, the *antichrist beast*, the enemy of Messiah and His saints. The harvest of souls out of the RCC was great, leading to the Popes' power being reduced. Catholics were starved for Scriptural truth, as the Papal Church priests taught in Latin. When Martin Luther and the Protestant Reformers preached the pure Gospel, millions were reaped unto Yah's harvest. Now Messiah, our crowned King, is reaping souls for His kingdom through the Protestant Reformation.

In Revelation 14:17-20, '*without the city*' is pointing to those outside of *Holy Jerusalem*, which we saw in Revelation 11:1-2 is pointing to the RCC, which is not part of the temple of Yah. The '*sharp sickle*' represents the coming bowl judgments of Revelation 16 against Catholics in France and Spain.

In *The Rise and Fall of the Papacy* (1701, Robert Fleming says, *And the winepress was trodden without the city, and blood came out of the winepress, even unto the horse bridles, by the space of a thousand and six hundred furlongs. Rev 14:20 Now what place can we imagine to be so properly meaning by this as the territory of the see of Rome in Italy, which, from the city of Rome to the furthermost mouth of the River Po and the marshes of Verona,* is extended the space of 200 Italian miles, that is exactly 1600 furlongs; the Italian mile consisting of eight furlongs.

Joseph Benson's Commentary on Revelation (1847) says, *The stage where this bloody tragedy is acted is without the city, by the space of a thousand and six hundred furlongs, which, as Mr. Mede ingeniously observes, is the measure of stato dello chiesa, or the state of the Roman Church, or St. Peter's patrimony, which, reaching from the walls of Rome unto the river Po and the marshes of Verona, contains the space of two hundred Italian miles, which make exactly sixteen hundred furlongs. The time of God's vengeance, his appointed time is fully come, for the iniquities of the inhabitants of the earth have made them fully ripe for destruction.*

The Popes of Rome, the kings who *revered* and *obeyed* him, and the Catholics who carried out his orders to kill the saints; all deserved punishment. In the bowl judgments, our Messiah faithfully answers the saints' prayers for vengeance to be poured out on those who persecuted them. HalleluYah!

And I saw another sign in heaven, great and marvelous, seven angels having the seven last plagues; for in them is filled up the wrath of God. And I saw as it were a sea of glass mingled with fire: and them that had gotten the victory over the beast, and over his image, and over his mark, and over the number of his name, stand on the sea of glass, having the harps of God.

And they sing the song of Moses the servant of God, and the song of the Lamb, saying, Great and marvelous are thy works, Lord God Almighty; just and true are thy ways, thou King of saints. Who shall not fear thee, O Lord, and glorify thy name? for thou only art holy: for all nations shall come and worship before thee; for thy judgments are made manifest.
Revelation 15:1-4

CHAPTER 57 - REBEL WITHOUT A CAUSE
16ᵀᴴ CENTURY

To understand the mindset of the FPJSG, who controls the Roman beast kingdom in the end times, we need to look more into the life of Ignatius Loyola. This narrative from a Catholic priest, Father Cyprian, paints the picture well.

The Devil sat in hell and doubled himself up with pain, because the monk Luther was courageous enough to encroach on the round world, and to upset the old order of things. "Is it not sufficient," he screamed, "that it resounds from afar that the wicked one dares to venture an attack on the spiritual power; must he also be bold enough to turn everything upside down in my own kingdom and dominion? He has taken up a position and will rob hell if I do not oppose him by a greater power. And who will help me in this severe exigency, when the world threatens to depart from its course?" Thus howled Satan, and flogged his brains in such a way as to make his black forehead the color of blood. At this juncture the Serpent, the old poisonous beast, who nearly burst his belly with malice, deceit, and cunning, whispered softly a couple of words. The Devil lost not a syllable in his innermost thoughts. Up he sprang, and his swollen breast was relieved, and his eye shone again with pleasure and lust. Nine months after that a woman gave birth to a youngster whose name was Don Inigo de Loyola.

You may think that vision is hyperbole, but you will see that it's not. Ignatius Loyola, born as Don Inigo Lopez de Recalde, was born at Loyola's castle in 1491. His family was wealthy. His older brother reportedly sailed to the *New World* with Christopher Columbus, which is interesting, given the Jesuits' influence in America. Ignatius was friends with the powerful Charles Habsburg, King Charles I of Spain, Emperor Charles V of Rome.

In his book *The History of the Jesuits* (1914), Hector Macpherson gives us the sordid story of Inigo's evil calling.

In due course Ignatius entered upon a military career, in which he greatly distinguished himself, but in the course of which he met with an accident, which completely changed the current of his life. A wound which he received in battle laid him aside for a time from active duties. During his tedious illness he took to reading Roman Catholic literature. He underwent a spiritual change. He longed to devote himself as whole-heartedly to the Church as he had done to the army. He gave himself up to asceticism of the extremist type. We are told that he clothed himself in black filthy garments, and allowed his uncurled hair to fall over his unwashed face.

As the result of his long fasts he had fainting fits, and in his trances, on his own affirmation, he had visions of the saints, especially of the Virgin Mary. His delusions led him to imagine that he had been translated directly to heaven, where God with His own hand had placed him close beside His own Son, Jesus Christ. His brother, alarmed no doubt for his sanity, urged Ignatius to give up all his nonsense and act like other men. All in vain. Ignatius persisted in his new career, In order to chastise himself for his former love of pleasure; he flogged his body till the blood flowed. He took himself to a hospital in order to live with beggars and sick people. We are told that he never slept in a bed, not even on straw, but upon the bare naked ground, and subsisted during the whole week on nothing but water and bread, which he obtained by begging in the streets.

He girded himself round the body with an iron chain, with which he duly flogged himself three times a day; he no longer made use of any comb or scissors, so that his appearance became perfectly horrible to a degree that, whenever he made his appearance, he was surrounded by the street boys who ran screaming after him, bespattering him with rotten eggs and mud. Accidentally the discovery was made of his noble birth, and, as a consequence, interest in him was greatly increased. To avoid publicity Ignatius found a convenient cave, which he made into a hiding place. In the cavern he increased his penance, abstaining from food and drink for several days. When he did eat, his food consisted of roots which grew in front of his cave, and old bread which he had brought with him from the hospital.

He flogged himself with his chain six times a day instead of three times, prayed for seven hours on his naked knees. In order to increase his bodily mortification he reduced his sleep to the minimum. Impressed with the idea that in the matter of penance and mortification he had fallen short, Ignatius was afflicted with remorse. As the result of his unnatural way of life and his morbid broodings, his imagination in a state of disorder called up pictures of the devil, with claws, horns, club-feet, and black face. He had also visions of the Savior surrounded by heavenly hosts, ready to engage in conflict with Satan and his hirelings. Imagination ran riot.

On one occasion Ignatius, we are told, saw "the Holy Spirit in the form of three piano notes closely bound together hanging upon a stalk, and to his holy eyes, moreover, the Host was transformed into the true God-man."Ignatius was on the point of paying with his life for his pious experiments. For eight days he lay unconscious, and would certainly have died had he not been accidentally discovered by some passers-by and conveyed to the hospital, where he received proper attention.

His prolonged penances, his ecstatic raptures his marvelous visions, brought Ignatius no peace of mind. As the result of conversation with the priests to whom he made confession, he was led to see that he had a mission which demanded all his energies. He realized that as the outcome of the work of Luther a crisis had arisen in the Romish Church. "The Romish Church, the Papacy, and the Pope himself," said Ignatius, "and the whole religious fabric must collapse, owing to its former supports being now thoroughly worm-eaten, unless some entirely new foundation pillars can be found." It was borne in upon him that he had a mission, the rooting out of the heresy of the Reformers and the conversion of the heathen.

Ignatius carried out an all-night vigil at Mount Montserrat, where he put his military shield and sword on the altar of the Madonna, the *Shrine of the Black Virgin*. He committed his service to the *Queen of Heaven*, who is Semiramis of the Babylonian Mystery Religion.

Much like Mohammed, who received visions of the text of the Qur'an while in a cave, Loyola was in the *Cave of Manresa* when he was given the militant, self-mortifying *'Spiritual Exercises,'* which he went through as Satan used them to form his mindset. And the JSGs have used them ever since to shape the minds of SOJ leaders to die to themselves.

Ignatius carried out the ritual mysticism of Spain's illuminated ones, called the *Alumbrados*, the *Spanish Illuminati*. Their rituals caused them to believe that the Holy Spirit was leading them, and they were given vision and revelation. But no doubt it was a different spirit working.

And no marvel; for Satan himself is transformed into an angel of light. 2 Corinthians 11:14

Just as Satan responded to the falling Roman Empire by creating his masterpiece, Romanism, to seek to destroy the true faith from within, now he is empowering a military army to bring the saints and the whole world back under his authority. To counter the Protestant Reformation, the ACBP empowered Loyola and his company of Jesuits. He is called the JSG because he commands an army of soldiers fighting against Messiah and His saints, and the whole world, to bring everyone under the authority of the ACBP.

On September 27, 1540, Pope Paul III, after carefully studying Loyola's Plans, christened them by the famous bull *Regimini Militantis Ecclesiae (On the Supremacy, or Rulership of the <u>Church Militant</u>)*, thus inaugurating Loyola's grand geopolitical design.

In June 1541, Paul III gave Loyola's company the parish *Santa Maria Della Strada – Our Lady of the Road –* a church dedicated to Mary, under whose patronage Loyola's company was consecrated. <u>Loyola credited his conversion to his vision of the Madonna and dubbed himself a knight of the Holy Virgin.</u>

In *Romanism And The Reformation*, Henry Grattan Guinness says,
Look at this other book (the Constitutions of the Jesuits, their war manual). It is the volume of the laws and constitution of the Jesuits. Here, on p. 10, the Jesuit

is taught that his superior, whoever he may be, must be recognized, reverenced, and submitted to with perfect and complete subjection of act and thought, as occupying the place of Jesus Christ. Thus the priest in the confessional and the superior in the Jesuit order, and the bishop and archbishop and cardinal, all reflect the sacerdotal supremacy of the pope, who sits there in God's very temple, the temple of conscience and of the Christian Church, as a usurping god quasi Deus, as if God Himself.

Rise up, O Luther! cry out concerning "the Babylonian captivity of the Church," burn the Papal bull, rouse Germany; but you shall have your match. Satan shall bring forth his Loyola, and Loyola his Jesuits subtle, learned, saintly in garb and name, protean in form, infinite in disguises, innumerable, scholars, teachers, theologians, confessors of princes, politicians, rhetoricians, casuists; instruments keen, unscrupulous, double-edged; men fitted to every sphere and every enterprise they shall swarm against the Church of the Reformation, each one wise in the wisdom and strong in the strength which are not from above but from beneath.

In *The Power and Secrets of the Jesuits* (1930), Rene Fulop-Miller says, *At the very time when Ignatius was attempting, with the help of his newly founded order, to bring the world "under the dominion of God," Calvin was making the same attempt in the narrow confines of the Republic of Geneva. Just as the foundation of the Society of Jesus called his efforts "military service for God," so Calvin called his work a "holy military service for the Supreme Captain," and the Genevan reformer, too, often spoke of the "glory of God when he summoned his followers to the campaign against sin.*

This sets up the battle between Martin Luther, a former Catholic monk, led by the Spirit to expose the ACBP and his *harlot* church. And Ignatius Loyola, who is led by Satan to counter Luther and the Protestant Reformers. That battle is still playing out, and sadly, the SOJ seems to be winning the war, as they have deceived the end-times saints about prophecy fulfillment so that they're not protesting against the enemy of Messiah anymore. I pray that there's a great awakening so that the saints overcome the enemy for the glory of our Warrior King!

CHAPTER 58 - LOYOLA VERSUS LUTHER
16ᵀᴴ CENTURY

The parallels and contrasts of the lives of Ignatius Loyola and Martin Luther are profound. Both of their lives were committed to the RCC, but the impact of what took place in the sixteen century has been felt for five hundred years. It's no exaggeration to say that it affects the whole world even today.

In *The Jesuits: Their Moral Maxims And Plots Against Kings, Nations, And Churches* (1881), James Aitken Wylie contrasts Loyola and Luther.

Loyola was rapidly rising to the proud position of the first solder in Spain, and to be the first soldier in Spain was to occupy no second place among the champions of Christendom. Luther was the first name in the university of Erfurt; and now he saw opening to him the gate which led to the office of the State and the dignities of the Church, where he hoped to leave a name that would shine like a star in the future of his country's history.

It was at this stage of their career that a hand was put forth, and a sudden arrest was laid on both. Each became the subject of a solemn and awful dispensation, which said to them plain as articulate speech, "No farther can you proceed on this path. Henceforth the current of your life must be diverted into another channel."

As Luther, one day, was returning to Erfurt, from a journey which he had made into the country, the heavens suddenly grew black; an awful tempest broke over him, the thunders rolled through the sky, and flashes of unwonted brightness blaze all round him, and to add to the horrors of the scene, a bolt struck a companion who was journeying with him, and laid dead at his feet. Luther expected every moment to appear before the great tribunal. Trembling and horror fell upon him, and he stood riveted to the spot. When he emerged from the cloud his whole thoughts had undergone a change. He had been baptized in the cloud and in the fire.

It was in the battlefield that Loyola underwent his great change. He was fighting at the siege at Pampeluna, the capital of Navarre, and whilst contending against fearful odds he was wounded, and laid senseless, and almost lifeless on the field. He was carried to a hospital to be cured, where he endured month of excruciating pain, relieved by periods of intense mental excitement and visionary rapture, produced by the "Lives of the Saints," which were given him to read, and which he greedily devoured in the solitude of his chamber. Thus were both men, in the full tide of the success – their honors on the point of blossoming – lead hold upon, and brought in a moment to the grave's brink.

Luther submitted to the Word of God, which is truth, and filled with the Spirit of God, which is love, led the nations out of their prison-house. Loyola, full of pride and rebellion, and hating the truth, strove by every Satanic device, and by every unholy and cruel weapon to compel the nations to return to their prison, and lie down in their old chains. Loyola hung up his sword and shield at the shrine of Mary, and took a vow to be her servant and soldier. He would go round the world doing battle in her cause, and offering to all blasphemers and impugners of the deity the alternative of "conversion or the sword."

At this state in his career, he had a vision shown him, in which he plainly beheld two cities or camps, and two armies engaged in mortal combat. "These gloomy towers and dungeon-keeps on the left," said a voice to him, "which murky clouds overhang, are the strongholds of Babylon. You see her dark warriors mustering phalanx on phalanx at her gates. These shining battlements on the right are Jerusalem, and these soldiers in bright armor, posted on her walls, are her defenders. You are the chosen captain who is to lead in this great war. Go forth and conquer, thou mighty man!" So spake the voice in the ear of his imagination.

In *The Black Pope: A History of the Jesuits* (1896), M.F. Cusack says,
The one uplifts the banner of light and spiritual freedom; the other forges new chains for the enslaving of the human race – spiritually and intellectually – and transmits the worst evils of the dark ages to posterity. Loyola consecrates himself to the service of the Virgin Mary and puts on her livery. Luther puts on the whole armor of God. Loyola fasts, flogs himself, and sees visions, but does

not find peace; the more he flogs himself and fasts, the more visions he sees. Luther cries aloud "the just shall live by faith."

The close of the fifteenth century witnessed the birth of two children who were destined to make history. Luther was born in 1483. Eight years afterwards Don Inigo Lopez de Ricalde was born. The one was destined to be the precursor, who proclaimed Gospel liberty to the enslaved; the other was destined to forge new chains for the souls of men and to bind them with cords of steel.

For Luther, born of a humble family, an unnoticed career would have been anticipated; he might, indeed, have aspired to the cloister, for it was then the resort of the poorest and the least educated in the community. But for Loyola, the descendant of Spanish grandees, a brilliant career in court and tented field would have seemed little short of a certainty. But when the pages of life came to be unfolded for these two men, how different was the result to the anticipation.

The fame of the lowly-born Luther has echoed down the stream of time, as the champion of religious liberty, and if he was somewhat rude in his mode of denouncing error, his rudeness was as much the outcome of his earnestness and sincerity, as of the habits of the times in which he lived.

As for Ignatius Loyola, he also has had his fame and his applause, but his fame has not been the fame of an enlightener of mankind, or of one who has advanced civil or religious liberty. His applauders have not been those who have loved truth and hated dissimulation. Sad indeed that the once chivalrous and knightly Loyola should have become the founder of an institution which has reduced the practice of deceit to a fine art, and taught its members how to conceal and practice evil under a semblance of virtue.

Loyola was empowered to counter the Protestant Reformation, make war with the saints, and bring the Protestants and all of the world under the ACBP's authority.

Luther was declared a heretic, anathematized, and excommunicated. A Jesuit priest hated Luther so much that he cursed him but would not utter his name, *"I may not make mention of this hellish monster by name, this traitor to the Catholic religion, this fugitive from the cloister, this restorer of all heresy, this hideous wretch before God and man."*

Can you see the historical battle that was set up in the sixteenth century? The militant army of the SOJ was created to counter Messiah and His saints. Luther shined the Gospel's light, and the SOJ sought to extinguish it with their dark works. Luther followed Scripture to serve His Heavenly Father and Messiah; Loyola followed the Babylonian Talmud and Egyptian Kabbalah to serve the god of this earth, Satan.

Luther sought to bring the Scriptures to the people and preach the Gospel; Loyola sought to create corrupt Bibles and push false gospels through apostate Christian churches.

Loyola's SOJ leaders go through all of his *Spiritual Exercises* to reprogram their minds so that they die to themselves and obey the General without question. Luther urged people to read the Scriptures, to transform their thoughts so that they have the mind of Messiah to die to themselves and obey the Father.

Even today, we see this battle for the crux of the narrative is that the SOJ leaders are making war with Messiah's saints, though they now do it covertly through people groups.

We're at war. Satan has programmed the minds of the enemy to serve him at all costs. Messiah is looking for brave soldiers who will lay down their lives for the glory of their King.

> *Also I heard the voice of the Lord, saying, Whom shall I send, and who will go for us? Then said I, Here am I; send me.* Isaiah 6:8

We win the war by teaching the truth about prophecy's fulfillment, which validates Scripture's authority and Messiah's deity. This casts down the power of Satan, the ACBP, and the FPJSG over people so that the captives are set free and redeemed for the kingdom.

CHAPTER 59 - ENGINEER CORPS OF HELL

Ignatius calls his army of Jesuits *'the Society of Jesus,'* but the leaders are the opposite, *'the Society of Satan,'* for this is who they serve. The lower tier of SOJ priests believe that they're serving Jesus, but the SOJ leaders have been programmed to believe that the Black Pope, the JSG, is Jesus. In the Jesuit *Constitutions*, their Bible, it repeats five hundred times that the trainee must see Christ in the person of the JSG.

So when a Jesuit, or one of their minions, says that they're serving *'God,'* they are pointing to serving the cause of the ACBP, who have proclaimed to be God. And when a Jesuit, or one of their minions, says that they're serving *'Jesus,'* they're pointing to serving the JSG.

The *Spiritual Exercises* of the SOJ leaders involve systematic trained and testing, which lasts over fourteen years. The training of high-level Jesuit priests is the most extreme form of mind-control programming. It breaks their spirit to become *as dead* so that they serve the JSG's orders without question. It takes the trainee through emotion-inducing exercises, through visualization, through self-flagellation, through self-denial, through fasting, etc. They are taken mentally and physically through heaven and hell, tortured by burning pain, and blessed with spiritual visualizations.

They're taken through the life of Messiah, putting themselves through all that He experienced, from being beaten, spit on, flogged with the Roman whip, and crucified. Every detail is magnified so that they experience it to the full. All of that seems like a noble thing until you realize that it's all done to program their minds to defend Christ, their JSG, with all of their vigor and even their life. They are put through the experience of being in hell, focusing on what they see, hear, taste, and feel; so that they are overwhelmed with a terror of the fiery pit. And again, that seems noble until you realize that it's all done to program their minds to serve God, the ACBP.

Can you see how the SOJ trainee thinks that he is carrying out pious exercises but is being led to blindly serve the JSG for the ACBP's glory? Their psyche is formed so that every human impulse is put under intense discipline not to be subject to normal men's arbitrary moods. Their emotions are put aside by their will to serve and carry out their mission. This explains how they, and their minions, can carry out heinous crimes against humanity and not have any remorse, as they do it all for *'the glory of God,'* the ACBP.

They become devout officers in the militant order, whose role is to conquer Protestantism and the whole world. They have no will of their own; they will obey any assignment given to them, even that of a despised Jew or a Protestant pastor. If the General says white is black, they believe it. They revere the JSG as infallible, as God, as Jesus Christ.

The SOJ leaders are the military of Satan. Many books have been written about the *Spiritual Exercises* that form their minds and their Oath, which binds them to obedience at the cost of their life; and their *Constitutions,* their war manual. You can search for their *Spiritual Exercises,* their *Oath,* and their *Constitutions* on Google and YouTube and find much more information if it's not been suppressed.

Hector Macpherson, in his book *The History of the Jesuits* (1914), says, *Ignatius conceived the idea of creating a new organization with which to combat the Reformation. He gathered round him six associates, four Spaniards, one Portuguese, and one Savoyard. For the purpose of dedicating themselves to the "Holy Vow," the seven assembled themselves in the crypt of Notre-Dame de Montmarte (Church of the Queen of Heaven, Mary) on 15th August 1534, where they bound themselves by oath to follow the course which had been mapped out. Ignatius placed himself before the altar and swore upon the Bible to live henceforth a life of poverty, chastity, and obedience. Ignatius swore to fight to all eternity only for the things of God (effectively, the Pope), of the Holy Mary (the Queen of Heaven), and her Son, Jesus Christ (effectively, the Jesuit General) - a true spiritual knight; as also for the protection of the Holy Romish Church.*

After him the six others took the same oath. As they at last rose up from their knees, Ignatius Loyola marked upon the altar three large capital letters - I.H.S. "What do these signify?" demanded the others. "They signify," answered Ignatius, 'Jesus Hominum Salvator ' (Jesus the Savior of Mankind)- and they shall henceforth be the motto of our institution."

Edwin A. Sherman in Engineer Corps of Hell (1883), says, *Imagine an association whose members having destroyed all ties of family and of country, to be singled out from among men, and whose forces are to be concentrated at last to one united and formidable end, its plan devised and it establishes its dominion by all possible means over all the nations of the earth.*

Imagine this immense conspiracy having in place substituted its rules and its policy, yet, to the same principles of religion, that, little by little, they have arrived to dominate over the princes of the church, to maintain a royal slavitude, although not confessed, and of such a manner, that those who officially have the titles and assume the responsibility, are nothing but the docile instruments of a force hidden and silent. Such are the Jesuits. Always expelled, forever returning, and little by little clandestinely and in the darkness throwing out its vigorous roots.

Henry VI, "the one king of whom the people have treasured his memory," found three assassins successfully, and died under the knife of a fanatic, at the same time he was about to attack the favorite government of the Jesuits – Austria. Its society grows and increases in riches and influence by all sorts of means; and no one can attack them, for everywhere we find men prompt to serve them, to obtain from them some advantage of position or pride.

Some of the chapter titles of the Monita Secreta of the Jesuits: 'System that must be employed with widows and the manner to dispose of their properties;' 'Methods by which the sons of rich widows are to be made to embrace the religious state or that of devotion.' 'The method by which me must charge the confessors and preachers to the great of the earth.' 'Mode of making profession of despising of riches.'

Having ceased to care for the widow, to capture the inheritances, to rob the children from their families, of intriguing near the great, of influencing in the politics of the nations, of working to the last with but one object that is not the triumph of religion, but the engrandisement of the "Company of Jesus" and the establishment of its dominion on the earth.

The formidable "Company of Jesus" is a society of dead men! Established and directed with the proposition of universal domination, this Society presents in the means of its organization such power of invasion that we cannot think of it without being oppressed by a species of fear.

For themselves, that are nothing, not having pompous titles, no sumptuous ornaments, no crosiers, no mitres, no capes of the prebendaries, but pertain to that one Order everywhere governing and directing. Of command, others have the appearance; but these possess the reality. In whatever place of the Catholic world a Jesuit is insulted or resisted, no matter how insignificant he may be, his is sure to be avenged – and this we know.

Who are they? The agents of espionage, intrigue, and accusations; the prime moves of the leagues, civil wars and dragonnades, schisms, murderers; that is what they are! Incarnate enemies of legitimate liberty, partners of despotism; that is what they are! Disturbers of the peace of all states and of all families, seducers and conspirators; instructors of the assassinations of kings; authors of slavery and the stolidity of peoples; vassals and oppressors in the name of God to popes, kings, peoples and to the most holy and illustrious men; THAT IS YOUR HISTORY!

In *The Babington Plot*, J.E.C. Shepherd says, *Between 1555 and 1931, The Society of Jesus was expelled from at last 83 countries, city-states, and cities for engaging in political intrigue and subversive plots against the welfare of the state. We read in the sentence given by the parliament of France in 1662: The institute of the Jesuits is inadmissible, for its nature in its whole estate is contrary to natural right, opposed to all authority, spiritual and temporal, and on the road to introduce under the cloak of a religious institution, a body politic, whose essence consists in the continual activity, to reach by whatever* *way their desire, direct or indirect, secret or public, until first an absolute independence, and successively the usurpation of all authority.*

The sentence of 1762 contained the following paragraph relating to the morals of the Jesuits. The moral practice of the Society of the Jesuits is perverse, destructive of all religious principle and probity; injurious to the Christian morality; pernicious to civil society; seditious and contrary to the rights and nature of the royal power, and to the sacred persons of the sovereigns, and to the obedience of the subjects; they are adapted to excite the greater revolts in the States and to re-form and sustain the most profound corruption in the hearts of men. (1)

From 1759-1773, Catholic leaders of Europe were preoccupied with abolishing the SOJ. Emmett McLaughlin's book, *An Inquiry in to the Assassination of Abraham Lincoln* (1963), summarizes these events very succinctly. *Even their own Catholic countries finally came surfeited with Jesuit political intrigue and financial avarice and, in self-preservation, were forced to expel them. Portugal, Angola, Goa, and Brazil took the lead in 1759. France followed in 1764. Several Italian states such as Parma, Sicily, and Naples followed suit. By sealed imperial orders sent to her colonies around the world, Spain threw out the Jesuits in 1767. This decree suppressed them in the Philippines, Argentina, New Granada (Columbia), Peru, Chile, Ecuador, Guatemala, Cuba, Puerto Rico, Mexico, New Mexico, and Arizona. Austria did the same in 1773.*

Finally, Pope Clement XIV, in 1773, issued the document, Dominus ac Redemptor, abolishing the Jesuit Order altogether, listing eleven poses that tried to curb their excesses. Among them were Benedict XIV, Innocent XI, Innocent XIII, and Benedict XIV. He cited the Jesuits for opposition to "other religious orders.' For 'revolts and intestine troubles in some of the Catholic states,' and 'persecutions against the church in Europe and Asia. There remained no other remedy to so great evils... and this step was necessary in order to prevent the Christians from rising one against the other and from massacring each other in the very bosom of our common mother, the holy church. Therefore, he wrote, "after a mature deliberation, we do out of our certain knowledge and the fullness of our apostolic power, suppress and abolish the said company.

In *The Jesuits: Their Moral Maxims And Plots Against Kings, Nations, And Churches (1881)*, **James Aitken Wylie says,** *The very Mother out of whose bowels they sprung was compelled to confess that she had given birth to a progeny that would devour her unless she should find some means of ridding herself of them. Clement did the bold deed, knowing that he risked his life in doing it. On laying down his pen after affixing his name to the Bull of Suppression, he gave vent to the presentiment that oppressed him. "I have signed my death-warrant," he proclaimed.*

The mightiest Catholic nations of Europe banished the SOJ from their realms. These Catholic monarchs demanded that the Catholic Church abolish the society forever. Clement XIII, the pope at that time, initially resisted their wishes but finally capitulated. The night before he planned to do this, he was poisoned to death.

Now that you see the evil of the *Engineer Corps of Hell* and how Satan has formed their minds to die to themselves for their church's purpose, I want to remind you that to be useful for our Commander In Chief, we need to die to ourselves.

Then said Jesus unto his disciples, If any man will come after me, let him deny himself, and take up his cross, and follow me. Matthew 16:24

CHAPTER 60 – THE CONTEXT OF THE SEVEN BOWLS

Revelation 14 points to the great harvest of souls during the Protestant Reformation and the coming judgment of those who *revere* and *obey* the ACBP. Revelation 15 proclaims the wrath of Yah, which is directed at those who tortured and killed the saints during the 16th-18th centuries, so it's directed at Catholics and the Pope.

The Inquisition was the most notorious and devilish thing in human history! It was devised by the ACBPs and JSGs and used by them for hundreds of years to maintain their power. More than a million French Protestants were killed or run out of the country, many of which had their heads cut off in France's major cities and who were killed all around France. Spain and other Catholic countries also followed the Pope's orders in killing the saints.

In *The Approaching End Of The Age*, Henry Grattan Guinness says, *The Apocalypse presents us with two great companies of martyrs; one slain by pagan Emperors, on account of their testimony against heathen idolatry; the other slain by Christian Popes, on account of their testimony against Christian idolatry, against the corruptions and false doctrines of the Papacy. The martyrs represented in the fifteenth chapter of the book, standing as victors on the sea of glass, having "gotten the victory over the beast, and over his image, and over the number of his name," must be those slain by papal Rome. A previous group of martyrs are represented in the sixth chapter, who must therefore be those slain by Pagan Rome in the ten great persecutions of the church by the Caesars.*

In Yah's economy, every martyr who does not deny Messiah is a *victory* over the beast. The saints sang the *'song of the Lamb'* as they revere Messiah's blood sacrifice as the Passover Lamb, which paid the price for their sins, as opposed to the Catholic Church, whose mass of Transubstantiation denies Messiah's one-time atonement.

Psalm 75:8 shows us that a *'vial,'* a *'cup,'* in Scripture can represent Yah's judicial infliction upon His enemies. *For in the hand of the LORD there is a cup, and the wine is red; it is full of mixture, and he pours out of the same: but the dregs thereof, all the wicked of the earth shall wring them out, and drink them.*

Before we get to the fulfillment of the bowl judgments, let's note where we're at on the Revelation fulfillment timeline to see the bowl judgments' proper context. The Popes gained civil authority over the Roman Empire in 538, so their 1,260-year reign of power was coming to an end, and the next phase of the Roman beast, called the *earth beast*, was set to begin.

But there's a subplot, as Yah uses pagan armies to carry out His righteous judgment. During the 18th century, the SOJ had been serially expelled from the Portuguese Empire (1759), France (1764), the Two Sicilies, Malta, Parma, the Spanish Empire (1767), Austria, and Hungary (1782). In 1762, an Act of Parliament in France dissolved and banished the SOJ, noting: *Their doctrines destroy the law of nature; they break all the bonds of civil society, by authorizing theft, lying, perjury, the utmost licentiousness, murder, criminal passions, and all manner of sins; their doctrines root out all sentiments of humanity, overthrow all governments, excite rebellion, uproot the foundation of religion, and substitute all sorts of superstition, irreligion, blasphemy, and idolatry.*

Finally, in 1773, anti-SOJ forces succeeded in persuading Pope Clement XIV to sign the brief of dissolution *"Dominus ac Redemptor."* Clement knew that by signing their death warrant, he was signing his own as well, *"This suppression is done at last, and I am not sorry about it. I would do it again if it was not done already; but this suppression will kill me."*

The bull labeled them the *"bane of all nations."* It further accused them of *"tumults, disturbances, violences, and of disturbing the peace the Church and the nations."* In enumerating their faults, the Pope said that they were so great as to outweigh their services.

The SOJ are a vengeful bunch, and they wanted to carry out revenge against France primarily and the other countries which had kicked them out. But it started with Pope Clement XIV, who was poisoned to death by the SOJ in 1774. He lamented, *"Alas, I knew they would poison me; but I did not expect to die in so slow and cruel a manner."* (3)

In the bowl judgments, you will see how the countries which had kicked the SOJ out are the ones whose blood is spilled. And you will see that the Jesuits were used to remove the ACBP from power, ending his Yah-determined 1,260-year reign of power in 1798. So though the SOJ leaders are an evil group who serve Satan's plan, they're being used to carry out Yah's righteous judgments.

In *Notes on the Handbook of Revelation* (1852), Albert Barnes says, *The scenes which occurred in the times of the French revolution were such as would be properly symbolized by the pouring out of the first, the second, the third, and the fourth vials. With acts of atrocity and horror accompanying, scarce paralleled in the history of people; and suffering and anguish of correspondent intensity throbbing throughout the social mass and corroding it; what, from France as a center, spread like a plague throughout its affiliated societies to the other countries of papal Christendom, and was, wherever its poison was imbibed, as much the punishment as the symptoms of the corruption within.*

Interestingly, before the bowl judgments were poured out, a natural phenomenon happened in France.

In *Horae Apocalypticae*, Edward Bishop Elliott says, *Even the elements contributed to swell the public discontent, and seemed to declare war on the falling monarch. A dreadful storm of hail in July 1788 laid waste the provinces and produced such a diminution in the harvest as threatened all horrors of famine: while the severity of the succeeding winter exceeded anything that had been experienced since that which followed the disasters of Louis the XIVth.*

The Encyclopedia Britannica records that even the elements seem to have declared war on the French monarchy and citizens: On Sunday, July 13, 1788, about 9 am, without any eclipse, a dreadful darkness suddenly overspread parts of France. It was the prelude of such a tempest as is unexampled in the temperate climates of Europe. Wind, rain, hail, and thunder, seemed to content in impetuosity; but the hail was the greatest instrument of ruin.

Instead of the rich prospects of an early autumn, in the space of an hour presented the dreary aspect of universal winter. The soil was converted to a morass; the standing corn beaten into the quagmire; the vines broken to pieces; the fruit trees demolished. Even the forest trees were unable to withstand the fury of the tempest. Such a calamity must at any period have been severely felt, but occurring on the eve of the great political revolution, and amidst a general scarcity throughout Europe, it was peculiarly unfortunate and gave more embarrassment to the government than perhaps any other even whatever.

How amazing that even the weather was used to conspire against the people of France, as their judgment drew nigh!

The book *Paraphrase of the Revelation of Saint John According To E.B. Elliott* (1862) says, *As the book, in which the divine predictions were recorded, was sealed with seven seals, and each seal was in turn opened, and as on the opening of the seventh seal seven trumpets were in succession sounded, as the events of the seventh seal were to be successively developed; so now upon the sounding of the seventh trumpet, are seven angels bringing the seven bowl judgments.*

Judgment Of The Popes And Their Church
CHAPTER 61 - THE FIRST BOWL JUDGMENT

And I heard a great voice out of the temple saying to the seven angels, Go your ways, and pour out the vials of the wrath of God upon the earth. And the first went, and poured out his vial upon the earth; and there fell a noisome and grievous sore upon the men which had the mark of the beast, and upon them which worshipped his image.
Revelation 16:1-2

In *The Last Prophecy,* **Edward Bishop Elliott says,** *The similarity of the four first vials to the four first trumpets cannot escape observation. The localities, as well as other figures, are almost identical. The earth, the land division of Western Roman Christendom; the sea, its maritime colonies; the rivers, those two boundaries, the Rhine and Danube, and their valleys; the sun, the ruling emperor of one-third of the Roman earth, all these symbols, and their significations remain much the same.*

In *A Dissertation On Prophecies* **(1806), George Stanley Faber says,** *It may be observed that the contents of one vial are not represented as being fully poured at before another begins to be emptied; though it is evident that they commence in regular chronological succession. Hence it is not unreasonable to conclude that two or more of the vials may be pouring out at the same time, though the effusion of one commenced before that of another.*

The earth is the Roman empire: the men, who bear the mark of the beast and worship his image, are the once superstitious, but now atheistical, members of the Latin Empire and Church: and <u>the noisome and grievous sore, is the delusive spirit of atheism,</u> or that gross lie of Antichrist the denial of the Father and the Son. An open profession of Atheism was made by a whole nation once zealously devoted to the papal superstition, then commenced the eruption of the noisome sore.

The *'earth'* is still the Roman Empire, and judgment is coming upon the Catholics in this area, as they *revered* and *obeyed* the ACBP in killing the saints. The SOJ is being used to carry out these bowl judgments, though they do it out of selfish revenge.

Some of the best people who contributed to the great country of France were now gone. The *salt* and *light* of the Protestants had been killed or cast out, and France descended into darkness and decay. What would America be like if you removed all of the saints? It would quickly fall into great apostasy, to be sure. That's what happened to France.

> Isaiah 1:4-7 describes the House of Judah as a *sinful nation, a people laden with iniquity, a seed of evildoers, children that are corrupters... the whole head is <u>sick</u>, and the whole heart faint... <u>corrupted and full of putrefying sores</u>*.

The SOJ used people like French poet, dramatist, and historian Francois-Marie Arouet, better known by the pen name *Voltaire*, to guide the minds of the French in philosophy, as to cause them to throw off the chains of all religions. Voltaire mocked the Scriptural faith and reportedly proclaimed, *"It took twelve ignorant fishermen to establish Christianity, I will show the world how one Frenchman can destroy it."* Voltaire was the leader of *The Enlightenment*, whose writings caused France to enter an *'age of reason,'* which became their god. He declared that the Bible was false, and thus by association, so was the RCC.

Ironically, within thirty years of Voltaire's death, his home was purchased by the *Geneva Bible Society*, and it became a Bible storage building, while his infidel printing press was used to print an entire edition of the Bible. HalleluYah!

The Jansenists, an SOJ-led society utterly corrupt in morals and literature, propagated infidelity and sowed the seeds of revolution. Before the French Revolution, France was flooded with atheistic literature, from Voltaire, Diderot, Boyle, and Rousseau.

They waged a literary war with the Roman Church, which agitated the French people and led to massacres of Catholic priests and the aristocrats and Royalty that supported them. The people had witnessed the wholesale slaughter of the Protestant Huguenots, which shook their faith in the Papal Church. Now their minds were filled with atheism and rage, and the stage was set for the bloody French Revolution.

On August 26, 1792, the denial of God in France was for the first time formally established by law. The country fell into total apostasy, as the plague of infidelity and immorality, like an ulcerous sore, covered the nation from head to foot. This caused them to seek liberty from any religious institution, and they turned on the RCC. The result, which is explained in the next few bowls of judgment, resulted in the mighty Catholic nation of France being thrown into a civil war, which was deluged with its Catholic leaders' blood.

In *Horae Apocalypticae,* **Edward Bishop Elliott says,** *that tremendous outbreak of social and moral evil, of democratic fury, atheism, and vice, which characterized the French Revolution.*

Pere Bernard Lambert, a Dominican monk of Province, southern France, described the condition of France as *a sick man covered with ulcers.* (1)

The first bowl judgment was poured out when the SOJ caused the foul and loathsome *sore* of atheism to spread across France. The French Protestants had been killed, so the Catholic religion was all that was left. Yah allowed the abomination of atheism to turn the French people away from the RCC, so they were left with no hope.

In *Light for the Last Days,* **Henry Grattan Guinness says,** *About the year 1750 Voltaire began his scoffing attacks on Christianity in France, and for fifty years from that time he and his colleagues in the task of undermining all religious faith in the masses of the people, Rousseau, Diderot, and the Encyclopaedists, and others, were indefatigable in their attacks on the only form of Christianity with which they were acquainted-Popery.*

They succeeded in producing in France an intense hatred and contempt for the priesthood and the Church of Rome.

In *Horae Apocalypticae*, Edward Bishop Elliott quotes Voltaire, *"From this filthy Cocytus (river of hell) flowed those streams of impurity which disgraces France during the reign of Louis XV, and which continued in that of Louis XVI to affect society, morals, and literature." Such was the state of French morals, and so originated, at the time of the outbreak of the Revolution."*

In *The Life and Letters of Barthold* (1852), George Niebuhr says, *The revolution of 1789 is the <u>breaking out of local disease</u>, peculiar to the Roman Catholic nations and governments of southern Europe. The <u>malignity of the disease</u>, exclusively proper to the countries where it was indigenous - France and the South of Europe.*

In *Apocalyptic Sketches* (1850), John Cumming says, *Burke, the most eloquent orator of the day, called it "<u>the fever of Jacobinism</u>," – "the epidemic of atheistical fanaticism," – "such a plague, that the precaution of the most severe quarantine ought to be established against it." The result was "the corruption of all morals," "the decomposition of all society." It was during this terrific era that "the whole head was sick, and the whole heart faint: from the sole of the foot even unto the head there was no soundness in it, <u>but wounds, and bruises, and putrefying sores</u>."*

In *Lectures on the Book of Revelations* (1860), Rev. C.M. Butler says, *The French Father Lambert calls the irreligion of the period "a horrible ulcer," "moral gangrene." <u>Burke constantly uses the phrases, "the fever of the atheistical fanaticism," "the malignant French distemper," "the plague," and "the living ulcers,"</u> as expressive of the moral corruption of the revolutionary principals and practices. The Revolution was preceded by wide-spread infidelity and atheism. Blanco White, in his memoirs, tells us how infidelity was the inevitable revolt of reason against the dogmas and cruelties of the Papacy. If Popery were Christianity, no thoughtful mind could accept it.*

The infection spread to the other nations which had the mark of the beast and worshiped his image; for the emissaries and apostles of Jacobinism spread their principles widely over every part of Europe. Such as the terrific emptying of the first vial of the wrath of God. (5)

In *Notes on the Handbook of Revelation* (1852), Albert Barnes says, *The symbol would properly denote that "tremendous outbreak of social and moral evil, of democratic fury, atheism, and vice, which was especially seen to characterize the French Revolution that of which the ultimate source was in the long and deep-seated corruption and irreligion of the nation; the outward vent, expression, and organ of its Jacobin clubs, and seditious and atheistic publications; the result, the dissolution of all society, all morals, and all religion. The result of this was to affect the Papacy--a blow, in fact, aimed at that power.*

Of course, all the infidelity and atheism of the French nation, before so strongly papal, went just so far in weakening the power of the papacy; and in the ultimate result, it will perhaps yet be found that the horrid outbreaks in the French revolution were the first in the series of providential events that will result in the entire overthrow of that antichristian power.

In *The Last Prophecy*, Edward Bishop Elliott says, *Republican clubs and cheap infidel publications served under their direction to undermine the principles of the different ranks of society; and without religion to control them, the mass of the people were ready for any <u>outbreak</u> against government and social order. A tremendous <u>outbreak of social and moral evil</u>, democratic and popular fury, atheism and vice, characterized the French Revolution. From France, as a center, the <u>plague rapidly spread</u> through its affiliated clubs, and the whole of Papal Christendom soon imbibed the poison and shared the punishment.*

As the Catholics killed the saints in France, the light of Scriptural truth faded, and the country grew dark. This led to the French being turned against Romanism and the RCC, and they became infected with the moral sore of atheism. All of this was by the design of the SOJ, as it set the stage for a bloody social cataclysm.

338

The book *Paraphrase of the Revelation of Saint John According To E.B. Elliott* **(1862) says,** *It represents an extraordinary outbreak of moral and social evil, the manifestation of deep-seated disease within. This was that tremendous outbreak of social and moral evil, of democratic fury, atheism, and vice, which was speedily seen to characterize the French Revolution: ' that of which the ultimate source was in the long and deep-seated corruption and irreligion of the nation; the outward vent, expression, and organ in its Jacobin clubs, and seditious and atheistic publications; the result, the dissolution of all society, all morals, and all religion, with acts of atrocity and horror accompanying, scarce paralleled in the history of man, and producing anguish of correspondent intensity, throbbing throughout the social mass and corroding it. From France, as a centre, it spread like a plague throughout its affiliated societies, to the other countries of Papal Christendom, and wheresoever its poison was imbibed, was as much the punishment as the symptom of the corruption within.*

We can see how the SOJ set up the moral environment in which people turn against their RCC leaders, killing them and the priests, and destroying their basilicas. The SOJ could repeat this process in the future judgment of the RCC, to cause the world to turn against the *harlot* church, to hate her because of her evil deeds in the world, and *burn her and desolate her.*

In recent headlines, Catholic churches are being attacked in Europe, in the U.S. and other places, as people take out their rage about the crimes of the RCC and their wicked priests who have carried out sexual crimes on children in parishes around the world.

> *But whoso shall offend one of these little ones which believe in me, it were better for him that a millstone were hanged about his neck, and that he were drowned in the depth of the sea. Woe unto the world because of offences! For it must needs be that offences come; but woe to that man by whom the offence cometh!* Matthew 18:6-7

CHAPTER 62 - THE SECOND BOWL JUDGMENT

And the second angel poured out his vial upon the sea; and it became as the blood of a dead man: and every living soul died in the sea. **Revelation 16:3**

In striking parallelism with the judgments under the trumpets, the second bowl judgment is on the waters.

Two scenarios point to the *sea becoming as blood*, both fulfilled during this period. A '*sea*' can point to a large group of people, as the French leaders and Catholic priests' blood was poured out in Paris where many saints had been killed. The *Reign of Terror* commenced in Paris, and the blood of the French people flowed. French politician and Freemason Bertrand Barère exclaimed on September 5, 1793, in the Convention: *"Let's make terror the order of the day!"*

The royal guard and some five thousand leading royalists were killed. They dethroned, imprisoned, tried, and condemned King Louis XVI (of the French Royalty who had initiated the *St. Bartholemew's Day Massacre* and Revocation of the *Edict of Nantes* and Dragonnades against Protestants) and Queen Marie Antoinette (of the Hapsburgs who had persecuted Bohemian and Netherlands Protestants). They were beheaded, and with that fell the government of France, laden with the crimes of centuries of oppression, corruption, and cruelty.

SOJ trained Maximilien Robespierre, a French lawyer, and politician, as well as one of the best known and most influential figures associated with the French Revolution and the *Reign of Terror*; said: *If the basis of popular government in peacetime is a virtue, the basis of popular government during a revolution is both virtue and terror; virtue, without which terror is baneful; terror, without which virtue is powerless.* <u>*Terror is nothing more than speedy, severe, and inflexible justice; it is thus an emanation of virtue.*</u> (1)

The People's New Testament by Barton Johnson (1891) says, *The French Revolution, the uprising of enslaved masses who were maddened into fury, sent Catholic king, royal families, nobles, and priests to the guillotine by tens of thousands, impelled the nation in its madness to publicly declare itself atheistic, leavened it with skepticism, and broke the hold of Rome to such a degree that she can never more control France. As the result of breaking forth of this ulcer, the mightiest Catholic nation was convulsed with civil war, every Catholic country in Europe was deluged in blood, and the Papal power received a shock from which it can never recover.*

In *A Dissertation On Prophecies* (1806), George Stanley Faber says, *The second vial relates to the dreadful massacres of revolutionary France which commenced early in the September of 1792, which, extending from the metropolis to the provinces, converted that unhappy country into one great slaughter-house. The sea symbolizes a nation in a violent state of effervescence and revolution: and, when it is said to become as the blood of a dead man, we are evidently led to conclude that the nation this was deeply stained with the blood of its slaughtered citizens. For a considerable time, in the interior of France, each recent event surpassed in horror that which preceded it; and the metropolis was the center of the massacre, atheism, and anarchy.*

In *History Unveiling Prophecy*, Henry Grattan Guinness says, *Initially, those who fell victim to the guillotine were the aristocrats, the clergy, and the members of the royal family. The "reign of terror" witnessed the slaughter of one million and twenty-two thousand persons, of all ranks and ages, and of both sexes, till the streets of Paris ran with blood, and the guillotines could not overtake their work. Thousands were mowed down by grape-shot fusillades; drowned in "noyades," where in loaded vessels, hundreds of victims were purposely sunk in the rivers. They were roasted alive in heated ovens or tortured to death by other infernal cruelties. Christianity was publically renounced, and a prostitute enthroned as 'goddess of reason' at Notre Dame, and worshipped by the National Convention, and by the mob of Paris, with the wildest orgies of licentiousness.*

The great massacre of St. Bartholomew was cast into the shade by "the St. Bartholomew of five years," as the massacre of the Revolution has been called. More than 30,000 were massacred in the city of Lyons; at Nantes, 27,000; in Paris 150,000; in la Vendee, 3,000. In all France, about two millions of persons were massacred, of whom 250,000 were women; 230,000 children; and 24,000 priests.

At Lyons, the scaffold opposite the Hotel de Ville, where the trials were conducted, was kept in ceaseless employment. Around its bloody foundations, large quantities of water were daily poured, but they were inadequate to wash away the ensanguined stains or remove the fetid odor. So noxious did they become, that Dorfeuille, the functionary entrusted with the executions, was obliged to remove it to another situation; where it was placed directly above an open sewer, ten feet deep, which bore the gore away to the Rhone. The washerwomen there were obliged to change their station from the quantity of blood which became mingled with its waters. At length, when the executions had risen to thirty or forty a day, the guillotine was placed in the middle of the bridge at Mo-rand in the center of the Rhone, into which the stream of blood at once fell, and into which the headless trunks and severed heads were precipitated. Yet even this terrible slaughter, which went on without intermission for three months, appeared insufficient to the Jacobins. So immense were the numbers of those who were cut off by the guillotine or mowed down by the fusillades that three hundred men were occupied for six weeks in covering with earth the vast multitude of corpses that filled the trenches which had been cut in place of the Department at Nantes to receive the dead bodies. Ten thousand died of disease, pestilence, and horror in the prisons of that department alone.

France became drenched in blood, and the whole territory converted into a vast slaughter-house. The French Catholics had stolen the saints' wealth, and now the people confiscated the RCC's vast revenues and all the estates of refugee nobles for the state's use. Notre Dame in Paris was converted into the *'Temple of Reason,'* and 40,000 churches were turned into stables.

In *History of Europe from the Commencement of the Revolution* (1815), **Sir Archibald Alison noted,** *From Samur to Nantes, a distance of 60 miles, the Loire was for several weeks red with human blood; the ensanguined stream, far a sea, divided the blue waves of the deep. The multitude of corpses it bore to the ocean was so prodigious that the adjacent coast was strewn with them; and a violent west wind and high tide having brought part of them back to Nantes, followed by a train of sharks and marine animals of prey, attracted by so many human bodies, they were thrown ashore in vast numbers.*

Do you see how Yah has carried out vengeance against people who *revered* and *obeyed* the ACBPs in killing the saints?

The secondary fulfillment points to the 'sea' as literal waters. The sphere of this judgment was in a special sense a maritime one.

In *Notes on the Handbook of Revelation* (1852), **Albert Barnes says,** *The proper application, according to this interpretation, would be the complete destruction or annihilation of the naval force that contributed to sustain the papacy. This we should look for in respect to the naval power of France, Spain, and Portugal, for these are the only papal nations that have had a navy. We should expect, in the fulfillment of this, to find a series of naval disasters, reddening the sea with blood, which would tend to weaken the power of the papacy, and which might be regarded as one in the series of events that would ultimately result in its entire overthrow.*

In the year 1793, the greater part of the French fleet at Toulon was destroyed by Lord Hood; in June, 1794, followed Lord Howe's great victory over the French off Ushant; then the taking of Corsica, and nearly all the smaller Spanish and French West India Islands; then, in 1795, Lord Bridport's naval victory, and the capture of the Cape of Good Hope; as also soon after of a French and Dutch fleet, sent to retake it; then, in 1797, the victory over the Spanish fleet off Cape Vincent; and that of Camperdown over the Dutch; then, in succession, Lord Nelson's three mighty victories — of the Nile in 1798, of Copenhagen in 1801, and in 1805 of Trafalgar.

Altogether in this naval war, from its beginning in 1793 to its end in 1815, it appears that there were destroyed near 200 ships of the line, between 300 and 400 frigates, and an almost incalculable number of smaller vessels of war and ships of commerce. The whole history of the world does not present such a period of naval war, destruction, and bloodshed."

The sea became as the blood of a dead man; and may show also that, on the supposition that it was intended that these events should be referred to, an appropriate symbol has been employed. No language could more strikingly set forth these bloody scenes.

The People's New Testament by Barton Johnson (1891) says, *Protestant England and Catholic Europe strive together upon the ocean. The old Catholic powers, those which in the past have been the vile instruments of Papal wrong, the nations whose kings have committed fornication with the great spiritual harlot, suffer the loss in this long and deadly struggle of six hundred ships of the Line, the largest war vessels that then went to sea, besides the thousands of ships of war of smaller size. At the close of the contest, the naval power of Catholic Europe had been swept from the ocean.*

In *The Last Prophecy*, Edward Bishop Elliott says, *There was the destruction of the maritime power and commerce of the colonies of Papal Christendom. The democratic revolutionary spirit of France and the naval force of England contributed to effect the purpose of Divine Providence.*

We can see that the symbolic '*sea*' of people in the large cities of France had their blood shed, and we can see that the literal '*sea*' was full of French naval personnel's blood.

This devastation of the nation of France was their punishment for *revering* and *obeying* the ACBP in killing the saints. The French Catholics had terrorized the Protestants, and the Reign of Terror came against them! Yah truly does exact vengeance on the enemy of the saints. HalleluYah!

CHAPTER 63 - THE THIRD BOWL JUDGMENT

And the third angel poured out his vial upon the rivers and fountains of waters; and they became blood And I heard the angel of the waters say, Thou art righteous, O Lord, which art, and was, and shalt be, because thou hast judged thus. For they have shed the blood of saints and prophets, and thou hast given them blood to drink; for they are worthy. And I heard another out of the altar say, Even so, Lord God Almighty, true and righteous are thy judgments. **Revelation 16:4-7**

Again we see the parallel between the third trumpet judgment, which was on the *rivers and fountains of water*.

The people of France killed many saints around the Rhine, Danube, and Po River Valleys. Lutherans, Moravians, Albigenses, Waldenses, Vaudois, Hussites, and Huguenots; were killed for their faith. Now, France's people were killed in the same places, and the rivers filled with their blood.

In *The Last Prophecy*, Edward Bishop Elliott says, *This judgment was to take place on those countries watered by the Rhine and Danube, as well as upon Northern Italy. Even so it fell out. During the year 1792, war was declared by France against Germany, and the next year against Sardinia; consequently, all those towns watered by the Rhine and Alpine streams became scenes of carnage.*

Metz, Worms, Spires, the towns formerly desolated by Attila, suffered. In 1793 and 1794, war still raged in the same quarters. The French advanced to Holland. In many places, the success fluctuated, but in most instances, they were victorious, Moreau and Jourdan, and their armies to the Rhine. In 1797 Bonaparte attacked the Sardinians and Austrians. The course he tracked was from Alpine river to river through Northern Italy, till he reached Venice. Every river was a scene of carnage, and he cross seven in succession. The Alpine rivers were turned to "blood."

It was in 1797 that Bonaparte uttered the remarkable threat, "I will prove an Attila to Venice." Again in 1799, the "fountains of waters" were dyed in blood, the French having suffered reverse and been driven out of all the places they occupied in North Italy with much bloodshed. The war soon recommenced: In 1800, that terrible and decisive battle of Marengo was fought, and the Danube became the scene of judgment. Once victory after another succeeded, till the memorable battle of Austerlitz completed the overthrow of the Austrian power.

The reason given by the angel for the judgment is remarkable, "They are worthy, for they have shed the blood of saints and prophets, and thou hast given them blood to drink." Was it not so that the cruelties – of the French and Piedmontese and the rulers of Savoy against the Waldenses and Albigenses, the Huguenots and Calvinists, from the end of the thirteenth to the end of the eighteenth century, and of Austria against the Hussites, the Waldenses and Lutherans in Lombardy, Moravia, and the Netherlands already related did call out for retributive justice?

Indeed, 'the rivers and springs of water became bloody,' as Messiah poured out His vengeance on the people and countries who *revered* and *obeyed* the ACBPs in killing the Protestants. HalleluYah!

In *Notes on the Handbook of Revelation* (1852), Albert Barnes says, *In regard to the application of this, there are several things to be said. The following points are clear: (a) That this judgment would "succeed" the first-mentioned, and apparently at a period not remote. (b) It would occur in a region where there had been much persecution. (c) It would be in a country of streams, and rivers, and fountains. (d) It would be a just retribution for the bloody persecutions which had occurred there. The nations here referred to had been engaged in scenes of bloody persecution, and this is a just recompense. To wit, by turning the streams and fountains into blood. Blood had been poured out in such abundance that it seemed to mingle with the very water that they drank.*

In *A Dissertation On Prophecies* **(1806), George Stanley Faber says,** *The first three vials relate to the French Revolution, describing at once the principles upon which it was founded, and the miseries both internal and external which it has produced. This tremendous revolution, which more or less has affected the whole Roman Empire, I conceive to be the first period of the third woe-trumpet, which John figuratively describes under the image of a harvest; a harvest not of mercy, but of God's wrath against the nations.*

The People's New Testament by Barton Johnson (1891) says, *There are two marks given which help us to locate the seat where the plague of the third vial is poured. One, it must be a region of rivers and fountains of waters. Two, it has evidently been the scene of terrible persecutions of the people of God. This very region, which was full of rivers, was the home of the Albigenses. Against them, the Papacy had hurled its fanatical legions from generation to generation. The blood of the Protestants of the Alps had for centuries dyed the rocks and streams with crimson.*

Revelation of Saint John According To E.B. Elliott **says,** *The judgments of the third vial were a righteous retribution from God on the counties and nations judged, for murders previously committed by them on His saints and prophets.*

The third bowl judgment was poured out as the bloody French Revolution spread out from the major cities (*seas*) to the rural areas where they had shed the blood of saints, and now it was time for them to drink the same fate.

Recall the medals that the ACBP and the King of France had minted to commemorate the murders of the Huguenots during their evil St. Bartholomew's Day Massacre.

With the first three bowl judgments, the country of France was filled with blood. This is the punishment for them having the *mark of the beast*, as they *revered* the ACBP and *obeyed* him in killing Messiah's saints. The Heavenly Father's wrath continues to be poured out against the ACBP and Catholics in the remaining bowl judgments.

CHAPTER 64 - THE FOURTH BOWL JUDGMENT

And the fourth angel poured out his vial upon the sun; and power was given unto him to scorch men with fire. And men were scorched with great heat, and blasphemed the name of God, which hath power over these plagues: and they repented not to give him glory.
Revelation 16:8-9

Once more, the parallelism with the trumpet judgments is seen, as it is poured out on the *sun*.

The People's New Testament by Barton Johnson (1891) says, *Since these vials of the wrath of God are "poured into the earth" (Rev 16:1), the sun must be used as a symbol. It is a symbol of a supreme ruler—a ruler or king. Anyone who becomes a great light and occupies a pre-eminent position may be indicated by this symbol. The Saviour is described as the Sun of Righteousness in Malachi 4:2.*

As you've already seen in the apocalyptic vision, the *'sun'* symbolically represents a primary ruling leader. *'Fire,'* the instrument of bitter pain, is a symbol of *suffering*. Therefore, it is evident that the ruler, symbolized by the *sun*, shall be the means of inflicting great suffering upon men. The fourth bowl is pointing to Napoleon Bonaparte, who had seized power after the French Revolution.

From 1796 to 1815, Napoleon and his armies, referred to by historians as the *'scourge of Europe,'* *scorched* the European continent, causing much bloodshed in the places they had shed the saint's blood.

In *Notes on the Handbook of Revelation* (1852), Albert Barnes says, *"A revolution in France," said Napoleon, "is sooner or later followed by a revolution in Europe."*

In *Vision Of The Ages* (1881), Barton Johnson says, *He converted Europe into a great camp, and every nation was blackened and torn with wars. In his wars, it is estimated that 2,000,000 men perished by the sword, and none* can tell of the want and misery and despair that brooded over the bleeding and desolated lands that were tracked by his armies.

Dr. Alexander Keith (1792–1880), a historian and Church of Scotland minister known for his biblical prophecy writing, said, *Napoleon performed the miracles of genius. His achievements still dazzle while they amaze the world. Within the space of eight years, he scorched every kingdom in Europe, from Naples to Berlin, and from Lisbon to Moscow. Ancient kingdoms withered before the intense blaze of his power… Kingdoms were unsparingly rift like garments… <u>like the sun</u>; there was nothing hid from his great heat*

In *History Unveiling Prophecy*, Henry Grattan Guinness said, *The overthrow of Roman Catholic governments and enormous destruction of life connected with the wars of Napoleon. With the rise of Napoleon, the French Revolution took a new character, and became the scourge of Europe. The armies of France were now led on an unparalleled career of conquest by that man who was the most "gigantic manifestation of mental power and despotic will" the world had ever seen.*

Arrogant, unscrupulous, selfish, remorseless, ambitious, self-reliant, with indomitable vigor, unwearying energy, marvelous military genius, surpassing administrative ability, uniting a lofty comprehensive intellect with utter disregard for moral considerations, Napoleon sacrificed the lives of millions, overturned the throne of Europe, revived the Empire of Charlemagne, and strove to obtain monarchy of the world.

Within the space of eight years, <u>he scorched every kingdom in Europe</u>, from Napes to Berlin, and from Lisbon to Moscow. Ancient kingdoms withered before the intense blaze of his power. <u>Like the sun</u>, there was nothing hid from his great heat, and the exercise of his power was the misery of millions.

The Catholic nations which had warred for centuries against the Reformed faith were successively crushed under the feet of this ruthless despot; thrones overturned, crowns trampled in the dust; armies scattered; cities pillages; provinces wasted with war; and reduced to desolation. Spain, which had crushed the Reformation within in her own borders, and in other lands, by the

349

horrors of the Inquisition, and the Auto da Fe, was delivered over to the dreadful bloodshed and miseries of the seven years Peninsular war: the Inquisition suppressed; and a revolutionary spirit awakened which has made the country since the theater of endless strife, disaster, and decay.

It was as if the sun were smitten in the heavens, and power was given to scorch men with fire. Europe seemed to be on fire with musketry and artillery and presented almost the appearance of the broad blaze of a battlefield. The number that perished was immense. These wars were attended with the usual consequences – blasphemy, profaneness, and reproaches of God in every form. But the Pope did not repent; he did not acknowledge Elohim's righteous judgment against the Church of Rome.

The first four bowl judgments are against Catholics who had that *mark of the beast*, as they *revered* and *obeyed* his command to kill the saints. The driving force was the Jesuit's revenge against countries that had kicked them out, but Yah used them to pour out His wrath on the people who had killed the saints.

In *Codeword Barbelon*, P.D. Stuart says, *In the raising up of their great avenger Napoleon Bonaparte whose Catholic adviser was the Jesuit-trained cleric Fr. Abbe Emanuel Joseph Sieyes. Father Sieyes was the second Consul in the Napoleonic regime, and according to Robertson, Sieyes was also a French Illuminati (a disciple of Jacobinism.) It was the hidden hand of the Jesuits, through their Illuminati disciple, the so-called 'ex-Jesuit' Adam Weishaupt, that devised, used, and funded Jacobinism to instigate the French Revolution and the carnage that followed. Speaking of this period of upheaval and revolution, Prince de Ligne wrote to Madame de Choisy: "if the Jesuits had not been expelled, we would not be seeing this accursed spirit or turbulence spreading like a torrent that threatens all the thrones of Europe." Rev. James MacCaffrey, S.J., all but admits that it was the Jesuits who fomented the volatile and unruly elements which later erupted into the Revolutions that swept away the monarchies of Frances and those nations that had called for the suppression.*

"In a few years," wrote MacCaffrey, "the Revolution was in full swing; the thrones of France, Spain, Portugal, and Naples were overturned, and those members of the royal families, who escaped the scaffold or the dungeon, were themselves driven to seek refuge in foreign lands, as the Jesuits had been driven in the days of Clement XIV."

In *A Dissertation On Prophecies* (1806), George Stanley Faber says, *In the language of symbols, the sun of a kingdom is the government of that kingdom; and the sun of an empire, if it be a divided empire, is the government of the most powerful state within that empire. When the political sun shines with a steady lustre and yields a salutary warmth, it is a blessing to the people. But when it glares with a fierce and unnatural heat, scorching all the productions of human industry with the intolerable blaze of a portentous tyranny, it is the heaviest curse which can befall a nation. The present Popish states were France, Austria, Spain, Portugal, Naples, Sardinia, and Etruria. Of these, France is by many degrees the most powerful, and consequently that its government must inevitably be esteemed the sun of the system. To observe then the accurate completion of the prophecy of the fourth vial, in which it is said that power was given to this sun to scorch men with fire and that they were scorched with great heat, we have only to cast our eyes over the continent. A system of tyranny, hitherto unknown in Europe except in the word periods of the Roman history, has been established, and is now acted upon by him who styles himself Emperor of the French: and the scorching rays of military despotism are, at this moment felt, more or less, throughout France, Holland, Switzerland, Italy, Spain and the west of Germany.*

On the Revelation timeline, we've seen how Messiah's apocalyptic vision describes these key historical figures: the Cretan Roman Emperors, Emperor Constantine, Alaric, and the Heruli, Genseric and the Vandals, Attila the Hun, Odoacer, and the Heruli, the last Western Roman Emperor Augustus Romulus, the Popes of Rome, Mohammed and Muslim army, the Ottoman Empire, the last Eastern Roman Emperor Constantine XI, Ignatius Loyola, and the SOJ, Martin Luther, the King of France and Marie Antoinette, and Napoleon Bonaparte. It all validates the authority of Scripture and the deity of Messiah!

CHAPTER 65 - THE FIFTH BOWL JUDGMENT

And the fifth angel poured out his vial upon the seat of the beast; and his kingdom was full of darkness; and they gnawed their tongues for pain, And blasphemed the God of heaven because of their pains and their sores, and repented not of their deeds. **Revelation 16:10-11**

The previous bowl judgments were against Catholic countries who *revered* and *obeyed* the ACBP in killing the saints. Now the judgment is aimed directly at the office of the papacy, as the *'seat of the beast'* points to his stately seat, his civil authority.

The People's New Testament by Barton Johnson (1891) says, *By the throne of the beast must be meant the seat of his power. There are few students of the Bible, whether Catholic or Protestant, who deny that Italy and Rome are the throne of the great world power of which the seven-headed beast is the symbol. Then, the scene of the calamities of the fifth vial will be Italy and Rome. That has been the seat of the beast for 1300 years. In the very seat of his power, the beast shall receive a blow that will fill his kingdom with darkness and those who worship him with anguish.*

When Yah desires to carry out judgment against an apostate people, He uses pagan armies to carry out His justice. In the bowl judgments, He is using the SOJ. The JSG is taking control of the Vatican, as Yah uses his zeal to end the Popes' 1,260-year reign of power, which started in 538 and ended in 1798.

I want to emphasize the dual stories here because though we look at the evil deeds of the SOJ, they are ultimately just being used by Yah to fulfill prophecy in His perfect timing. What the SOJ intends for their evil purposes is used by Yah to carry out righteous judgments. Keep this in mind as we watch events take place in these end times. Our Heavenly Father is always in control, and He can protect us against the enemy.

352

Napoleon Bonaparte told us exactly who the Jesuits are, *"The Jesuits are a military organization, not a religious order. Their chief is a general of an army, not the mere father abbot of a monastery. And the aim of this organization is power – power in its most despotic exercise – absolute power, universal power, power to control the world by the volition of a single man (the office of the Superior General of the Jesuits). Jesuitism is the most absolute of despotisms; and, at the same time, the greatest and most enormous of abuses. Their society is by nature dictatorial, and therefore it is the irreconcilable enemy of all constituted authority. Every act, every crime, however atrocious, is a meritorious work if committed for the interest of the Society of Jesus, or by the order of the general."*

In *Visions of the Ages* **(1881), B.W. Johnson says,** *This scorching sun, which parched, burnt and blackened the earth, exerted a most baleful influence on the power of the Papacy. In 1796 Bonaparte entered Italy; in 1797, his armies entered the Papal dominions, and a peace was made by which the Pope was not only shorn in half his provinces but was compelled to buy off the invader with the payment of large sums of money. The next year (1798), the French armies entered Rome, tore the Pope from the Vatican, sent him a prisoner to France to die, and robbed Rome of its hoarded wealth. It was despoiled of its treasures of art, which were sent to Paris as legitimate spoils of war.*

In *The Papal Drama: A Historical Essay* **(1866), Thomas Hornblower Gill says,** *French military office Berthier marched upon Rome, set up a Roman republic, and laid hands upon the Pope. The sovereign Pontiff was borne away to the camp of the infidels… from prison to prison, and finally, carried captive into France. Here he breathed his last at Valence, in the land where his priests had been slain, where his power was broken, and his name and office were a mockery and by-word, and in keeping of the rude soldiers of the unbelieving commonwealth, which had for ten years held to his lips a cup of such manifold and exceeding bitterness.*

At the end of the narrative of the ACBP led *sea* beast phase of the Roman-beast kingdom, it says.

If any man have an ear, let him hear. He that leadeth into captivity shall go into captivity: he that killeth with the sword must be killed with the sword. Here is the patience and the faith of the saints. Revelation 13:9-10

The Popes caused many saints to be taken into captivity, interrogated, tortured, and killed. They caused Catholics in countries like France to kill the Protestant saints, promising them forgiveness for their sins of murder. Now the Pope has been taken captive. The term *'must be killed with the sword'* isn't literal; it's pointing to the Popes' judicial punishment, taking him captive and removing him from civil authority.

Arthur R. Pennington, M.C., F.R., of the Historical Society, says of this event. *"On a sudden, the shouts of an angry multitude penetrated to the conclave, intermingled with the strokes of axes and hammers on the doors. Very soon a band of soldiers burst into the hall, who tore away from his finger his pontifical ring and hurried him off, a prisoner, through a hall, the walls of which were adorned with a fresco, representing the armed satellites of the papacy, on St. Bartholomew's Day."* (4)

The 1990 Encyclopedia Britannica 1990 says, *"The ultimate humiliation of the Church came when Pius VI was driven out of Rome by the French armies in 1798 and in the following year was taken captive by them and dragged back to France, where he died."* (5)

In *The Visions of Daniel and of the Revelation Explained* (1918), E.P. Cachemaille says, *The Temporal dominion of the Rome Papal has already been consumed. Not a nation in Europe remained under it, and men marvel that they ever bowed beneath it. In the estimation of many, its downfall is the severest blow that has fallen upon Rome for a thousand years past. But the spiritual power of the Papacy remains and will remain to the end.* (6)

The Pope's kingdom was in darkness, and the Papal States were repeatedly attacked, being absorbed by other people groups. The Popes' authority progressively disintegrated, while the Gospel was preached through worldwide missions and Bible societies. HalleluYah!

In 1848, the people of Rome arose in rebellion against the Papal authority and drove Pius IX into exile. A few months later, he was restored by a French army, and he stayed under the protection of French bayonets. The continuous loss of power and its once-mighty papal empire caused the papacy to *"gnaw their tongues for pain,"* but no repentance was found. They continued to hurl their anathemas, but they had no power behind them. They continued to blaspheme by introducing new false doctrines, which Paul the apostle called the *doctrine of devils.*

> *Now the Spirit speaks expressly, that in the latter times some shall depart from the faith, giving heed to seducing spirits, and doctrines of devils; Speaking lies in hypocrisy; having their conscience seared with a hot iron.* 1 Timothy 4:1-2

They issued ex-cathedra declarations about the *Immaculate Conception of the Virgin Mary* (1854) that Mary was born without a sin nature; the *Syllabus of Errors* (1864), and the *Bodily Assumption of the Virgin Mary* (1950) up into heaven like Messiah.

In 1870, Pope Pius IX assembled a Vatican council to declare the *Infallibility of the Pope*. They set up mirrors in St. Peter's to reflect the sun towards the Pope, as to illuminate him, but a dark storm moved in, which darkened the scene and terrified them with lightning and thunder. HalleluYah!

Interestingly, just as Emperor Justinian began the process of exalting the Pope's authority in 533, but it wasn't completed until 538; so too did the 1793 declaration of France for the abolition of Romanism, begin the process of removing the Pope's authority, which took place in 1798.

The result of the fifth bowl judgment is that the ACBP was removed from power, ending their 1,260-year reign of power from 538-1798. The office of the papacy *'had the wound by a sword, and did live,'* meaning the Pope was removed from civil power, but their office did not end, as it still exists to this day.

The Black Pope Takes Power Over The Roman Beast

CHAPTER 66 - REVELATION 13 – THE JESUIT GENERALS
1798-PRESENT

Some historicists teach that the second beast of Revelation 13, the *earth beast,* is the USA; because it was created out of a large, mostly unpopulated *land* and because America *appears* to be the most powerful nation in the world. But as you saw in *The Beasts of Daniel* chapter, Daniel only described four beast kingdoms that would rule the world; and we can see how they have been fulfilled by Babylon, Medo-Persia, Greece, and Rome. Revelation 12-13 picks up the narrative of the Roman beast kingdom to show us the leaders of the different phases: pagan Roman Emperors > ACBPs > FPJSGs. We are now in the last phase.

And I beheld another beast coming up out of the earth; and he had two horns like a lamb, and he spoke as a dragon. **Revelation 13:11**

As you saw in *The Antichrist Beast Versus Messiah* chapter, the term *'beast'* in Revelation 13 is not pointing to a kingdom, but a man, the Roman beast kingdom leader, a *liar*, a *deceiver*, who subverts Messiah's Ekklesia. The one who is called the *'beast'* by John in Revelation is the office of the papacy, the Popes of Rome. Now John declares that another *'beast,'* another *liar,* another *deceiver*; the Black Pope, rises to power over the Roman kingdom. Instead of being called the *'beast,'* this Pope is called the *'false prophet.'*

John Gill's Exposition of the Entire Bible (1748) says, *And I beheld another beast. The same with the first, only in another form; the same for being and person, but under a different consideration; the same antichrist, but appearing in another light and view: the first beast is the pope of Rome.*

The word *'earth'* in Strong's Greek is *'ghay,'* which means: *soil; by extension a region, or the solid part or the whole of the terrene globe (including the occupants in each application):—country, earth(-ly), ground, land, world.*

John is pointing to a new phase of the Roman beast and saying that the leader would rise to power out of the *region*, the *land*, of the Vatican, the headquarters of the previous leader, the ACBP. And that's what the JSG did. It was the JSG who was empowered in 1540, who lived in the *land*, the *earth*, of the Vatican for over 250 years.

It was the JSG who caused the bowl judgments to be carried out against Catholic countries that had kicked the SOJ out. And it was the JSG who used Napoleon's army to take the Pope captive, ending his 1,260-year reign of power in 1798.

Notice that the narrative of the *earth* beast in Revelation 13:11-16 is pointing to *'he,'* a man, the leader of the end times phase of the Roman beast. Just as the *antichrist beast* is pointing to the office of the papacy, the *'he'* of the *earth beast* narrative is pointing to the office of the JSG, which started in 1541.

'Horns' in prophecy point to *leaders*. The *little horn* of Daniel 7 is fulfilled by the office of the papacy, the Popes of Rome. The goat with the *'large horn'* in Daniel 8 is pointing to Alexander the Great. The *'little horn'* in Daniel 8 is Antiochus Epiphanes, a less powerful leader.

The end-times phase of the Roman beast has *two horns like a lamb*, which means that it has two leaders who pretend to be Messiah's priests, *lamb-like*; the Black Pope and the White Pope, the FPJSG, and the ACBP.

We see more proof that there are two leaders of the end-times Roman beast in these verses: Revelation 16:13 says that *three unclean spirits* come out of the dragon (Satan), the *antichrist beast,* and the *false prophet.* Revelation 19:20 tells us that the *antichrist beast* and *false prophet* will be captured and thrown into the fiery pit. Revelation 20:10 says that the *antichrist beast* and *false prophet* are in the lake of fire.

Note that the text does not declare that the beast would start *like a lamb* and then become like the *dragon* (Satan), as some people proclaim about America. It's saying that they do both things at once; they pretend to be priests of the *Lamb*, but they serve Satan the *dragon*.

Francesco Borgia, the third JSG (1565-1572), said, *"We came in like lambs and will rule like wolves. We shall be expelled like dogs and return like eagles."*

This lines up with Messiah's words in Matthew 7:15. *Beware of false prophets, which come to you in sheep's clothing, but inwardly they are ravening wolves.*

Thomas Coke's Commentary on the Holy Bible (1803) says, *For the false prophet no more than the beast is a single man, but a body or succession of men, propagating false doctrines and teaching lies for sacred truths. Another beast, or the same power under another form, appears, like a lamb with two horns, the symbol of his dominion temporal and spiritual, who, with all pretended meekness and humility, has all the pride and rage of the old dragon, exercising all the power of the first beast, and causing all the earth to worship him, and own his universal, temporal as well as spiritual, jurisdiction, with lying miracles supporting his idolatrous worship, deceiving the inhabitants of the earth, and leading them to erect the image of the first beast, whose deadly wound was healed, and pay their adoration to the idol, blindly and implicitly submitting to the authority of the Pope, and the constitutions of Paganism revived in the church of Rome; giving life to the image of the beast, enforcing all the canons and laws of his idolatrous worship, by ex-communications, fire, and sword; making it death to refuse obedience to the Papal power; setting a mark upon all the votaries of the beast, and excluding those who would not submit to make profession of this system of error and blasphemy, from all intercourse with the worshipers of the beast, as unworthy of every blessing of society.*

In *The Jesuits: Their Moral Maxims And Plots Against Kings, Nations, And Churches* (1881), James Aitken Wylie says, *Never was the description more applicable, or the warning that accompanies it more needful. The Jesuits come to us in the name of Him who was "holy, harmless, undefiled, and separate from sinners." They call themselves the "Companions or Company of*

Jesus." The name is but "the sheep's clothing." Let us apply the test. "By their fruits, ye shall know them." Their teaching is "the doctrine of devils," and their deeds are the works of Satan.

And he exerciseth all the authority of the first beast in his presence, and causeth the earth and those who dwell in it to worship the first beast, whose deadly wound was healed. Revelation 13:12

Recall that the SOJ had been kicked out of many countries, including Catholic ones, so the JSG can't openly rule the Vatican, as they knew his evil ways. So the Black Pope stays in the background and uses the White Pope to be the spokesman for the Vatican. But it is the JSG who controls the city-state corporation of Vatican City, and he *exercises his authority* in front of the White Pope.

Alexander Robertson puts it thus, *"The General of the Jesuits, the 'Black Pope,' is the real and only Pope. The one who bears the title is but a figurehead. It is the Jesuit's policy he pursues, their voice that speaks through him, their hand that guides him. When illustrating this fact to me, Count Campello, who was a great friend of the late Pope Pio Nono (Pius IX), drew a circle, and said, "Within that circle he (the Pope) is free; if he crosses it, he is a dead man.'"*

Michelangelo Tamburini, JSG from 1706-1730, said, *"See, sir, from this Chamber, I govern, not only to Paris but to China; not only to China but to all the world, without anyone knowing how I do it."* It was Ignatius Loyola who said, *"... we are called to win to God, not only a single nation, a single country, but all nations, all the kingdoms of the world."* By 'God,' Ignatius is pointing not to the Heavenly Father but to the Pope, who has proclaimed to be God.

Romanism, the Pope's apostate version of the true faith, was created to make war with Messiah and His saints by infiltrating Messiah's Ekklesia from within. During the Pope's 1,260 year reign, they did exactly that, as they falsely proclaimed to be the leader of the *one true church* while teaching doctrine contrary to Scripture, teaching a false salvation message, and persecuting the true Ekklesia.

And now, the JSG has taken the deception to the next level. They've sent SOJ priests around the world to teach a false salvation message. Over the past century, the number of Catholics worldwide has more than quadrupled, from an estimated 291 million in 1910 to nearly 1.2 billion as of 2010, according to a comprehensive demographic study by the Pew Research Center. The Sub-Sahara had 1.2 million in 1910, and now there are 171 million in 2010. Latin America-Caribbean had 70.6 million in 1910, and now there are 426.5 million in 2010. Asia-Pacific had 13.9 million in 1910, and now there are 130.5 million in 2010. That's a staggering growth rate of Catholics who *revere* (*worship*) the ACBP.

John Gill's Exposition of the Entire Bible (1748) says, *To worship the first beast; to be subject to the temporal power of the Papacy, or to submit to the pope as a temporal lord, to give homage and tribute to him, and the like, in order to support his worldly power and grandeur; and this was caused or brought about by his emissaries, his spiritual vassals, his legates, cardinals, priests, etc. by their exhortations, persuasions, and commands, delivered both in writing and preaching. Whose deadly wound was healed; which deadly wound was given the Roman empire under its sixth head, the emperors, when they ceased and was healed by the pope, the seventh head, being set as a temporal monarch over the ten kingdoms in it.*

Brigadier General Thomas M. Harris, a physician, and Union General during the American Civil War, reportedly said, *"The organization of the (RCC) Hierarchy is a complete military despotism, of which the Pope is the ostensible head; but of which, the Black Pope (the Superior General), is the real head. The Black Pope is the head of the order of the Jesuits and is called a General. He not only has command of his own order but directs and controls the general policy of the (Roman Catholic) Church. He is the power behind the throne and is the real potential head of the Hierarchy. The whole machine is under the strictest rules of military discipline. The whole thought and will of this machine, to plan, propose and execute, is found in its head. There is no independence of thought, or of action, in its subordinate parts. Implicit and unquestioning obedience to the orders of superiors in authority is the sworn duty of the priesthood of every grade."* (4)

And he doeth great wonders, so that he maketh fire come down from heaven on the earth in the sight of men, And deceiveth them that dwell on the earth by the means of those miracles which he had power to do in the sight of the beast; saying to them that dwell on the earth, that they should make an image to the beast, which had the wound by a sword, and did live. Revelation 13:13-14

Thomas Coke's Commentary on the Holy Bible (1803) says, *Miracles, visions, and revelations are the mighty boast of the Church of Rome; the contrivances of an artful, cunning clergy, to impose upon an ignorant or credulous laity.*

In 1917, the SOJ caused an event where 70,000 witnesses supposedly saw the sun, contrary to cosmic laws, twirl in the sky, throw off colors, and descend to earth. This event, which occurred in Fatima, Portugal, caused even non-believers to drop onto their knees and beg for forgiveness immediately. The '*Miracle of the Sun*' supposedly confirmed the validity of the '*Message of Fatima,*' a message from the Virgin Mary, which warned about future calamity if people did not participate in the Eucharist communion. It served to draw the Muslim community towards the RCC, as they too revere Mary and believe that she was speaking through Fatima, Muhammad's daughter.

"Fire coming down from heaven" may refer to a future time when the SOJ uses Tesla-inspired HAARP technology, military Directed-Energy Weapons, holographic images in the sky from Project Blue Beam, etc.

Revelation 13:14 says that the FPJSG is a *deceiver*. Webster's 1828 Dictionary, which is based on the KJV, has the following definitions.

Jesuit: *One of the Society of Jesus, so-called, founded by Ignatius Loyola, a society remarkable for their cunning in propagating their principles.*

Jesuitism: *The arts, principles, and practices of the Jesuits. Cunning, deceit; hypocrisy; prevarication; deceptive practices to effect a purpose.*

That is the perfect definition of the FPJSG and his army of priests!

361

Thomas Coke's Commentary on the Holy Bible (1803) says, *In short, he is the most perfect likeness of the ancient Roman emperors; is as great a tyrant in the Christian world, as they were in the Heathen; presides in the same city; usurps the same powers; affects the same titles; and requires the same universal homage and adoration. The influence of the two-horned beast, or corrupted clergy is farther seen, in persuading and inducing mankind to make an image of the beast, &c. that is, an image and representation of the Roman empire, which was wounded by the sword of the barbarous nations, and revived in the revival of a new emperor in the West.*

Recall that the *'deadly head wound'* described in Revelation 13:3 is pointing to the last Western Roman Emperor being removed from power in 476. The lineage of Western Roman Emperors *died*, the position ceased to exist. The *healing of the deadly head wound* occurred early in the narrative of the *sea beast* phase, pointing to the ACBP being given civil authority in 538. They took the title of the Emperors, *Pontifex Maximus,* and they took his place, as leader of church and state, over the Roman beast; thus, the *deadly head wound was healed.*

The phrase *'had the wound by a sword, and did live'* in Revelation 13:14 is pointing to the office of the papacy, who was removed from civil power in 1798. They were *wounded by the sword,* but the office of the papacy *lives* on. And the *'image of the beast,'* the popes being propped up as a civil and ecclesiastic leader, causes people to *revere* and *obey* them again.

***And he had power to give life unto the image of the beast, that the image of the beast should both speak, and cause that as many as would not worship the image of the beast should be killed.* Revelation 13:15**

John Gill's Exposition of the Entire Bible (1748) says, *that is, that as many as will not embrace and profess the Popish religion shall be put to death; and these are the known orders and decrees of the Papacy, which have been executed by the Inquisition, and other hands, in innumerable instances; the blood of all the saints and prophets is found in Rome Papal, and will be avenged.*

CHAPTER 67 - THE FALSE PROPHET

In the last chapter, you saw how the *earth beast* of Revelation 13 describes the last phase of the Roman beast kingdom, which is now controlled by the Black Pope, the JSG. The White Pope is called the *'beast'* by John, and the Black Pope is another *'beast.'* It's not pointing to a new kingdom; it's pointing to another Pope. The Roman beast kingdom is now controlled by *'two horns,'* two leaders, the FPJSG and the ACBP.

They both pretend to be priests of Messiah to covertly make war with Him and His saints and deceive the nations to push the world into their One World Government.

The SOJ has been kicked out of many countries, including Catholic ones, which shows how badly their *'fruits'* stinketh! Many people have declared what a Jesuit represents, as they *steal, kill, and destroy*, to take control of countries. The title of *'false prophet'* is associated with the leader of the Roman beast kingdom's *earth beast* phase. Let's see how.

The Strong's Greek word for *'false prophet'* is 5578 *'pseudoprophetes'* from 5571, which means; *a spurious prophet, i.e., pretended foreteller or a religious impostor: a false prophet*. 5571 *pseudes* means; *untrue, i.e., erroneous, deceitful, wicked:—false, liar*.

The *false prophet* is a *religious imposter* who is deceitful and wicked. That's the JSG! He pretends to be a priest of Messiah to better make war with Him and His saints. He can't rule openly because of the bad reputation of the SOJ, so he rules in the shadows.

In 185, Irenaeus held that this *lamb-like* leader would be *'a false prophet.'* In 380, Tichonius said that the leader of the *earth beast* would be a *'false priest.'* In 1259, Ubertino of Casale, an Italian Francisca, even equated it with the *'Romanist clergy.'*

363

Andreas, the Bishop of Caesarea in Cappadocia during the 5th century, describes the false prophet, *"exhibiting a show of piety, and with pretense of being a lamb when in fact a wolf."* (2)

Primasius, the Bishop of the Carthaginian province, in his 6th-century *Commentary on the Apocalypse*, views the second beast of Revelation 13, the *two-horned* beast, as ecclesiastical rulers, *hypocritically feigning likeness to the Lamb, in order the better to war against him: and by the mask of a Christian profession, under which mask the devil puts himself before men, acting out the Mediator.* (3)

The Venerable Bede (672-735) similarly interprets the *lamb-like* beast of Revelation 13 as meaning *Antichrist's pseudo-Christian false prophets: He shows the horns of a lamb that he may secretly introduce the person of the dragon. For by the false assumption of sanctity, which the Lord truly had in Himself, he pretends that a matchless life and wisdom are his. Of this beast, the Lord says: 'Beware of false prophets' which come to you in sheep's clothing but inwardly are ravening wolves.* (4)

Ambrose Anspert, a Latin expositor in the 8th century, interpreted the second beast of Revelation 13 as, *Signifying the preachers and ministers of antichrist; feigning the lamb, in order to carry out their hostility against the Lamb; just as antichrist too, the first beast's head wounded to death, would,* he says: *exhibit himself pro Christo, in Christ's place.* (5)

In his *Commentary on the Apocalypse* (1183), Joachim Abbas declared, *The harlot city reigning over the kings of the earth undoubtedly meant Rome, and that the false prophet foretold in the Apocalypse would probably issue out of the bosom of the Church.* (6)

John Wesley wrote, *"The false prophet — so is called the second beast (the earth beast of Revelation 13) frequently named, after the kingdom of the first (the ACBP) is darkened; for he can then no longer prevail by main strength, and so works by lies and deceits."* (7)

They understood that the *false prophet*, the leader of the last phase of the Roman beast kingdom, would rise to power out of the *earth*, out of the *land*, out of the Vatican of the ACBP. They foretold that they would pretend to be a priest of Messiah to make war with Him and His saints.

Beyond the JSG causing SOJ priests to spread around the world to preach a false Gospel, which now causes 1.3 billion Catholics to *revere* the ACBP; let's look at the many ways that the FPJSG has used his militant army to create deception after deception.

They created false, futuristic prophecy fulfillment explanations.

As you saw in the **Historicism vs. Futurism** chapter, the JSG had SOJ priests create these explanations in the 16th century to counter the Reformers, who rightly identified that the office of the papacy fulfills prophecy as the *son of perdition* and the *antichrist beast*. The SOJ explanations didn't take hold for a few centuries, but they have gained a stronghold during the last century so that they deceive the majority of people. They also created false, Preterism deceptions, which proclaim that all of Revelation was fulfilled in the first centuries and that Nero was the antichrist.

They created false, corrupt Greek, and English Bibles.

Since they couldn't stop the *little book* of Revelation 10, the printed Bible, from spreading, they set out to corrupt it. A major step in the process took place in the 19th century when they used heretics Brooke Foss Westcott and Fenton John Anthony Hort to create a *Greek New Testament* in 1881. Instead of being based on the *Textus Receptus*, it borrowed from the corrupt *Sinaiticus* and *Vaticanus*, which removed many words that validate Messiah's deity.

Codex Sinaiticus (Aleph or a) was found in a trash heap by Saint Catherine's Monastery's monks. On nearly every page of the manuscript, there are corrections and revisions done by ten different people. It is, indeed, worthless trash. *Codex Vaticanus* (B) is kept at the Vatican of the ACBP. In the Gospels alone, it leaves out 237 words, 452 clauses, and 748 whole sentences. The early saints rejected these manuscripts, so they were cast aside for a thousand years until they were later dug up and called *'ancient manuscripts.'*

The *Greek New Testament* of Westcott and Hort has 5,337 deletions compared to the *Textus Receptus Greek*; many of them are words that validate Messiah's deity. Westcott and Hort helped create the 1885 *English Revised Version Bible*, which is based on their corrupt Greek Bible, so it's also missing many relevant words.

Then the SOJ helped create the *Nestle-Aland* (NA) and the *United Bible Societies* (UBS) *Greek New Testaments,* which are based on the Westcott-Hort Greek Bible. It has 8,000 differences from the Textus Receptus.

The *Nestle-Aland Greek New Testament* is the basis for nearly every modern Bible translation, including the NIV and ESV. This is why they're missing many words that validate Messiah's deity. For example, the NIV has 64,576 fewer words than the KJV.

Because the corrupt Greek Bibles and modern Bible versions are both missing words and verses, most Pastors don't notice the deception. As you can see, the FPJSG and Satan have been very effective.

They created false religions, which are *daughters* of the mother, the *harlot* church of Rome.

There was no way to stop the saints from proclaiming the Gospel, so the SOJ used Freemasons to create false 'Christian' denominations, which pervert the Gospel. This includes Mormonism, Jehovah's Witnesses, and other Christian sects, whose teachings are contrary to Scripture. These Christian cults mislead people and cause division. The SOJ have infiltrated Protestant denominations to bring them back under Rome's teachings and in alliance with Rome. The only denomination that declares that the Popes are the *antichrist beast* is the Seventh-Day Adventist Church. But they now appear to have been infiltrated, as their explanations deflect blame away from the ACBP and the FPJSG.

Looking at the Revelation Fulfillment Chart, we're now in the third phase of the Roman beast kingdom.

On the 1st Layer, you see that the 1,260-year reign of the ACBP ended in 1798, and now the FPJSG controls the Roman beast kingdom. The office of the papacy was *'wounded by the sword,'* but it didn't end, so it wasn't a *'deadly head wound.'* The ACBPs are still around, but they no longer control the Roman beast kingdom; the FPJSG does. The White Pope is now the spokesman for the Black Pope.

On the 2nd Layer, we see the *two lampstands*, the two church eras of Thyatira and Sardis, carried out their mission of *witnessing* against the ACBPs during their 1,260-year reign of power. During the last phase of the Roman beast kingdom, the church era of Philadelphia plays its role in the great harvest of saints. And then the last church era of Laodicea will see the rest of the prophecies in Revelation fulfilled.

On the 3rd Layer, we see that Yah used the JSG to carry out the first four bowl judgments against the Catholic countries that had killed the saints. During the fifth bowl, the JSG used Napoleon's army to take the Pope captive, removing him from civil power.

We're in the last phase of the Roman beast kingdom, which is led by the FPJSG, the Black Pope. During this time, the FPJSG uses his SOJ priests to spread around the world, proclaim Catholicism's false gospel, to cause people to *revere* the ACBP.

Messiah's Ekklesia proclaims the Gospel through worldwide missions and via Bible Societies. We see the stage for the final phase of the battle between the Satan-empowered Roman beast kingdom, called *'Babylon the great,'* and Messiah's Ekklesia of saints, called *'Holy Jerusalem.'*

CHAPTER 69 – THE PHILADELPHIA CHURCH ERA

This church era of Philadelphia narrative is in Revelation 3:7-13.

The *'open door'* was an unprecedented opportunity to preach the Gospel throughout the world to people who were ripe to receive it. This time saw the rise of the evangelical church in North America and the British Isles, as they took the Word of Yah to the whole world. The *Great Awakening* in America and worldwide Gospel preaching crusades redeemed souls from the enemy, and Bible Societies flooded the world with the Holy Scriptures.

Here are some of the great men of Yah who preached the Gospel during this glorious church age. Francis Asbury (1745-1816) was the first of many Methodist *'Circuit Riders.'* He traveled 270,000 miles and preached 16,000 sermons, despite persecution.

William Carey (1761-1834) was the Baptist father of modern missions. In 1809, he finished the *Bengali Bible* and published many more Bibles in other languages. Carey sailed for India, where he found an *open door* to preach the Gospel, and since then, Messiah opened the door into China, Japan, Korea, India, and Africa.

Charles Finney 1792-1875 was an American Presbyterian minister and leader in the *Second Great Awakening* in the United States. Adoniram Judson 1804-90 was a missionary to the Burmese people and completed the translation of the Bible into Burmese.

The *British and Foreign Bible Society* was formed in 1804, and the *American Bible Society* in 1816, which spread many millions of Bibles worldwide. Charles H. Spurgeon (1834 – 1892) was a strong figure in the Reformed Baptist tradition, known as the *'Prince of Preachers.'*

Hudson Taylor 1832-1905 was a British Protestant Christian missionary to China for fifty-one years, founder of the *China Inland Mission,* responsible for bringing over 800 missionaries to the country who then began 125 schools.

Henry Grattan Guinness was part of the Evangelical awakening and preached during the *Ulster Revival of 1859*, which drew thousands to hear him. He was responsible for training and sending hundreds of *faith missionaries* all over the world.

The church age of Philadelphia shined the *light* of the Gospel throughout the world. The saints and the Scriptures spread worldwide, preaching the pure Gospel and exposing Rome's false gospel. Messiah did not have one word of condemnation for this church era, only praise for their faithful love and service. Ah, that we would be like them during these end times.

Regarding the *'Jews who say they are Jews but are not,'* I'll cover this in **The Kings of the East In The 6ᵗʰ Bowl** chapter

Regarding them being kept *'from the hour of temptation,'* I believe that it's pointing to all of the deceptions that have been poured out on the next church era of Laodicea, which have misled them.

Here's what Messiah says about the end-times church age.

> *So then because thou art lukewarm, and neither cold nor hot, I will spue thee out of my mouth. Because thou sayest, I am rich, and increased with goods, and have need of nothing; and knowest not that thou art wretched, and miserable, and poor, and blind, and naked.* Revelation 3:16-17

Our world is full of the SOJ's deceptions, yet most believers just dismiss it as *'conspiracy theories.'* Trials have come upon Laodicea's last church era because the saints are undiscerning and apathetic and negligent. Evil triumphs when good people do nothing.

CHAPTER 70 - IT'S A PYRAMID SCHEME

People act as if a one-man antichrist can suddenly take control of the whole world, but that's ridiculous. It took the ACBPs hundreds of years to gain control of the ten kingdoms of the fallen Western Roman Empire. Taking authority over the whole world is a much bigger task.

The JSG took command of the Vatican in 1798, but he worked for many years beforehand to take power over the world. Since then, he has worked systematically to take power over most countries in the world, the money supply, the banking systems, the media, etc.

The SOJ can't rule openly because people still know their sordid past, so they control the world through many front organizations, hiding their power and causing people to blame other people groups. They use the front organization's lower levels as a disguise of sorts, as these people don't understand the beliefs and plans of the people at the top of the power pyramid.

Visualize a company pyramid-shaped organizational chart with the CEO at the top, VP's on the next level, supervisors on the next level, managers on the next level, and workers on the bottom level. The workers are part of the company, but they don't know what the CEO and VP's discuss in meetings.

The org chart of the JSG is the same, with him at the top. What I want you to notice is that he's created many organizations with high-level leaders, mid-level leaders, and then members at the bottom. They all provide a function to the organization, but the lower levels have no idea what is the agenda of the higher-level leader. And the JSG sits as the capstone of every organization.

A key function of each is to find people who will serve their agenda, which they promote and illuminate with knowledge. The higher one moves in the organization, the more they learn. They serve in an intelligence-gathering capacity, meaning that the leaders report to the JSG about what's going on in business, government, etc., which might endanger the JSG. They take blood oaths to protect the secret knowledge, and they all act as an internal spy agency, meaning they rat out people in the organization who have gone astray.

Take the SOJ, for example. At the top is the JSG, and below him are the provincial leaders, who serve Satan and know the full plan. Below them are different levels of Jesuits who carry out high-level agendas, who know some of what's going on, but not all. And below them are SOJ priests who perform good works in their community, who are oblivious to the leaders' evil agenda. They simply preach Roman Catholicism, which causes people to believe in a false salvation message and *revere* and *obey* the ACBPs. The world sees the good works of the lower-level Jesuits and the priests dressed in black, proclaiming to be working for Jesus; so they would never suspect the JSG in Rome as being the enemy of mankind.

The SOJ has spread around the world, whether as a priest taking confessions or as a crypto-Jesuit businessman or politician, gathering intel for their JSG. This intel on government and corporate leaders is used against them in blackmail to take control of the country. The priests of every parish and in every country are the kingpins in this web of spying – regularly reporting to their bishops every item of interest shared in the confessional; in turn, the bishop to his archbishop; the archbishop to the cardinal, and the cardinal to the JSG. It's how he keeps his eyes on the whole world.

In *History of Protestantism* (1870), James Aitken Wylie says, *From his chamber in Rome, the eye of the General surveys the world… to the farthest bounds; there is nothing done in it which he does not see; there is nothing spoke in it which he does not hear… to the general of the Jesuits the world lies "naked and open." He sees by a thousand eyes, he hears by a thousand ears; and when he has a behest to execute, he can select the fittest agent from an innumerable host, all of whom are ready to do his bidding.*

Every year, a list of the houses and members of the society, with the name, talents, virtues, and failings of each, is lead before the General. In addition to the annual report, every one of the thirty-seven provincials must send him a monthly report of the state of his province; he must inform him minutely of its political and ecclesiastical condition. Every superior of a college must report once every three months. The heads of houses of residence, and the house of novitiates, must do the same. In short, from every quarter of his vast dominions come a monthly and a tri-monthly report." (1)

It was Sun-Tzu who wrote in *The Art Of War*, *"The General sees all. Hears all, does all, and (yet) in appearance is not involved with anything."* This is the hallmark of the JSG.

The JSG used Adam Weishaupt to create the Bavarian Illuminati.

Adam Weishaupt began his formal education at age seven at a Jesuit school. Weishaupt became a Jesuit professor (1772) of Vatican canon law, a position held exclusively by the SOJ. On May 1, 1776, Weishaupt formed the Bavarian Illuminati.

They infiltrated Freemasonry to find like-minded people they can use for their agenda and be a massive front organization.

Freemasonry is a pyramid organization of learning their secrets through degrees of illumination. The people at the highest degrees know that they are serving the JSG and Satan, and they understand the agenda of pushing the world into the One World Government. Even the top Freemasons have been deceived into believing that their actions are for the good god, who they are told is Lucifer, which helps them justify killing Yah's followers.

Below are people with various enlightenment levels who carry out the JSG's agenda but don't know the whole plan. On the lower levels are many people who are Masons for business and social reasons. They're oblivious to the evil plans of the leaders at the top levels. The world sees them as decent people, including some Christians who are Freemasons, so they dismiss that Freemasonry is evil.

372

Through Freemasonry and other organizations, the JSG controls the world's political, financial, and business leaders. They have repeated this process, creating front organizations with different levels; to hide their agenda from the world and even from the people on the lower levels of their organizations.

In *The Jesuits: Their Moral Maxims And Plots Against Kings, Nations, And Churches* (1881), James Aitken Wylie describes the SOJ.

The whole condition of the vast empire of which he is monarch, is lead before the General at short and regular intervals. From every Provincial there comes to him once a month a full and minute account of the state of matters in his province. Every head of college, residence, and mission is bound to send in a similar report once a quarter. He is thus able intently to watch the progress of the battle at all points and to know what is going on in every part of the field. What an organization! Shape monstrous and dreadful! Its dark wings stretched out to the ends of the earth, and its iron strength gathered up in its one autocratic head at Rome! To counter the Reformation in Germany, the Jesuits, under guise, took university seats, and colleges such as Ingolstadt soon fell entirely under their influence. They infiltrated governments and schools; to shape the minds of the youth, especially the sons of Protestants, in their schools.

Abbate M. Leone, an ex-Jesuit, said, *"There are in the central house, at Rome, huge registers, wherein are inscribed the names of… all the important persons, friends, or enemies. It is the most gigantic biographical collection that has ever been formed. When it is required to act in any way upon an individual, they open the book and become immediately acquainted with his life, his character, his qualities, his defects, his projects, his family, his friends, his most secret acquaintances."* [2]

Over the last four hundred years, the SOJ has succeeded in establishing the largest worldwide network of schools and universities, with many well-known alumni. Thus, the SOJ has shaped and molded the thinking of many famous world leaders and produced generations of political and religious leaders who are favorable to the JSG, the RCC, and her doctrinal agenda.

Whole books have been written about the United States of America's founding by the SOJ, so I won't spend time explaining it. In this summary, I want to stir your mind to question the official narrative we've been told. This is important because some historicists teach that America is the *earth beast* of Revelation 13, but it's just a city-state corporation of *'the great city'* of Rome, the Roman beast kingdom.

Before the USA was founded, 98% of settlers were Protestants, who fled Europe to escape the SOJ Inquisition. They banned Catholics from being a lawyer, voting, and holding public office because they understood the SOJ's evil nature. Once these laws were nullified by the Maryland Constitution of 1776, Jesuit Daniel Carroll was elected to the Maryland Senate, serving from 1777–81.

Jesuit Daniel Carroll (1730–1796) was a plantation owner from Maryland and is one of the Founding Fathers. He was one of three commissioners appointed to survey for land for the new federal capital. The new United States Capitol was built on the wooded hill, owned by his nephew, Daniel Carroll of Duddington.

The land bordered Virginia and Maryland, which, when combined, means the "*VIRGIN MARYland.*" The area was settled by a man named *Francis Pope*, who called his 400-acre farmstead *'Rome'* and renamed *'Goose Creek,'* the tributary of the Potomac River as *'Tiber Creek,'* once again pointing to Rome. None of this was a coincidence, as the SOJ had planned it all out long ago.

His Jesuit cousin, Charles Carroll (1737–1832), was an early advocate of independence from Great Britain. He served as a delegate to the Continental Congress and Confederation Congress and later as the first United States Senator for Maryland. He was the only Catholic and the longest-lived signatory of the Declaration of Independence, dying fifty-six years after the document was first signed.

His Jesuit brother John Carroll (1735–1815) founded Jesuit Georgetown University. He was the richest man in America. He became the first Catholic bishop in America and presided over the *See of Baltimore*. He founded Jesuit Georgetown University in 1789, which to this day is used to train people's minds to carry out the JSG's agenda. Founding that major university at the very beginning of the USA is a major clue about the role of the SOJ in this country.

The eagle on Georgetown's seal carries two objects in its talons: a terrestrial globe (the symbol of rational knowledge) and a cross. Its beak carries a scroll with the Latin inscription '*Utraque Unum,*' which translates as "*Both are one.*" It's pointing to the SOJ using the USA to take control of the world to cause people to revere the ACBP.

In *The Life Of Charles Carroll of Carrollton* (1918), Lewis A. Leonard says, George Washington had no truer, no stauncher friend than (Jesuit) Charles Carroll, *though the world has partially blinked the fact. Others of the Colonial fathers might waver here and falter there, but Charles Carroll always upheld the hands of Washington as Aaron and Hur upheld the hands of Moses in his battle with Amalek. Charles Carroll of Carrollton easily ranked next to Washington in the value of the services rendered the patriot cause in our Revolutionary struggle.*

He devoted more of his time and more of his money to the cause of the people than any other patriot. He spent more time with Washington at army headquarters than any other civilian and was more closely identified with the purposes, impulses, and activities of the great commander than any other man in or out of the army. During the critical year of 1776, he was a member of Congress, a member of the Maryland Assembly, a member of the Convention to draw a new constitution for the state, member of three different provincial committees, member of the War Board charged with the conduct of the war, and a commissioner from the United States to Canada. And in every position, he was either the most active or one of the most active in the work.

He was the richest man that signed The Declaration of Independence, the first man that signed, the most useful man that signed, the only Roman Catholic that signed, and the last man to die of those who signed it. (1)

Charles Carroll was the SOJ handler of George Washington. Given their sordid past, no Jesuit would have been elected as President, but they don't need to, as long as they controlled the President. George was a Freemason who is deified on the Capitol dome as a god on the *Apotheosis of Washington*. Pagan gods surround him. *Freedom*, also known as *Columbia*, is the personification of war. *Minerva*, the Roman goddess of crafts and wisdom. *Neptune*, the Roman sea-god. *Mercury*, the Roman god of commerce. *Vulcan*, the Roman god of fire and the forge. *Ceres*, the Roman goddess of agriculture.

That the Jesuits and their French Illuminatists were the instigators behind the American War of Independence was hinted at by President George Washington himself. In response to a letter from SOJ Bishop Carroll congratulating the President on his election, Washington wrote back on March 12, 1790, saying: *"To the Roman Catholics of the United States... your fellow-citizens (non-Catholics) will not forget the patriotic part which you took in the accomplishment of their Revolution, and the establishment of their Government, or the... assistance... received from a nation in which the Roman Catholic faith is professed."* (2)

The Jesuits changed the laws to allow Catholics to take control.

The SOJ covertly had the 1st Amendment created, not to establish religious freedom for Christians, as they already had it. The SOJ did it to create religious freedom for Catholics and pave the way for them to control the country. The *Establishment Clause* is a limitation placed upon the United States Congress preventing it from passing legislation respecting an establishment of religion. The second half inherently prohibits the government from preferring any one religion over another. Christians today believe that it was declared to ensure their religious freedom, but it really was designed to allow Catholics to practice their faith and set up churches, as they had previously been banned.

The SOJ's layout of Washington D.C. invokes Satanic energy.

YouTube videos and websites reveal the Satanic design, with the bottom point of the Satanic upside-down pentagram on the White House. The U.S. Capital layout features a Masonic owl, which points to the pagan god Moloch. The *White House* is named after Andrew White (1579-1656), an English SOJ missionary involved in the Maryland colony's founding. He is considered a forefather of Georgetown University and is memorialized in the name of its White-Gravenor building, a central location of offices and classrooms on the campus. *Capitol Hill* is named after *Capitoline Hill* in Rome, showing the District of Columbia's direct connection to Rome.

The woman on the top of the Capitol dome is the *goddess of war*.

The American form of *Asherah* is known as *Columbia*. The name *'The District of Columbia'* is saying that it's her territory where she rules. At the top of the U.S. capital is the Statue of Freedom—also known as *Armed Freedom*, which faces East towards the sunrise, towards Rome.

She sits on a circular shape, representing the earth, and has *'E Pluribus Unum'* inscribed around its base, which means *'out of many, one.'* This points to the SOJ's mission for the USA, to use it to push the world into their One World Government. She has many fasces symbols under her feet, which represent that the capital is under Roman authority. A fasces is a bundle of rods and a single ax which were carried as a symbol of magisterial and priestly authority in ancient Rome.

The *Great Seal* on the U.S. One Dollar Bill proclaims the JSG's mission for the District of Columbia.

It was first used publicly in 1782. The phrase *'ANNUIT COEPTIS'* means *"He favors our undertaking."* The *'he'* is the JSG and Satan. *'NOVUS ORDO SECLORUM'* means *'New Order of the Ages.'* The SOJ helped found the country to use it to push the world into their One World Government. The MDCCLXXVI numbers point to Rome and the 1776 founding of the Bavarian Illuminati, and 13 levels of the pyramid.

On the right side is a Satanic hexagram above the head of the eagle (phoenix); which has 32 feathers on one side and 33 on the other, pointing to the levels of Freemasonry; 13 stripes on the shield, 13 leaves, 13 arrows, and 13 tail feathers; and the motto '*E Pluribus Unum*,' which means '*Out of many, one*,' pointing to the One World Government.

The motto 'IN GOD WE TRUST' does not point to the Yah of Scriptures, but rather to the god represented on the dollar bill with the all-seeing eye, the JSG, and Satan. The District of Columbia acts as the JSG's intelligence agency. The top leaders of the intelligence agencies protect the JSG and his leaders.

The pyramid on the Great Seal on the U.S. Dollar Bill has 1776 on it because it's pointing to the founding of the SOJ Bavarian Illuminati. Interestingly, San Francisco (Spanish for *Saint Francis*) was founded on June 29, 1776, when colonists from Spain established the *Presidio of San Francisco* and the *Mission San Francisco de Asís* named for St. Francis of Assisi, a few miles away.

San Francisco is an SOJ stronghold. The University of San Francisco is a premier SOJ university, rooted in the symbolic vision of St. Ignatius of Loyola, the founder of the SOJ. Reverend Anthony Maraschi, S.J. (1820 - 1897), an Italian-born priest of the SOJ, founded the *University of San Francisco* and *Saint Ignatius College Preparatory* and was the first pastor of *Saint Ignatius Church* in San Francisco, California.

On the San Francisco city seal is a phoenix, Freemasonry symbolism which points to the New World Order rising out of the ashes. The SOJ had plans for America long before it was founded, which we see in her design and institutions.

Today, the USA government is filled with people who were trained at SOJ schools. Catholics rule D.C., as we see with Joe Biden, Nancy Pelosi, Mike Pence, Rudy Giuliani, etc. The Supreme Court is now stacked with Catholics in Chief Justice John Roberts, Samuel Alito, Clarence Thomas, Sonia Sotomayor, Brett Kavanaugh, and Amy Coney Barrett.

The political battle between left and right is an illusion, created to distract Americans while the leaders on both sides promote the agenda of the JSG. They pretend to fight while they both work to push the U.S., and the world, into the JSG's One World Government.

CHAPTER 72 - WITNESSES AGAINST THE SOJ

Those who control a country rewrite history to hide incriminating facts. In this chapter, I will focus on what U.S. Presidents said about the JSG because they didn't teach us this at school.

John Adams wrote to Thomas Jefferson in 1814 about the SOJ's rebirth and its danger to America. *"I do not like the resurrection of the Jesuits. They have a General now in Russia, in correspondence with the Jesuit in the United States, who are more numerous than anybody knows. Shall we not have swarms of them here, in as many disguises as only a king of gypsies can assume. If ever any congregation of men could merit eternal perdition on earth and in hell, it is this company of Loyola."* Jefferson replied, *"Like you, I disapprove of the restoration of the Jesuits, for it means a step backward from light into darkness."*

Adams wrote back to Jefferson, *This society (Jesuits) has been a greater calamity to mankind than the French Revolution or Napoleon's despotism or ideology. It has obstructed the progress of reformation and the improvement of the human mind in society much longer and more fatally.* (1)

John Adams and Thomas Jefferson, who both opposed the SOJ, both died on the same day, on July 4, 1826, the 50th anniversary of the Declaration of Independence.

What are the odds? They opposed the JSG, and the SOJ upheld their oath to use poison to take out opposition, no matter the rank. And no autopsies were performed to prove that they were poisoned.

President James Monroe died five years later, on July 4, 1831.

Again, what are the odds? He supposedly died from TB, but the symptoms are basically the same as arsenic poisoning. The Monroe Doctrine opposed the JSG and paid the price.

President William Henry Harrison was elected on March 4, 1841, and served for only 35 days, then he got sick and died.

He defied the JSG in his inauguration speech, and he also opposed the annexation of Texas, which the SOJ needed to push the slavery issue. John Tyler took his place, and the annexation of Texas was approved within a few months.

President Zachary Taylor only served from March 1849 until his death in July 1850, when he got violently sick on July 4th. Go figure! He fought the poison for five days and died on the 9th.

He opposed the expansion of slavery and refused to sign a compromise that the JSG wanted. Millard Fillmore took his place and was more malleable to the JSG's will, and he signed the compromise that Taylor had refused.

President Abraham Lincoln opposed the JSG and the SOJ.

Lincoln said to his friend Charles Chiniquy, *"I am so glad to meet you again. You see that your friends the Jesuits have not yet killed me. But they would have surely don't it when I passed through their most devoted city, Baltimore, had I not passed by incognito a few hours before they expected me. We have proof that the company which had been selected and organized to murder me was led by a rapid Roman Catholic called Byrne.*

I saw Mr. Morse, the learned inventor of electric telegraphy: he told me that when he was in Rome, not long ago, he found out the proofs of the most formidable conspiracy against this country and all of its institutions. It is evident that it is to the intrigues and emissaries of the pope that we owe in great part the horrible civil war, which is threatening to cover the country with blood and runs.

So many plots have already been made against my life, that it is a real miracle that they have all failed, when we consider that the great majority of them were in the hands of the skillful Roman Catholic murderers, evidently trained by Jesuits. But can we expect that God will make a perpetual miracle to save my life? I believe not. The Jesuits are so expert in those deeds of blood that Henry IV said it was impossible to escape them, and he became their victim, though he did all that could be done to protect himself. (3)

Abraham Lincoln said to Charles Chiniquy, *"I will be forever grateful for the warning words you have addressed to me about the dangers ahead to my life, from Rome. I know they are not imaginary dangers. If I were fighting against a Protestant South, as a nation, there would be no danger of assassination. The nations who read the Bible fight bravely on the battlefield, but they do not assassinate their enemies. The pope and the Jesuits, with their infernal Inquisition, are the only organized powers in the world which have recourse to the dagger of the assassin to murder those who they cannot convince with their arguments or conquer with the sword.*

Unfortunately, I feel more and more every day that it is not against the Americans of the South alone; I am fighting, it is more against the Pope of Rome, his perfidious Jesuits and their blind and bloodthirsty slaves. As long as they hope to conquer the North, they will spare me; but the day we route their armies, take their cities and force them to submit, then, it is my impression that the Jesuits, who are the principal rulers of the South, will do what they have almost invariably done in the past. The dagger or the pistol will do what the strong hands of the warriors could not achieve. This civil war seems to be nothing but a political affair to those who do not see, as I do, the secret springs of that terrible drama. But it is more a religious than a civil war. It is Rome who wants to rule and degrade the North, as she has ruled and degraded the South, from the very day of its discovery. There are only very few of the Southern leaders who are not more or less under the influence of the Jesuits through their wives, family relations, and their friends. Several members of the family of Jeff Davis belong to the Church of Rome.

But it is very certain that if the American people could learn what I know of the fierce hatred of the priests of Rome against our institutions, our schools, our most sacred rights, and our so dearly bought liberties, they would drive them away tomorrow from among us, or they would shoot them as traitors. But you are the only one to whom I reveal these sad secrets, for I know that you learned them before me. The history of these last thousand years tells us that wherever the Church of Rome is not a dagger to pierce the bosom of a free nation, she is a stone to her neck, to paralyze her, and prevent her advance in the ways of civilization, science, intelligence, happiness, and liberty."

If the American people could learn what I know of the fierce hatred of the priests or Rome against our institutions, our schools, our most sacred rights, and our so dearly bought liberties, they would drive them out as traitors. This war would never have been possible without the sinister influence of the Jesuits. We owe it to popery that we now see our land reddened with the blood of her noblest sons…. I pity the priests, the bishops and the monks of Rome in the United States when the people realize that they are, in great part, responsible for the tears and the bloodshed in this war.

Lincoln was murdered, and a trial was held for some of the Catholic perpetrators, but the history books point to a lone rogue gunman.

Catholic John F. Kennedy defied the JSG when he sought to avoid a war, and he started the process of taking control of the U.S. money supply from the Federal Reserve by printing $5 bills with "UNITED STATES NOTE" on them instead of "FEDERAL RESERVE NOTE." Because of those actions, he was taken out.

Do you now see the SOJ's oath fulfilled against the U.S. Presidents?

It says, *'That when the same cannot be done openly, I will secretly use the poisoned cup, the strangulating cord, the steel of the poniard or the leaden bullet, regardless of the honor, rank, dignity, or authority of the person or persons.'*

Giovanni Battista Nicolini, an Italian poet, and playwright wrote the following in his book *History of the Jesuits* in 1854.

The Jesuits are dreaded and detested on all sides as the worst species of knaves, whose arts the (Jesuit) fathers have earned for themselves a disgraceful celebrity. They are not Americans or Englishmen, but their country is Rome; their sovereign the Pope; their laws the commands of their General.

I cannot too much impress upon the minds of my readers that the Jesuits, by their very calling, by the very essence of their institution, are bound to seek, by every means, right or wrong, the destruction of Protestantism. This is the condition of their existence, the duty they must fulfill, or cease to be Jesuits. They must be considered as the bitterest enemies of the Protestant faith; and bad and unworthy priests; to be equally regarded with aversion and distrust.

The main difficulty of my subject, as will be readily understood, lies in discovering and delineating the true character of the Jesuits: for, take the Jesuit for what he ought or appears to be, and you commit the greatest blunders. Draw the character after what the Jesuit seems to be in London, and you will not recognize your portrait in the Jesuit of Rome.

The Jesuit is the man of circumstances. Despotic in Spain, constitutional in England, republican in Paraguay, bigot in Rome, idolater in India, he shall assume and act out in his own person, with admirable flexibility, all those different features by which men are usually to be distinguished from each other.

He will accompany the gay woman of the world to the theatre and will share in the excesses of the debauchee. With solemn countenance, he will take his place by the right side of the religious man at church, and he will revel in the tavern with the glutton and the sot. He dresses in all garbs, speaks all languages, knows all customs, is present everywhere through nowhere recognized – and all this, it should seem (O monstrous blasphemy!), for the greater glory of God – ad majorem Dei gloriam.

Loyola had but one end in view – one fixed idea – namely, to establish an order which would domineer over society; and that his successors have been arrested by no scruples as to the means to be employed for obtaining this end. With the exception of this fixed rule, to which the Jesuits have adhered with undeviating constancy, it may be asserted that they have no principle whatever.

To accomplish their ends, they have all along thought that money would be the most efficient instrument; hence their insatiable desire for wealth, to accumulate which, they violated all laws, divine, and human. The riches got by illicit means have been ever expended for more culpable purposes.

384

Ministers of different sovereigns are bought over by princely largesses, and even the ruling beauties of courts are bribed to serve the order with costly and suitable presents. From the beginning, the establishment of the Society was everywhere opposed, and in all places where it was finally admitted, it was subsequently, at different epochs, persecuted and convicted of iniquitous and abominable crimes.

Founded by that bold, despotic, and ambitious man, it seems as if his spirit had transmitted itself into the whole Society and presided over all its acts. "The moment," says an author of the beginning of the seventeenth century, "a great crime is committed; the public voice at once and unanimously accuses the Jesuits of being its perpetrators."

"The end justifies the means" is the Jesuit's favorite maxim, and as his only end is the order, at its bidding, the Jesuit is ready to commit any crime whatsoever.

Such, then, is the history of the Society dreaded and relied upon, worshipped and abhorred, which has produced little good, and infinite mischief, and which, having been hurled down from the pinnacle of splendor and glory, attempts no, with renewed vigor and unceasing activity, to regain the summit of its ancient pre-eminence. An appalling prospect, foreboding no good to the welfare of mankind!

With such a vile reputation, you can understand why they hide who they are and work through front organizations. But every President knows who controls D.C., the JSG, and they know that they will be taken out if they defy him. They push his agenda while pretending to represent the American people.

Slowly but surely, Americans' rights have been removed, and their wealth is stolen so that they're slaves of the corporation of the JSG-led District of Columbia. The labor and money of Americans fund the endless wars against other countries so that the JSG controls every country. This is why Iran, Syria, and North Korea have been demonized recently by Presidents and the media because they don't have an SOJ Rothschild central bank yet.

CHAPTER 73 - THE TAKEOVER OF AMERICA

Though the SOJ helped establish the USA, they've had to systematically work to take more control of the government.

The rights of states, and the citizens of those states, were nullified in 1868 when the SOJ had the 14th Amendment, called the *Reconstruction Amendment*, ratified.

It was written under the guise of an amendment to give rights to former slaves following the Civil War, but in reality, it created a new empire, one that serves the Jesuits. Before this amendment, people were citizens of their state, not the federal government. Now everyone has a Social Security Number, and they are U.S. Citizens.

Part of the 14th Amendment says, *"No State shall make or enforce any law which shall abridge the privileges or immunities of citizens of the United States."* That declares that the Federal government rules supreme and that all of the rights that we were given in our Constitution are now just privileges that can be taken away by the Federal government. Before this amendment, the Federal government was the servant of the states. Now, the states are subservient to the national government, and the citizens are slaves to their new master.

The *'Act of 1871'* created the SOJ-owned city-state corporation of the 'UNITED STATES OF AMERICA.'

The SOJ used the Civil War to cause the United States of America to go bankrupt. Under no constitutional authority to do so, Congress being in dire straits, created a separate form of government for the District of Columbia. They created the city-state corporation of the UNITED STATES OF AMERICA that uses an altered version of the constitution, titled in all capital letters as 'THE CONSTITUTION OF THE UNITED STATES OF AMERICA.'

The United States of America, as founded by our forefathers, is bankrupt and dead. The UNITED STATES OF AMERICA of the SOJ controls the people of America via their corporation. The leaders in the city-state corporation of the District of Columbia work for the corporation's interest, not the people. Still, they fake working for Americans as not to incite a revolt. Search YouTube for *"Act of 1871"*

They control the money supply via their Federal Reserve Bank.

The evil ones sunk the Titanic (it was really the Olympic) on purpose to get rid of some key people who opposed the creation of their Federal Reserve Bank. Benjamin Guggenheim, Isador Strauss (the head of Macy's department stores), and John Jacob Astor (the world's wealthiest man) were killed when it sank. These three men, the main opposition to the creation of the Federal Reserve Bank, were eliminated.

Thomas Jefferson warned, *"If the American people ever allow private banks to control the issue of their money, first by inflation and then by deflation, the banks and corporations that will grow up around them will deprive the people of their property until their children will wake up homeless on the continent their fathers conquered."*

Since the Federal Reserve Act was established in 1913, the US Dollar has lost 95% of its value in relation to gold. Not only are they enslaving our country in debt, but they also reduce the value of our hard-earned money. Their money printing debt scheme is the biggest fraud ever conceived, yet U.S. Presidents say nothing about it.

Daniel Webster said, *We are in danger of being overwhelmed with irredeemable paper, mere paper, representing not gold nor silver; no sir, representing nothing but broken promises, bad faith, bankrupt corporations, cheated creditors and a ruined people."*

The Fed creates credit out of thin air via their computers, or they pay the treasury a small printing fee for currency. For every dollar they create, our government has agreed to pay them interest. Every year our national debt increases from the cost of wars, bailouts, social programs, etc., so we have to pay more interest. The U.S. debt is now so large that it can't be paid off, so we're enslaved forever paying interest to the Fed. This is what Thomas Jefferson warned us about!

The stock market crash of 1929 was engineered by the SOJ when they suddenly withdrew money from the system, which collapsed the market, and then the evil ones bought the major corporations for pennies on the dollar. That's how you take over a nation!

President Franklin D. Roosevelt signed Executive Order 6102 on April 5, 1933, *'forbidding the hoarding of gold coin, gold bullion, and gold certificates within the continental United States.'*

They've removed the gold and silver, which backed our money supply. Each monetary note was legal tender; a silver certificate could be traded at the bank for the corresponding silver amount. They gave us *Federal Reserve Notes*, which are not backed by gold or silver, and can be devalued at any time. When you compare the modern bills to Monopoly money, you see how they mock us with similar coloring.

President Johnson removed silver from our coins, which used to be 90% silver, but now they are made of worthless junk metals. And President Nixon took us off of the gold standard. One ounce of gold will buy the same amount of goods today as it did 100 years ago, and that's even with the suppression of the price of gold and silver. But a Federal Reserve Note is worth about 5% of what it was 100 years ago.

They created the IRS, which was never ratified by all states, to collect taxes from the American people. People went to war over a 3% tea tax, but now Americans complacently give up a huge amount of money in income tax, and then with their remaining money, they're taxed on every good and service. You get taxed to fish, hunt, drive, etc.

Senator Thomas Watson (1856-1922) said, *"Rolling upon the horizon are these appalling storm clouds and few there be who will take warning. The Protestant Churches are blind to the awful danger. The State authorities are indulging a fatal security.*

The general public is strangely apathetic – indifferent at the growth of a religion which openly denounces freedom of speech, freedom of conscience, and freedom of education – a religion which is implacably antagonistic to the very principles upon which our Republic stands."

"It was but yesterday that the Roman peril was only a small cloud, no larger than a man's hand, upon the distant horizon. Now, it is the storm-cloud which darkens the whole land. It was but yesterday that the Roman Catholic priest avoided the public eye and passed you on the street with a humble, deprecatory smile, which seemed to mutely plead for permission to exist. Today, the Roman priest is the most insolent and arrogant man in America. The laws will not touch him. The politicians do his bidding. The press is afraid of him. Protestant pulpits no longer dare to fulminate against him.

His powerful hand controls Congress and the President. He is forcing his church into a union with the state. His greedy paws are raking public funds out of municipal, state, and national treasures for the use of the church. Our juvenile courts are furnishing slaves to his Houses of the Good Shepherd. "Make America Catholic" is the slogan now publicly proclaimed at monster Romanist gatherings."

"For American people to close their eyes to the efforts of the Church of Rome, to extend her influence and to secure to herself dominion over your country is criminal. And for those whom God has placed as watchmen upon the walls, to refrain from sounding the alarm in the holy mountain is to render themselves responsible for all the injuries which the cause of Christ or your common country or individual persons, would suffer from such negligence!"

"Our forefathers knew that the Roman Catholic hierarchy was. Its record – reeking with crime and fraud – was familiar to them... But the children forget the reason why the fathers dreaded the Roman Catholic Church. The children know not the record of crime and devastation, which caused our forefathers to detest the Roman hierarchy. Consequently, the Pope has found our Republic an easy prey to his designs."

There's so much more to the story, but that's not the focus of this book. The point I'm making is that the SOJ has stolen Americans' wealth to use it for their trillion-dollar war machine, which they are using to push the world into their One World Government.

Our duty is to expose *'the great city'* of Rome and her SOJ army and to pray for the utter destruction of their deceptions over mankind. Prayer is our most powerful weapon against the SOJ, the enemy of Messiah, His saints, and humanity.

They will not prevail, the *harlot* church of Rome will be destroyed, the FBJSG and ACBP will be cast down from their pinnacle of power. The saints will prevail for the glory of our Warrior King.

The bottom line is that the leaders in the District of Columbia ultimately work for the JSG. We will see the city-state corporation of D.C. in *The Seventh Bowl Judgment* chapter, as it's one-third of the *'Empire of the City'* which is used to control the world.

When you see how the JSG controls the District of Columbia, you're not deceived by the puppet show. The SOJ controls both political parties, and they have them play out their roles to cause Americans to be caught up in the political narrative, instead of seeing *The Wizard of Oz*, who is behind the curtain and controls it all, the JSG.

They fill the media with stories of the battle between left and right so that Americans are distracted and divided. They're causing emotions to run high on both sides, pitting Americans against each other so that they don't realize who is their collective enemy.

Is it *'risky'* to expose these truths? Perhaps, but it a crime against humanity, and the Heavenly Father, to know the truth and not warn others. The Spirit shows us the truth, not just so that we are aware, but so that we can share it with others.

CHAPTER 74 – THE LAODICEA CHURCH ERA

The Laodicea era Church era is described in Revelation 3:14-22.

Messiah says that we're *lukewarm* and self-satisfied. The flames of the Protestant Reformation and the Great Awakening have been quenched. The passion for winning souls has been passed off to Pastors and missionaries instead of being born by Yah's temple priests, the saints.

The name *'Laodicea'* points to the *'power and rule of the laity,'* which is a fitting description for our church era, as people give all of the power to the Pastor and maybe some deacons. Churches have to liven up the worship and arts and teachings to entertain their members. Instead of making a public profession of one's belief in Messiah, now they quietly slip up their hand when everyone's eyes are closed.

The church is compromised in sin and doesn't stand out from the rest of the world when it comes to divorce, drinking, watching evil movies, etc.

> *By this we know that we love the children of God, when we love God, and keep his commandments. For this is the love of God, that we keep his commandments: and his commandments are not grievous.* 1 John 5:2-3

The desire to fight against the ACBP has been lost because most don't know that the office of the papacy fulfills that role, as the enemy is *hidden in plain sight*. The passion for helping Catholics come out of the *harlot* church has faded, as most think that the RCC is just another Christian denomination. Pastors teach personal development instead of proclaiming who is the enemy of Messiah.

Many people believe that they'll be raptured out, so they've become complacent. They don't seem to care who the *antichrist* is, as they think they won't have to face him. They don't care about the fulfillment of Revelation because they think that they won't be here to see it. They think that they're ready to meet their Messiah. Based on their lack of understanding, that perspective is problematic.

The SOJ has infiltrated Protestant churches to compromise their teachings and return them to unity with Rome's ACBP. We see that with Franklin Graham, Rick Warren, Kenneth Copeland, Paula White, etc. Pastors should have nothing to do with the ACBP of Rome, other than exposing their false teachings.

The majority of Christians follow man's traditions, such as pagan-based Easter and Christmas, instead of the Father's seven Holy Feast Days, which Messiah is fulfilling to redeem the set-apart saints. The fall Feast of Trumpets represents His return, Atonement His judgment, and Tabernacles, His marriage to His bride; so they have not been fulfilled yet, and they have not been done away with. Every set-apart believer should celebrate them as they are the whole Gospel message.

Those who do study prophecy think that they are rich in understanding of prophecy. They think that they know how the end-times will play out and do not need to learn more truth. Sadly, most are believing the well-schemed deceptions of the SOJ.

> *Because thou says, I am rich, and increased with goods, and have need of nothing; and knows not that thou art wretched, and miserable, and poor, and blind, and naked.* Revelation 3:17

> *For the time will come when they will not endure sound doctrine, but according to their own desires, because they have itching ears, they will heap up for themselves teachers; and they will turn their ears away from the truth, and be turned aside to fables.* 2 Timothy 4:3-4

False prophets have infiltrated churches and seminaries.

> *For such are false apostles, deceitful workers, transforming themselves into apostles of Christ. And no wonder! For Satan himself transforms himself into an angel of light. Therefore it is no great thing if his ministers also transform themselves into ministers of righteousness, whose end will be according to their works.* 2 Corinthians 11:13-15

Beloved, do not believe every spirit, but test the spirits, whether they are of God; because many false prophets have gone out into the world. 1 John 4:1

Messiah gives the end-times saints this admonition.

I counsel thee to buy of me gold tried in the fire, that thou may be rich; and white raiment, that thou may be clothed, and that the shame of thy nakedness do not appear; and anoint thine eyes with eyesalve, that thou may see. Revelation 3:18

Pray for the Spirit to give you *eye salve* to be able to see the truth.

Do not quench the Spirit. Do not despise prophecies. Test all things; hold fast what is good. 1 Thessalonians 5:19-21

We should no longer be children, tossed to and fro and carried about with every wind of doctrine, by the trickery of men, in the cunning craftiness of deceitful plotting, but, speaking the truth in love, may grow up in all things into Him who is the head—Christ. Ephesians 4:14

Be *clothed* with the truth, so you're not *naked* when He returns.

Behold, I am coming as a thief. Blessed is he who watches, and keeps his garments, lest he walk naked and they see his shame. Revelation 16:15

Messiah closes with a promise to the *overcomers.*

As many as I love, I rebuke and chasten. Therefore be zealous and repent. Behold, I stand at the door and knock. If anyone hears My voice and opens the door, I will come in to him and dine with him, and he with Me. To him who overcomes I will grant to sit with Me on My throne, as I also overcame and sat down with My Father on His throne. He who has an ear, let him hear what the Spirit says to the churches. Revelation 3:19-22

Will you accept His rebuke, repent of your misunderstandings, and overcome the deceptions of the enemy, to be an overcomer?

In *Romanism And The Reformation*, Henry Grattan Guinness says,

The Reformation of the sixteenth century, which gave birth to Protestantism, was based on scripture. It gave back to the world the Bible. It taught the Scriptures; it exposed the errors and corruptions of Rome by the use of the sword of the Spirit. It applied the prophecies and accepted their practical guidance. Such Reformation work requires to be done afresh. We have suffered prophetic anti-papal truth to be too much forgotten. This generation is dangerously latitudinarian – indifferent to truth and error on points on which Scripture is tremendously decided and absolutely clear.

This point strikes at the heart of the issues with Protestantism today. The plain truths of the Scriptures have given way to an era of SOJ-infused compromise, leading the Protestant world to become part of Babylon, just as the Bible foretold.

Oh, how much worse is the state of affairs today? Guinness would be appalled at the lack of understanding of who the *antichrist beast* is and how Revelation has been fulfilled historically.

Deception has become the order of the day. The adage is that *"If you repeat a lie often enough, it becomes the truth."* This is sometimes called the *'illusion of truth effect,'* which is useful for establishing and entrenching deceptions. Since the 19th century, the enemy has repeatedly programmed the futuristic prophecy fulfillment deceptions into people's minds so that they can't comprehend explanations outside of their paradigm.

I pray that this book causes the saints' minds to be filled with the glorious truth about prophecy fulfillment, which the enemy has hidden. I pray Messiah's Ekklesia will be raised from their slumber and use the authority that Messiah has given to her to cast down the enemy's power with Scriptural truth and fervent prayer.

CHAPTER 75 - THE IMAGE OF THE BEAST
1929

There seems to be two applications to the fulfillment of the *'image of the beast,'* both applying to the ACBPs. This reference in Revelation 13:14-15 is pointing to something that the FPJSG did, not the ACBP.

And deceiveth them that dwell on the earth by the means of those miracles which he had power to do in the sight of the beast; saying to them that dwell on the earth, that they should make an image to the beast, which had the wound by a sword, and did live. And he had power to give life unto the image of the beast, that the image of the beast should both speak, and cause that as many as would not worship the image of the beast should be killed. **Revelation 13:14-15**

The word *'image'* is Strong's 1504 *eikon*, which means: *a likeness, i.e. (literally) statue, profile, or (figuratively) representation, resemblance:—image.*

The *'beast,'* the Popes of Rome, had civil and ecclesiastic authority over the Roman beast kingdom for 1,260 years until 1798 when they lost their civil power. During the 19th century, they lost more authority over people. Though the Black Pope controls the Vatican, he can't rule openly, as people know his evil deeds; so he needed to prop the White Pope back up to power. A *'likeness,'* an *'image,'* is something that makes it appear that the Popes have civil authority again.

In 1929, the SOJ got Benito Mussolini to sign a concordat at the *Lateran Treaty* in Rome on behalf of King Victor Emmanuel III. It established Vatican City as a sovereign state and guaranteed full and independent sovereignty to the Holy See.

Pope Pius XI reigned from 1922-1939, and he had this coin made that says *'Face Christi Italiae Reddita'* in Latin, which in English means *'Returning the Italian face of Christ.'*

It's pointing to the underline image of the *Italian Christ*, the Pope, the *Vicar of Christ*, returning to power, so the *'image of the beast'* was established. On the back is the blasphemous Eucharist ceremony golden cup of abominations. In the background are the two main temples of the Popes, the *Lateran Basilica* and *St. Peter's Basilica*. Notice that it has an IHS Jesuit sun, showing the authority of the JSG, as the true leader, the *sun*.

Here's a 1929 coin from Pope Pius XI that says *'Stato Della Cittadel Vaticano,'* which means *'State of Vatican City.'* The city-state corporation of Vatican City, with the ACBP as the spokesman, is the *'image of the beast'* as the Pope appears to be the leader of Rome's church and state. But it's just an *image*, as the Black Pope controls the Vatican.

Since the Lateran Treaty of 1929, Vatican coins have said '*Citta Del Vaticano*,' which means '*Vatican City*.' Best as I can tell, that phrase was never used beforehand, which points to the significance of this event, as the Popes now have the *image* of being a civil leader again.

The JSG props up the ACBP as the world leader to use him and the Vatican to gather the world under their power. Only this time, they're pretending to be nice.

Remember that in the 12th-15th centuries, the Popes were at their height of power, and they controlled kings and princes, and they controlled Christendom. That approach worked in the Dark Ages, but it won't work now. Today, the Popes are playing nice and saying things to draw all people unto them. Pope John XXIII led the *Second Vatican Council* in St. Peter's Basilica at the Vatican in September of 1962. A total of 2,540 cardinals, patriarchs, archbishops, and bishops from around the world attended the opening session.

They used to teach that the Catholic Church is the '*one true church*' and that everyone outside of it was a heretic who they condemned to be killed, but now they're preaching ecumenism to draw people of all faiths until them. They issued the *Decree on Ecumenism, Unitatis Redintegratio*: It said that ecumenism should be everyone's concern and that genuine ecumenism involves a continual personal and institutional renewal.

They used to condemn people of other religions as heretics, but now they're teaching against religious discrimination. They issued the Declaration on the *Relationship of the Church to Non-Christian Religions, Nostra Aetate*: It said the Catholic Church rejects nothing that is true and holy in non-Christian religions, called for an end to anti-Semitism and said any discrimination based on race, color, religion or condition of life is foreign to the mind of Christ.

They used to proclaim that if you disagreed with their doctrine, that you are a heretic and deserve to be burned without pity, but now they're saying that people have the freedom to act according to their beliefs. They issued the *Declaration on Religious Freedom, Dignitatis Humanae*: It said that religious liberty is a right found in the dignity of each person and that no one should be forced to act in a way contrary to his or her own beliefs.

They used to force people to accept their religion by the pain of torture, but now they say that missionaries should not force anyone to accept their faith. They issued the *Decree on the Church's Missionary Activity, Ad Gentes*: It said missionary activity should help the social and economic welfare of people and not force anyone to accept the faith.

Why would they do this? Because the ACBP isn't going to be able to demand that everyone bow down to his authority out of fear like they used to do. Instead, they're going to appeal to all Christian denominations, and all religions, and even atheists, to join with them in the name of *'love and unity.'* They've changed their language to acceptance of all people; instead of saying *'convert to Romanism or die.'*

Pope Francis made a video in 2016 that featured religious leaders from Judaism, Catholicism, Islam, and Buddhism, all proclaiming that they believe in the same God. Look at how many Christian leaders have joined with the Pope in the name of love and unity. They gather with the Pope at conferences and recognize his authority. Churches like Hillsong have held the Roman Catholic Mass. They promote the One World Religion at their ecumenical Alpha conferences. Founder Brian Houston has said that *'Allah of Islam and the God of the Bible are the same.'*

Joel Osteen thinks the Pope is fantastic. Kanye West now proclaims to be a Christian and has already demonized people who point to Catholicism's false salvation message. Kenneth Copeland has aligned with the Pope. Tony Palmer, an Evangelical Anglican Bishop, proclaimed at a Copeland event that "*the Protest against Rome is over.*"

This paves the way for their One World Government when, after a religious-based WW III between Muslim countries and Israel, people will cry out for an end to religious division and wars. And the ACBP will be used to unite the world, drawing it under his power.

Just keep in mind that Papal bulls and statements are permanent declarations until the RCC rescinds them, and none of the blasphemous statements by Popes that condemned heretics have been rescinded.

The references to the *'image of the beast'* in Revelation 14:9, 15:2 and 16:2 seem to point to the following explanation.

The ACBPs removed the second commandment, *'Thou shall not make graven IMAGES nor bow to them.'* Revelation 13:18 points to the image of the crucifix, which equates to 666; that is in every Catholic Church and home. So that seems to be an *image of the beast*, which keep Messiah on the cross to mock Him per Galatians 3:13.

> *Christ hath redeemed us from the curse of the law, being made a curse for us: for it is written, Cursed is every one that hangs on a tree.*

Recall that the word *'image'* is Strong's 1504 *eikon*, which means: *a likeness, a statue, profile, or (figuratively) representation, resemblance: —image.*

The crucifix started to be used around the time of Emperor Constantine and the creation of Romanism. Then it was used more widely in the sixth century, when the ACBPs were given civil and ecclesiastic authority.

Since then Catholics have revered (worshipped) the image of the crucifix. The Roman Rite requires that "*either on the altar or near it, there is to be a cross, with the figure of Christ crucified upon it, a cross clearly visible to the assembled people. It is desirable that such a cross should remain near the altar even outside of liturgical celebrations, so as to call to mind for the faithful the saving Passion of the Lord.*"

So we see two applications to the fulfillment of the *'image of the beast,'* both applying to the ACBPs. Don't revere him or his wicked crucifix.

CHAPTER 76 - THE SIXTH BOWL JUDGMENT

And the sixth angel poured out his vial upon the great river Euphrates; and the water thereof was dried up, that the way of the kings of the east might be prepared. **16:12**

The Turks who were symbolized by the *Euphrates River* during the sixth trumpet judgment became the Ottoman Empire. Wikipedia records the expansion and peak (1453–1566), the stagnation and reform (1566–1827), the decline and modernization (1828–1908), and the defeat and dissolution of the Ottoman Empire. The Ottomans' territory was vast, but it was *'dried up'* so that they only possessed the country of Turkey. Once again, we see how Messiah's apocalyptic vision is about major world events.

In *The Approaching End Of The Age,* **Henry Grattan Guinness says,** *Nor had it been under judgment of the sword alone. It is miserably perishing in its own corruption. Internal discord and insurrection, provoked by cruel tyranny and monstrous misgovernment, have weakened the state. Polygamy and other vices have caused depopulation so rapid as to be almost incredible. Pestilence, conflagration, earthquakes, civil commotions, massacres, slaughters all have tended to reduce the population and weaken the empire. Attacks from without, rebellions from within, and this steady process of internal decay have reduced Turkey.*

In *The Rise and Fall of the Papacy* **(1701), Robert Fleming says,** *The sixth vial will be poured out upon the Mahometan Empire, as the former on the papacy. And seeing the sixth trumpet brought the Turks from beyond the Euphrates, from crossing the river they date their rise, this sixth vial dried up their waves and exhausts their power. Supposing, then, that the Turkish monarchy should be totally destroyed between 1848 and 1900.*

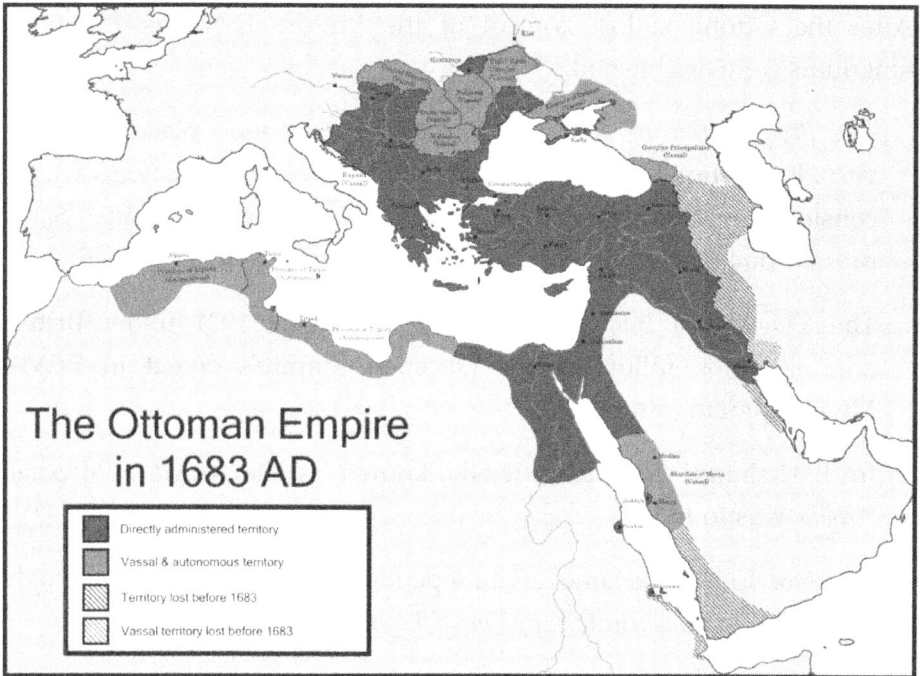

The Ottoman Empire
in 1683 AD

Directly administered territory

Vassal & autonomous territory

Territory lost before 1683

Vassal territory lost before 1683

One of the most important territories that they lost control of is the Middle East. In 1917, the *Battle of Jerusalem* occurred during the British Empire's *'Jerusalem Operations'* against the Turks, during the *Sinai and Palestine Campaign* of World War I. Fighting for the city led to the surrender of the Turks. British General Allenby liberated Jerusalem on December 11, 1917.

After the First World War, the *Armistice of Mudros* decreed that Allied Forces would occupy Istanbul. On November 1, 1922, the newly founded parliament formally abolished the Sultanate, ending 623 years of Ottoman rule. The *Treaty of Lausanne* of July 24, 1923, led to the international recognition of the sovereignty of the newly formed *Republic of Turkey* as the successor state of the Ottoman Empire. Amazingly, modern Turkey, a small country in Asia Minor, possesses the source of the Euphrates. So indeed, *the River Euphrates dried up*!

After the Ottomans lost control of the Middle East, the following kingdoms were established.

The *Proclamation of the Arab Kingdom of Syria* took place in March 1920. Interestingly, the mission of the *Syrian National Congress* was to consider the future of "Syria," by which was meant *Greater Syria*: present-day Syria, Lebanon, Israel, Palestine, and Jordan.

The *Kingdom of Iraq* was founded in August 1921 under British administration following the Ottoman Empire's defeat in WWI's Mesopotamian campaign.

In 1932, Saudi Arabia, officially known as the *Kingdom of Saudi Arabia*, was founded.

In 1946, Jordan became an independent sovereign state officially known as *The Hashemite Kingdom of Transjordan*.

Though the kingdoms of Syria, Iraq, Saudi Arabia, and Jordan; were created after the Ottoman Empire lost control of the Middle East, I don't believe that they are the *"kings of the east,"* who are foretold in the sixth bowl. I believe that they will play a role in the end times, as we witness the ongoing confrontation between Zionist Israel, Syria, and Iran, which sets the stage for WW III.

Many prophecy teachers point to China and countries from the Far East as the *"kings of the east,"* but those countries were already in place before the Ottoman Empire was dried up. It makes sense to look for something that happened due to the Ottoman Empire drying up, so *'that the way of the kings of the east might be prepared.'* And it makes sense that it's in a place that's going to play a significant role in fulfilling the sixth and seventh bowls.

The *"kings of the east"* are directly tied to the *'drying up'* of the Ottoman Empire, but they have a more sinister nature, which will shock most believers.

CHAPTER 77 - THE KINGS OF THE EAST

When you think of the Middle East, what people group and nation comes to mind? Is it not the Jews in Israel?

For a long time, I didn't see where the modern state of Israel fit into Bible prophecy, given that most of the prophecies that people cite are not pointing to the modern state of Israel. But now I see that the Jews in Israel fulfill prophecy as the *"kings of the east."*

Let me preface this explanation by saying that our pastors have conditioned us with certain beliefs, so I pray that you will seek Scriptural truth. The topic of the Jews in the modern state of Israel can be an emotional subject, so please pray for discernment.

To understand this, we have to look back to the medieval Khazarian kingdom, which was in Eastern Europe, part of modern-day Russia, and Ukraine. They dominated this area and controlled trade through the region from 650-965. The Khazars were Turkish, generally described by Arab sources as having a white complexion, blue eyes, and reddish hair. They appear to descend from Esau, as he was red and hairy. Keep that in mind as we move forward.

They were warriors who worshiped many false gods, making them ripe for invasion, as Orthodox Christians and Islamic Muslims surrounded them. The ruling elite reportedly converted to Judaism in the 8th century; to deflect the Arabs and Byzantines outside pressure to accept either Islam or Orthodoxy. It's reported that Talmudic Rabbi's were brought in to teach the people Jewish traditions.

The people were fully converted to their beliefs. They were steeped in Judaism rituals and became 'self-styled' Jews with their clothing, beards, long hair on the side, etc. After several generations, they stopped remembering that their ancestors converted to Judaism, and they believed that they were the true Jews of Scripture.

The Khazars were warriors who used to be hired out by other countries for battles, as they were domineering. The Jewish Babylonian Talmud told them they could rule the world and have all of the wealth, and the Egyptian Kabbalah gave them the sorcery to *steal, kill, and destroy.*

Then in the 10th century, they were pushed out of Khazaria. They migrated west, primarily into Russia and Poland, and also Hungary and Germany. In Russia, they pretended to be Christians, so they were crypto-Jews, Jews in secret.

They were involved in the *Bolshevik Revolution* to seize control of Russia, which caused tens of millions of Orthodox Christians to die. Once again, this may have been part of Yah's judgment, as most Orthodox Christians believe in salvation through the sacraments, that Mary is the intercessor to the Father, and they have many idols.

To help justify the creation of the modern state of Israel, the enemy caused the persecution of Jews in Germany and other countries.

The great majority of Jews in the modern state of Israel are *Khazar* Jews. Today they're called *Ashkenazi* Jews, but they're Jews by religion, not by blood. Most of them have Turkish-Mongol DNA. With that in mind, consider what Messiah declares in Revelation 3:9

> *Behold, I will make them of the synagogue of Satan, which say they are Jews, and are not, but do lie; behold, I will make them to come and worship before thy feet, and to know that I have loved thee.*

Messiah wrote that to the church era of Philadelphia, which is when these Khazar Jews were active in pushing to be allowed to go live in Palestine and justify a state in the Middle East.

In *Notes on the Apocalypse* (1870), David Steele says: *By the "kings of the east" may be understood the Jews.* (1)

Listen to these Jews who proclaimed the truth.

In 1867, Russian Jewish scholar Abraham Harkavy, who studied Oriental languages and mastered in History, wrote *The Jews and Languages of the Slavs*. He declares that the Jews in Russia did not come from Germany but the Black Sea region (from Khazaria) and that the Slavonic language was integrated with their Biblical and Talmudic commentaries. In other words, the Yiddish language came from the Khazars, not the Hebrews.

The *1906 Jewish Encyclopedia* page on *Chazars* documents the Turkish Khazars conversion to Judaism.

The *Jewish Encyclopedia* documents that in the 8th century, King Bulan of Khazaria questioned the Mohammedans and the Christians about which of the other two religions they considered the better. When both gave preference to the Jews, that king perceived that it must be the best option. He, therefore, adopted it.

The *Jewish Virtual Library* documents the same narrative that the Turkish Khazars converted to Judaism in 740 AD.

The *Encyclopedia Of Ukraine* documents that at the beginning of the 8th century, Jews from Iran and Byzantium settled among the Khazars in northern Daghestan. Although some Khazars soon converted to Judaism, it was only at the beginning of the 9th century that Khagan Obadiah proclaimed non-Talmudic Judaism the state religion.

Britannica.com documents that trade and the collection of tribute were major sources of income. But the most striking characteristic of the Khazars was the apparent adoption of Judaism by the Khagan and the greater part of the ruling class in about 740. The circumstances of the conversion remain obscure, the depth of their adoption of Judaism difficult to assess, but the fact itself is undisputed and unparalleled in central Eurasian history.

The *Universal Jewish Encyclopedia* documents the same narrative that the Turkish Khazars converted to Judaism in the 8ᵗʰ century. (8)

Encyclopedia.com reports that Khazars are a national group of general Turkic type, independent and sovereign in Eastern Europe between the seventh and tenth centuries. During part of this time, the leading Khazars professed Judaism. (9)

I cite all of those sources to show that it's common knowledge available if you look for it, but you won't hear it from your pastor.

Abraham Nahum Polak, Professor of Medieval Jewish History at Tel Aviv University wrote an essay on the Khazars in 1941, titled 'The Khazar Conversion to Judaism!' This work appeared in 'Zion,' a Hebrew publication. He wrote a book called *Khazaria*, published in Hebrew in Tel Aviv in 1944. <u>Professor Poliak severed the 'mystic tie,' that umbilical cord that tied modern Jewry to Israel's Biblical tribes.</u> (10)

In 1976, a prominent Jew named Arthur Koestler published a book called 'The Thirteenth Tribe: The Kazar Empire and Its Heritage.' He wrote: *"The large majority of Jews after World War II in the world, were of Eastern origin-and thus perhaps mainly of Khazar origin. If so, this would mean that their ancestors came not from the Jordan, but from the Volga; not from the Canaan but from the Caucausus, once believed to be the cradle of the Aryan race. Genetically, they are more closely related to the Hun, Uigur and Magyar tribes than to the seed of Abraham, Isaac, and Jacob."* (11)

In the 1993 book *The Ashkenazic Jews: A Slavo-Turkic People in Search of a Jewish Identity*, Dr. Paul Wexler, a Tel Aviv University linguist, says: *"Yiddish began as a Slavic language whose vocabulary was largely replaced with German words. Going even further, he contends that the Ashkenazic Jews are predominantly converted Slavs and Turks who merged with a tiny population of Palestinian Jews from the Diaspora."* (12)

In 1999, Kevin Brooks wrote the book, 'The Jews of Khazaria,' which provides historical information on the Khazarian culture and their conversion to Judaism. *The Khazar people belonged to a grouping of Turks who wrote in a runic script that originated in Mongolia. The royalty of the Khazar kingdom was descended from the Ashina Turkic dynasty. In the 9th century, the Khazarian royalty and nobility as well as a significant portion of the Khazarian Turkic population embraced the Jewish religion. After their conversion, the Khazars were ruled by a succession of Jewish kings and began to adopt the hallmarks of Jewish civilization, including the Torah and Talmud, the Hebrew script, and the observance of Jewish holidays*

In 2007, University of Tel Aviv history teacher Schlomo Sand verified their Turkish-Mongol heritage in his book *Invention of the Jewish People*, saying, *"Jews are not a race and have no Israelite connection."*

DNA research science from Dr. Eran Elhaik (a Jew) and associates at the McKusick-Nathans Institute of Genetic Medicine, Johns Hopkins University School of Medicine, have confirmed that <u>97% of the 17 million of the world's Jews are not descendants of Abraham</u>.

Dr. Dan Graur is a world-famous Jewish geneticist who served on Tel Aviv University's faculty for twenty-two years and is now at the University of Houston. Graur is the recipient of the prestigious Humboldt Award, given to the world's top biological scientist. He declared that Dr. Elhaik's research is *"very honest."*

In 2001, Dr. Ariella Oppenheim of Hebrew University's genetics research department in Tel Aviv produced the same results as Dr. Elhaik. Oppenheim's study also found that the Jew's origins are in Khazaria and that they are of a Turkic bloodline. She also reported that some Palestinians have the chromosome in their blood indicating they are Cohanim and Israelite.

Do you see how these fake Khazar Jews are deceiving the world? Just like Satan created a counterfeit to the true Ekklesia of Messiah when he caused the RCC to be formed, Satan created a counterfeit to the true Israel of Scripture when he caused the Zionist state of Israel to be formed. Jews are telling the truth about the Zionists in Israel; why do people ignore their witness?

CHAPTER 78 - THE GOG AND MAGOG INVASION

The Khazar Jews are Jews by religion, not by blood. They fulfill Bible prophecy as the *'kings of the east'* in the sixth bowl, and Messiah points to them in saying that they're *'of the synagogue of Satan, which say they are Jews, and are not, but do lie.'* But they also fulfill another role, which takes the deception to a whole new level!

The book of Ezekiel points to *'Gog and Magog'* invading the Holy Land, attacking the citizens. People associate Gog and Magog as coming from Russia. The shocker is that it has already taken place! Let me state how and then I'll provide the proof. Lord Rothschild is *Gog,* and the Khazar Jews are *Magog.* They have already come against Palestine, taken control of the land, and have already persecuted the people who live there, killing many of them.

Let me explain. When the Khazar Jews were driven out of Khazaria, they fled primarily into Russia and Poland, and also into Germany and Hungary. In 1743, Mayer Amschel Bauer, a Khazar Jew, was born in Frankfurt, Germany. He is the son of Moses Amschel Bauer, a money lender. Moses placed a red sign above his counting-house, with a Satanic hexagram on it. When you investigate this family, you see that they worship the god of mammon and have sold their soul to Satan to gain immense wealth.

When Moses Amschel died, Mayer Amschel returned to Frankfurt to take over his money lending business. He understood the significance of the hexagram's symbolism, so he changed his last name to Rothschild, which means *Red Shield. Rot* is German for *Red, Schild* is German for *Sign.* The family shield is red with a white HEXagram on it.

A hexagram is used in sorcery. It represents two triangles, one pointing up, the other down. It symbolizes *'as above, so below.'* It has six points, six triangles, and it's a six-sided hexagon. The hexagram represents sun worship, which is Satan worship. Luciferians revere the hexagram.

The compass of Freemasonry represents a hexagram. This becomes significant when you realize why the six-pointed star, the HEXagram is on the Israeli flag and not a menorah.

Baron James Mayer Rothschild was born in Germany in 1792. His youngest son, Baron Edmond de Rothschild, is called the "father" of Palestine colonization. In the book *The Times And The Great Consummation*, which was written in 1856, Joseph A. Seiss noted: *There are already thousands of Jews in Jerusalem and its vicinity. A goodly portion of the Holy Land is at this moment under mortgages in the hands of those rich Jewish bankers, the Rothschilds of Europe.*

Zikhron Ya'akov (which means *Jacob's Memorial*) is a town in Israel, 22 miles south of *Haifa*, which overlooks the Mediterranean Sea. It was one of the first Jewish settlements of Halutzim in the country, founded in 1882 by Baron Edmond James de Rothschild.

It was Joseph Feinberg, the leader of the pioneers in *Rishon-Le-Zion*, the first of the Jewish colony in Palestine, who obtained 50,000 Francs from the Baron to enable the settlers to overcome their difficulties. The early settlers belonging to the *Bilu Society* received generous financial and moral help from the Baron to establish the important colonies of *Petach Tikvah*, *Zichron Jacob*, *Hederah*, *Rosh Pinah*, *Yesod Ha' Ma'aleh*, and most of the older Jewish colonies in Palestine.

In 1898, the *First Zionist Congress* called for establishing a home for the Jewish people in Palestine secured under public law, well before the persecution of Jews and WW II. The Rothschild-financed *Jewish National Fund* was founded in 1901 through Theodor Herzl. They began buying up land from mostly absentee Turkish landlords, and they kicked the Arabs off the land that had been in their family for centuries. Any land acquired by the Fund had the stipulation that it was never to return to Arab possession. Over thirty of these colonies were founded with his aid between 1880 and 1895.

Chaim Azriel Weizmann, born in Belarus (a part of the Russian Empire), was a Khazar Jew and Zionist leader, and Israeli statesman. He served as President of the *Zionist Organization* and later as the first President of Israel. He founded the *Weizmann Institute of Science* in Rehovot, Israel, in 1934; and was instrumental in establishing the *Hebrew University of Jerusalem*.

Baron Edmond de Rothschild established the *Palestine Jewish Colonization Association* (PICA) in 1924, which acquired more than 125,000 acres of land and set up business ventures. He spent an estimated $50 million to develop an electric generating station. With the great wine-cellars in *Rishon-le-Zion* and *Zichron Jacob*, the important Palestine wine industry owes its development to Baron. He was instrumental in establishing the other enterprises such as the big flour mills in *Haifa* and the silk factory at *Rosh Pinah*.

Edmond de Rothschild is honored on Israel's 500-shekel note as the 'Father of Israel.'

חמש מאות שקלים בנק ישראל 500 500

Rothschild Boulevard is one of the first streets built in Tel Aviv, Israel, a little over 100 years ago. It's one of the most expensive streets in the city and one of the main tourist attractions.

410

Named originally as *Rehov HaAm* (the *street of the people*), it was renamed to reflect Baron Edmond James de Rothschild's generosity in creating the nation of Israel. *Independence Hall*, where Israel's Declaration of Independence was signed in 1948, is located on Rothschild Boulevard. The Rothschild Hotel was designed in tribute to the Zionist vision and activities of Baron Edmond de Rothschild.

November 1917 was a key month for the enemy, as they made two bold moves.

I believe that this began the prophecy of Ezekiel 38 and 39. The British Balfour Declaration prepared the way for the Gog and Magog invasion of the land. On November 2, 1917, Britain issued the *Balfour Declaration*, giving the Jews the country of Palestine. This 'Declaration' of British support is addressed to Lord Rothschild. The letter certainly clarifies who is in charge of the Zionist movement, Lord Rothschild. He says that *"the reason the letter was written to him is that it was primarily a movement from Eastern Europe (Ashkenazi) Jews."*

If you search online, you can find a photo of Israel Prime Minister Benjamin Netanyahu with British Prime Minister Theresa May and Rothschild, viewing the original Balfour Declaration during the 100th-anniversary event.

Another major event took place in 1917, which also points to the Rothschild family. On November 7, 1917, the Rothschild-financed Khazar Jew Bolshevik Communists took over Russia, and *Gog* became the *"Prince of Rosh (Russia), Meshech (Moscow), and Tubal (Tolbolsk)."*

Gog (Lord Rothschild) and *Magog* (the Khazar Jews) conquered the Orthodox Christian nation of Russia, and they control the leader of Russia, who right now is Vladimir Putin. Putin puts on a show about opposing the New World Order, but he's just a puppet of Rome.

The Bolshevik Revolution leaders, including Lenin and Marx, were Khazar Jews, who caused an estimated fifty million Russian Orthodox Christians to die. The first legislative act passed by the Bolshevik's was the *Antisemitism Act*, making it a criminal offense to defame Jews and Judaism, which shows you who controls Russia.

All of this took place decades before Israel became a state. The Khazar Jewish population in 1922 was 84k; by 1931, it was 175k; by 1941, it was 474k; in 1946, there were 608k Jews in Israel; all before the Zionist state was created in 1948. These Jews came in peacefully, as not to cause a red flag.

On May 15, 1948, when Israel declared its independence, it was well-armed by the British, French, and Americans. Then the Khazar Jews revealed their true nature in killing Palestinians, destroying their villages, and taking control of their land.

That may all seem unbelievable, as it's so contrary to what Pastors have taught us. But we see clear evidence that Lord Rothschild is the father of modern-day Israel. He is the one who funded communities and industries to use it for his agenda.

Here's another proof that the Khazar Jews controls Zionist Israel. All of the Israeli Prime Ministers came from Russia and Poland, the very places where the Khazarian Jews lived. And they, or their parents, all changed their names to sound more *Jewish*.

David Ben-Gurion, the 1st Prime Minister of Israel, was born David Grun in Congress Poland. Moshe Sharett, 2nd PM, was born Moshe Shertok in Russia. Levi Eshkol, the 3rd PM, was born Levi Shkilnik in Russia. Golda Meir, the 4th PM, was born Golda Mabovitch in Kiev, Russia. Yathak Rabin, the 5th PM, had the family name Rubitzov and had Ukrainian parents.

Menachem Begin, the 6th PM, was born to Zeev Doc in Russia. He went to a Polish government school and then studied law at the University of Warsaw. He was the leader of the *Irgun Gang*, which blew up the King David Hotel in Jerusalem.

Yithak Shamir, the 7th PM, was born Titzhak Yezernitsky. He was born in Russia. Shimon Peres, the 8th PM, was born Szymon Perski in Wiszniew, Poland. Ehud Barak, the 10th PM, was born Ehud Brog. He was born in Palestine. His mother was born in Russia. Arial Sharon, the 11th PM, was born Ariel Scheinermann. His parents were born in Russia. The father of Benjamin Netanyahu was born with the last name Mileikowsky. His father was born in Warsaw, Poland.

Indeed, they are *Jews, who say they are Jews, but are not*. Do you get it now? The Rothschilds financed the Zionist state of Israel's main government buildings. The Israeli Knesset, where the legislative branch of the Israeli government works, was financed by James de Rothschild as a gift to the State of Israel in his will and was completed in 1966.

The Israeli Supreme Court building was funded and designed by the Rothschild family, and it features many Satanic, Illuminati symbols. A painting at the Israeli Supreme Court entrance shows the Rothschilds with Shimon Perez and Isaac Rabin.

The most prominent symbol is the green pyramid with the all-seeing eye on it, representing Satan, the god of this earth, who is to be exalted in their One World Government. Search YouTube for *"Know Your Enemy Part 71 - Israeli Supreme Court"* to see the many Satanic/Masonic symbols, such as the 33 steps which point to the levels of Freemasonry; symbols of female and male anatomy; and an obelisk, which represents sun god worship, which ultimately is Satan worship.

Lord Rothschild is *Gog*, and the Khazar Jews are *Magog*.

Khazar Jews like Lord Rothschild study the Satanic Babylonian Talmud and Egyptian Kabbalah and use sorcery to *steal, kill and destroy*. And that's what the Jesuit-Rothschild family has done, worship the god of mammon and take control of the money supply of almost every country in the world. The Rothschild family are the keepers of the Vatican treasury. They serve the agenda of the FPJSG and ACBP.

They call the Rothschild family leader by the titles of *'Baron Rothschild'* and *'Lord Rothschild.'* There have been four Lord Rothschilds. Nathan Mayer died in 1915, succeeded by eldest son Lionel Walter; succeeded by his eldest son Nathan Mayer Victor; and today, Lord Jacob is running the show. You might think that if Lord Rothschild is Jewish, that it's normal for him to help the Zionist state of Israel to be created, but he is a fake Jew of the Syna<u>GOG</u>ue *of Satan,* whose desires he is carrying out. They needed control of Jerusalem for the headquarters of their One World Government.

Six times in Ezekiel 38:12-13, it spells out the Zionists' economic policy: *"to take spoil... to take prey... to take silver... gold... cattle, and goods."* Five times *'take'* is translated from the Hebrew *'bazaz'* meaning *'to seize or plunder.'* That fits the Talmudic Khazar Jews mentality to a T, as they have stolen the Palestinians' land, homes, and resources.

Ezekiel 38:10-11 foretold Gog's army coming against *"unwalled villages"* which have *"neither bars or gates."* The Khazar Jews met little resistance in Palestine, the *'land of unwalled'* villages because the Palestinians had lived in peace with Jews, Arabs, and Christians, in the area. These Khazar Jews forced 700,000 Palestinians from their homes, and 531 Arab villages were destroyed or depopulated. Ironically, Zionist Israel is now the most walled up, barred up, and gated up place in the world.

In *Exposito in Matthaeum Evangelistam,* ninth-century Benedictine monk Christian of Stavelot noted: *At the present time, we know of no nation under the heavens where Christians do not live. For Christians are even found in the lands of Gog and Magog -- who are a Hunnic race and are called Gazari (Khazars) (they are) circumcised and observing all (the laws of) Judaism.* (1)

Does the story of Gog and Magog surprise you? If you've read to this point in the book, you know that the SOJ works by deception. Pastors have taught us that many things are off the mark, and they've neglected to give us the full narrative of the fulfillment of Scripture.

CHAPTER 79 - THE EDOMITES TAKE CONTROL

Now that we've seen how the Khazar Jews fulfill prophecy as the *"kings of the east,"* the *'Jews who say they are Jews, and are not, but do lie,'* and that Lord Rothschild is *Gog* who leads the vast organization of Khazar Jews, *Magog;* we're going even further down the rabbit hole to see how it relates to the story of Esau and the Edomites.

According to the Septuagint in Numbers 24:7, *'Edom'* is synonymous with *'Agag,'* which is a generic term used for the kings of Amalek. In Genesis, it shows us that Amalek was Esau's grandson, who is also called Edom. Amalek was Esau's grandson. Just as Ephraim, Jacob's grandson, became head of Israel's leading tribe, Amalek became the leading tribe of Esau/Edom. Agag was the king of the Amalekites. Agag is not someone's name; it's a title, like king or czar. Agag was the ruler of the Edomite tribe of Amalek.

Ezekiel 35:5 tells us that the Edomites have a perpetual hatred for the Israelites.

> Because thou hast had a perpetual hatred, and hast shed the blood of the children of Israel by the force of the sword in the time of their calamity, in the time that their iniquity had an end:

Esau gave up his birthright, and his descendants, the Edomites, have continually made war with the Israelites and Jews. They even burned down the temple after the Babylonians took the Jews captive.

Adam Clarke's Commentary on the Bible (1832) says, *A perpetual hatred - The Edomites were the descendants of Esau; the Israelites, the descendants of Jacob. Both these were brothers, and between them, there was contention even in the womb, and they generally lived in a state of enmity. Their descendants kept up the ancient feud: but the Edomites were implacable; they had not only a rooted but perpetual enmity to the Israelites, harassing and distressing them by all possible means; and they seized the opportunity, when the Israelites were* *most harassed by other enemies, to make inroads upon them, and cut them off wherever they found them.*

Edom disappeared into Jewry beginning 126 BC, so that some of the Jewish leaders were Edomites.

The Edomites and Jews battled each other, and the Edomites could not prevail, so they joined with the Jews. One can press the case that they joined with them to defeat them from within. After Messiah proclaimed that His disciples know the truth that sets them free, the Jewish leaders proclaimed that they had never been in bondage.

> *They answered him, we be Abraham's seed, and were never in bondage to any man: how sayest thou, Ye shall be made free?* John 8:33

We know that the Israelites were in bondage in Egypt, and the Jews were in bondage in Babylon, so it seems that these 'Jewish' leaders were really Edomite Jews who had never been in bondage.

Gog/Edom became the '*King of the Jews*' beginning with King Herod the Edomite.

Less than a hundred years after being defeated by the Maccabees and absorbed into Jewry, an Edomite became King of the Jews, as King Herod and his descendants were Edomites. The Roman Empire officially gave Herod the Great the title *King of Judea* in 37 BC. His wife, Mariamne, was a Jew and descendant of the Maccabees. Herod the Edomite, as king, was fulfilling the role of Agag/Gog.

He's the one who had all the young male children killed to try and kill Messiah as a child. His son, Herod Antipas, conspired with Pontius Pilate in the crucifixion of Messiah. The grandson, Herod Agrippa I, persecuted the early Christians and had James, the brother of John, executed. Herod Agrippa II presided over Paul the Apostle's trial. So we see a history of Gog battling against Messiah and His saints.

The Edomites reportedly infiltrated the *'house of Togarmah,'* the Khazars, and caused them to convert to Judaism and study the Satanic Babylonian Talmud and Egyptian Kabbalah.

These are the Edomite/Khazar Jews who fled primarily to Russian and Poland and then were sent to populate Zionist Israel.

Many believers deem the Jews in Israel as *'God's Chosen People,'* when they are really *'Gog's Chosen People.'*

The Khazar Jewish leaders are of the *'synaGOGue of Satan,'* as Messiah proclaimed in Revelation 3:9.

> *Behold, I will make them of the synagogue of Satan, which say they are Jews, and are not, but do lie;*

It's interesting that when the Khazars were pushed out of Khazaria, they migrated west, primarily into Russia and Poland, and also Hungary and Germany. Billionaire George Soros, born György Schwartz, and his father are from Hungary. He's another Edomite Khazar Jew who uses the Babylonian Talmud and Egyptian Kabbalah to *steal, kill and destroy.* He's a puppet who is used to fund evil agendas to carry out the will of the JSG and deflect blame from Rome.

Can you see it now? The Edomites, the enemies of the true Jews, have taken control of the land. They tolerate the true Jews in Israel, as they give credibility, but they also mistreat them very harshly.

Gog and Magog, Lord Rothschild and the Khazar Jews, are the Edomites, who have taken back the land to use it for their evil plans.

The enemy has tricked Christians into blessing *Gog and Magog* and giving them money. Ironically, the battle is being set up for when *Gog and Magog* will make war with *Holy Jerusalem*, Messiah's saints, to try to wipe them out once and for all.

417

CHAPTER 80 - THE ZIONIST STATE OF ISRAEL

When you present evidence about the Jews in the Zionist state of Israel, people make accusations. But the Jewish leaders and most of the Jews in Israel are not descendants of Abraham, so the racist rhetoric falls flat. And ironically, Jews make some of the most acute accusations against the Khazar (Ashkenazi) Jew.

Israeli Professor Nurit Peled-Elhanan said in a speech, *"Israel has reached an unimaginable peak of evil. And indeed many people all over the world find it hard to imagine that this is so. The only possible conclusion must be that Israeli evil has nothing to do with Judaism and that what is manifested in Israeli behavior is not Jewishness. It was the great Prof. Yeshayahu Leibovitch who said: National Judaism has with Judaism what National Socialism had with Socialism. What drives Israeli behavior is pure colonialist nationalist and chauvinistic racism that should be treated as such."* (1)

Rabbinical Torah Jews believe that the Zionist state of Israel is illegitimate in the eyes of Yah and that it does not represent true Jews or Judaism. They protest in New York and Jerusalem, but the media and most Christians ignore their witness. They believe that the Ashkenazi Jews have illegitimately seized the name *'Israel'* and have no right to speak in the name of the Jewish people! Groups such as *True Torah Jews* (www.truetorahjews.org) and *Jews United Against Zionism* (www.nkusa.org) protest against the Zionist state of Israel, and they support the Palestinians.

Dr. Hajo Meyer, whose Jewish parents died in Germany, said: *"If we want to stay really human beings, we must get up and call the Zionists what they are: Nazi criminals,"* Meyer said. *The hate of the Jews by the Germans "was less deeply rooted than the hate of the Palestinians by the Israeli Jews,"* he observed. *"The brainwashing of the Jewish Israeli populations is going on for over sixty years. They cannot see a Palestinian as a human being."* (2)

Miko Peled, the son of Israeli General Mattityahu Peled, proclaims that Israel's Zionist leaders are not Jewish. Miko has proclaimed that *"Israel is a racist criminal state that uses "security" as an excuse to murder innocent Palestinians and assassinate Palestinian political leaders, intellectuals, and clergy. This has been going on for over six decades."*

Michael Chabon, a Jewish Pulitzer Prize-winning novelist, said: *"Israel's occupation of Palestine is the most grievous injustice I've ever seen."*

Do you see how the enemy has tricked us? All they had to do was put people called *'Jews'* in a land called *'Israel,'* and most Christians are faked out. This is one of Satan's grandest end-times deceptions! Because most of the Jews in Israel are not descendants of Abraham, they have no right to the land.

Messiah proclaims that they are of the *Synagogue of Satan* because they revere the Satanic Babylonian Talmud and Egyptian Kabbalah. They despise Messiah and His saints and wrote evil, blasphemous things about Him in their Talmud. They only tolerate Christians because of the tourist income it brings to the state and because American Christians support them financially.

Christians blindly support Zionist Israel, despite their brutal treatment of the Palestinians, despite them repeatedly violating U.N. Council resolutions by using banned chemical phosphorous weapons and by not allowing inspection of their nuclear facilities.

Do you see the grand deception here? Because Zionist Christians blindly support the Khazar Jews in Israel, they are getting away with genocide. And sadly, most Christians would probably cheer if Israel nuked Muslim countries, killing millions because they've been programmed to believe that they're the enemy of *'God's Chosen People.'*

The creation of the state of Israel reinforces the enemy's false prophecy fulfillment explanations about a futuristic one-man antichrist, which deflects blame away from the ACBP. The Jesuits use the Ashkenazi Jews and Zionist Israel to deflect blame away from them; as many people point to the Jews as the enemy trying to control the world.

Zionist Israel will be involved in WW III, which will help usher in the New World Order. The NWO government will be based in Jerusalem, so the FPJSG needed to control Israel to prepare it for their agenda. This will lead to '*the battle of that great day of God Almighty*,' which will pit the FPJSG and ACBP in their fake Israel against Messiah and His saints, who are the *true Israel* of Scripture.

We've covered some profound information, and when I learned it, I was greatly grieved, and I repented about my former beliefs. I prayed for forgiveness for supporting the enemy of Messiah and His saints. I prayed for forgiveness for supporting them, as they've killed many Palestinians and Muslims. I pray that you've been able to see the truth, for in that there is much rejoicing!

I realize that what I've described in the last few chapters is a lot to take in because we've been taught to support the state of Israel. My statements aren't one of judgment or hatred for these people called Jews. I'm simply explaining Revelation's fulfillment, and part of that exposes truths about people groups. I pray that all Jews come to have a covenant relationship with their Heavenly Father, through Messiah.

One of the deterrents to Jews seeing how Messiah has already come and fulfilled prophecy is Christians' explanations. The seventy weeks of Daniel 9 prophecy points to the exact time that Messiah appeared and died for their sins as the Spotless Lamb. But most Christians proclaim that the 70th week of Daniel is yet future, which hides the amazing, exacting fulfillment from the Jews.

Jews are told not to read Isaiah 53, Daniel 9, and the New Testament, as evil leaders know that they will see how Messiah has already come to fulfill the prophecies that point to Him. If you don't know how to share the truth about the fulfillment of the 70th week of Daniel 9 with Jews, have them read my *The 70th Week Of Daniel 9 Decoded* book.

CHAPTER 81 - THE THREE UNCLEAN SPIRITS

And I saw three unclean spirits like frogs come out of the mouth of the dragon, and out of the mouth of the beast, and out of the mouth of the false prophet. For they are the spirits of devils, working miracles, which go forth unto the kings of the earth and of the whole world, to gather them to the battle of that great day of God Almighty.
Revelation 16:13-14

In the New Testament, the term *'unclean spirits'* describes a demonically possessed person. It may be pointing to Satan, the *dragon,* demonically possessing the ACBP and FPJSG as they carry out his agenda.

Out of their mouths come three things that gather the world's leaders, to the confrontation with Messiah's saints. When you look at the context, the *drying up* of the Ottoman Empire involved battles, and it's pointing to the earth's leaders being gathered to a *'great battle.'*

Revelation 19:19-20 points to the FPJSG and the ACBP gathering to make war with Messiah and His saints.

> *And I saw the beast, and the kings of the earth, and their armies, gathered together to make war against him that sat on the horse, and against his army. And the beast was taken, and with him the false prophet that wrought miracles before him.*

Up until this point, Revelation has only pointed to events that occurred on the *'earth'* (Strong's #1093 *ge*), the *land* of the Roman Empire. But now, a shift in the focus has occurred, as the *"whole world"* (Strong's #3625 *oikoumene*) is pointing to all of the earth.

I believe that it's pointing to the ACBP and FPJSG contriving three World Wars to push the world into their One World Government, which is described in the seventh bowl. They *'creak like frogs'* through their people when they *create a problem, to cause a reaction, to justify their solution.* This generates their desired outcome.

Freemasonry leader Albert Pike wrote a letter to Mazzini on August 15, 1871, in which he outlined plans for three world wars that were seen as necessary to bring about the One World Order. For a short time, this letter was on display in the British Museum Library in London. It was copied by William Guy Carr, former Intelligence Officer in the Royal Canadian Navy.

It calls for *Communism, Nazism,* and *Political Zionism,* to be used to foment three global world wars. Let's look at how Satan used the FPJSG and ACBP to help instigate them.

WW I

Albert Pike foretold, *"The First World War must be brought about in order to permit the Illuminati to overthrow the power of the Czars in Russia and of making that country a fortress of atheistic Communism. The divergences caused by the "agentur" (agents) of the Illuminati between the British and Germanic Empires will be used to foment this war. At the end of the war, Communism will be built and used in order to destroy the other governments, and in order to weaken the religions."*

The SOJ and ACBP fomented World War I, causing the overthrow of Russia's Czars, which brought in atheistic *Communism,* which has been used to destroy other governments and weaken the religions. They caused the Ottoman Empire to lose control of Palestine, to *prepare the way* for the Khazar Jews, *the kings of the east,* to populate it.

WW II

Albert Pike, *"The Second World War must be fomented by taking advantage of the differences between the Fascists and the political Zionists. This war must be brought about so that Nazism is destroyed and that the political Zionism be strong enough to institute a sovereign state of Israel in Palestine. During the Second World War, International Communism must become strong enough in order to balance Christendom, which would be then restrained and held in check until the time when we would need it for the final social cataclysm."*

The SOJ ACBP fomented World War II by empowering Hitler and the Nazi regime to persecute Jews to strengthen *Political Zionism* and justify the creation of their sovereign state of Israel. The *drying up* of the Ottoman Empire led to the creation of the kingdoms of Syria, Iraq, Saudi Arabia, Jordan, and the Zionist state of Israel, which set up the theater of the last world war between Muslim countries and Israel.

WW III

Albert Pike foretold, *"The Third World War must be fomented by taking advantage of the differences caused by the "agentur" of the "Illuminati" between the political Zionists and the leaders of Islamic World. The war must be conducted in such a way that Islam (the Moslem Arabic World) and political Zionism (the State of Israel) mutually destroy each other. Meanwhile, the other nations, once more divided on this issue will be constrained to fight to the point of complete physical, moral, spiritual, and economical exhaustion."*

The three created ideologies of *Communism*, *Nazism*, and *Political Zionism*; are the political forces that led to two world wars. The power of countries was changed forever, and hundreds of millions of people died. We can see how those events were intertwined with *Political* Zionism to justify the creation of the state of Israel.

Is it not feasible to see that WW III between Muslim countries and Israel, with Russia and the USA becoming involved, will cause severe damage to countries and people, and to the economy, and push the world into the One World Government? I think so.

The sixth bowl may be referring to the three World Wars or the three false ideologies created to cause those wars. When we look back, we can see the Popes' involvement in the World Wars; out of their mouth came words that pushed the wars' agenda. History shows that the three World Wars fit the time frame, as WW I started in 1914, just as the Ottoman Empire had dried up. As a *river is dried up,* frogs issue from its bed and banks and fill the air with their croakings.

423

As the Ottoman Empire dried up, the Muslim countries came to power; and they continually talk, *croak*, about war with Israel.

The first two World Wars have significantly shifted the balance of power globally and allowed the SOJ to take over large countries, such as Germany, Russia, etc.

We can see how the SOJ causes countries' leaders to continually talk, *croak like frogs*, and promote their agenda. They speak to agitate the people, to create division. They create problems, to create a reaction, to provide a solution, and so advance the cause of the SOJ.

Interestingly, the term *'frog-marched'* applies to countries' leaders being forced to do something against their will. *Harrap's Essential English Dictionary* says: *You are frogmarched somewhere when you are forced to walk there by two people holding you firmly in each arm.*

The prophecy points to two demon-possessed leaders (*unclean spirits*), the FPJSG and the ACBP of Rome, who exert their influence on nations' leaders to carry out three World Wars to push the world into their One World Government. No doubt, the SOJ control countries' leaders through financial manipulation, through blackmail for their many evil deeds, etc. Then they can strong-arm these leaders to do what they want them to do, including taking their country to war.

The Roman beast kingdom (*iron*) controls the powerful Muslim countries (*miry clay*), such as Saudi Arabia, and they control Zionist Israel through the Rothschild family. WW III will take place when the enemy wishes to push their agenda to the next level.

These three contrived political agendas and the three world wars; will push the world into the One World Government. If/when the enemy uses WW III to cause a worldwide economic collapse, we can see how the United States would be forced to submit to a One World Government. Americans would not be able to buy and sell, and the commerce system, which provides food, water, and fuel, would be shut down. This would cause people worldwide to beg for a One World Government, to end religious wars, and stabilize the economy.

The world's wars and revolutions occur because the Jesuits want to establish a one-world government with the Papacy at its head. 19th-century theologian Luigi De Sanctis tells us: *At what then do the Jesuits aim? According to them, they only seek the greater glory of God; but if you examine the facts, you will find that they aim at universal dominion alone. They have rendered themselves indispensable to the Pope, who, without them, could not exist because Catholicism is identified with them. They have rendered themselves indispensable to governors and hold revolutions in their hands, and in this way, either under one name or another, it is they who rule the world.*

In *The Secret History of the Jesuits*, **Edmond Paris says,** *The public is practically unaware of the overwhelming responsibility carried by the Vatican and its Jesuits in the starting of the two world wars – a situation which may be explained in part by the gigantic finances at the disposition of the Vatican and its Jesuits, giving them power in so many spheres, especially since the last conflict.*

Dr. Dennis L. Cuddy says, *Mazzini, with Pike, developed a plan for three world wars so that eventually every nation would be willing to surrender its national sovereignty to a world government. The first war was to end the czarist regime in Russia, and the second war was to allow the Soviet Union to control Europe. The third world war is to be in the Middle East between Moslems and Jews and would result in Armageddon.*

Albert Pike also made this interesting statement in his vision.
"We shall unleash the Nihilists and the atheists, and we shall provoke a formidable social cataclysm which in all its horror will show clearly to the nations the effect of absolute atheism, origin of savagery, and of the most bloody turmoil. Then everywhere, the citizens, obliged to defend themselves against the world minority of revolutionaries, will exterminate those destroyers of civilization, and the multitude, disillusioned with Christianity, whose deistic spirits will from that moment be without compass or direction, anxious for an ideal, but without knowing where to render its adoration, will receive the true

light through the universal manifestation of the pure doctrine of Lucifer, brought finally out in the public view. This manifestation will result from the general reactionary movement, which will follow the destruction of Christianity and atheism, both conquered and exterminated at the same time."

A few things stand out about that statement. First of all, Pike described *'atheists and Nihilists'* (a person who believes that life is meaningless and rejects all religious and moral principles), saying that they would be provoked to create a *'bloody turmoil.'* Look around today, and you see the godless Antifa and BLM organizations whose leaders proclaim to be trained Marxists. Look at how they conduct themselves, violently attacking other people, looting, and destroying property.

Antifa and BLM are not organic movements, but rather are well-funded controlled opposition groups that are being used to carry out an evil agenda. We can see the fulfillment of Pike's vision being set up.

The second thing that stands out is the statement *'those destroyers of civilization, and the multitude, disillusioned with Christianity.'* Look at what's taking place right now in America, with the strong association of President Trump and Christians. When the godless Antifa and BLM take to the streets again, they may target Christians to take out their rage on those who supported Trump, whom they hate.

Trump has surrounded himself with 'Christian' pastors. He has repeatedly proclaimed that the prayers and votes of Christians have supported him. This incites hatred from the left towards Christians, who may become the target of their attacks. The desire of the Roman beast kingdom leaders is to seek to wipe out Messiah's saints.

So this theater, which is being played out in Washington D.C., may be a planned operation to bring about the fulfillment of Albert Pikes' vision, to bring division in the USA and civil war.

We are in the '*the hour of temptation, which shall come upon all the world, to try them that dwell upon the earth,*' which Messiah foretold about the end times church age. The enemy has thrown a myriad of deceptions at us. And only those who hunger for truth find it. If you've read this far and can see how most of Revelation has already been fulfilled during the last 1,900 years, no doubt you're saddened that the enemy has deceived the end-times church era saints so badly! And you're rejoicing for being shown the truth.

> *Blessed is he that reads, and they that hear the words of this prophecy, and keep those things which are written therein: for the time is at hand.* Revelation 1:3

We're in the midst of the sixth bowl in which Messiah proclaims these words.

> *Behold, I come as a thief. Blessed is he that watchs, and keeps his garments, lest he walk naked, and they see his shame.* Revelation 16:15

We live in the generation of saints who may see Messiah's return! HalleluYah!

So what will happen next? I believe that we're waiting on WW III between Muslim countries and Israel, with other countries joining in. This would cause the world to cry out for '*peace and safety*' to prevent another religious war. Of course, that is the enemy's desired outcome, who will offer it in their One World Government.

I believe that there will be a worldwide economic collapse, perhaps caused by WW III and the CV19 agenda. This will lead us into the One World Government described in the seventh bowl, as there will be great political upheaval, as the nations and great cities will submit their authority to the One World Government.

CHAPTER 82 - THE BATTLE OF ARMAGEDDON

In this chapter, I want to give you the perspective of the end-times battle between the Roman beast kingdom, called the *'great city,'* fighting against Messiah and His saints, called *Holy Jerusalem*. In Revelation 19, we see the bride of Messiah, dressed in white, pointing to her righteousness. She has *come out of Babylon* and kept herself pure and renounced the things of this world to keep herself set-apart for a better kingdom.

Satan wants to control the whole world, but more than that, he wants to defeat Messiah and His saints. It will come down to a great battle in the end times when Satan will work through his Roman beast kingdom, to seek to eliminate Messiah's saints. And the Father will use this time of tribulation to refine His bride, to test her faithfulness and resolve, even to the point of death.

To me, that's what the *'battle of Armageddon'* is symbolizing. I don't think that it's a physical battle in the Middle East, but the spiritual battle that is taking place. The enemy controls the countries' leaders, and they will exert their power to war against the saints.

Satan's goal is to push the world into a One World Government, where he is exalted, just like he tried to do in Babylon. And he will use the kings of the earth to make one last attempt to wipe out Messiah's saints.

The *'battle of that great day of God Almighty'* will happen when the FPJSG and ACBP have pushed the world into their One World Government, which will push aside all religions, and make Messiah and His assembly of saints the enemy of the world.

CHAPTER 83 - THE 7TH BOWL NEW WORLD ORDER

Some people say that the Scriptures don't point to a One World Government, but I think that the seventh bowl of Revelation describes exactly that. Because people don't understand the symbolism used, they don't know who the *'great city'* represents, the Roman beast kingdom, and what *earthquakes* in prophecy represent, which is *political upheaval*.

WW III may be waged primarily against the outer portions of Israel, Tel Aviv, and other places, and perhaps in the Palestinian regions, as the Zionists seek to eliminate them. But I believe that the evil ones will protect Jerusalem, as that's the capital from which they seek to rule.

The enemy may gather in Jerusalem, the capital from which they will govern their One World Government. The three major religions are focused on Jerusalem, and it's where Messiah carried out His ministry and died for our sins, and where He said that He would return; so this is why the enemy desires to rule from Jerusalem.

And the seventh angel poured out his vial into the air; and there came a great voice out of the temple of heaven, from the throne, saying, It is done. **Revelation 16:17**

The bowl judgments are against the ACBP and Catholics who revere him, so the seventh bowl will bring about more judgment on them. Interestingly, it points to the vial being poured out on the *air*, and Satan is the *"prince of the power of the air,"* so the judgment ultimately is on him.

> *Wherein in time past ye walked according to the course of this world, according to the prince of the power of the air, the spirit that now worketh in the children of disobedience.* Ephesians 2:2

It's Satan who empowers the FPJSG and the ACBP, the two leaders of the end-times *earth* beast phase of the Roman beast kingdom. It's Satan who uses them to push the world into a One World Government, in which he desires praise and to steal glory from the Heavenly Father.

And there were voices, and thunders, and lightnings; and there was a great earthquake, such as was not since men were upon the earth, so mighty an earthquake, and so great. **Revelation 16:18**

As we saw in the sixth seal when the Roman Empire was *falling*, an *earthquake* in Bible prophecy represents *political upheaval*. This points to the greatest political upheaval in history, as all countries become subservient to the One World Government. After WW III and a worldwide economic collapse, every country will beg for a One World Government to provide a solution. This is the only way that the United States will agree to become subservient to a global government.

The enemy has been planning this for many years. They've taken control of every country's money supply, stolen their wealth, and put them into massive debt, which will cause their economy to collapse. This will fulfill the dream and plans of SOJ founder Ignatius Loyola to control the world.

And the great city was divided into three parts, and the cities of the nations fell: and great Babylon came in remembrance before God, to give unto her the cup of the wine of the fierceness of his wrath. **Revelation 16:19**

The *great city* represents the Roman beast kingdom. It's pointing to the FPJSG, the end-times Roman beast kingdom leader, controlling the world through three city-state corporations, which form one interlocking empire called the '*Empire Of The City*.' These three countries have their own government and laws and are accountable to nobody.

The city-state corporation of *'Vatican City'* is an independent country located within the city of Rome. With an area of 110 acres and a population of about 1,000, it's the smallest country in the world by both area and population.

The Popes have historically helped control the religious and political leaders of the world. U.S. Presidents and the leaders of most countries have flown to Vatican City to meet with the Pope. Many religious leaders, including Protestant Christian leaders, have traveled to Vatican City to meet with the Pope.

The city-state corporation of the *'City of London'* is not a London borough, a status reserved for the other 32 districts. It's a separate county which is surrounded by Greater London. It's a small county in the United Kingdom. Lord Rothschild and others control the world's financial and trade organizations from this city to determine who can buy and sell. They trade everything there, including men's souls, as people are deemed a corporate entity. Every major bank in the world has a branch in the City of London. It's the world's financial power center and the wealthiest square mile on the face of the Earth. It houses the Rothschild controlled Bank of England, Lloyds of London, the London stock exchange, all British banks, the branch offices of 385 foreign banks and 70 US banks. It is also the headquarters for worldwide English Freemasonry & headquarters for the worldwide money cartel known as *'The Crown.'*

The city-state corporation of the *'District of Columbia'* is ten square miles. It is yet another small country within a country. It's not part of the United States, but it's used to control the United States. Washington, D.C., controls the world's intelligence agencies and military powers. The District of Columbia Constitution operates under a tyrannical Roman law known as *Lex Fori*, which bears no resemblance to the US Constitution. The FBI and CIA operate under the guise of protecting Americans, but their primary role is to identify and eliminate threats to the JSG and his leaders.

D.C. has military bases worldwide, not to protect Americans' freedom but to control the world and overthrow people who don't bow down to the JSG's authority. The District of Columbia flag has three red stars representing the three city-state corporations of the Roman beast empire.

The world's great cities will lose their independent powers and be subservient to the One World Government and controlled by these three city-state corporations.

And every island fled away, and the mountains were not found. **16:20**

Jeremiah 51:25 points to the kingdom of Babylon, using the symbolism of being a destroying mountain.

> *Behold, I am against you, O destroying mountain, says the LORD, who destroy all the earth: and I will stretch out my hand upon you, and roll you down from the rocks, and will make you a burnt mountain.*

Zechariah 4:7 points to a mountain of people who opposed the building of the temple after the Jews were released from Babylon.

> *Who art thou, O great mountain? before Zerubbabel thou shall become a plain: and he shall bring forth the headstone thereof with shoutings, crying, Grace, grace unto it."*

As we saw in the sixth seal judgment of the pagan Roman Empire, it's not pointing to literal islands and mountains; but is symbolic of small and large people groups who were affected by the political upheaval.

> *And the heaven departed as a scroll when it is rolled together; and every mountain and island were moved out of their places.* Revelation 6:14

The seventh bowl points to small and large countries losing their independence and becoming subservient to the One World Government. This has been the plan of the JSG, via the *League Of Nations*, via the *United Nations*, for a long time.

And there fell upon men a great hail out of heaven, every stone about the weight of a talent: and men blasphemed God because of the plague of the hail; for the plague thereof was exceeding great. **Revelation 16:21**

It could be pointing to WW III with many missiles, as the previous verses describe the One World Government, which seems to happen after WW III. But it seems to be describing something that takes place after the One World Government is formed.

It may be pointing to the *harlot* RCC's desolation, as the FPJSG and ACBP may be in power in Jerusalem. They pretend to be Messiah's priests, *like a lamb*, but they serve Satan *the dragon*. They have no allegiance to Catholics, and the SOJ is a spiteful bunch who may seek final revenge against the Catholic countries that kicked them out. But in the big picture, they will just be pawns in Yah's hand as He uses them to carry out His righteous judgment of the apostate *harlot* church.

This book shows how Daniel, Paul, and John all point to the RCC of the ACBP. I don't declare these things out of spite or hate; it's the very opposite; it's out of love for Catholics, as I want them to know the truth. Pray for Catholics and proclaim the pure Gospel to them so that they have a covenant relationship with the Heavenly Father through the Son.

We know that Messiah has saints in the RCC because in Revelation 18:4 He tells them to *Come out of her, my people, that ye be not partakers of her sins, and that ye receive not of her plagues.* In Revelation 18:23, Messiah says that after the *harlot's* judgment, *the light of a candle shall shine no more at all in thee; and the voice of the bridegroom and of the bride shall be heard no more at all in thee;* meaning that Catholics won't have the witness of the saints in her anymore. I pray that this book causes a great awakening so that many Catholics are redeemed for the kingdom.

I believe that the Father will allow the One World Government of the ACBP and the FPJSG to be formed, as it provides the environment in which the saints can declare their allegiance to their King. It allows truth to be declared and the pretenders to be exposed.

CHAPTER 84 - THE MARK OF THE BEAST REVISITED

Six passages in Revelation (13:16-17, 14:9/11, 15:2, 16:2, 19:20, 20:4) mention the *mark of the beast*, but only one links it to whether people can buy and sell. People apply all of the instances to one time, when people can't buy and sell, but that's not what Messiah is proclaiming.

The mention of the mark in Revelation 14 is about the Catholics in France and other countries who revered and obeyed the ACBP when he commanded that they kill the saints. It had nothing to do with buying and selling, and their judgment came during the bloody French Revolution and Napoleonic wars of the bowl judgments.

The fulfillment of the first bowl judgment tells us exactly what the *mark of the beast* is; as the Catholics in France *revered* (*mark* on *forehead*) and *obeyed* (*mark* on the *right hand*, actions) the ACBP of Rome in killing the Protestants. Their judgment was the *sore* of national atheism, which set up the reign of terror in the French Revolution when the King of France, the Catholic priests, and France's people had their blood shed. Then the Napoleonic Wars shed the blood of even more people in Catholic countries.

The *mark of the beast* is about whether you *revere* and *obey* the ACBP, who is the Satan-empowered enemy of Messiah. Today, 1.3 billion Catholics already have the *mark of the beast* because they *revere* and *obey* the ACBP as their leader. In the One World Government of the seventh bowl, the *mark of the beast* will be the same thing; *revering* and *obeying* the ACBP.

Seventh-Day Adventists say that the *mark* is a Sunday law from the Pope, but do we think that our Heavenly Father will condemn people for gathering together to praise Him, pray to Him and learn about Him because it's supposedly on the wrong day? No! Going to church on Sunday is not a conscious decision to *revere* the ACBP.

It seems that the SDA church has been infiltrated and that this Sunday law narrative serves to deflect blame away from the true mark. That said, the evil ones could make a Sunday law to promote this false *mark of the beast* narrative and their climate change agenda.

And he had power to give life unto the image of the beast, that the image of the beast should both speak, and cause that as many as would not worship the image of the beast should be killed. **Revelation 13:15**

The word '*worship*' doesn't describe worshiping the *antichrist* as god, but to *fawn or crouch to, to prostrate oneself in homage, to venerate.*

This verse points to the <u>act</u> of *revering* and *obeying* the ACBP to be able to continue to live. When people can't buy and sell and have no food and water, they will fawn over, venerate, the ACBP when he offers them a solution. The threat of not joining means that you will be cut off from the financial system or killed.

Albert Barnes' Notes on the Bible (1870) says, *That the image of the beast should both speak. Should give signs of life; should issue authoritative commands. And cause that as many as would not worship the image of the beast. Would not honor it, or acknowledge its authority. The "worship" here referred to is civil, not religious homage, Cmt. on Re 13:4. The meaning is that what is here called the "image of the beast" had power given it, by its connection with the second "beast," to set up its jurisdiction over men and to secure their allegiance on pain of death.*

Just as Messiah is the *image of Yah,* whose Gospel provides *light* to the world; the ACBP is the *image* of Satan who *darkens* the world with his false religion. *Revering* the Pope, who is the *idol* of the Catholic Church, *revering* the idols of Mary (Semiramis) and the crucifix; causes Catholics to have the *mark of the beast.*

Look at the sequence of events. Revelation 13:15 points to an action, *revering* the ACBP. Revelation 13:16 points to the result of taking that action, *being marked.* Revelation 13:17 points to the result of not revering the ACBP, *not being able to buy and sell.*

And he causes all, both small and great, rich and poor, free and bond, to receive a mark in their right hand, or in their foreheads.
Revelation 13:16

This verse points to the <u>result</u> of getting the physical mark *after* you *revere* and *obey* the ACBP. It ties directly into the narrative of a worldwide financial collapse when nobody will be able to buy and sell. Many will join with the Pope in his One World system, to be able to *buy and sell* again, to have food and water. An RFID chip or tattoo may be implemented in their financial system, but it would be the result of *revering* the ACBP.

The goal is simple, a one-world government with the ACBP and the FPJSG controlling the world.

And that no man might buy or sell, save he that had the mark, or the name of the beast, or the number of his name. **Revelation 13:17**

This verse points to the <u>result</u> of not *revering* and *obeying* the ACBP.

> Revelation 20:4 points to this time *And I saw thrones, and they sat upon them, and judgment was given unto them: and I saw the souls of them that were beheaded for the witness of Jesus, and for the word of God, and which had not worshipped the beast, neither his image, neither had received his mark upon their foreheads, or in their hands; and they lived and reigned with Christ a thousand years.*

The evil ones may mandate medical vaxx and a tracking chip or tattoo, but the Father isn't going to condemn people for ignorance about these things, though they will pay the price for it. The importance of them playing out this narrative and getting this vaxx in the worldwide population should be a huge signal to the evil nature.

WW III and CV-19 may lead to a worldwide economic collapse, which will prevent people from buying and selling. Imagine what your life would be like if you were shut out of the financial system; if you couldn't get paid because you have no access to a checking account, if you couldn't make any withdraws from your checking account, if you couldn't use a credit card, and if you couldn't pay your mortgage/rent or utility bills. Would you be able to survive?

Imagine that your country's commerce is shut down; delivery trucks are not moving, restaurants and grocery stores are closed, gas stations are closed, banks are closed, etc. People will turn to violence to be able to get food and water, gasoline, etc. This scenario will set the stage for the One World Government of the ACBP and FPJSG, and they may say that they've developed a One World financial system backed by gold (which they stole from the nations), which will allow people to buy and sell again.

Most people in the world will deem the Pope as a *'savior'* of sorts and will join with him in the One World Order, and thus they will have the *mark of the beast* on them. This includes 1.3 billion Catholics, and the Popes have already set the stage by drawing in Muslims and leaders of all religions, who will undoubtedly be used to draw their people into unity in the One World Government.

Those who don't understand that the office of the papacy is the *antichrist beast* may deem him as a *'Christian'* who offers to help them in their time of need. Most people will be so desperate that they will join with the Pope. People will be tired of religious wars, so the Pope will draw all of the major religions together, and even atheists, in the name of p*eace and safety*. People, cities, and countries will be in massive debt, so the Pope may offer debt forgiveness.

The evil ones are putting tens of thousands of satellites in space, and they may offer free access to the internet worldwide. Of course, that would be their surveillance tracking system. The evil ones have been hiding advanced technology, which they may then provide, such as free electricity to people so that everyone has power. I think people will be incredibly desperate, and the offer that the Pope makes will be too hard to pass up.

437

An interesting side note is that *The Illuminati*, created by the Jesuits in the 18th century, has recently taken the strategy of coming out of the closet. They've remained in the background for hundreds of years, conducting private meetings, but now they have a public website, www.illuminati.am, and they're active on Facebook.

Their strategy is to make themselves appear as heroes, working in the background, for the good of mankind. People can become an Illuminati member and take their oath. They even published a book called *'Illuminatiam – The First Testament Of The Illuminati.'*

Here is part of the description: *Fear not for your war-stricken, poverty-ridden planet: help is on the way. The Illuminati's path for humanity - our Universal Design - has spanned centuries to safeguard the human species from extinction. For the first time in history, the Illuminati has broken its silence with Illuminatiam: a testament of this planet's future, wisdom previously available only to elite members, and your life's guide to all that is ahead. Humanity's age of War is finally nearing its end. A new dawn awaits to usher in a society where all people in all places can live in Abundance. Fear not for the bursting sounds that echo across your red horizons. We are always watching out for you.*

They, too, are positioning WW III to be the catalyst to push the world into their One World Government, which will promise to end wars between countries and people groups. They position themselves as a hidden force, working behind the scenes for the good of mankind. They point to a worldwide economic collapse, which will usher in a new age.

John Gill's Exposition of the Entire Bible (1748) says, *And that no man might buy or sell. Either in an ecclesiastical sense, as to, be in any church office, or perform any such service, to say Mass, hear confession, give absolution, sell pardons and indulgences, etc. or in a civil sense, as to trade, and exercise merchandise, and this was forbidden by several Popish councils and synods; the Lateran council, under Pope Alexander, decreed against the Waldenses and Albigenses, that no one should presume to retain or encourage them in their houses or countries, or "trade" with them; and the synod of Tours in France* *forbid any reception of heretics or protection, and that any communion should be had with them "in buying and selling," as Mr. Mede has observed; and it was ordered by a bull of Pope Martin the Fifth, that no contract should be made with such, and that they should not follow any business and merchandise:*

Save he that had the mark; took the oath to be true to the pope, or made a public profession of the Popish religion: or the name of the beast; Papists, so-called from the pope; thus, the antichristians are called from antichrist, as the Christians from Christ: or the number of his name; which is either the same with the number of the beast in Revelation 13:18 or is something distinct it; and those who have it may be such persons who neither have the indelible character of the Romish clergy, nor are open professors of the Popish religion, but are in heart inclined to it, and privately and secretly promote it, by their doctrines and practices; and so are numbered, reckoned, esteemed, and accounted of by the Papists, and receive favors from them; or rather such who openly "furnish the drink offering" in the Mass.

Those who were obliged to receive the mark in the right hand seem to be the clergy, such who entered into holy orders; who lifted up their right hand, and swore and vowed allegiance to the pope, and testified they were ready to defend and support his religion and interest; and who in their ordination are said to have an indelible character impressed on them: and those who received the mark in their foreheads are the common people in general, who one and all have the same impress upon them; which may intend either the sign of the cross in baptism or rather their open confession of the Popish religion, which they as publicly avow and declare as if it had been written on their foreheads."

Yah's *mark* is on those who have a covenant relationship with Him through Messiah, who seek to obey His will. *The mark of the beast* is on those who *revere* and *obey* the ACBP, whose teachings are contrary to Scripture. The bottom line is that the *mark of the beast* is about *revering* and *obeying* the ACBP. If you get a vaxx, an RFID tattoo or chip, but you didn't *revere* the ACBP, then those aren't the *mark of the beast*. That said, I would avoid the sorcery of a vaxx and a RFID tattoo or chip.

CHAPTER 85 - THE RICHES OF BABYLON THE GREAT

And the kings of the earth, who have committed fornication and lived deliciously with her, shall bewail her, and lament for her, when they shall see the smoke of her burning, Standing afar off for the fear of her torment, saying, Alas, alas, that great city Babylon, that mighty city! for in one hour is thy judgment come. And the merchants of the earth shall weep and mourn over her; for no man buys their merchandise any more. **Revelation 18:9-11**

People proclaim that the USA is the *earth beast* of Revelation 13 and that it's *Babylon the Great*, but that's a false narrative. Revelation 17 describes the *harlot* church of the ACBP, which rides on the Roman beast kingdom described in Revelation 13, which has *seven heads, ten horns, and is full of names of blasphemy.*

The Satan-empowered Roman beast kingdom uses the Babylonian Talmud and Egyptian Kabbalah sorcery to *steal, kill, and destroy.* Goodness knows what takes place below the Vatican in the catacombs of the Temple of Cybele. The proclamation that the Vatican has *'become the habitation of devils'* points to the top leaders being demon-possessed.

When you look at the history of the Popes of Rome, you see how leaders of countries have been intoxicated with power and riches as they carried out the orders of the ACBP. No authority on earth has historically interacted with the world's leaders (*the kings of the earth*) more than the Popes. Every U.S. President visits the Pope, as do the leaders of most other countries.

Vatican City is the biggest financial power, wealth accumulator, and property owner in existence, possessing more material wealth than any bank, corporation, giant trust, or government anywhere on the globe. The *'kings of the earth'* point to the Rothschild's, the Rockefellers, etc., who have become enormously wealthy because of their alliance with the ACBP and the FPJSG.

According to *The Vatican Billions* by Avro Manhattan, *"The Vatican has billions of shares in the most powerful international corporations such as Gulf Oil, Shell, General Motors, Bethlehem Steel, General Electric, International Business Machines, T.W.A., etc."* Note that it was not billions of dollars but billions of shares!

In Revelation 18:4, Messiah is giving one last plea to His saints to come out of the influence of the Babylonian *harlot* church. He's not saying to come out of the USA or New York City, as people say that they're Babylon. Her primary influence is the over 1.3 billion Catholics who *revere* (*mark* on their forehead) and *obey* (*mark* on their right hand) the ACBP. Her secondary influence is over the daughter churches, who teach concepts created by the Roman beast kingdom's councils, who teach a false Gospel and a false Messiah.

Joseph Benson's Commentary on Revelation (1847) says, *Probably the voice of Christ, graciously warning his people of their danger of being infected by the prevailing corruptions of the mystical Babylon, and, in consequence thereof, of being involved in her ruin; saying, Come out of her, my people — Immediately forsake the communion of so corrupt a church; that ye be not partakers of her sins — Which you surely will be if you do not separate yourselves from her; and that ye receive not of her plagues — That ye share not in that guilt which would render you liable to all the plagues and judgments with which she shall assuredly be punished.*

The Popes and priests of the RCC are proud, boastful, and arrogant, proclaiming to be Messiah's *one true church*, when all the while they've been misleading people with teachings that are contrary to Scripture, and they're led by the ACBP. The judgments against the *harlot* RCC will come quickly.

Messiah is saying that when the *harlot* church of Rome is destroyed, that will end her purchases from the kings of the earth. It's pointing to her riches, which she has given to the kings of the earth, for their services and goods. So she is the one who is making the purchases. It's not saying that she's a city or country which produces a lot of goods.

It's saying that her purchases enrich the kings of the earth who serve her. This is why they'll mourn when she is desolated.

The RCC is the largest non-governmental provider of higher education in the world. As of 2016, the church supports 43,800 secondary schools, 95,200 primary schools, and 1,358 Catholic college universities. The RCC is the largest non-government provider of health care services in the world. It has around 18,000 clinics, 16,000 homes for the elderly and those with special needs, and 5,500 hospitals.

The Vatican owns not only the 110 acres of Vatican City but roughly 177 million more acres of various lands throughout the world, including the hundreds of Vatican embassies that are legally titled to *The Holy See* as an independent nation.

Joseph Benson's Commentary on Revelation (1847) says, *For all nations have drunk of the wine of her fornication, &c. — She hath not only been guilty of idolatry herself, and with great wrath persecuted the true Christian faith, worship, and practice, but hath also corrupted the princes and nations of the earth, as if she had given them a cup of poisonous composition, to disorder their reason and inflame them into rage and fury, having prevailed upon them to commit the same sins of which she was guilty, and to propagate her corruptions by ambitious views, incitements to luxury, and prospects of gain.*

And the merchants of the earth are waxed rich through the abundance of her delicacies - "The Romish clergy," says Daubuz, "by trading in spiritual matters, have gotten vast wealth; these are the merchants of the earth, who by their Popish tricks and trinkets have gotten a good part of the wealth of the world into their hands. In short, Rome is a great mart; the Romish clergy are the merchants and factors; the secular, inferior clergy, the monks and friars, are the peddlers and hawkers which retail the merchandise. As for the luxury of Rome, procured by this trade, it needs no proof.

'Standing afar off' may point to seeing it take place on TV or internet video, just like we watched Notre Dame burning on April 15, 2019. Or it may point to distancing themselves from any association with her.

The merchandise of gold, and silver, and precious stones, and of pearls, and fine linen, and purple, and silk, and scarlet, and all thyine wood, and all manner vessels of ivory, and all manner vessels of most precious wood, and of brass, and iron, and marble. **Revelation 18:12**

Though the many universities and other institutions that she owns are grand in their own right and cost a lot of money to build and maintain, this part of the description seems to be pointing specifically to her purchases for her many church affairs.

As of May 2018, the Catholic Church in its entirety comprises 3,160 ecclesiastical jurisdictions, including over 645 archdioceses and 2,851 dioceses, and 221,700 parishes in the world.

Can you imagine how much money it cost to build those institutions and the fortune spent to maintain them? An *Economist* magazine investigation offered a rough-and-ready estimate of $170 billion in annual spending by the RCC per year!! This money is to run the organization and salaries.

Google images of "*catholic monasteries*" to how large and grand they are, for some, are like fortresses. Google "*Catholic basilicas,*" and you will find the Wikipedia page. On the top of the page are listings for the major basilicas, the grandest and most expensive of them all: *St John Lateran, St Peter's, St Paul Outside the Walls*, and *St Mary Major*.

I recommend clicking on each link and then viewing the church's images to see how luxurious they are so that you can see how much money was spent to make them.

The rebuilding of St. Peter's Basilica in the 16th century involved the genius skill of Michelangelo, Bernini, Raphael, and the other great artists of the day. The riches and treasures lavished on the stately buildings of the Roman Catholic Church are beyond description.

Scroll down the list of basilicas. As of November 2019, there were 1,690 basilicas in the world, 573 in Italy alone! You can see the buildings' images to see how large and ornate they are, and if you click on the image of the building, you can see photos of the interior, to see the riches that have been spent on these places, which are like art museums. They're filled with the goods that Revelation 18 describes.

Google images of *"catholic basilica gold,"* *"catholic basilica art,"* and *"catholic basilica marble."* You will see their basilicas filled with gold, silver, marble, wood, brass, and iron. Gold and silver adorn the buildings, with gold leaf and solid gold in many of the designs. Her priests are decked with gold crosses. The bishops mitres are decorated *with gold, and silver, and precious stones, and of pearls.* This is the merchandise that they purchased from the merchants of the earth.

Google images of *"catholic cardinals bishops silk,"* and what do you see? Her priests are dressed in fine linen and silk garments.

An alb is a long, white *linen* tunic-like robe worn by liturgical ministers. It is worn under the chasuble. A cassock is a full-length robe made of watered *silk*. It is black for priests, *purple* for bishops, *red (scarlet)* for cardinals, white for the pope. The *purple* cassock for bishops has *red* cuffs on the sleeves.

Cardinals wear a simar at non-liturgical functions, made of black *silk* with *scarlet* piping, *silk* stitching, and buttons. They are like a cassock but have an optional elbow-length shoulder cape. A simar is worn with a *scarlet* sash made of *silk*. A mozzetta is a short, elbow-length *silk* cape that surrounds the prelate, twelve *silk*-covered buttons. A ferratuolo is a full cape is made of *scarlet* watered *silk* that is worn at solemn, non-liturgical occasions.

A *silk* zucchetto is a close-fitting, saucer-shaped skull cap, which is contrary to Scripture, as it says that men should not wear a cap when praying. A mitre, made of layers of white damask *silk*, is worn by cardinals when they're in the presence of the Pope.

Can you see how the RCC fulfills the description of being adorned with *silk* and *fine linen* and *purple* and *scarlet* colors?

Google images of *"catholic cardinals bishops purple scarlet,"* **and what do you see? Her priests are dressed in the RCC mandated colors of** *purple* **and** *scarlet.*

'Thyine wood' can point to Algum trees or Cypress and Cedar, used in temples for rafters. The word *'vessels'* can point to a bowl or cup, but the Strong's Greek word points to equipment or apparatus or goods, so it can simply point to construction materials for their grand basilicas. It says that she has purchased *'all manner of ivory, precious woods, brass, iron, and marble.'*

Their basilicas are lavishly adorned with these types of materials. For example, the *Basilica of the Sacred Heart of Paris* opened in 1914. It took seven architects and nearly forty years to complete the structure. Its ornate exterior is constructed of costly travertine *marble.*

Interestingly, the Vatican Gift store near St. Peter's sells merchandise made of gold, silver, precious stones, pearls, graven images of Mary and others, etc. They bought merchandise from the companies of the kings of the earth to resell at high prices.

And cinnamon, and odors, and ointments, and frankincense, and wine, and oil, and fine flour, and wheat, and beasts, and sheep, and horses, and chariots, and slaves, and souls of men. **Revelation 18:13**

Her ceremonies are filled with incense made from *frankincense* and *cinnamon*, which is burned in *iron* and *brass* censers. The Eucharist ceremony uses wafers made of *fine flour*. They carry out this ceremony many times a week in every church, so imagine how much they use. *Wine* is for the chalice, used in daily Masses, and drank by the priests. They use three holy *oils* for Chism at baptism, and the sacrament of anointing of the sick, and the Extreme Unction when administered to the dying. 221,700 parishes require a lot of these products.

Horses and *chariots* were used for Popes, Cardinals, Archbishops, and Bishops to ride in state and grandeur.

'*Slaves*' may be found in celibacy and servitude in those who give their lives without remuneration to serve the Papacy. The '*souls of men*' they trade in are all those lost to Messiah by believing that the false christ and the false church can save them. What is the whole system of masses for the dead, paid for out of the money drawn from mourning relatives, but traffic in the *souls of men*?

So how did the Vatican accumulate all that wealth? One method was to put a price-tag on sin. They actively marketed guilt, sin, and fear for profit by selling indulgences. Worshippers were encouraged to pre-pay for sins they hadn't yet committed and get pardoned ahead of time. Those who didn't pay-up risked eternal damnation. Pope Leo V rebuilt St. Peter's Basilica by selling tickets out of hell and tickets to heaven, *selling souls*.

Another method was to get wealthy landowners and widows to hand-over their land and wealth to the church on their deathbed in exchange for a blessing that would supposedly enable them to go to heaven.

Apart from the hoarded gold, thousands of church buildings, thousands of estates, they have purchased art, books, sculpture, and relics that are impossible even to guess their value. The Vatican vaults are filled with this merchandise.

There's one additional aspect regarding '*slaves and the souls of men.*' *Unam Sanctam* is a papal bull issued by Pope Boniface VIII in 1302. It gave them legal authority over all people using Roman law, temporal as well as spiritual. Using *Lexi Fori* maritime law, they designate every person as a corporate entity. They assign people a birth certificate with a taxpayer ID#. People are stocks to be owned and traded, so in essence, they are trading in the *souls of men*.

The merchants of these things, which were made rich by her, shall stand afar off for the fear of her torment, weeping and wailing, And saying, Alas, alas, that great city, that was clothed in fine linen, and purple, and scarlet, and decked with gold, and precious stones, and pearls!

446

For in one hour so great riches is come to nought. And every shipmaster, and all the company in ships, and sailors, and as many as trade by sea, stood afar off, And cried when they saw the smoke of her burning, saying, What city is like unto this great city! And they cast dust on their heads, and cried, weeping and wailing, saying, Alas, alas, that great city, wherein were made rich all that had ships in the sea by reason of her costliness! for in one hour is she made desolate.
Revelation 18:14-19

Prophecy teachers say that the *'great city'* can't be Rome because it's not a large manufacturing city and it doesn't have a great seaport, but John is not saying that the great city is making and selling the goods. It's saying that when the *great city* is destroyed, then the *harlot* church won't <u>buy</u> the merchants' goods anymore. It's saying that the RCC is the one who is buying the merchants' goods and that they will weep when that ends.

The RCC basilicas, cathedrals, parishes, monasteries, nunneries, and schools; are worldwide, where the merchants *ship* the goods. The evil elite will lament her desolation, for, by her, they were made wealthy.

There's another aspect of the RCC being related to *water*. The *Holy See* reportedly controls the world via *Admiralty Law*, also known as *Maritime Law*, the *Law of the Sea* through which their banks control currency (*current-sea*). Their fiat money *flows* around the world, stealing the wealth of the nations through inflation. Since the 11th century, it has governed vessels' operation and ownership on the oceans, transport, and insurance of cargo, commerce, bills, navigation, liability, liens, and finance.

There's no mistaking that the *'great city'* of Revelation is Rome, home of the Satan-empowered Roman beast kingdom. Physical Babylon, Jerusalem, America, New York, etc., do not have the distinction of fulfilling the detailed description in Revelation 17 and 18.

In *Key To The Apocalypse,* **Henry Grattan Guinness says,** *Further, we identify Papal Rome as the Harlot of the Apocalypse by her characteristic attire. Her garments of purple, scarlet, and gold, adorned with precious stones and pearls, what are these but the notable and characteristic dress of the popes, cardinals, archbishops, bishops, and priests of the Church of Rome — the dress they wear in their churches, in their conclaves, in their processions? Is it not notorious that the robes and miters of Romish popes and bishops are covered with gold and silver and adorned with "diamonds, sapphires, emeralds, chrysolites, jaspers, pearls, and all precious stones"? Is it not a fact that the papal diadem surpasses all other diadems — that it is more richly wrought, more marvelously magnificent with costly jewels, than any crown of mere terrestrial monarchy.*

Revelation is the historical narrative of the Satan-empowered ACBP's and their RCC, called *Babylon,* waging war on Messiah's saints, called *Holy Jerusalem.* Can you imagine being alive when this judgment happens and seeing it on the news?

Though we don't want people to be killed and lost in their sins, there will be rejoicing when the *harlot* church is rightly judged. This recalls the vision in Daniel 2 when the uncut stone will be thrown at the feet of the statue.

> *Thou sawest till that a stone was cut out without hands, which smote the image upon his feet that were of iron and clay, and brake them to pieces.* Daniel 2:34

> *Forasmuch as thou sawest that the stone was cut out of the mountain without hands, and that it brake in pieces the iron, the brass, the clay, the silver, and the gold; the great God hath made known to the king what shall come to pass hereafter: and the dream is certain, and the interpretation thereof sure.* Daniel 2:45

I pray that the leaders of Laodicea's church era will be used to teach the truth about prophecy fulfillment, and expose the deceptions of the enemy, to set the captives free; thus, her power is cast down, destroyed!

And the voice of harpers, and musicians, and of pipers, and trumpeters, shall be heard no more at all in thee; and no craftsman, of whatsoever craft he be, shall be found any more in thee; and the sound of a millstone shall be heard no more at all in thee; And the light of a candle shall shine no more at all in thee; and the voice of the bridegroom and of the bride shall be heard no more at all in thee: for thy merchants were the great men of the earth; for by thy sorceries were all nations deceived. **Revelation 18:22-23**

The *'craftsman'* are the artisans who made the basilicas, many of them in the 19ᵗʰ century. The *'great men'* point to people like the Rothschild's, Rockefeller's, Hapburg's, Carrington's, Bronfman's, Oppenheimer's, etc., who have become immensely wealthy by the RCC.

The word *'sorceries'* is Strong's Greek Dictionary word 5331 **pharmakeia**, which means; *medication ("pharmacy"), i.e. (by extension) magic (literally or figuratively):—sorcery, witchcraft*.

It's based on the Greek word 5332 *pharmakeus*: from *pharmakon*, which means *a druggist ("pharmacist") or poisoner, a magician:—a sorcerer*.

Google '**Medical Association**' and you see the *Rod of Asclepius*, a snake around a pole, seen throughout the modern medical profession's symbolism. Another symbol recognized through the medical field is known as a *Caduceus*, also called the *Staff of Hermes*, which has a pole, two intertwining snakes, and wings on the top.

The *American Medical Association* logo now has a pole with a snake encircling it, which forms three '6' shapes, symbolizing 666, pointing to their sorcery.

One of the ways that they've become extraordinarily rich is through the *sick-care* industry. They've taken control of how doctors treat patients. It's not based on health care, as doctors don't focus on nutrition, water intake, minimizing toxin intake, detoxification, exercise, etc.

449

Instead, it's focused on prescribing medications that treat the symptom but not the cause. This is what Revelation 18:23 is pointing to, as they've created a culture with foods that lack nutrition, toxins in food and body-care products, metals in shots, chemicals in the air and water, etc.

The system is designed to poison our bodies so that they can control us. In 1983, 10 shots were given to children, now it's 74 and increasing. It sets people up to have health issues for life, which keeps them going to doctors to continue this vicious cycle. This makes the *great men* wealthy.

Aldous Huxley (1894-1963) said, *"There will be in the next generation or so, a pharmacological method of making people love their servitude and producing dictatorship without tears, so to speak. Producing a kind of painless concentration camp for entire societies so that people will, in fact, have their liberties taken away from them, but will rather enjoy it because they will be distracted from any desire to rebel by propaganda or brainwashing enhanced by pharmacological methods. And this seems to be the final revolution."* (1)

Fluoride and lithium in the water supply *'dumb people down'* so that they don't see all of the deceptions and don't fight back. Be sure to filter your water. Today, there's a massive push for people to get shots! It's *sorcery* that gives the evil ones control over people, and you want no part of it! Please do your research!

And in her was found the blood of prophets, and of saints, and of all that were slain upon the earth. Revelation 18:24

People argue that it's pointing to Jerusalem because that's where the prophets were killed. But Revelation describes what takes place after it was written, not before. The saints have not been killed in Jerusalem, the Roman beast kingdom has killed them. We've already seen how the ACBP made war with the saints, killing tens of millions during the Dark Ages and the Inquisition, and no doubt many tens of millions covertly.

CHAPTER 86 - BABYLON THE GREAT DESTROYED

And the ten horns which thou saw upon the beast, these shall hate the whore, and shall make her desolate and naked, and shall eat her flesh, and burn her with fire. **Revelation 17:16**

Revelation 17:1-15 describes the *harlot* church of the ACBP, who rose to power after seven forms of government of the pagan Roman Empire. He exerted his authority over the ten kingdoms of the fallen Empire. Revelation 17:16-17 points to the judgment of the *harlot* church of Rome.

When this is fulfilled, it will be by the hand of the FPJSG. That may seem contrary, as he's supposedly a Catholic Church priest, but he's the *false prophet,* a fake priest. He controls the ten European countries of the fallen Roman Empire, the *ten horns.* After the One World Government of the seventh bowl is fully formed, he may command these countries to forsake their allegiance to the RCC.

Recall what took place during the first, second, and third bowl judgments. The people were turned against their Catholic leaders and priests, and they systematically killed them.

An example of a *harlot* being desolated is given in Micah 1:7.

> *And all the graven images thereof shall be beaten to pieces, and all the hires thereof shall be burned with the fire, and all the idols thereof will I lay desolate: for she gathered it of the hire of an harlot, and they shall return to the hire of an harlot.*

I can see a time when the Roman Catholic basilicas are attacked, all of the graven images destroyed, and the buildings burned down.

For God hath put in their hearts to fulfill his will, and to agree, and give their kingdom unto the beast, until the words of God shall be fulfilled. **Revelation 17:17**

The SOJ is a spiteful bunch who always looks for ways to exact revenge upon their enemies. The FPJSG is just using the Vatican and the RCC to gather the world under his power. Once that is achieved, and he is ruling from Jerusalem, he may cause the *harlot* church's grand basilicas to be desolated and her priests killed.

The *ten horns* are pointing to the ten kingdoms of the fallen Roman Empire in Western Europe. Here's a list with the number of basilicas in each. France (168), Spain (123), Portugal (12), Britain (4), Austria (35), Luxemburg (1), Switzerland (12), Belgium (27), and the Netherlands (27). There are 573 basilicas in Italy alone, with 66 of them in Rome.

When you look at what's taking place in these countries right now, you see Muslims' massive immigration. When they reach a majority, they may be used to carry out this judgment on the *harlot* church. Recall that they are the '*miry clay*' of the *iron-clay feet* of the statue in Daniel 2, which don't *mix* well with each other.

RCC priests' rampant homosexuality and their sexual crimes against children could lead to a worldwide revolt against the Catholic priests, leading to their destruction. And wouldn't that be a righteous judgment after they've been getting away with their crimes for so long?

It could be that the judgment is partially fulfilled by the RCC being exposed for her many crimes against humanity so that Catholics cease to support her and leave her. France has historically played a huge role in the bowl judgments, so perhaps it will be France leading the way of Europe's ten kingdoms to attack the Vatican.

Joseph Benson's Commentary on Revelation (1847) says, *Rome, therefore, will finally be destroyed by some of the princes who are reformed, or shall be reformed, from Popery; and as the kings of France have contributed greatly to her advancement, it is not impossible nor improbable that some time or other they may also be the principal authors of her destruction.*

In *Elucidations on the Apocalypse of St. John* (1687), Jacques Philipot says, *As the king of France did his utmost to enhance the glory of Popery, it will be the king of France who shall most contribute to her ruin.*

And the woman which thou sawest is that great city, which reigneth over the kings of the earth. Revelation 17:18

Keeping in mind that the apocalyptic vision is from John's perspective, it's easy to see that the *'great city'* is Rome, as the Roman Empire reigned supreme. And after reading this book, I hope you can see that the Roman beast kingdom still controls the whole world.

Recall the parable of the *'wheat and the tares.'* The *tares* were initially *planted* when Satan used Simon the Sorcerer in the first century to go to Rome and feign to be an apostle of Messiah. He combined the *Babylonian Mystery Religion* with the true faith, which was the *'mystery of iniquity.'* Then Satan used Constantine to exalt the *tares* church in the Roman Empire and hold councils and create mandates that hid the Scriptural faith, which led to the *falling away* of 2 Thessalonians 2.

Satan has used the ACBPs to nourish the *tares* church, making it seem like the church of Messiah. Messiah's Ekklesia, the *wheat*, and Satan's RCC, the *tares*, have grown side by side. *Wheat* and *tares* look similar until they bear fruit. *Tares* are a weed known as *Darnell* or *Bastard Wheat*, which has black and poisonous fruit.

When we look at the fruit of the RCC, we see darkness and sorcery. Indeed, she is the *'Bastard Wheat'* of Satan and the ACBP! We see the vast difference between the *wheat* of Messiah's Ekklesia and the *tares* of the RCC, and the time of judgment has come.

> *Let both grow together until the harvest: and in the time of harvest, I will say to the reapers, Gather ye together first the tares, and bind them in bundles to burn them: but gather the wheat into my barn.* Matthew 13:30

We need to proclaim Scriptural truth to Catholics so that they're not in the *harlot* church, for the time of her judgment is quickly approaching.

The Great Triumph Of The Saints
CHAPTER 87 – MESSIAH WINS THE VICTORY!

There are many perspectives about the one-thousand years and the timing of Messiah's return. I'm not including an explanation of Revelation 19-20 in this book because I'm still researching it. I have a different theory than what I've seen taught, but I'm not ready to share it at this time. Once I prove it out, I will publish my explanation. For now, I'll give you a few things to ponder.

Reading Revelation 19, the literal understanding is that Messiah's wife has made herself ready, Messiah returns for her, and then they come on white horses. The ACBP and the *kings of the earth* are ready to make war against them, the FPJSG and ACBP are captured, and those with them are killed.

Given that most of Revelation uses symbolic language to point to a literal fulfillment, it may be pointing to Messiah's bride coming out of the influence of Babylon/Roman teachings and returning to the ancient path of Scriptural truth so that she is pure. I've seen that taking place during the last few years, as people have come out of false teachings.

Recall that Revelation is about two women, the *harlot* church of the ACBPs, called *'Babylon the Great,'* and Messiah's Ekklesia, which is called *'heavenly Jerusalem.'* When the *harlot* is judged, the bride will appear radiant; she will shine before the world as a beautiful bride.

The FPJSG and ACBP will make one last attempt to wipe out Messiah's Ekklesia. Many saints will be killed when they won't deny their faith, which will be an amazing witness before the world. And history shows that Messiah's Ekklesia grows during persecution. Messiah gains the victory over the enemy through His saints as they cast down the power of the FPJSG and ACBP by exposing their deceptions.

Reading Revelation 20, the literal understanding is that Satan is bound for one thousand years and that the saints' rule and reign during this time. Then Satan is released to stir up Gog and Magog to battle against the saints, and Yah devours them with fire.

The challenge is that none of the time references in Revelation have been literal. The *'ten days'* in Messiah's message to the Smyrna church era martyrs points to ten years from 303-312. The *'forty-month'* reign of power of the ACBPs points to 1,260-years. The *'five months'* of the fifth trumpet points to 150 years. And the *'day, and a month and a year'* in the sixth trumpet points to 391 years. So why would we think that the one thousand years in Revelation 20 is literal?

Regarding the *'souls'* of those who are *beheaded for the witness of Messiah*, recall that the souls of the Symrna church era martyrs symbolically cried out for vengeance, which came during the seal and trumpet judgments against the pagan Roman Empire. Here, the witness of those who died for their faith is fresh in the minds of those who are still alive, compelling them to proclaim the Gospel and expose the enemy.

Revelation 3:21 gives the promise to the Laodicean church era saints.

> *To him that overcometh will I grant to sit with me in my throne, even as I also overcame, and am set down with my Father in his throne.*

We should not think that it's talking about His heavenly throne at the right hand of His Father. Rather, it may point to the overcoming saints sitting on earthly thrones, meaning they reign in power.

Satan is exalted in the heavenly realm when the world worships false gods or no god, so when his evil agenda is exposed to the world when they see how he has warred against them, his power will be bound. I envision the Spirit-empowered saints winning the victory for Messiah with the *'rod of iron,'* the Scriptures, which is *powerful and sharper than a two-edged sword*. No matter the fulfillment of Revelation 19-20, our role is the same, to preach the Gospel and expose the enemy's deceptions so that the captives are set free.

CHAPTER 88 - THE END-TIMES MILITANT BATTLE

In this book, you've seen how most of the prophecies in Revelation have been fulfilled during the historical war between the Roman beast kingdom's Satan-empowered leaders who are fighting against Messiah and His saints. I pray that you can now see who is the ACBP and the FPJSG. The mission of the FPJSG is to control the world and cause everyone to *revere and obey* the ACBP. After seeing how Satan has used the pagan Emperors and the ACBPs to try to wipe out Messiah's Ekklesia of saints, the FPJSG will try to do the same in the end-times.

We're at war, and the stage of the final battle is now in place. Let's survey the scene to see what we're up against so that we know how to fight to gain the victory for our beloved Messiah. Let me start by saying that too many believers are focused on what political and corporate leaders are doing. At this point, the enemy controls almost every country, the political and business leaders, the media, etc., which they use to promote their agenda and hide their crimes against humanity.

So though we should defend our Yah-given rights, our fight is not against flesh and blood.

> *For we wrestle not against flesh and blood, but against principalities, against powers, against the rulers of the darkness of this world, against spiritual wickedness in high places.* Ephesians 6:12

We could spend our lives battling in the physical realm, against the servants of the SOJ, in government, in corporations, in media, etc. I'm not saying that we shouldn't take a stand against evil. But military leaders know that they need to fight against the enemy's leaders to win the battle. Our spiritual end-times battle is against the FPJSG, his SOJ leaders, and against the ACBP.

The JSG is effective because he has absolute control of the minds of his leaders. They deny themselves and are *as dead men*. They trust and obey the JSG without question. They will do anything for him, including *steal, kill and destroy*. They're programmed to believe that *'the end justifies the means.'* The SOJ leaders regard the JSG as Jesus Christ, so they think their actions are justifiable. They have been mind-controlled to carry out the JSG orders of persecuting Messiah's saints and taking control of the world, even if it means killing to accomplish their goal.

The SOJ is a worldwide military organization that is well-organized, well-funded, and well-armed. They're of one mind, and they have one agenda, to take control of the whole world, cause the world to revere the ACBP, and fight against Messiah and His saints.

Now look around at Messiah's Ekklesia of saints, and what do you see? A disorganized mess, with no real leader and no cohesive strategy.

We're at war and living in one of the most important eras in church history, as the FPJSG and ACBP push the world into their One World Government. We may be the generation who sees Messiah return.

Yet most believers don't even know who the enemy is, and they aren't equipped for the end-times battle. Can an army win a war if they don't know who the enemy is? No! Sadly, most believers don't even believe in being a militant soldier in Messiah's army; they're resigned to waiting for the supposed *pre-trib rapture*.

For the saints to prevail over the enemy, they have to understand who the enemy is, where we're at on the Revelation timeline, and what's left to be fulfilled so that the enemy's deceptions do not mislead them. I hope that you will share this book with all of the teachable people you know so that we can form a mighty army of well-equipped warriors.

Messiah could come and destroy the ACBP, the FPJSG, and their military order at any time. But I believe that He is glorified by defeating the enemy through His faithful saints. Just as the JSG has an army carrying out his Satanic agenda, I believe that Messiah will work through His army of set-apart saints.

Just as the SOJ leaders are sold-out to their Satanic agenda, the warrior saints need to be sold-out for the glory of their King, the *lion of the tribe of Judah*. Messiah has to have absolute control of the minds of his leaders. We need to deny ourselves and be as *dead men* for Him. The Jesuit leaders only have Satan's power to work with, but the saints have the Ruach Spirit's power.

Psalms 94:16 beckons us, *Who will rise up for me against the evildoers? Or who will stand up for me against the workers of iniquity?*

The Jesuits have provincial leaders around the world. They have leaders in the major cities of the world. Who will stand against them in the power of the Ruach Spirit, with prayer, in each country, in each major city? Who will lead people to the truth of prophecy fulfillment, which destroys the power of the enemy? Who will abandon the selfish things of life (TV, movies, sports) to carry out the battle plan?

We will be held accountable for not sounding the alarm!

> *But if the watchman see the sword come, and blow not the trumpet, and the people be not warned; if the sword come, and take any person from among them, he is taken away in his iniquity; but his blood will I require at the watchman's hand.* Ezekiel 33:6

We win the battle, not by killing with the sword, but by wielding the *rod of iron* by which we cast down the enemy with the Word. We defeat the enemy by teaching the truth of prophecy, which exposes the enemy's deceptions, to set the captives set free.

> *Know ye not that they which run in a race run all, but one receives the prize? So run, that ye may obtain. And every man that strives for the mastery is temperate in all things. Now they do it to obtain a corruptible crown; but we an incorruptible.* 1 Corinthians 9:24-25

John Wycliffe said, *"I believe that in the end, the truth will conquer."*

CHAPTER 90 - HOW TO PREPARE AND FIGHT

Pray against the enemy. Evil ones pray against us; they cast spells over states, cities, and neighborhoods. They only have the power of Satan; we have the power of the Almighty One. Fight back by praying over your state, city, neighborhood, home, workplace, etc., to cast down the enemy's strongholds. Visit **www.Antisa.org** for more information.

Disengage from the enemy's mind control programming, Tele-lie-vision, news, and movies pervert thoughts and create a fear mindset. Engage in Bible study, prayer, and praise, as truth is only found in our Heavenly Father, beloved Messiah, the Ruach Spirit, and the Word.

Attack the enemy by using their social media platforms against them. Teach the truth of fulfillment of the 70th week of Daniel 9, the Olivet Discourse, and Revelation, as they validate Scripture's authority and Messiah's deity. Share the books and websites to expose the enemy's deceptions, to cast down their power, to set the captives free.

Minister to those who are sick and lonely, those in prison, widows and orphans, the hungry and homeless. They need the message of hope of the Gospel of our Heavenly Father and beloved Messiah. Every person who is redeemed for the kingdom is a victory against the enemy.

Stay focused on productive actions. Fighting against people who aren't seeking the truth is not a productive use of your time, and they will suck the life out of you. *Cast not your pearls before swine*. Pour out your life in helping those who are teachable and seeking the truth.

Prepare for tough times ahead, as the enemy enforces mandates about masks, vaxx, medical certificates, etc. Prepare for a time when the power may be shut down, civil war, being cut off from the financial system, etc. Our Heavenly Father will protect His saints, but a prudent person sees trouble and gets out of the way. I created a Prep page on the **www.RevelationTimelineDecoded.com** website to provide basic tips.

CHAPTER 91 - WHO WILL BE THE OVERCOMERS?

I don't see the two-millennium story of fulfilling the prophecies in Revelation ending with Satan defeating the saints. It just seems like such a major let down after the saints have battled so hard against their enemy. Do we think that's how the narrative ends, that Messiah has to come to destroy the enemy for us because we've been so weak that we've not won the victory for Him?

Being beheaded by the enemy because we refuse to *revere* the ACBP is victory over the enemy, as we saw that take place with the pagan Roman Emperors' martyrs. Denying ourselves and laying down our lives for the glory of our King gives powerful testimony to the watching world. The martyrs are exalted in the heavenly realm; they are the heroes of the faith. Keep that in mind if that time comes in your life.

That said, I believe that Messiah wants to win the victory through His saints by using them to teach the truth about prophecy fulfillment, to expose the many deceptions of the enemy, to validate Scripture's authority and the deity of Messiah, to set the captives free from their bondage, to redeem countless souls for the kingdom in the last days.

To him that overcomes will I grant to sit with me in my throne, even as I also overcame, and am set down with my Father in his throne. He that hath an ear let him hear what the Spirit said unto the churches. **Revelation 3:21-22**

Is longing for a supposed pre-trib rapture the attitude of an overcomer? What kind of saint would want to leave? What kind of saint doesn't want to fight for souls until the end? What kind of saint doesn't want to play a role in how the narrative of Revelation finishes? Do you think that all saints are going to be deemed as an *overcomer*?

Friend, you've seen some of the testimonies of the saints who have gone before us, some who gave their lives to proclaim the truth. Do you want your testimony to be told in heaven as stories are shared about the heroes of the faith?

> *Wherefore seeing we also are compassed about with so great a cloud of witnesses, let us lay aside every weight, and the sin which doth so easily beset us, and let us run with patience the race that is set before us, Looking unto Jesus the author and finisher of our faith; who for the joy that was set before him endured the cross, despising the shame, and is set down at the right hand of the throne of God.* Hebrews 12:1-2

The word *'overcomes'* in the Greek is *'nikao.'* It's a name that has been important to me since I learned the truth about the historical fulfillment of Revelation, and knew that I had a calling to share it with others.

How will this Laodicean church age be remembered?

Like the *Dark Ages*, when the ACBP banned and burned the Scriptures, there was a famine for the truth; it's dark today because the FPJSG has hidden the truth about prophecy fulfillment. Like it was in 1514 when it was proclaimed that all of Christendom lies under the control of the ACBP; today, the saints are *as good as dead*, for they're not fulfilling their role in protesting against the ACBP. Messiah says that the end-times saints think that they're *rich* but that they're *blind*.

Recall the vision in Daniel 2, which foretold the four beast kingdoms, the last one being the Roman beast.

> *His legs of iron, his feet part of iron and part of clay. Thou sawest till that a stone was cut out without hands, which smote the image upon his feet that were of iron and clay, and brake them to pieces.* Daniel 2:33-34

Daniel also foretold that the Son of Yah would set up His kingdom, which happened in the 1st century.

> *And in the days of these kings shall the God of heaven set up a kingdom, which shall never be destroyed: and the kingdom shall not be left to other people, but it shall break in pieces and consume all these kingdoms, and it shall stand for ever.* Daniel 2:44

461

Daniel proclaims that a *'stone'* will be *'cut out'* of the mountain.

> *Forasmuch as thou saw that the stone was cut out of the mountain without hands, and that it brake in pieces the iron, the brass, the clay, the silver, and the gold; the great God hath made known to the king what shall come to pass hereafter: and the dream is certain, and the interpretation thereof sure.*
> Daniel 2:45

So what does that stone represent? To see it, I want you to visualize a pyramid that serves as an organizational structure, such as you saw that the enemy has done with their many pyramid structures. Messiah has a pyramid organization, He's the capstone, and His leaders make up the levels below Him.

And there's a *great mountain* of saints that make up the bulk of the pyramid. I believe that Messiah will cast the leaders, the upper part of the pyramid, the *'stone that was cut out of the mountain;'* at the enemy, to expose their many deceptions, which would destroy their power over the world.

Regardless of the fulfillment, I'm going to wage war against the enemy to bring them down.

I just can't visualize Satan persecuting the saints, cutting them off from buying and selling, and killing them, and winning the battle. I want the classic movie ending when the hero seems like they're dead when all hope is lost, but then the hero is empowered with enough strength to stage a comeback and defeat the enemy. I want that victory for my Heavenly Father and beloved Messiah! I want it for the saints who have gone before us, who fought the good fight!

You and I are blessed to live in the age when the battle between the Satan-*empowered* FPJSG and his army against Messiah and His set-apart saints; comes to its glorious ending! There's an epic opportunity to impact Catholics right now, as Pope Francis teaches many things that go against the Catholic Church's core beliefs.

Martin Luther posted his 95 Thesis, which exposed how what the Popes taught is contrary to Scripture, and sparked the Protestant Reformation when millions of captives were set free and redeemed for the kingdom.

I believe that a remnant of set-apart saints will rise up and expose the enemy's deceptions to spark an epic movement such as Luther did, which will lead to many millions of people coming out of Babylon, coming out of the teachings of the *harlot* church of Rome.

I pray that the saints will cast aside the many teachings which originated from the Roman beast, and are contrary to Scripture, and be *restored* to the ancient path of Scriptural truth. I pray for an army of saints who fight against the enemy with fervent prayers because the enemy has an army of people praying to Satan against us.

We're not just waiting for Messiah to return. We're at war. Doing nothing only causes our side to lose ground to the enemy.

This is the grand finale. The rest of Revelation may be fulfilled, and Messiah may return in our lifetime. If not, then we are called to *prepare the way* for the saints who will follow in our tracks.

We're on the verge of entering the promised land, but a battle lies ahead as the enemy seeks to oppose us. Satan has an end-times army of people who fight against Messiah and His saints.

We're the end-times militant army of Messiah. We're called to battle against the enemy with the sword of truth.

> *For says the Lord: Call together the archers against Babylon: all ye that bend the bow, camp against it round about; let none thereof escape: recompense her according to her work; according to all that she hath done, do unto her: for she hath been proud against the LORD, against the Holy One of Israel.* Jeremiah 50:39.

> *Put yourselves in array against Babylon round about: all ye that bend the bow, shoot at her, spare no arrows: for she hath sinned against the LORD.* Jeremiah 50:14

We're called to protest against the FPJSG and the ACBP, and their *harlot* papal church. We're called to declare that the Catholic and Orthodox Church's Gospel is a false salvation message of works through the sacraments and revering Mary as the Intercessor to the Father. We do this not out of judgment or hate, but out of love, to help them have a covenant relationship with the Father through the Son alone. The enemy has created a mountain of deceptions, and it's our role to use Scripture to cast that mountain into the sea.

As a kid, did you ever dream of being a superhero? Well, now's your chance. In the movie *The Gladiator*, Maximus said, *"What we do in life echoes in eternity."* I believe that what the end-times saints achieve for the kingdom by the power of the Father's Spirit will be talked about by the saints forever.

The righteous shall be in everlasting remembrance. Psalm 112:6

Wanting to escape the battle is an act of selfishness. Wanting to save your life while leaving others behind on the battlefield is cowardliness. We are to lay down our lives for the glory of our King!

How do you want to be remembered?

Heavenly Father, I pray that you bind Satan, his demons, and his spirits, and cast them away from the readers of the book; for the enemy hates that they now understand the fulfillment of Revelation.

I pray that you perform a mighty work in these last days to raise an army of set-apart saints who can explain the fulfillment of prophecy, expose the many deceptions of the enemy, and set the captives free.

I pray that everyone who reads this book will come out of the influence of *Mystery, Babylon the Great* and that our witness will bring about the desolation and burning of the Babylonian *harlot* system.

May we be the *stone* cut out of the great mountain of saints, which is cast at the Babylonian-Roman beast kingdom to break it into pieces.

All glory and honor go to you, Heavenly Father and our beloved Messiah, for in seeing the exacting fulfillment of the prophecies in Revelation, we see how you have faithfully worked through your set-apart saints to execute your perfect plan.

> *And from Jesus Christ, who is the faithful witness, and the first begotten of the dead, and the prince of the kings of the earth. Unto him that loved us, and washed us from our sins in his own blood, And hath made us kings and priests unto God and his Father; to him be glory and dominion for ever and ever. Amen.* Revelation 1:5-6

> *The four and twenty elders fall down before him that sat on the throne, and worship him that liveth for ever and ever, and cast their crowns before the throne, saying, Thou art worthy, O Lord, to receive glory and honor and power: for thou hast created all things, and for thy pleasure they are and were created.* Revelation 4:10-11

We long for your return Messiah but until then,

> *Let us run with endurance the race that is set before us, looking to you, our Prince and the Perfecter of our belief.*

Thank you, Spirit of Yah, for guiding our path of learning. HalleluYah!

David Nikao Wilcoxson

Be a lion in a world of wolves and sheep!!!

> *But thanks be to God, which gives us the victory through our Lord Jesus Christ.* 1 Corinthians 15:57

> *Thou therefore, my son, be strong in the grace that is in Christ Jesus. And the things that thou hast heard of me among many witnesses, the same commit thou to faithful men, who shall be able to teach others also. Thou therefore endure hardness, as a good soldier of Jesus Christ. No man that wars entangles himself with the affairs of this life; that he may please him who hath chosen him to be a soldier.* 2 Timothy 2:13-4

THE 70TH WEEK OF DANIEL 9

The context of the 70th week of Daniel 9 is that the House of Judah was due to be released from their seventy-year captivity in Babylon, and Daniel was praying about what would happen to them.

The *'covenant'* of Daniel 9:27 is the same *covenant* that Daniel was praying for the Heavenly Father to remember regarding the Jews in Daniel 9:4; the *everlasting covenant* of mercy that was made to Abraham, which needed to be ratified with the blood of the Spotless Lamb.

Daniel's 70th week was fulfilled on time, after the 69th week, from 27-34 AD, and that is the exact timeframe that we know that Messiah died on Calvary for our sins, and He rose again.

What took place in the 70th week of Daniel 9 was the pinnacle of human history, for in it Messiah carried out His ministry and died for our sins, which ended the need for temple animal sacrifices. The Heavenly Father marked this event by tearing the temple curtain in two.

It has nothing to do with the end times or the antichrist. That is a deception from the enemy to deceive the end-times saints, to deflect blame away from the ACBPs.

The 70th week of Daniel 9 prophecy is extremely important because it validates Scripture's authority and Messiah's deity. And it's vital to know because the enemy's false, futuristic explanations of the fulfillment of Revelation are based on it, including the concept of a *'pre-trib'* rapture.

The 70th Week Of Daniel 9 Decoded book explains it in easy to understand terms so that you can be confident that it was fulfilled on time. You can get a copy of the book @ **www.70thWeekOfDaniel.com**

THE OLIVET DISCOURSE

Messiah's Olivet Discourse ties in with the 70th week of Daniel 9 prophecy, which points to Messiah being delivered up by the Jews, being *'cut off,'* killed, and that their wicked actions cause the *desolation* of Jerusalem, the temple, and the Jewish nation. The context is the desolation of the temple that He was just in when He rebuked the Jews and said, "*That upon you may come all the righteous blood shed upon the earth. Verily I say unto you, all these things shall come upon this generation.*"

All of the things that Messiah described from Matthew 23:36 to Matthew 24:33 were fulfilled by 70 AD when the Romans desolated the Jewish nation. The enemy has deceived people about the symbolism of the *sun, moon, and stars being darkened*; Messiah *coming in power and glory*; and the *elect being gathered into the kingdom*. The Bible gives the definitions for the symbols to see the fulfillment.

We need to take Messiah at His Word and look at how the things that He described were about the Jewish nation, for their punishment of continuing their rebellion against the Father, for delivering Messiah up to be killed, and for persecuting His disciples. They faced a time of great tribulation during the Jewish-Roman War of 66-70 AD when 1.1 million Jews died in and around Jerusalem from famine, pestilence, infighting, suicide, evisceration, crucifixion, and the Roman sword.

The fulfillment of the Olivet Discourse prophecy is extremely relevant because it validates Scripture's authority and Messiah's deity. It will help you see that it's not about the end times so that you're not misled as we await Messiah's promised return. It's also important to understand that the 1,290 and 1,335 days in Daniel 12 were pointing to the time of great tribulation during the Jewish-Roman War of 66-70 AD.

The Olivet Discourse Decoded book explains it in easy to understand terms so that you can be confident that it was fulfilled on time. You can get a copy of the book @ **www.TheOlivetDiscourse.com**

ADDITIONAL RESOURCES

In the Revelation Timeline Decoded book, I added the most important information to give you the fulfillment of the prophecies, but there's more to the story. If I would have added it to this book, then it would have made it even longer.

Here's a list of additional studies for you to continue your research:

There's much more to the story of the religion of Islam being created by the Roman bishops. I have studies which provide more detail on this website: www.ironclayfeet.com   remove link on this

I created a Revelation Timeline Decoded book resource page, so that you can link to studies about topics about Simon Magus, the Jesuits of Rome, the city-state corporation of the District of Columbia, etc. You can access it at www.revelationtimelinedecoded.com/resources

BOOK REFERENCES

CHAPTER 1 - THE BEASTS OF DANIEL
1 – Key To The Apocalypse, H. Grattan Guinness, p.17

CHAPTER 11 - THE FIRST SEAL
1 - The Decline and Fall of the Roman Empire, Edward Gibbon, Vol 1, p. 82

CHAPTER 13 - THE MYSTERY OF INIQUITY
1 - Dictionary of Christian Biography, Vol. 4, p. 682

CHAPTER 14 - THE SECOND SEAL JUDGMENT
1 - Sismondi's Fall of the Roman Empire, Vol. I. p. 36.
2 - The Decline and Fall of the Roman Empire, Edward Gibbon, Vol 1, c. 6

CHAPTER 15 - THE THIRD SEAL JUDGMENT
1 - The Decline and Fall of the Roman Empire, Edward Gibbon, Vol 1, p. 174

CHAPTER 16 - THE FOURTH SEAL JUDGMENT
1 - The Decline and Fall of the Roman Empire, Edward Gibbon, Vol 1, p. 180
2 - The Collected Works of Edward Gibbon by Edward Gibbon

CHAPTER 17 - THE FIFTH SEAL
1 - The Decline and Fall of the Roman Empire, Edward Gibbon, Vol 1, p. 190
2 - Horae Apocalypticae Vol. 1 - Page 164

CHAPTER 19 - THE FALLING AWAY OF 2 THESSALONIANS
1 - Stefano Assemani, Acta Sanctorum Martyrum Orientalium Vol 1, p 105

CHAPTER 21- THE SEVENTH SEAL SILENCE
1 - The Decline and Fall of the Roman Empire, Edward Gibbon, Vol 1, c. 30
2 - Ammianus Marcellinus - Roman Antiquities, Book XXVI, p. 589
3 - Hutton Webster, Early European History, Part 2, p 243
4 - Philosophy of History Karl Wilhelm Friedrich Schlegel, p. 305

CHAPTER 22 - THE FIRST TRUMPET JUDGMENT
1 - The Holy Roman Empire by Viscount James Bryce Bryce, p. 267
2 - The Decline and Fall of the Roman Empire, William James Reid 1878 - Page 229
3 - Philostorgius Ecclesiastical History, Book Xi, Chapter 7
4 - The History of Rome: The Republic (Volume 1) by Mike Duncan

CHAPTER 23 - THE SECOND TRUMPET JUDGMENT
1 - Dynasty of Theodosius by Thomas Hodgkin, pp 219-220
2 – The Decline and Fall of the Roman Empire, Edward Gibbon, Vol. 2, p 363-364

3 - Universal Naval History by John Frost p. 181

4 - An History of Marine Architecture (1810) John Charnock, p. 166

5 - Osprey – The Cutter's Guide, World History, Rome's Enemies.

6 - Italy and Her Invaders by Thomas Hodgkin, Book III, Chap. II, par. 49.

CHAPTER 24 - THE THIRD TRUMPET JUDGMENT

1 - The Decline and Fall of the Roman Empire, Edward Gibbon, Vol. 2 pp. 314,315.

2 - Attila the Hun: The Scourge of God - Demonic Savage or Inspired Leader?

3 - Revelations from Revelation by Patrick M. Jones

4 - Italy and Her Invaders, Hodgkin, Book III, Chap. I, p 212-213

5 - Hawera and Nomanby Star, April 2, 1910

6 - J.B. Bury History of the Later Roman Empire, Vol. I. p 161

7 - J.B. Bury Cambridge Medieval History, Volume 1, p. 417

8 - A View of Ancient Geography and Ancient History, P. 52

9 - Time Magazine, December 17,1973, Volume 102

CHAPTER 25 - THE FOURTH TRUMPET JUDGMENT

1 - The Decline and Fall of the Roman Empire, Gibbon vol. ii. pp. 440,441

2 - The Decline and Fall of the Roman Empire, Gibbon. vol. ii. pp. p. 446

3 - Horae Apocalypticae, Volume 1, p. 359

4 - Brittanica.com Barbarian migrations and invasions - The Germans and Huns

5 - Outlines of History (1864) Marcius Willson

6 - The Rise of Dennis Hathnuaght (1915) James Philip MacCarthy

7 - A History of the Later Roman Empire, AD 284-641

CHAPTER 26 - TRANSITION FROM EMPERORS TO POPES

1 - The Seventh Vial (1848), James Aitken Wylie, p. 39

2 - Frank Frost Abbott, A short history of Rome, 1906, p. 236

CHAPTER 28 - REVELATION 13 - THE ROMAN POPES

1 - E.B. Elliott in The Last Prophecy p. 163

2 - Daniel and the Revelation (1898), Joseph Tanner. p. 193

3 - Duc de Broglie, 'Histoire de L'Eglise,' VI, pages 424-456, 1856-66

4 - Acta Sanctae Dedis, Deeds of the Holy See, V, page 324 said of Pope Pius IX

5 - Pope Pius IX, 'Discoursi' I, page 253

6 - Pope Pius XI: Encyclical Letter, Ubi Urcano Dei Consilio, Dec. 23 1922

7 - Laetentur Coeli, Council of Florence, 1439

CHAPTER 29 - THE LITTLE HORN OF DANIEL 7

1 - M. H. Brown, The Sure Word of Prophecy, pp. 54, 55

2 –History of the World, by Ridpath, Vol. 4, chap. 74

3 - Nelson's Encyclopedia, Vol. XII, art. "Vandals."

4 - Outlines of Prophecy, Dr. George Dawe, p15

5 - Pope Pius IX, Apostolic Letter Cum Catholica Ecclesia, March 26, 1860

6 - Decretal, de Tranlatic Episcop. Cap. Ferraris Ecclesiastical Dictionary

7 - The Morning Watch Quarterly Journey On Prophecy, 1831, p. 823

CHAPTER 30 - THE SON OF PERDITION

1 – A Commentary on the Greek Text of the Epistles of Paul, John Eadie, William p. 345

2 - St. Paul's Epistles; The General Epistles; The Book of Revelations 1872, p. 31

3 – Pope Pius IX, in his "Discorsi" I., p253

4 - Duc de Broglie, 'Histoire de L'Eglise', VI, Pages 424-456, 1856-66

5 - Editor of the 'Acta Sanctae Sedis,' (Deeds of the Holy See), V, page 324

6 - Temporal Power" by Cardinal Manning, Preface, p 42-46

7 - Decretals of Gregory IX," Book 1, chapter 3

8 - Decretals. par. Distinct 96 ch. 7 edit. Lugo 1661

9- Pope Pius V, quoted in Barclay, Cities Petrus Bertanous Chapter XXVII: 218.

10 - Pope Leo XIII Encyclical Letter, June 20, 1894

11 - City of God, Book XX, Chap 19

12 - Concordia Theological Monthly, Sept. 1942, Vol XIII

13 - John F. Coltheart, What I saw In Rome, 1958, chap. 1

CHAPTER 31 - THE MAN OF SIN

1 - Pope Leo XIII, Sapientiae Christianae: On Christians as Citizens, 01-10-1890

2 - Pope Innocent III, Papal Bull, 1198 A.D

3 - Pope Gregory IX, Council Tolosanum, 1229 A.D.

4 - The Papal Antichrist: Martin Luther - Influence of Lorenzo Valla, p. 61

5 - Pope Innocent III, Denzinger-Schönmetzer, Enchiridion Symbolorum 770-771

6 - Pope Innocent II, The Council of Toulouse, Canon 14

7 - Pope Pius IV, Catholic Church Council of Trent, Rule III

8 - Pope Leo XIII, Great Encyclical Letters of Leo XIII, pp. 412-413

9 - Pope Pius XII: Exhortation, Menti nostri, September 23, 1950) — [p. 14, no. 23]

10 - Pope Pius XII : The Raccolta, Benzinger Brothers, Boston, 1957 A.D., No. 626.

11 - Pope John Paul II: Redemptoris Mater, #41

12 - Pope Pius IX, Ineffabilis Deus, December 1854

13 - Pope Pius XI: Quas Primas, Encyclical promulgated on 12-11-1925, #18.

14 - Pope Leo XIII: Encycl., Jucunda Semper, September 8, 1894.) — [p. 19, no. 43]

15 - Pope Leo XIII: Encycl., Octobri mense, September 22, 1891.) — [pp. 13,14, no. 19]

16 - Pope Leo XIII: Encycl., Adiutricem Populi, September 5, 1895.) — [p. 12, no. 13]

17 - Pope Pius IX: Encycl., Ubi primum, February 2, 1849.) — [p. 12, number 12]

18 - Pope Pius X: Allocution to the Franciscans, November 12, 1910.) — [p. 14, no. 20

19 - Pope Benedict XV, Quas Primas, Encyclical promulgated on 12-11-1925, #18.

20 - Pope John Paul II: Los Angeles Times, December 12, 1984.

CHAPTER 32 - MYSTERY, BABYLON THE GREAT

1 - Peter M.J. Stavinskas, ed., Catholic Encyclopedia, 1991, pp. 175-176

2 – Our Sunday Visitor's Catholic Encyclopedia, 1991, p. 175, 178, 466

3 - Robert Broderick, The Catholic Encyclopedia, 1976, pp 103-104

3 - The Trentine Creed or The Creed of Pius IV. , A.D. 1564.

4 - An abridgment of Doctor Newton, Volume 2 By Thomas NEWTON 1768. p. 57

5 - Vatican.va Catechism of the Catholic Church, Part One, Section One

6 - Johann Albrecht Bengel's Gnomon of the New Testament Revelation 17

7 - St. Cyprian, De unit. 6: PL 4, 519

8 - The Catholic Encyclopedia, 1976, p. 529

9 - William J. Reid, Lectures on the Revelation, 1878, p.400

10 - The Testimony of The Reformers, E. Bickersteth, 1836, p. 46

11 - Foxes Book of Martyrs, op cit., p. 445

12 - Foxes Book of Martyrs, p. 45

13 - History of Redemption, Jonathan Edwards, 1793, pp. 452, 460

CHAPTER 34 - ROME IS BABYLON

1 - Martin Luther, First Principles, pp. 196-197

2 - Tertullian chap. Ix

3 - A Woman Rides the Beast By Dave Hunt

4 - Faith of our fathers 1917 ed. Cardinal Gibbons, p. 106

5 - City of God, book xviii., chapt. xxii

6 - Outline of Dogmatic Theology" Vol I, p. 410

7 - Annals, sec xvi, p. 344

8 - De Rom. Pont.." c. iii, 2, Preterea, Tome I, p 232, Colon 1615

CHAPTER 37 - THE THYATIRA CHURCH ERA

1 - History Unveiling Prophecy By H. Grattan Guinness

2 - Sismondi's History of the Albigenses, p. 7

3 - History of the Christian Church, Volume 2 By John Fletcher Hurst, p. 48

4 - Tracts and Treatises of John de Wycliffe, p. 90

CHAPTER 38 - WHAT IS ANTICHRIST?

1 - Pope Boniface VIII, Papal bull Unam sanctam, 1302 A.D.

2 - Pope Pius IX, History of the Christian Church, by Henry Charles Sheldon, p. 59.

3 - Pope Pius X, Evangelical Christendom Vol. 49, Jan 1895 p. 15

4 - Pope Pius Xi, The Bulwark, Oct 1922, p. 104

5 - McGinn, Bernard, Visions of the End. Apocalyptic Traditions 1979. p. 64

6 - The Sacred Writings of Hippolytus p. 50

7 - Codeward Barbelon by P.D. Stuart

CHAPTER 40 - THE CHURCH OF SATAN

1 – Richard Noll (1999). When Catholics Die: Eternal Life Or Eternal Damnation? p. 126

2 - Behold a White Horse By Cisco Wheeler · 2009, p.180

3 - Henry Edward Manning, The Fourfold Sovereignty of God, 2nd ed, 1872, pp 171-172

4 - Henry E. Manning, Caesarism and Ultramontanism, 1874, p 35

5 - Cardinal John Henry Newman, Essays Critical & Historical, Vol. II, 1890, pp 116-117

CHAPTER 41 - THE POPES BLASPHEME

1 - Pope Innocent III, Denzinger 423

2 - Pope Boniface VIII, Papal Bull Unam Sanctam A.D. 1302

3 - Papal Bull Unam Sanctam 1302

4 - Pope Eugene IV, The Bull Cantate Domino, 1441

5 - Pope Gregory XVI Encyclical, Summo Jugiter

6 - Pope Pius IX, Denzinger 1647

7 – Pope Clement VI, "Super Quibusdam," Apostolic Digest, Book V

8 - Pope Leo XII, Encyclical, Ubi Primum

9 - Pope Leo XIII, Satis Cognitum, Acts of Leo XIII: Supreme Pontiff",1896

10 - Pope Leo XIII Encyclical, Annum Ingressi Sumus

11 - Pope Saint Pius X Encyclical, Jucunda Sane

12 – Pope Pius XII, The Raccolta, Benzinger Brothers, Boston, 1957, No. 626.

13 – Pope Pius XII, Orientalis Ecclesiae, quoted in "Acta Apostolicae Sedis," 36:129

14 - Pope Pius XII Allocution to the Gregorian, October 17, 1953

15 - Pope Benedict XV Encyclical, Ad Beatissimi Apostolorum

16 - Pope Pius XI Encyclical, Mortalium Animos

17 - Pope John XXIII, Coronation Homily, Nov. 4, 1958.

CHAPTER 45 - THE FIFTH TRUMPET JUDGMENT

1 – The Decline and Fall of the Roman Empire, Edward Gibbon, Vol. V, p 396-397

2 - Sahih Bukhari, Hadith # 6611

3 - Towards Understanding Islam by Sayyid Abul Ala Maududi, archive.org

4 - William S. Davis, A Short History of the Near East p. 100

5 - The Decline and Fall of the Roman Empire, Edward Gibbon, Vol.V. p 466

6 - The Decline and Fall of the Roman Empire, Edward Gibbon, Vol.V p. 425-426

7 - Antar, A Bedoueen Romance, c.1, p.7

8 - Travels' Vol. II. p 337

9 - Muir's book The Caliphate (p. 44), as cited in Emmerson's op. cit. p. 484.

10 - Edward Upham, The Ottomam Empire! Vol. I. p 40

11 - William Samuel Cardell, Essay on Language, p. 20

12 - Henry Hart Milman History of Latin Christianity. p 218

13 - Forster's Mohammedanism Unveiled 1:217

14 - The History of the Saracens by Simon Ockley, 1848, p. 94

15 - Antar - A Bedoueen Romance · Volume 1, p. 6

16 - The Decline and Fall of the Roman Empire, Edward Gibbon, Vol.V, p. 413 -414

17 - Barnes, Forster's Mohammedism Unveiled (vol. i, 401.

18 - A. Keith, Signs of the Times, Vol.1, p 312

19 – Notes on the Book of Revelation, Albert Barnes, Poem of Antar, 274

CHAPTER 46 – THE ANTICHRIST HEIGHT OF POWER

1 - Pope Saint Nicholas wrote an envoy from Constantinople.

2 - Decretals of Gregory IX," Book 1, chapter 3.

CHAPTER 47 - THE SIXTH TRUMPET JUDGMENT

1 – The Works Of Thomas Goodwin, c. V, p. 57

2 - The Collected Works of Edward Gibbon, c XLII

3 - Oman, "Art of War" p.22

4 - Elliott "Horae Apocalyptica" ch VII p.508

5 - Al-Hind: The Making of the Indo-Islamic World, Vol. 2, p 76-77

6 - The Decline and Fall of the Roman Empire, Edward Gibbon, Vol VII p. 192

7 - The Decline and Fall of the Roman Empire, Edward Gibbon, Vol VII p.193-195

8 - The Diadem of Histories by Sa'd Al-Dīn ibn Hasanjān

9 - The Decline and Fall of the Roman Empire, Edward Gibbon, Vol VII

10 - The Byzantine Achievement: An Historical Perspective, A.D. 330-1453

11 - The Decline and Fall of the Roman Empire, Edward Gibbon, Vol VII p.203.

12 - Constantinople: The Last Great Siege 1453 Roger Crowley Faber & Faber, 2006

CHAPTER 49 - 1514 AD TIMELINE ANALYSIS

1 - Pope Innocent III, Denzinger-Schönmetzer, Enchiridion Symbolorum 770-771

2- Concil Tolosanum, Pope Gregory IX, Anno. Chr. 1229.

3 - D. Lortch, Histoire de la Bible en France, 1910,p. 14.

4 - The Western Watchman, August 9, 1894, "The Word of God, page 7.

CHAPTER 50 - THE LITTLE BOOK OF REVELATION 10

1 –History Of The Christian Church c. 4, 62

2 - John Foxe, Actes and Monuments of These Latter and Perillous Dayes p. 570

3 - The Obedience of A Christian Man (1528)

4 - A history of England, Henry Walter, P. 445

5 - Pope Innocent II, The Council of Toulouse, Canon 14

6 - Pope Innocent III, Denzinger-Schönmetzer, Enchiridion Symbolorum 770-771

7 - Pope Pius IV, Catholic Church Council of Trent, Rule III

8 - Pope Leo XIII, Great Encyclical Letters of Leo XIII, pp. 412-413

CHAPTER 52- MEASURING THE TEMPLE

1 - History of the Reformation in the Sixteenth Century, Jean-Henri Merle d'Aubigné ·

CHAPTER 53 - THE TWO WITNESSES OF REVELATION 11

1 – John's Revelation Unveiled by Dr. Francis Nigel Lee p. 209

2 - Third Lateran Council, p. 27

3 - A Comparative Study of the Constitution, George Leo Leech, 1922

4 - William Cuninghame Dissertation on the seals and trumpets. p. 98

5 - Elliott, 2:402, 403

6 - Fulfilled Prophecy, in Proof of the Truth of Scripture, Bourchier Wrey Savile p. 182

7 - European History Foretold, Harold Hemenway p. 83

8 - What Luther says: an anthology, Volume 1

CHAPTER 54 - THE HISTORICAL WITNESSES

1 - In the Homily of Obedience, Part iii. Sermon against Wilful Rebellion, Part v

2 - The Testimony of The Reformers, E. Bickersteth, 1836, pp. 43, p. 44)

3 - The Smalcald Articles.

4 - Article 31 of the Confession of Faith adopted in 1603 in the Synod held at Gap

5 - Article 80 of the Irish Articles of Religion of 1615. Froom, PFF, volume 2, p. 553.

6 - Westminster Confession of Faith 25.6

7 - 1689 Baptist Confession Chapter 26, point 4

8 - Phillip Schaff, History of the Christian church, 8 vols., reprint of the 3d (1910) edition

9 - The case of Berengar of Tours by Margaret Gibson Cuming, pp 61-68)

10- LeRoy Edwin Froom, The Prophetic Faith of our Fathers)

11 - (Ibid, p. 90)

12 - Froom, PFF, volume 2, p. 40.

13 - Froom, PFF, volume 2, p. 88.)

14 - Guinness, op. cit., p. 134

15 - The Acts and Monuments of the Church by John Foxe. p 341

16 – The Obedience of A Christian Man (1528)

17 – Principle Works of Zwingli, Vol. 7, p. 135.

18 - John Calvin, Tracts, Vol. 1, pp. 219,220. John Calvin, Institutes.

19 - L. Froom, Prophetic Faith of our Fathers Volume 2 (1948): 437.

20 - Martin Luther, First Principles, pp. 196-197

21 - D'Aubigne, History Of The Reformation Of The 16th Century, V II, Book VI, Ch IX

22 - Froom, PFF, volume 2, p. 305., Furnemliche und gewisse Zeichen, sig.A2r.,v.

23 - Translated from Melanchthon, Disputationes, No. 56, vol. 12 col. 535

24 - Froom, PFF, volume 2,p. 47

25 - Froom, PFF, volume 2, p. 382

26 - Froom, PFF, volume 2, p. 378

27 - Froom, PFF, volume 2, p. 45

28 - Froom, PFF, volume 2, p. 45

29 - Works by Cranmer, vol.1, pp.6-7

30 - The Testimony of The Reformers, E. Bickersteth, 1836, pp. 44,45

31 - Froom, PFF, volume 2, p. 392

32 - http://www.exclassics.com/foxe/foxe340.htm

33 - John Knox, The Zurich Letters, p. 199.

34 - Froom, PFF, volume 2, p. 423

35 - Taken from The Prophetic Faith of Our Fathers by Froom, Vol. 3, pg. 52.

36 - Froom, PFF, volume 3, p. 113.

37 - A Discourse on the Man of Sin, p. 12

38 - Sir Isaac Newton, Observations Upon the Prophecies (London: 1831 edition), p. 75.

39 - History of Redemption, Jonathan Edwards, 1793, pp. 452, 460

40 - Explanatory notes upon the New Testament, John Wesley, Vol. II, 1813, p. 431

41 - The Papacy is the Antichrist, J.A. Wylie, preface.

42 - Sermons of the Rev. C.H. Spurgeon, of London, Volume 20 p. 76-77

43 - WELS Topical Q&A. Wisconsin Evangelical Lutheran Synod.

CHAPTER 57 - REBEL WITHOUT A CAUSE

1 - The Jesuits: A Complete History Volume 1 Theodor Griesinger. p.2

CHAPTER 58 - LOYOLA VERSUS LUTHER

1 - Theodore Griesinger, The Jesuits: A Complete History. Op. cit, p. 152

CHAPTER 59 – ENGINEER CORPS OF HELL

1 - Justin Dewey Fulton in his book Washington in the Lap of Rome (1888)

2 - Emmett McLaughlin, Assassination of Abraham Lincoln, Lyle Stuart, Inc., pp 84-85

3 - The Jesuits, (1881), James Aitken Wylie p. 76

CHAPTER 60 – THE CONTEXT OF THE SEVEN BOWLS

1 - The Secret Instructions of the Jesuits by W. C. Brownlee, 1857, p. 15

2 - Caraccoli: Vie de Pape Clement XIV Desant, Paris 1776, p. 313

3 - Hector Macpherson, The Jesuits in History (1914), p. 148

CHAPTER 61 - THE FIRST BOWL JUDGMENT

1 - Prophetic Faith of our Fathers Vol 3 LeRoy Edwin Froom

2 – Light for the Last Days (1888), Henry Grattan Guinness, p. 79

3 - The Life and Letters of Barthold George Niebuhr, Volume 3, xxvii

4 - Apocalyptic sketches: Lectures on Revelation, John Cumming (1850) p. 342

5 - Lectures on the Book of Revelations , Clement Moore Butler, p. 237, 247-248

CHAPTER 62 - THE SECOND BOWL JUDGMENT

1 - The Bolshevik Revolution, Vol. 1 (1951) by Edward Hallett Carr, p. 154

2 - Alison, vol. 2 p.281

CHAPTER 64 - THE FOURTH BOWL JUDGMENT

1 - The Signs of the Times, David Alexander Keith

2 - Codeward Barbelon by P.D. Stuart

CHAPTER 65 - THE FIFTH BOWL JUDGMENT

1 - General Montholon, Memorial of the Captivity of Napoleon at St. Helena, p. 62, 174

2 - Vision Of The Ages or Letters On The Apocalypse by B.W. Johnson

3 - The Approaching End Of The Age by Henry Grattan Guinness, p 361

4 - Arthur R. Pennington, Epochs of the Papacy, 1881, pp. 449-450 SOURCE

5 - The Encyclopedia Britannica, 1990, Vol.26, p.938

6 - The Visions of Daniel and of the Revelation Explained by E.P. Cachemaille, 1911

CHAPTER 66 - REVELATION 13 – THE JESUIT GENERALS

1 - Alexander Robertson, The Roman Catholic Church in Italy, op. cit. p. 51f

2 - Fifty Years in the Church of Rome by Charles Paschal Telesphore Chiniquy, p. 681

3 - Dominique Bouhours, Life of Ignatius, bk. 1, p. 248.

4 - The Schism of the Roman-Catholic Church By Nikolay Dmitrievich Talberg

CHAPTER 67 - THE FALSE PROPHET

1 - John's Revelation Unveiled, Dr. Francis Nigel Lee, p.164

2 - History Unveiling Prophecy, Henry G. Guinness

3 - Elliot, Horae, IV, p. 342

4 - Bede on the Apocalypse, Ch. XIII, p. 11

5 - Elliott, Horae, IV, P. 351

6 - History Unveiling Prophecy, H, Grattan Guinness

7 - John Wesley's Notes on the Bible

CHAPTER 70 - IT'S A PYRAMID SCHEME

1 - James Aitken Wylie, History of Protestantism, Vol. 2, Bk. 15, Chap. 3

2 - Codeword Barbelon by P.D. STUART Chapter 1, pages 13-19

CHAPTER 71 – THE SECRET DESTINY OF AMERICA

1 - The Life Of Charles Carroll of Carrollton (1918), Lewis A. Leonard,p. 13

2 - George Washington: A Collection, compiled and edited by W.B. Allen, 1998.

CHAPTER 72 - WITNESSES AGAINST THE JESUITS

1 - Codeword Barbelon by P.D. Stuart

2 - Fifty Years in the Church of Rome, by Charles Chiniquy. p. 292

3 - Fifty Years in the Church of Rome, by Charles Chiniquy, p. 302

4 - Fifty Years in the Church of Rome, by Charles Chiniquy, p. 294-295

5 - Fifty Years in the Church of Rome, by Charles Chiniquy, pp. 296-297.

6 - History of the Jesuits Giovanni Battista Nicolini, preface

CHAPTER 73 - THE TAKEOVER OF AMERICA

1 - Thomas Jefferson in 1802 in a letter to Secretary of the Treasury, Albert Gallatin
2 - Congressional Record Proceedings and Debates of the Congress · Volume 2, Part 5
3 - Thomas Edward Watson The Roman Catholic hierarchy, p. 8
4 - The Roman Catholic hierarchy; the Deadliest Menace to American Liberties. 1913, p.
5 - Thomas Edward Watson, The Roman Catholic Hierarchy, 1912, p. 35

CHAPTER 77 – THE KINGS OF THE EAST

1 - Notes On The Apocalypse, by David Steele, The Project Gutenberg
2 - 1906 Jewish Encyclopedia page on Abraham Harkavy.
3 - 1906 Jewish Encyclopedia page on Chazars.
4 - http://www.jewishencyclopedia.com/articles/4279-chazars
5 - https://www.jewishvirtuallibrary.org/khazars
6 - http://encyclopediaofukraine.com/display.asp?linkpath=pages\K\H\Khazars.htm
7 - https://www.britannica.com/topic/Khazar
8 - The Universal Jewish Encyclopedia, Volume 6 1939 376-377
9 - https://www.encyclopedia.com/history/asia-and-africa/central-asian-history/khazars
10 - Smithsonian, How Hebrews Became Jews, p. 19.
11 - https://en.wikipedia.org/wiki/The_Thirteenth_Tribe
12 - https://en.wikipedia.org/wiki/Paul_Wexler_(linguist)
13 - http://www.khazaria.com/brook.html
14 - https://en.wikipedia.org/wiki/The_Invention_of_the_Jewish_People
15 - https://www.sciencedaily.com/releases/2013/01/130116195333.htm
16 - http://www.khazaria.com/genetics/abstracts-jews.html
17 - http://www.khazaria.com/genetics/abstracts-jews.html

CHAPTER 78 - THE GOG AND MAGOG INVASION

1 - https://en.wikipedia.org/wiki/Expositio_in_Matthaeum_Evangelistam

CHAPTER 80 - THE ZIONIST STATE OF ISRAEL

1 - Closing Session of the Russell Tribunal on Palestine, Nurit Peled-Elhanan
2 - Adri Nieuwhof interview of Hajo Meyer. electronicintifada.net
3 - The General's Son: Journey of an Israeli in Palestine by Miko Peled.
4 - Haaretz.com Michael Chabon: Israeli Occupation 'The Most Grievous Injustice

CHAPTER 81 - THE THREE UNCLEAN SPIRITS

1 - Popery, Puseyism & Jesuitism, Luigi Desantis, 1905, p.139

CHAPTER 85 - THE RICHES OF BABYLON THE GREAT

1 - Aldous Huxley, Tavistock Group, California Medical School, 1961

CHAPTER 86 - BABYLON THE GREAT DESTROYED

1 - The Prophetic Faith of Our Fathers Volume II Le Roy Edwin Froom

Made in the USA
Monee, IL
13 October 2024

67019810R10266